Cities and Environmental Change

Environmental issues have always burdened cities and their residents. This volume analyzes how cities have solved past environmental challenges to provide a framework on which to build solutions to the problems caused by the climate crisis. It sets urban environmental crises within the socio-technical history of urban development. With six application chapters that provide rich and detailed examples of urban environmental transitions – including water resources, air quality, and public health – this book promotes better understanding of how urban environmental change takes place across a wide array of social–ecological–technological systems. It illustrates the process of urban environmental transition and the role crises play in shifts in urban environmental policy. Readers of the book will gain a deeper understanding of urban climate action and activities for future action. It is invaluable reading for students, researchers, and policymakers in environmental sustainability, climate change, urban studies and planning, and public policy.

WILLIAM SOLECKI is a professor in the Department of Geography and Environmental Science at Hunter College, City University of New York. He has studied the interaction of urbanization and climate change for almost 30 years. He has served as an author on several Intergovernmental Panel on Climate Change (IPCC) assessments and is a cofounder of the Urban Climate Change Research Network (UCCRN). He is a Fellow of the American Association of Geographers.

Cities and Environmental Change

From Crisis to Transformation

WILLIAM SOLECKI
City University of New York

CAMBRIDGE
UNIVERSITY PRESS

CAMBRIDGE
UNIVERSITY PRESS

Shaftesbury Road, Cambridge CB2 8EA, United Kingdom

One Liberty Plaza, 20th Floor, New York, NY 10006, USA

477 Williamstown Road, Port Melbourne, VIC 3207, Australia

314–321, 3rd Floor, Plot 3, Splendor Forum, Jasola District Centre, New Delhi – 110025, India

103 Penang Road, #05–06/07, Visioncrest Commercial, Singapore 238467

Cambridge University Press is part of Cambridge University Press & Assessment, a department of the University of Cambridge.

We share the University's mission to contribute to society through the pursuit of education, learning and research at the highest international levels of excellence.

www.cambridge.org
Information on this title: www.cambridge.org/9781108463027

DOI: 10.1017/9781108564144

When citing this work, please include a reference to the DOI 10.1017/9781108564144

First published 2025

A catalogue record for this publication is available from the British Library

Library of Congress Cataloging-in-Publication Data
Names: Solecki, William, author.
Title: Cities and environmental change : from crisis to transformation / William Solecki, City University of New York.
Description: 1. | New York : Cambridge University Press, 2025. | Includes bibliographical references and index.
Identifiers: LCCN 2024059588 | ISBN 9781108473972 (hardback) | ISBN 9781108463027 (paperback) | ISBN 9781108564144 (ebook)
Subjects: LCSH: Climatic changes – Law and legislation. | Environmental law, International. | Liability for climatic change damages.
Classification: LCC K3585.5 .S65 2025 | DDC 363.7/0561091732–dc23/eng/20241224
LC record available at https://lccn.loc.gov/2024059588

ISBN 978-1-108-47397-2 Hardback
ISBN 978-1-108-46302-7 Paperback

Contents

Foreword

As someone who is focused on practical action, let me get straight to the punch line of this foreword. If you have any interest in the intersection of the two most important megatrends of the twenty-first century, urbanization and climate change, you need to read and reread this book.

So why the hard sell? I have spent four decades working in an African city at the science–policy–practice interface – an experience that has been both a privilege and a monumental reality check. Getting to grips with issues such as climate change, biodiversity, sustainability, and resilience from a policy and practice perspective has left me with no illusions about the complexity and influence of the local political economy; the complex range of factors that govern local decision-making; and the extent to which local decisions are often immune to global influence. On the other hand, my scientific experience has deepened my understanding of the unprecedented environmental challenges and opportunities we face globally and has made me realize that now often the global narrative is misaligned with local needs. This book is important because it helps build a conceptual and practical bridge between those two experiences.

Cities are now a part of our civilization's DNA. By 2050, two out of three people are likely to be living in urban areas.[1] No surprise there given that we are living through the most rapid period of urbanization is our species' history. Humankind's transformation into an urban species has benefited billions of people, but it has also transformed the planet and contributed toward a changed

[1] D. Dodman, B. Hayward, M. Pelling, V. Castan Broto, W. Chow, E. Chu, R. Dawson, L. Khirfan, T. McPhearson, A. Prakash, Y. Zheng, and G. Ziervogel (2022). Cities, Settlements and Key Infrastructure. In: *Climate Change 2022: Impacts, Adaptation and Vulnerability. Contribution of Working Group II to the Sixth Assessment Report of the Intergovernmental Panel on Climate Change* [H.-O. Pörtner, D. C. Roberts, M. Tignor, E. S. Poloczanska, K. Mintenbeck, A. Alegría, M. Craig, S. Langsdorf, S. Löschke, V. Möller, A. Okem, and B. Rama (eds.)]. Cambridge University Press, Cambridge, UK and New York, NY, USA, pp. 907–1040, doi: 10.1017/9781009325844.008.

climate and escalating biodiversity loss. Urban areas are currently responsible for about 70% of global carbon dioxide emissions,[2] and urban expansion will lead to the loss of 11–33 million hectares of natural habitat by 2100.[3] This is significant because progress toward achieving global biodiversity targets remains variable, and it is increasingly unlikely that we will limit global warming to 1.5°C above preindustrial temperatures as outlined in the 2015 Paris Agreement. The recently released *United in Science* report indicates that "If current policies are continued, it is estimated … that global warming will be kept to a maximum of 3°C throughout the century."[4] At the same time, our ability to adapt to this level of climate change is becoming constrained as "progress on adaptation is slowing,"[5] and we may have already reached some adaptation limits that will have substantial implications for the loss and damage experienced by human and natural communities. Given these realities, it unsurprising that Dyke et al.[6] in a recent thought piece conclude that "claims from some that global warming can still be limited to no more than 1.5°C take on a surreal quality" and that the "time has come to accept that climate policy has failed, and that the 2015 landmark Paris agreement is dead."

Given these challenges, it is critical that cities around the world recognize that the risks they will be required to manage include ongoing biodiversity loss and temperature goal overshoot – creating a much-changed planet. The last time carbon dioxide levels were this high was in the Pliocene – 3 million years ago when the earth's climate was so warm that the High Arctic supported forests and roaming camels! The 64-million-dollar question of course is "how do we respond"? The most obvious place to start is to reflect on times in our past when we have confronted environmental challenges in our cities and to

[2] IPCC (2022). Summary for Policymakers. In: *Climate Change 2022: Mitigation of Climate Change. Contribution of Working Group III to the Sixth Assessment Report of the Intergovernmental Panel on Climate Change* [P. R. Shukla, J. Skea, R. Slade, A. Al Khourdajie, R. van Diemen, D. McCollum, M. Pathak, S. Some, P. Vyas, R. Fradera, M. Belkacemi, A. Hasija, G. Lisboa, S. Luz, and J. Malley (eds.)]. Cambridge University Press, Cambridge, UK and New York, NY, USA. doi: 10.1017/9781009157926.001.

[3] G. Li, C. Fang, Y. Li, Z. Wang, S. Sun, S. He, W. Qi, C. Bao, H. Ma, Y. Fan, Y. Feng, and X. Liu (2022). Global Impacts of Future Urban Expansion on Terrestrial Vertebrate Diversity. *Nature Communications* (2022) 13:1628 https://doi.org/10.1038/s41467-022-29324-2

[4] World Meteorological Organization (WMO); United Nations Office for Outer Space Affairs (UNOOSA); International Science Council (ISC); United Nations Environment Programme (UNEP); Global Carbon Project (GCP); European Centre for Medium-Range Weather Forecasts (ECMWF); UK Met Office; International Telecommunication Union (ITU); United Nations Convention to Combat Desertification (UNCCD) (2024). WMO, Geneva.

[5] United Nations Environment Programme (2023). Adaptation Gap Report 2023: Underfinanced. Underprepared. Inadequate Investment and Planning on Climate Adaptation Leaves World Exposed. Nairobi. https://doi.org/10.59117/20.500.11822/43796

[6] https://theconversation.com/the-overshoot-myth-you-cant-keep-burning-fossil-fuels-and-expect-scientists-of-the-future-to-get-us-back-to-1-5-c-230814

use that knowledge to better understand how we might address the urban challenges of the future. This is an enormous task that most of us do not have time or skills to undertake – but luckily Bill Solecki has done the work for us.

I have known Bill for over a decade now, and what have always impressed me about his scholarship are its mindfulness and sense of purpose. In this book, Bill brings both of those qualities to bear on his investigation of "what we can learn from past urban environmental crises and resulting policy transitions that might be applicable to understand how climate change will manifest as crises in cities increase and what can be done to help accelerate urban climate action." What Bill's careful and deep analysis of both theory and practice shows us is that while a biodiversity- and climate-changed world may require a new toolbox, it doesn't mean that we need to throw out all our existing tools. In fact, we can learn a great deal from how those tools have been used in the past and can use that knowledge to devise new ways of deploying old tools to deal with the emergent challenges. By grounding his analysis in a rich set of carefully curated case studies, Bill provides us with a realistic assessment of the art of the possible in the world's cities and makes it clear that there can never be a one-size-fits-all approach to urban environmental problem-solving. Different cities are going to need different tools over different timelines used by different actors to drive the system transitions that keep and expand the range of socioeconomic options on the table. We are not going to be able to create transformative change by using the same tools in the same ways as we have done in the past.

So read this book to get a clearer understanding of how the urban past speaks through the present to cities of the future and use it to begin reimagining how old tools can be repurposed to deal with the emerging, new, and unprecedented urban reality of the twenty-first century and beyond. Because of its pragmatism and textured analysis, I believe that this book will become a touchstone for urban researchers and practitioners alike, both now and in the future.

Dr. Debra Roberts
School of Life Sciences, University of KwaZulu-Natal, Durban, South Africa
Faculty of Geo-Information Science and Earth Observation, University of Twente, Enschede, The Netherlands

Acknowledgments

This book brings forward ideas that have been in my mind for a while. My thoughts received a significant push when reading Marten Scheffer's book, *Critical Transitions in Nature and Society* (2009) after I happened upon the book in 2010 in the back of Reiter's bookstore in Washington, DC. I had become interested in how, when, and why social–ecological–technological systems change and the transformations that result across the urban landscape. As my thinking advanced, I began to recognize that such transformations often come with stress, crisis, and moments of transition. Another component of this awareness was that, once resolved, these tumults are often largely forgotten and woven into the complex fabric of cities. The ambition of the book is help reveal and unearth what these past trials can tell us about how to best respond to the climate crisis that cities are now facing today.

I have made this intellectual journey into past urban environmental crises and transformations with a lot of help from others including from my family, friends, and colleagues and from my visits to cities near and far, old and new, big and small, and wealthy and not. The writing of the book took place during brief moments in between other responsibilities and over extended periods with more time to put pen to paper. A special thanks goes to Hunter College for the support during my sabbatical year in 2022 to really finish the work. I would also like to thank the folks at Cambridge University Press and Matt Lloyd specifically, who let me blow by some deadlines for the book while staying enthusiastic about the work and supportive of the effort. Extra special thanks go to Joy Cytryn, who did amazing work with book's graphics as well as providing other research and editorial support, and to Charlie Overton, who provided additional editorial review.

A wide range of conversations with friends and colleagues helped me formulate some of my ideas regarding systematic change, transitions, and transformations. The intellectual mixing within projects funded by US National

Oceanographic and Atmospheric Administration, the US National Science Foundation, and the Belmont Forum provided an opportunity to test out some of my research questions. The Transformation and Resilience on Urban Coasts project and the Arizona State University centered, Urban Resilience to Extremes Sustainability Research Network project were especially meaningful. Along the way, many individuals provided me with particularly valuable insights. These include Joern Birkmann, Erin Friedman, Allan Frei, Matthias Garschagen, Nancy Grimm, Mirosław Grochowski, Robin Leichenko, Hildegaard Link, Peter Marcotullio, Conor Murphy, Parisa Setayesh, Mark Pelling, Charles Redman, Debra Roberts, Cynthia Rosenzweig, Charles Vorosmarty, and John Waldman. The highest level of thanks goes to Robin Leichenko, who also provided me amazing encouragement and support to get the work done!

I would like to dedicate the book to Daniel Solecki and Helen Solecki. They are part of a next generation of people who are starting to take over the reins of the social–environmental problems that threaten this fragile world. I hope the book provides them with some additional knowledge on how to reconcile humanity's relationship with the earth, solve some of the pressing issues that climate change put in front of us, and advance sustainable and equitable life in our cities.

PART I

Framing Chapters

1

Introduction

Setting Climate Change within the Narrative of Urban Environmental Crises and Transformation

Environmental problems have always burdened cities and their residents. This book attempts to understand how cities address environmental concerns and develop opportunities for lasting solutions. Human settlements have had to respond to a broad range of challenges associated with access to natural resource access, well-being, and quality of life (e.g., drinking water supply, exposure to pollution and environmental hazards, and congestion and mobility). History shows us that the city building and urbanization are intertwined with environmental stresses, crises, and solutions. While significant environmental problems continue to be present in cities, there is also a history of making significant advances in addressing pressing environmental challenges. What are the key lessons from these actions?

Addressing urban environmental stresses and crises requires attention, day-to-day action, and long-term planning. Many of these ongoing threats are now exacerbated by climate change. Climate change also has begun to drive a series of new and emergent environmental problems for cities such as accelerated rise of sea level and increased extreme heating. Three critical questions are: How does the current climate change threat reflect past environmental challenges? How is it different? And what can be learned from past transformative character of cities, their residents, and their leaders that might inform society today?

In response, the central objectives of this book are to critically examine how cities resolve environmental problems, what key messages from these solutions can be translated to cities of today, and how they might promote enhanced opportunities for environmental sustainability (as well as economic development and social justice). The book is centered on evaluating the underlying social–ecological–technological processes and developing an analytical framework of urban environmental change and policy and management transitions. The volume includes case study material from a variety of cities throughout the world and is presented in a series of application chapters.

The earth is at a watershed moment for global environmental sustainability efforts. A broad consensus is now present – global climate change is underway. The earth's ecosystems and populations are facing the impacts of more frequent extreme climate events and gradual shifts in the everyday weather. Localities have begun to develop climate resilience efforts in response to these threats; however, conventional planning approaches and capacity-building strategies to tackle sustainability challenges such as increased vulnerability to extreme events have proven inadequate as the need for immediate and substantial action grows. Recent IPCC reports (IPCC 2023) indicate that greatly accelerated climate adaptation and mitigation action in the next 10 years is especially critical given the current rate of global warming.

The call has become louder for more transformative climate action that couples with sustainable economic development and social and environmental justice efforts (O'Brien 2012; Pelling et al. 2014; IPCC 2022). A climate resilient development framework (IPCC 2022) has been proposed to both serve as an outline for a transition to new kinds of broader scale adaptation and mitigation and enhance our understanding of the required transformational change. For some coastal cities, this might, for example, mean a shift from resiliency efforts that enhance the recovery from coastal storm surge flooding events to a transformative paradigm shift that includes the relocation of highly at-risk infrastructure and residential and commercial properties away from vulnerable shore locations. Conditions for meaningful and effective transformation require analysis on how significant policy and management regime shifts take place, whether there are particular moments when these types of actions are more effective and impactful, and whether there are early warning signals or conditions of such changes that can be utilized to further accelerate change.

This book directly responds to these intellectual and societal needs. It addresses this ambition by analyzing the conditions under which transitions in urban systems occur and how prospects for economically advantageous and socially just transformational change can be accelerated. The core of the analysis will be an examination of how transformational environmental action and policy change take place in cities and what lessons from this analysis can be translated into urban-focused climate adaptation and mitigation transitions and climate policymaking steps and procedures that could be coproduced by urban policymakers and practitioners (e.g., government officials) and stakeholders (e.g., nongovernmental organizations, community-based organizations, and private sector representatives).

1.1 Cities and the Climate Crisis

Human settlements and critical urban infrastructure now enduring climate change are facing more frequent flooding, droughts, heatwaves, and intense rain events as well as other climate change-related hazards (e.g., extreme wind events) (Rosenzweig et al. 2018; Dodman et al. 2022). Observed human and economic losses have increased in the past decade for urban areas and are expected to significantly increase in the future. Losses and damages from single events as well as compound, cascading, and systemic events have risen.[1]

Urban areas are now home to least 4.4 billion people, or approximately 55% of the world's population. Between 2015 and 2020, the global urban population grew by approximately 400 million people, more than 90% of this growth took place in low- and moderate-income countries. These trends are expected to continue through the next several decades. Upwards of 2.5 billion additional people are projected to live in urban areas by 2050, with up to 90% of this increase on the continents of Asia and Africa. The new population growth, coupled with the urbanization process, has brought a greater number of vulnerable and exposed urban residents and assets. Across the globe, the most rapid growth in urban vulnerability and exposure has been experienced in cities and settlements where adaptive capacity is low – particularly in informal and unplanned settlements in low- and moderate-income countries and in small- and medium-sized urban centers (Dodman et al. 2022). A key result of this is that climate impacts are experienced disproportionately in cities and urbanized areas with the most economically and socially marginalized, (Dodman et al. 2022).

Overall, the number of people expected to live in urban areas highly exposed and vulnerable to climate change impacts has increased substantially. Urban coastal locations are particularly of concern because they are often key administrative and transportation centers and suffer from multiple hazard threats including accelerated rise of sea level and related increased flooding (Pelling and Blackburn 2013; Glavovic et al. 2022).

More specifically, rise in the sea level and increases in tropical cyclone storm surge and rainfall intensity will enhance conditions for coastal city flooding. This is especially problematic given that more than a billion people

[1] Compound impacts arise from the interaction of a single climate hazard with at least one other hazard driver such as extreme heat with poor air quality. Cascade impacts are observed when damages occurring in one place or system reduce resilience or generate impacts elsewhere (e.g., when drought brings reduced hydroelectric power generation that in turn has economic consequences). Systematic impacts are associated with collapse or significant alteration of one system that has impacts on another system. The systems could be coincident or connected across space, for example, rural to urban linkages (derived from IPCC AR6, WG2 glossary).

located in low-lying cities and settlements are expected to be at risk from coastal-specific climate hazards by 2050 (Dodman et al. 2022). With respect to heat, the key drivers for increased exposure are the combination of global warming, urbanization, and the further exacerbation of local urban heat islands. Increasing urban water scarcity also is a growing challenge. Projections illustrate that 350 million people living in urban areas could be exposed to water scarcity from severe droughts at 1.5°C warming and 410.7 million at 2°C of warming (Dodman et al. 2022).

While some urban governments have been widely recognized as sites of new and innovative approaches to climate change action, most have not advanced (Rosenzweig et al. 2018; Dodman et al. 2022; New et al. 2022). Significant urban adaptation gaps exist across all different types of cities and localities. Governance capacity, financial support, and the legacy of past urban infrastructure investment now limit how cities are able to adapt (Dodman et al. 2022). Critical urban climate capacity gaps exist that hinder adaptation and mitigation.

For adaptation, these gaps include the limited ability to discern social vulnerability conditions and community strengths; the lack or minimal level of integrated planning to protect communities; and the absence or limited access to funding arrangements and minimal capability to manage finance and commercial insurance (Cutter et al. 2014; Dodman et al. 2022). For mitigation, the limitations are similar with respect to financing and technical expertise to measure and assess emissions reduction strategies. These deficits can be addressed through enhanced decision-making and action that (1) is locally accountable and utilizes local knowledge; (2) has sufficient access to the latest science, (3) is more transparent and equitable, and (4) is more focused on the rapid evaluation of these new climate solutions. Overall, it is recognized that accelerated climate change requires more responsive, flexible, and engaged action at the time when many municipal governments face constrained budgets, limited governance capacity, and increasing pressure to address significant social, economic, and environmental inequalities. A growing focus within climate change action has been to develop and implement strategies that simultaneously allow for climate adaptation, climate mitigation, and development within the context of sustainability for all. This possibility of fostering or guiding a transition that is integrative across multiple domains also is evident within the history of urban environmental transitions.

The link between climate change with urban development imperatives and demographic trends makes climate policy not only a key mechanism to safeguard development gains but also a well-defined and growing component of social struggles embedded within competing values and visions for the city

(Pelling 2010; Pelling et al. 2012; Solecki 2012; Wise et al. 2014; Garschagen and Romero-Lankao 2015; Sanderson et al. 2016). Climate risk management in the city not only affects the distribution of risk but also shapes the future of individual cities and cities collectively and the conditions faced by urban residents, leaders, and investors as well as the prospects for climate mitigation and sustainability (O'Brien 2012; Olsson et al. 2014; Pelling et al. 2014). At the same time, it has become clear that climate action is intensely local and requires people and institutions in places to make bold decisions about how to respond to climate change and to carry them out.

Cities have the potential for transformational change. Several factors are associated with this quality. These include cities' concentration of economic activity, high level of human resource capacity, dense social networks, concentration of infrastructure and building investment, relatively flexible local governments, close connection to surrounding rural and natural environments, and a tradition of innovation. Bringing financial and administrative resources from regional, national, and international sources also provides advantages for cities. Cities are increasingly seen as key potential sources of innovative solution-based policy transitions needed to address the global sustainability challenge (Dodman et al. 2022).

1.2 Environmental Stress and Crisis in Cities

Part I of the book focuses on how environmental stress and crisis are fundamental components of community development and the urbanization process. Every city present today has had to address and resolve drinking water, food, energy, and building material supply constraints during its history. The resolution of these issues is often imperfect, inequitable, unstable, and leads to unintended consequences that may cause other environmental conflicts and issues. For example, Cairo, Egypt, has water supply infrastructure that can provide water on a consistent basis to a few million people. However, the population of metropolitan Cairo is now well over 20 million. This gap must be met daily through a series of formal and informal adjustments and arrangements. Nonetheless, it is the process of addressing environmental constraints and inequities, the articulation of new policies and the transition to them that are profound elements of the city-building process that need to be better understood. These elements are examined individually and more importantly on how they link together and act synergistically, as a process of transition.

In this book, the conceptual structure of urban environmental policy transitions is developed through an integrative analytical approach that utilizes elements from urban development theory, complex system theory, resilience theory, and urban political ecology. Transitions are multifaceted and presented as fast or slow, intentional or forced, proactive or reactive, or planned or not. They are often associated with resultant regime shifts and tipping points along with early warning signals that denote the possibility of a shift is taking place (see Wallace and Wallace 2008; Smith and Sterling 2010; Ernstson et al. 2010; Westley et al. 2011; Markard et al. 2012; Beilin et al. 2013; Lin and Petersen 2013; Bentley et al. 2014; Rocha et al. 2015; Castilla-Rho et al. 2017; Milkoreit et al. 2018 for background discussion on social–ecological transitions and tipping points).

Policy regime or paradigm shifts are coupled with significant and persistent changes in the structure and function of a system that often are recognizable only afterward (Scheffer 2009; Scheffer et al. 2012). Urban environmental management transitions involve potentially foundational changes in broader governance structures or policy objectives (Solecki et al. 2019). Multiple nested policy systems also can change form or function in a cascade of adjustments. Policy transitions will have profound impacts on the valuation and spatial and temporal distribution of potential loss and damage (Solecki et al. 2019). As a result, transitions between climate risk management policies can become a central pivot point for planning pathways to sustainable and equitable development (Wilson 2013). It is during these transitions that the possibility of considerable progress toward sustainability emerges.

To frame the analysis in the book, four steps or phases toward a policy transition are defined. They include conditions of stress, crisis, transition, and transformation. While these four phases reflect the elements of the resilience focused, adaptive cycle, here they are presented as conceptually and operationally different. Each of these phases is associated with conditions that typically serve as a precursor to the next phase. For example, during conditions of stress, resource scarcity or decline takes place, and strategic conflicts emerge as a crisis and result in demands for a solution. Significant system-wide solutions are presented as moments of transitions, and their impact, aftermath, and consequence are defined as the broader conditions of transformation. Transitions and transformations are bracketed by contestation and debate between different interest groups and coalitions. In this way, the process of urbanization and city building and environmental problem-solving takes place through tension and dialogue across formal and informal linkages and networks. The application chapters, with case studies, presented in this book highlight different aspects of these connections within coupled societal, natural, and technological systems.

In this way, the book attempts to address fundamental questions regarding the relationship between cities and the environment. Most profound and straightforward are the questions of why cities indeed want to solve environmental problems, what drives them to do so, and how and why do these actions result in winners and losers being created. Furthermore, given that urbanization is typically associated with environmental stress, why do cities want to urbanize at all. Explanation of these questions has been framed by scholars around a variety of understandings and frameworks of how human societies are organized (i.e., paradigms including neoclassical economics, anthropological and sociological theory on traditional and informal social structures, and Marxist theory). In this book, the analysis utilizes a broadly defined political ecology framework where actions and decision-making are bounded by self-interest, culturally accepted norms, and structural limits.

Answering how cities solve environmental problems must be embedded in a conversation about why do cities face continuous environmental challenges? Urbanization often is associated with multiple stresses and conflicts across a range of topics that include environmental problems. A fundamental question often addressed is how and why does environmental stress and crisis emerge with development, demand, and technology choices? And why is it often the case that solutions to these environmental problems can lead to unintended consequences including new problems, inefficiencies, and inequities?

Embedded in the objective of the book, *Cities and Environmental Change: From Crisis to Transformation*, is the question of what or who is actually acting. Given that cities literally don't or can't act, what entity has the agency to actually attempt a solution to environmental problems? Any environment-related actions taken in cities is the product of the individuals or collectives deciding, arguing, debating, and compromising about which approach to take. Part of these activities is the articulation of capacity and power to pursue specific positions and defend or assert these positions over others. Contestation is part of the decision-making process, and these processes are motivated by a series of drivers including cultural beliefs, economic position, and social status and biases.

Part I of the book also addresses why cities are important sites for environmental problem-solving and what about the character of cities helps promote such problem-solving (and the important exceptions). Answers to these questions also help explain how these conditions vary across a spectrum of different cities. The key objectives here are to define how the urbanization process results in a range of environmental stresses and crises, the overall connection between urbanization and environment using coupled human–natural systems perspective, and how this connection emerges in different economic development contexts. One can look at each of these of questions in turn.

What makes cities places where environmental problem solving can occur, and why and when does it succeed or fail? The research literature is full of a variety of factors that are seen as contributing to environmental problem solutions emerging in cities. Cultural and social factors include the fact that cities are places where a diversity of opinions is present. Urban life requires the need for tolerance and acceptance. Diversity allows for a variety of approaches to be introduced and discussed and for solutions to be found through synthesis. Cities also are homes to social and economic elites, and often their interests and sensibilities are furthered when a city addresses its environmental problems and concerns. In pre–Civil War New York, for example, the families of the emerging wealthy merchant class were anxious to eliminate the squalor of the city's streets for reasons of health, economic, and social advancements. Internationally recognized author Charles Dickens first visited New York City in 1842 and wrote famously of its streets "reeking with dirt and filth."

Environmental problems of cities cannot be easily hidden away even when they become a part of the landscape. When they are "forgotten," they are eventually brought forward, as was done by Jacob Riis, a late nineteenth-century progressive era photographer, who illustrated how the "other half" lived in the gilded age of New York. His pictures depicted extreme poverty and unhealthy living conditions among many of the city's immigrant communities. As the problems became easier to identify, so were the potential impacts of the solutions. Environmental solutions, for example, cleaner air or streets, though challenging to attain, were often visual and tangible.

1.3 Urban Environmental Problems and Cities as Social Systems

The connection between environmental problems and a city's political and economic conditions is complex. Environmental problems often can be seen as both a product and a hindrance to further capital accumulation and effectiveness of the governing structure. In some cities, pollution became synonymous with progress and economic growth, such as steel production in early twentieth-century Pittsburgh and early instances of automobile-related pollution in Los Angeles. Since that time, chronic pollution has also become equated with decline or decay and the desire to address and mitigate the issue as a sign of progress. In this context, cities are sites that encourage solutions to environmental problems. Just as pollution is an externality from the urban industrial process, solutions to those same externalities promote economic growth.

A classic response to urban environmental problems is the removal and relocation to nearby but relatively less populated sites. In cities of the ancient world, removal was often achieved by burying or constructing onto existing buildings and structures like the tells[2] of ancient Middle East cities. By increasing security, declining the need for a city wall, and increasing population, cities began to spread horizontally. New areas of settlement are often presented as clean and less burdened by the perceived negative aspects of urbanization but still close enough to the opportunities that urban settings possess. Conversely, these outlying areas also were frequently used as dump sites for urban refuse and waste.

In capitalist market economies, these new lands beyond the city edge often are good sites for investment and continued money-making potential, and are defined by Harvey (1985) as part of the second circuit of capital in which existing wealthy urban elite can invest and expand their fortune while expanding the city. Under these conditions it is important that distance (whether literal or figurative) between areas of poor environmental quality and better environmental quality must be maintained in order to attract investors. Investors want unspoiled land that is well-drained, accessible, and easy to build on.

Cities' experimentation and innovation have long been connected (Mumford 1961). Various informal and formal social, economic, and political drivers have been introduced to explain this phenomenon. Interpersonal connections such as conversation and experience are one set of factors that lead to re-interpretation, fusion, and synergy. Economies of scale and agglomeration also provide conditions where innovation would occur – as the entrepreneurs attempt to fill emergent gaps in the market with new products and services. The rise of interior room air filter systems is one example of industry trying to fill the gap presented by the decline in ambient air quality. With respect to governance, cities provide opportunities for gathering and meeting from which solutions to urban problems are discussed. The close geography and networking potential also present environmental problems and their implications as things that can be witnessed, lived with, and in turn addressed.

A fundamental issue in cities is who has the right of the city, who is in control, and who makes the decisions regarding how its past is understood, how the present is managed, and how the future is created. The question of and demand

[2] A mound created over centuries through the accumulation of successive layers of civilization built one over the other.

for social justice and equity is central to the everyday experience of urban residents and has emerged as a critical component of contemporary urban research and questions of urban environmental management. Critical urban social science provides a valuable lens through which to understand how the decision-making and policymaking processes take place in cities. These processes involve multiple pathways and often involve both public or overt and private or covert deliberations and debate. Urban regime theory provides insight into how in many cities, the real power to affect change and resolve crises rests in the hands of elites, sometimes coalitions of elites or sometimes a very small number of elites. Central issues are how do elites gain power and assert power in these instances, and do the decisions made under these contexts hold up over time, are they durable, and seen as legitimate. Answers to these questions often depend on the circumstances and the root (i.e., historical, cultural), context (i.e., conditions of the underlying stress and crisis), and proximate (i.e., circumstances present when the crisis becomes acute and when a transition is underway) drivers present in the case at hand. That said, broad generalizations can be defined – power to drive a transition is either granted or seized, the process of the transition is always contested, transitions will involve winners and losers, engagement will result from a mixture of choice, bounded rationality, and coercion, and it is assumed that ambition to engage in the transitions process will be pressed by self-interest or at least a specific agenda that is reflective of a particular interest.

In all policy transitions, the issues of equity, justice, and legitimation are central to overall effectiveness[3] and the impact of the transition. Decisions that are made without successfully incorporating some or all of these factors are typically not as effective. Recent research has shown that policy debates and transitions that are co-produced or co-generated with the meaningful engagement of multiple stakeholders and interest groups in a way that recognizes outcome, procedural, and representational equity are typically more effective than otherwise (New et al. 2022).

1.4 A Framework of Urban Environmental Change and Policy Transitions

With addressing the question of how cities solve environmental problems, the book's focus reveals a more specific question – what happens at the moment when the environmental policy of cities changes. Or more directly, what are

[3] The effectiveness has many definitions and perspectives, including those associated with costs and benefits, level or amount of change, acceptance, or legacy.

the mechanisms of policy transitions in the context of a social, ecological, and technological system change? For example, what conditions might be a precondition or early warning of change, how do shifts in social systems affect ecological or technological systems and vice versa, and how do governance structures and policymaking either hinder or accelerate effective social and institutional responses to environmental threats? The structure and sequencing of these transitions will be evaluated, as will their societal and environmental implications. Social implications include those associated with economic development, sustainability, equity, and justice. Prospects for economic development have long been associated with urban environmental problem-solving and in the past two decades conditions of sustainability, equity, and justice have been added to the configuration. Because they are historical in nature, the book's application case studies, highlighted in Part II of the volume, often do not directly speak to these three more recent elements; however, aspects of how they do are highlighted as are how they might be relevant to contemporary climate change issues that will be presented.

Environmental implications involve shifts in natural capital and ecosystem services. In both instances, the policy implications and feedback can be a significant part of the transition aftermath. An important part of the narrative will be an analysis of how to predict or understand when a city is going through a policy transition and whether there are early warning signals or indicators of a transition. The book helps to scaffold and define the components of the framework and their interaction and operational issues. Chapters 2 through 4 present the background literature to be utilized in the book. At the end of Chapter 4, a framework to understand urban environmental policy transitions is presented.

The subsequent application chapters utilize the framework and provide empirical evidence for its potential adjustment and elaboration. The discussion examines these issues within several contexts, each one defining a different group of conditions presented within case studies across several domains. These include natural resource supply and scarcity, environmental degradation and quality, resource use efficiency including solid water management, disease and epidemics, environmental risks and hazards, and mobility and settlement. Each chapter includes a set of case studies that helps elucidate part of the internal mechanism of the framework.

Natural resource supply and scarcity is the most fundamental environmental question facing cities. The everyday life of cities can only be sustained with continuous access to water, food, energy, and other raw materials for shelter and other aspects of the built environment. Chapter 5 examines drinking water supply stress, crisis, and policy transition across a group of cases focused on Atlanta, US; Cairo, Egypt; New York City, US; and Tel Aviv, Israel. The objective of the studies focuses on how urban drinking water supply provision is a story of recurring catastrophic failure and impressive success and associated policy experimentation and transition.

Environmental degradation and quality represent another critical area of social and environmental change in cities. A result of urbanization is a local decline in environmental conditions and ecological function. These conditions include changes in water and air quality, solid waste, and land degradation. The case studies presented in Chapter 6 focus on urban air quality stress, crisis, and policy transition, including energy production switching. Examples of urban air pollution control include London, UK; Los Angeles, US; the Ruhr River Valley, Germany; and Tokyo, Japan, and present an evaluation of transboundary pollution and metropolitan-scale environmental problems.

Acute disease spread, epidemics, and pandemics have been a significant component of urban history. The COVID-19 pandemic has been only the most recent example since the initial outbreak in the early months of 2020. The virus spread rapidly around the world initially impacting global urban transportation hubs and then other urban areas generally especially hard. Cities have experienced and responded to past disease outbreaks that ravaged the health of residents and caused significant political and economic impact. Cities have reacted to these crises in a variety of ways and episodes have at times forced a rethinking of city form and function, and other transformative adjustments. The four narrative examples examined in Chapter 7 focus on how cities have attempted to solve these threats both within the moment of the outbreak and during the longer-term recovery. The examples include Marseille, France; Hong Kong, China; St. Louis, US; and Seoul, South Korea.

Cities are subject to environmental risks and hazards, both natural and technological. These events both as low-frequency/high-consequence and chronic events have played a significant role in the identity and structure of cities. Environmental risks and hazards result in a variety of stresses to cities and their residents that can result in crises and potential policy changes. These policy transitions can result in fundamental new types of human–environment interactions and patterns of resource use. Chronic risks, such as intense heat as well as catastrophic events such as a major hurricane/typhoon, steadily shape how communities manage and perceive their local environment. Understanding of how cities have been able to attend to and effectively respond to these events becomes a key exemplar of how other cities might be able to respond to current and future climate change. Case studies of urban risk management are presented in Chapter 8 to examine these issues. The set includes the cities of

Abu Dhabi, United Arab Emirates; Kolkata, India; New Orleans and Cedar Rapids, US; and Rotterdam, the Netherlands.

The drive to environmental sustainability in cities reflects attempts by cities to address resource use conditions and becomes the focus of the final two application chapters (Chapters 9 and 10). The capacity to respond to shocks is a key component of environmental sustainability. Equally fundamental are pathways to promote resource use efficiency such as the long-term use of the three Rs (reduce, reuse, recycle) and insights into slowly evolving crises and related policy transitions. These actions are critical for promoting the triple bottom line of simultaneous environmental, economic, and equity advance. The four cases that examine these questions are focused on Buenos Aires, Argentina; Johannesburg, South Africa; Seattle, US, and Taipei, Taiwan. These studies present the integration of environmental sustainability concepts into everyday practice within municipal government, businesses, and households.

A great challenge of urban development and city building is providing opportunities and conditions such that residents can live in a home within a clean and healthy environment and allowing them to move about the city in a way to promote economic advancement and equitable well-being. Achieving these factors requires cities to integrate conditions for urban sustainability, including social and environmental equity, economic development, and ecosystem integrity. This chapter is focused on examining how cities have dealt (or not) with this simultaneity of stresses and crises and the extent to which solutions presented have led to significant transitions and transformations. The chapter includes an examination of four cities that have struggled with these challenges and to one degree or another have addressed. These cities highlight this process of integrating livability and sustainability with the context of equity, economics, and ecology. The cities highlighted are Miami, US; Oslo, Norway; St. Georges, Grenada; and Shenzhen, China.

The results of the application chapters are reviewed and synthesized in Chapter 11. Several different perspectives are evaluated and considered, including character and structure of the crises, shifts in system resilience, and transition conditions. Comparisons are made across the application chapters and 25 case studies and within and between each crisis topic (i.e., water shortage, air pollution). This analysis serves as the foundation for the concluding chapter (Chapter 12), which is focused on translating these results and findings into specific conclusions and recommendations that are specifically relevant to urban-based stakeholders focused on advancing, if not accelerating, climate action in their city.

1.4.1 How the Book Can Contribute

In the past decade, significant research within geography and allied disciplines such as sociology, anthropology, economics, political science, and urban studies among others has been conducted that attempts to understand how urban social–ecological–technical systems (e.g., interconnected sets of systems) are organized, function, and respond to environmental stresses and crises and transition to solutions. The capacity of these systems to respond to stress is driven by the nature of the stresses and the structure and resiliency (i.e., ability to respond to shocks or other limitations) of the systems. The book directly addresses these issues through the development of a framework for urban climate policy transition analysis. The application chapters helps define pathways for testing the validity and robustness of the framework in a flexible adaptation context.

The history of how cities have responded to environmental problems (or not) has implications for an urban climate change transition theory and transformative climate adaptation and mitigation. The analysis also will bring forward findings that have relevance for stakeholders and practitioners, businesses and industries, and community-based organizations across a spectrum of cities and metropolitan regions of the Global South and North, which vary in vulnerability/resiliency, governance capacity, and human and financial resources, and the conditions of economic development. The results are directly germane to the ambition of the UN-driven climate-resilient development pathways and the related 17 sustainable development goals (SGDs) of the United Nations 2030 Agenda for Sustainable Development. The final chapter of the book will focus on defining how components of the framework, as an analytical tool, can be more concretely applied to understanding how cities are now and could potentially in the future respond to climate change. This discussion will present policy-relevant recommendations.

The book's analysis framework, application chapters, and case studies illustrate how the opportunities for transitions to transformative climate action can be enhanced for use by local policymakers and practitioners. Highlighted are specific tools and strategies, financing and governance, and knowledge co-production, and the role of boundary organizations. Underlying the analysis is how the framework can be applied in cities to promote transformative change. Explicit is the understanding that the framework can be used as a normative tool for enhanced climate action.

2

Why Do Cities Face Environmental Crises?

The London Fog was a frequent visitor to the British capital from the early nineteenth century almost through the entire twentieth century (Brimblecombe 2012). A primary source of the "fog" was the extensive burning of soft (high sulfur) coal in local homes and factories. Also known as the pea soup fog, black fog, killer fog, or what is now more regularly described as smog, the fog defined many aspects of daily life and was part of the experience and description of London (Brimblecombe 2012). As far back as the early nineteenth century, epidemiological studies at the time noted that the fog was a significant health hazard. The Great London Smog of 1952, lasting from December 5 to December 9 and responsible for up to 6,000 deaths, became a turning point and spirited a series of local and national clean air policies, such as the Clean Air of 1956 and 1968, that significantly improved the air quality of the city over the next several decades.

The case of the 1952 London Fog provokes a fundamental question: What is it about the urbanization process that results in such environmental stresses and crises? The question seems easy but in actuality is fairly complex. The answer to this question presses forward two others: What is the overall connection between urbanization and environment, and how does this connection result in different environmental conditions, which often can cause stress and crisis?

This chapter attempts to address these questions. In order to do so, a variety of framing elements have to be defined in an attempt to explain the pattern of interactions between humans and their physical environment. The elements highlight ways in which human and natural systems are coupled and the mechanisms whereby these linkages emerge and transform over time as a city changes. The character of these connections results in multiple development pathways.

2.1 Connection between Urbanization and the Environment

The urbanization process must focus on the constant demand of ensuring that the day-to-day life needs of urban residents are met. The conditions for town and city building and expansion require the acquisition and transport of food, energy, and water supplies and subsequent movement of waste products. These resources are intended to meet the biological needs of humans and their other material needs, such as shelter, the ability to move around the city, places to work, recreate, and take part in other activities of everyday life, such as politics, social interaction, and religion. While all humans require some sort of shelter, the cultural and economic contexts of a place define the character of that shelter (i.e., its size, organization, and construction material). Context can determine what is required (i.e., minimum standards such as indoor plumbing) or what is deemed as desirable. Of course, both of these conditions can also change over time and vary across space. For example, in the United States – the median floor space per capita for new single-family homes increased from 507 sq. feet in 1970 to 724 in 1990 and 926 in 2014 (U.S. HUD and ESA 2014). Meanwhile, the per capita floor space available in more developed countries is at least double and often more than that found in less developed countries (Harvey et al. 2014; González-Torres et al. 2022).

Urban development also requires more than just housing, it demands significant transformation of natural landscapes into built environments for places to conduct business, government, and state functions, and engage in recreation and the arts, as well as a means to get people and products in and out, and around cities. A connection between this transformation and its impact and the conditions of society is present, but the exact relationship is by no means simple or linear.

Often cited variables that drive the level of impact include the population, level of technology, and overall wealth or affluence. The I = PAT formula highlights this relationship by stating that the level of environmental impact is equivalent to the population, level of affluence, and technology available (Chertow 2000). While useful as a heuristic device, the formula has been largely portrayed as superficial and failing to address underlying social structure and power relations that result in environmental impact (Alcott 2010). Contemporary analyses focus more on the role of choice and how consumption is socially constructed and results in environmental impact. This perspective enables insights into how urbanization does not necessarily lead to environmental stresses and crises; they emerge from societal structures and processes. The impact of social conventions, attitudes, and norms is well illustrated by the different city densities around the world. For example, metropolitan Phoenix, a desert city in the southwest of the US, has a population density of 3,165 per square mile while, Cairo, Egypt, also in a desert, has a metropolitan population density of 50,180 per square mile. These vastly different densities illustrate different attitudes and societal contexts regarding the construction of everyday life.

As the global population shifts to become more urban, scholars have continued to debate the relative impact of the growing number of people experiencing an urban lifestyle on global resource consumption (Marcotullio 2003). On average, urban residents per capita consume more resources than rural residents; however, these ratios vary widely. In high-consumption countries like Australia and the United States, urban densities and distributional efficiencies often enable urban residents to be less consumptive per capita than rural residents. Conversely, in the Global South and otherwise less-developed settings, urban residents often consume many times more resources than their rural counterparts. In a recent study of water use in China, urban residents used 1.6–3.7 times the amount of water than rural residents (Sun 2019). Another factor that influences urban versus rural consumption rates is household dynamics specifically the size of households. The average household size has decreased globally, thereby further increasing the number of households. And, in general, urban households tend to have significantly fewer residents than rural households even in the same country. The greater number of households requires more separate spaces (e.g., apartments) and greater demand for items required for each household (e.g., appliances, furniture, and electronic equipment).

The spatial extent of urban areas expanded dramatically in the twentieth century and the trend is expected to significantly increase at least throughout the first half of the twenty-first century. Gao and O'Neil (2020), utilizing a range of datasets and a set of socioeconomic scenarios, projected that during the next decades the global total amount of urban land could increase by a factor of 1.8–5.9, and the per capita land use by a factor of 1.1–4.9. Although the fastest urban land expansion will take place in Africa and Asia, the Global North also will undergo a similarly large amount of new urban land development. In fact, even in areas of population no growth or even decline, the expansion of the urban footprint on the land can continue through decentralization and urban sprawl (Guneralp et al. 2020).

Consumption is driven by a vast array of social conventions and norms. Social science research is rich with explanations of the connections between consumption patterns and social conventions and norms and how these connections change over time. Most fundamental in this literature is that social organization and structures, including conditions of social and economic stratification, segregation, and subjugation, have significant impacts on the rate, site, and mode of resource consumption. Substantial evidence exists that societal inequity is a significant contributor to resource exploitation and inhibits progress toward sustainability (IPCC 2023). Urban sprawl and metropolitan growth in the United States is a classic example. The rapid growth of single-family suburban housing and associated environmental degradation in the US during the mid twentieth century emerged from a variety of push and pull factors, but underlying much of the process was systemic racism with wealthier whites moving from cities with increasing proportions of Black or minority residents to the outlying new suburbs. Suburban homeownership was further promoted by elite interest demands as a way to dampen the possibility of labor unrest among the white working middle class (Mollenkopf 1983). Ownership would require homeowners to attend to the property maintenance, employment (to pay the mortgage and taxes), and home value (as their most valuable asset).

2.1.1 Meeting Human Needs and Continuous Environmental Challenges

Cities, as agglomerations of people and structures they build, put demands on local environments and more distant locations where resources for cities to function are drawn. The process of meeting local population's needs is a continuous challenge for cities of all ages, locations, and sizes. Human settlements of any size beyond a few families can face biophysical limits, because the immediate local environment typically would have resources only enough to sustain the food, water, and other material demands of a small number of residents. These biophysical limits can be adjusted or socially constructed, meaning that institutions and human systems can foster conditions for increasing the supply of locally limited resources. The requirements to do so however can be very difficult or impossible to achieve because of significant costs, lack of technological capacity, and political conflicts, among other factors.

The story of Los Angeles and the greater Southern California region is relevant here. The Los Angeles basin and extended environs has a significant scarcity of natural freshwater. At the time of European contact, the region's hydrology might have been sufficient to supply up to approximately 100,000 residents with drinking water. As of 2021, the greater Los Angeles metropolitan area population is roughly 14.0 million. The difference in population is an illustration of the capacity of society to dramatically transform and expand the resource consumption capacity of a place. At the most fundamental level, humans require water, nourishment, and other basic things to survive. A human should consume at least several tens of liters of fresh, potable water and approximately 1,300–3,000 calories of nutritional input[1] per day. As the population of a settlement grows, the local infrastructure needs to increase the amounts of resources available. Resources must be accessible on a regular basis without significant interruption. Given the world's urban population is now about 4.4 billion, approximately 5.7–13.2 trillion calories of foodstuffs (~22.8–52.8 billion cups of rice and beans [at 250 calories per cup]) are consumed in the world's urban areas every day with almost all of that brought into these communities from outlying rural areas or over longer distances on a regular basis.

Water along with food and energy are critical resources to sustain urban populations. These resources take precedence, given that they are required day-to-day demands of hydration and nourishment. Without these three resources, the capacity of cities to act and even exist ceases. The most significant threat facing a city is the disruption of its drinking water supply. Without water, a settlement site loses its viability and within hours and most certainly days as local stocks are used up, the site could lapse into social unrest and collapse (Woolf 2020). Similar conditions exist for food supplies, but it is highly unusual that a full shutdown of food supplies would occur (e.g., resulting from a military blockade) but instead increased prices also could cause civil unrest before supplies were fully eliminated.

Meeting these basic physical human requirements has been a continuous struggle for all of human history. This history is complete with significant effort, failure, and achievement. Needs have been met by altering the immediate sites where human settlement occurs and through the ever-longer-distance transport of materials from source regions. While many hold the notion that in premodern times individual cities consumed what was locally available and functioned as a closed system, as illustrated by early nineteenth-century German economist Johann Heinrich von Thunen's notion of the isolated state, it is quite clear that in many cases foodstuffs and other consumer goods traveled long distances even at the dawn of settlements and cities. For example, more than 3,000 years ago, extensive commercial trade routes existed through the Mediterranean Sea region linking cities together (Rose 2014). The long-distance trade routes not only meant that settlements and distant source areas were linked, but it is also clear that these connections resulted in the resources of distant lands to be exploited. The growing archaeological record illustrates that the Mediterranean network was just one of many throughout the world that were already present at that time.

[1] Depending on one's age, size, and level of physical activity. Source: FAO FOOD AND NUTRITION TECHNICAL REPORT SERIES ISSN 1813–3932 Human energy requirements Report of a Joint FAO/WHO/UNU Expert Consultation Rome, October 17–24, 2001, www.fao.org/3/a-y5686e.pdf.

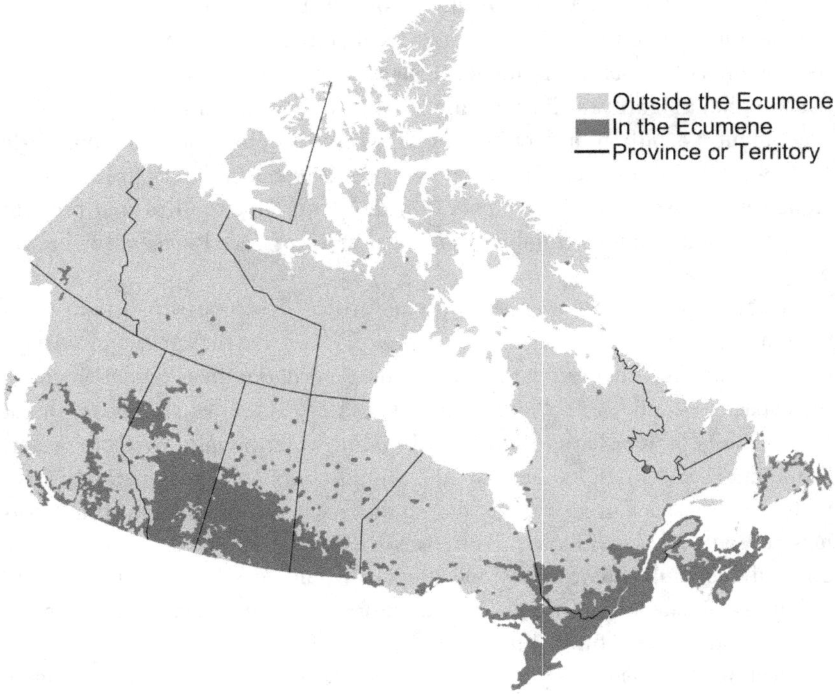

Figure 2.1 Ecumene of Canada. Highlighted as a dark gray shaded area. Source: Statistics Canada, Government of Canada, 2022, The 2021 Population Ecumene Boundary Files.[2]

Extraction, alteration, and utilization of local resources and the long-distance transport of resources from other locations have greatly expanded the livability of cities. Humans and human society are amazingly adaptable and have developed ingenious ways of surviving in a broad range of environmental conditions, including those that are notably wet, dry, hot, or cold, or a combination of two or more of these qualities. The term *ecumene* has been developed to define those lands permanently inhabited by humans. Typically, these are locations where the climate is favorable for some type of agriculture or other food resource extraction. The area of human settlement in Canada, for example, presents an image of extensive large-scale human occupation but an even larger area mostly devoid of human occupancy (see Figure 2.1). Of course, villages and communities are present throughout this larger area, but they are mostly quite small or in some cases not permanent.

[2] Source: www150.statcan.gc.ca/n1/pub/92-195-x/2011001/other-autre/ecumene-ecoumene/ec-eng.htm.

Over the past several hundred years, the ecumene of human settlement has significantly expanded. In large part, this resulted from an increase in human population settlement in ever more marginal locations (e.g., increasingly cold, hot, dry, or wet places). In other cases, and more importantly for our purposes, the ecumene has been significantly expanded as new technological advances such as air conditioning have made areas of the world more habitable or desirable to a broader population. For example, peninsula Florida has been occupied by humans for thousands of years, but broad application of air conditioning starting in the mid twentieth century made all-year occupancy much more attractive and was a significant factor in the growth of the permanent population (Arsenault 1984). In other localities the expansion of ecumene has been associated with the development of dramatically expanded drinking water supply, most often through the withdrawal of groundwater resources or long-distance conveyance of surface water. Growth in the ecumene often occurs as a result of multiple factors. This was the case in the desert areas of the US southwest and the Persian Gulf in the Middle East where advanced air conditioning and drinking water infrastructure and technology such as deep well drilling and now large-scale desalinization plants have greatly expanded resource supply.

The relationship between ecumene and biophysical limits is dynamic and complex. Some environments can sustain small human settlements – a few dozen to a few hundred – and are associated with local hunting and foraging. Human transformation of the environment has enabled places to develop much larger populations and exceed what could be understood as their settlement's "natural" carrying capacity. The story of the City of Jericho in the Middle East provides a brief example of humans' capacity to expand the ecumene even without access to modern technology.[3] Jericho, one of the oldest settlements in the world, is located along the west bank of the Jordan River and has a current population of 18,346. While its climate has changed over time, over the past 14,000 years it has consistently been an arid location with periods of extended drought. It currently receives approximately 145 mm of rain per year. Ten thousand years BCE, Jericho was a campsite for traveling hunter gathers, but by 9,600 BCE, permanent habitation began around the Ein as-Sultan spring (later called Elisha's Spring) that functioned as a sustained drinking water supply. By ~9,400 BCE, the permanent settlement grew to include almost 70 dwellings. Around 8,000 BCE, the settlement had a population of somewhere between 300 and 3,000. Over the thousands of years of occupation, humans have altered the local environment to enhance conditions for increased food

[3] Source: www.ancient.eu/article/951/early-jericho/.

cultivation and agrarian practice. Most important, irrigation was developed to provide an additional and consistent water supply, thereby allowing residents to maintain year-after-year food production (Mithen 2006). Jericho also emerged as a hub for ancient overland trade routes and as a result could acquire additional goods and provisions not available locally.

Cities and their residents face a multifaceted ecumene constraint that must be continually recognized and addressed if the community is to be sustained. Even if a constraint is resolved, the resolution and legacy (whether it be an infrastructure system, governance institutions, or form of social behavior) also often require continuous attention. For example, urban development in southeast Florida was significantly accelerated by addressing the local flooding problem through the construction of an intricate web of 3,500 kilometers of canals and water impoundment areas. This massive system is maintained through the operation of approximately 84 pumping stations, many of which operate on a continuous or near-continuous basis (SFWMD 2021). The pump stations move the water with a combined force of 100,000 horsepower (Swihart 2011), equivalent to that of two Boeing 737 jets.

Climate change will alter the ecumene of the world's human settlement. Urban areas in humid tropical equatorial nations will become subject to more frequent and higher temperature heat waves with humidity-related heat stress that will limit the capacity for outside physical activity for lengthy periods of time (Darmanto et al. 2019; Dodman 2022). In other settings, especially in arid sub-tropical areas, climate change will result in increased evaporation and droughtiness and in turn decreased freshwater availability resulting in more frequent water scarcity and supply vulnerability. Sea level rise will also make groundwater supplies vulnerable to increased saltwater intrusion. In still other locations, urban water supplies dependent on snow melt feeds streams also will experience water shortages as a result of reduced snow pack and irregular snow melt. High-density coastal communities with accelerating sea level rise also will experience more frequent flooding and potential storm surge damage. These threats to the human ecumene will require significant societal responses that might involve significant spatial shifts in human occupancy.

2.1.2 Conveyance Demands

Cities rely on a variety of mechanisms and infrastructure systems to convey resources to and from the city, and around the city. The process of city building results in significant demand on local and regional resources and is fundamental for urban growth. Materials for construction can be developed and extracted over a wide area. The globalization of the building supply industry has become increasingly extensive and involves vast global supply chains. City infrastructure and construction include a variety of natural resources that have been processed and fashioned into lumber, concrete, and steel as well as wires, pipes, and tubes. It is not enough to just get the resources to the city; they also must be continuously distributed about the city. In addition to basic water and foodstuff distribution, cities as systems are built around the question of how to bring energy to drive machines that provide water, heat and air conditioning, transportation, communications, and other essential services.

The physical infrastructure of a city becomes a significant part of the city itself but is often hidden from the view of its residents. Critical urban infrastructure, which supply needed resources and mechanisms to manage wastes and by-products, emerge as what environmental historian William Cronon describes as the "second nature" of a city. Before large-scale settlement, sites of future cities are dominated by what can be described as "first nature" – the local biophysical systems functioning without substantial human alteration. Yet in a fully built-out setting, the locality becomes dominated by a "nature" constructed by humans. This second nature includes reservoir systems, constructed landscapes including parks, and introduced biota.

This infrastructure becomes part of the lore and identity of the city. For example, in Victor Hugo's 1862 *Les Miserables* "Paris has another Paris under herself; a Paris of sewers; which has its streets, its crossings, its squares, its blind alleys, its arteries, and its circulation, which is slime, minus the human form." The city of Paris today has approximately 2,600 km of sewer lines, some of which include large tunnels and passageways. The historical development of urban sewers provides a fascinating vantage point to the tension between expanding the resource capacity of cities and the development of cities themselves (De Feo et al. 2014). This water and sewer infrastructure is actually a small part of the total amount of infrastructure that is built in cities, but it actually enables a tremendous amount of capacity for growth. In wealthier cities, the relationship between water supply infrastructure and growth especially is evident when examining drinking water supply. In such settings, the pattern and pace of urban development typically mirror the location of water supply pipes. New urban land conversion occurs typically on properties near to where this critical resource is conveyed.

Massive amounts of high-value natural resources are extracted, processed, and converted into urban infrastructure. The academic field of industrial ecology emerged in the past three decades to examine this process (Kendall and Spang 2020) and is defined as the study of material and energy flows through infrastructure systems. In the subfield of urban industrial ecology, research and analysis investigate how a network of industrial processes that extract Earth resources and transform them into commodities that are used to promote urban development and residential well-being, as well as how these resources can be managed and potentially recycled to promote sustainability.

Equally important is that cities require mechanisms and systems for waste removal. The history of waste management in cities is quite fascinating as humans are typically seen as messy and often foul their surroundings. Before the modern era, waste from cities was thrown out into the streets or just beyond the city walls, composted (along with human waste) for use as an agricultural fertilizer or used as fill for future construction. In the ancient city of Jerusalem, waste was landfilled in Kidron Valley, just outside the Roman-era walls of Jerusalem to a depth of 70 meters (Gadot 2022). To convey waste away from cities, work was done either by humans or animals or sometimes via water flow. Throwing waste into waterway flow was seen as an effective way to move wastes from a city and purify the wastes as they were mixed with the flowing water. The advent of the motorized carts and trucks brought a steep decline in the use of human and animal labor to move things around cities. In the City of New York, for example, a large fleet of garbage trucks removes approximately 6.4 million kg from residences each day (this number does include that material that is recycled and does not enter into the waste stream) of which approximately 80% is then put on a barge or train and taken to a landfill up to 1,000 miles from the city (Galka 2016).

2.1.3 Settlement Demands

The amount of wood, metal, stone, plastic, and other materials within the urban built environment is staggering. Cities contain what is described as embodied energy – the sum of all the energy required to produce any goods or services, considered as if that energy was incorporated or "embodied" in the product itself. Material flow analysis of Vienna, Austria, reveals the industrial ecology conditions of the mature city of approximately 1.5 million residents. Twelve to eighteen tons per capita per year of materials including construction materials and consumer products flow into the city. The stock material of the city is approximately 350 tons per capita and the number grows at four to ten tons per capita per year (Daxbeck et al. 1997). Industrial ecologists consider how large material stocks can represent potential future resources through recycling. In the case of Vienna, for example, there are approximately 20,000 tons of lead water pipes in the city's building and if repurposed could be refabricated into many other products requiring lead (Obernosterer and Brunner 2001).

It is clear that the process of extracting resources from the surrounding territory at ever-greater distances from the settlement has been part of the human experience. Neolithic people created extensive trade networks to acquire resources and supplies. Baysal et al. (2015) describe how the settlement of Çatalhöyük, Turkey, around 5,000 BCE, developed a complex and widespread chert economic network (i.e., rock material for tool making) that extended for hundreds of kilometers. This network facilitated the more rapid development and growth of some locations over others, creating conditions of comparative advantage and disadvantage.

Mobility is a key component of everyday life in cities. The growth of cities is often dependent on commensurate growth in the infrastructure to manage the movement of city-related functions. For infrastructure to provide this link, it needs to be consistently operational and resilient to stress and shocks. Transportation infrastructure also must overcome physical landscape challenges such as slope, topography, wetlands, and waterways. As the construction of transportation infrastructure takes place, it typically degrades and destroys local natural systems that cause a decline of local ecosystem services and often promotes increased exposure to environmental risks and hazards. This especially is true in cities with extensive waterfront areas where such ecotone sites have significant biodiversity but also historically have represented lands too economically valuable not to alter and fill, given that they provide space for port facilities, housing, and transportation infrastructure.

The natural environment can limit or place constraints on city expansion and land use conversion. Settlement sites with rugged terrain, steep slopes, and heavily bisected by waterways and water features such as wetlands illustrate well-recognized biophysical limits. The history of many cities is about overcoming these barriers and the breaching of them becomes significant benchmarks and turning points in their history. As an example, the completion of the first suspension bridge across the Bosporus (the strait that separates Asia from Europe, now known officially as the July 15 Martyrs Bridge and unofficially as the First Bridge, was opened in 1973) has dramatically changed the pattern of urban development in the Istanbul metropolitan region. The building of such a bridge had been first discussed in antiquity as a way to link the landmasses on either side of the Bosporus and further connect these two parts of the city. So important a site, the visionary inventor and designer Leonardo da Vinci also proposed such a bridge in 1502.

Another example of transformative infrastructure can be found further north in Europe. Oslo, Norway, is a city that historically has been hemmed in by low rolling mountains and deeply incising fjords. In the past decade, Norway has been able to apply its significant oil and natural gas wealth and begin one of the world's most expensive highway construction projects that involves tens of kilometers of tunnels cutting through or underneath the barriers that have blocked easy transit in Oslo and its hinterlands. In early 2019, Norway also proposed the E39 superhighway as a 47 billion USD project that will link Oslo with many cities in the western portion of the country along the coast in a long arc toward Norway's fjord-marked North Atlantic coast. When completed, the highway will hold many record-breaking engineering marvels including a suspension bridge with 1,500-foot-high towers and a span of 12,100 feet.

2.2 Urbanization and Environmental Stress and Crisis

How and why does the environmental stress and crisis emerge in a city with development, social organization, demand, and technology choices? As choices are made about how to work with or overcome biophysical limits of settlements, environmental stresses and crises can begin to emerge. These choices have consequences for the city's residents and its management, and in turn influence the rate of population increase, economic growth, and level and character of social differentiation resulting from competition and class divisions.

In this way, the question of choice reflects a series of basic questions about how societal development and transformation take place. Underpinning these secondary questions are foundational assertions regarding human behavior and collective action. More specifically, how and why are people motivated to act (or not)? Self-interest, including attainment of sustenance for oneself and one's family, and the quest for power and position are most often presented as reasons and can be expressed within the pattern and pace of city development. As an example, a community of boisterous business elite helped the early twentieth-century construction of Chicago's famous tall building Michigan Lake Front skyline to show the nation and the world that the city was taking its place among the great cities. At the same time, city building can be defined as rising from a collective and collaborative spirit that focuses on enhancing the everyday quality of life of residents. This expression can be associated with the opening of transformative infrastructure edifices such as New York's Brooklyn Bridge, which when opened in 1883 linked the cities of New York and Brooklyn and Manhattan Island and Long Island and simultaneously changed mobility in the emerging metropolitan and embodied the striving and dynamic spirit of the region.

The adoption of emergent technologies can well illustrate the connection between infrastructure choice and place building. While the technology by itself might enable or constrain specific options in the future, the decision to employ an available technology reflects underlying cultural norms and social biases. For example, as modern New York City was being built in the late nineteenth and early twentieth centuries, decisions were made about how to transform the congested, pedestrian, and horse-filled streets of Manhattan. Local elites and planners determined that the modern city should be more rational and efficient and in turn promote further economic development and capital growth. New transportation technologies and arrangements were being tested and co-existed. These included subways, internal combustion engine automobiles, bicycles, and yet fully developed flying machines. While a significant amount of subway tracks was laid during the first decades of the twentieth century, eventually the automobile became the dominant transport technology for the century. Bicycles became redefined as children's toys and local transit flying machines never developed as a viable mode of local transit, although helicopters do provide service for an elite segment of New Yorkers.

Cities of course can change choice of technologies and shift away from a locked-in technology but transitions can be difficult if not expensive. Decisions and choices made at one time will have influence in the future. Lock-in is a concept that illustrates how decisions made at one moment can be enabling or constraining for future decision-makers. Infrastructure or technology lock-in is a form of path dependency whereby a decision is made to select a specific type of infrastructure or technology and because of the cascading effects across time and space, the choices gain inertia.

Urban environmental histories of cities are full of conditions of lock-in where the legacy of choice can have significant implications. Lock-in can be presented as a single decision or connected to a broad-scale policy. A single decision example is the choice made in the 1930s not to construct rail lines on the George Washington Bridge linking northern Manhattan (and New York City) to the state of New Jersey. If added, this rail line would have linked the city's subway system with the rapidly suburbanizing area of northern New Jersey and as a result would have enabled more widespread, railroad-focused public transit development instead of the automobile-oriented development that rapidly transformed the agricultural landscape of northern New Jersey. A broad policy example of lock-in also comes from New York. As mentioned earlier, in the late nineteenth and into the early twentieth centuries, there were multiple modes of urban transit being proposed and tested, among them were dedicated lanes for bicycle users. By the 1920s and especially by the mid 1930s, bicycles were pushed to the side as a viable mode of urban transportation and the dedicated bike lanes were eliminated. Now in the first decades of the twenty-first century, the ambition for increased bicycle use has grown stronger but existing lock-in of other modes of transportation makes it difficult for another mode (such as bicycles) to be integrated back into the suite of options.

In situations where development is especially rapid and the government's capacity to dictate change is powerful, the transition from one technology to another can be dramatic. In the early 1990s, Beijing was a heavily bicycle-dominated city, but by the 2008 Olympics, throngs of cars filled the city's streets. By the late 2010s, however, bicycles were making an impressive resurgence as the city leaders attempted to control the intense local air pollution and enhance sustainability. These sorts of shifts can be implemented when strong central government control of the development and execution of public policy is present such as in Chinese cities. It should be noted that many cities in other governance contexts where the central authority does not have as much control are also experiencing a significant increase in bicycle use and grassroots and bottom-up discussion about how to reconfigure the use of urban space. Debate regarding which process is more successful remains.

Choices become important break points in any decision-making process. Implicit in the concept of choice are decision pathways or decision trees where branches illustrate divergent options. While we need to recognize that decisions are potentially reversible, iterative, and dynamic, once a decision is made, a certain amount of lock-in emerges. Choices come with resource allocation, governance adjustments, and physical alterations that are often difficult to reverse or significantly change. Choice and binary decision-making can limit future flexibility by directing cities toward one direction as opposed to another.

In this context, choice can generate environmental problems through two primary pathways. Most basic is that choices not taken could have been more in sync with the city's environmental limitations in ways in which the desired outcome (e.g., providing transit, energy provision, housing) could have been achieved with fewer environmental costs (or other costs). And second, specific choices while they might seem practical and effective in the short term could limit future flexibility and promote lock-in where the focus on a specific mechanism of resource management might become an issue at a larger scale application. As an example, automobiles in US cities in the early twentieth century were presented with great fanfare and as symbols of modernity and enhanced freedom for those who had access to them. At the same time, they also brought well-recognized and numerous social and environmental problems. And now that the highways have been built and opportunities for public transit diminished, it is hard to retrofit the cities' landscapes into a different urban form.

It is not only lock-in the built environment that is difficult to change. Built environments also can engrain in local populations specific social patterns of use and consumption. People become used to their mode of everyday life and change can be hard. At the same time, built environment choices also facilitate the development of governance institutions that surround the use of specific technologies, and in the same context they limit the development of the capacity of the other forms of technology. For instance, the rules and regulations of automobile use are quite extensive. Attempts to reintroduce public transit including bike riding and bike share programs in many cities however have been met with delays and conflicts because cities lack the governance capacity to manage competing road uses. The development and assertion of private property rights represent an excellent example of the cumulative effects of social and cultural norms and governance capacity. Extensive scholarly debate exists over the role and significance others of private property in urban environmental problems, but it is clear that private property rights when connected to specific policy promote individual interests over collective or community interest, foster increased environmental degradation, and also limit environmental protection strategies.

Choice also comes with uncertainty and lack of knowledge of the full implications of any decision. The need for environmental impact assessment statements in which potential effects of any decision can be illuminated reflects this recognition, but they themselves are quite limited in application and often fail to take into account all potential considerations. While rational resource decision-making based on a utilitarian philosophy often promotes the choice of the most beneficial option, empirical evidence shows that flexibility and capacity to act with uncertainty can promote a diversity of strategies that also allow for experimentation across a range of potential strategies. Policy diversity and flexibility are especially valuable when the conditions are highly dynamic, such as with rapid urban development and now with the onset of climate change.

2.2.1 Solutions and New Problems, Inefficiencies, and Inequities

Underlying the issue of choice is a question about how choice is constructed and by whom. Choice by definition is socially constructed in that they are not natural categories but emerge through a process of contestation based on norms and divergent interests. For example, public policy choices are often mediated through the actions and interests of elites, and often these might be in conflict with the common good or actions that promote environmental protection. Furthermore, these interests can promote or enable modes of consumption that also have negative environmental ramifications.

The story of the unintended consequences emerging from solutions is quite richly detailed in the urban environmental problem literature. What is attempted here is an unpacking of this relatively simple narrative and a more detailed examination of how and why solutions lead to these negative outcomes. Addressing human resource demands in cities often leads to consequences that become problems, resulting in inefficiencies and can entrench or foster inequities. Urban environmental histories are full of crises and solutions, or at least in many cases partial solutions. These solutions frequently lead to unintended consequences, including new problems, inefficiencies, and inequities. The most immediate and accessible solution and the most easy to achieve some measure of success is often the option given the greatest interest and is most attractive. It is well documented how current solutions might lead to unintended or unforeseen negative consequences, and as often described as costs not taken into account or external to the decision-making process. Of course, solutions also have intended consequences where solutions knowingly can adversely affect specific groups, communities, or locations. An underlying question is which of these consequences were intended or unintended and to what extent does this difference matter?

Several key reasons have been identified as to why solutions to environmental stresses can lead to unintended consequences or undesirable outcomes. The lack of system perspectives or lack of understanding feedbacks are specific reasons that are well documented. The history of urban environmental problems is full of attempts to solve problems with limited knowledge or lack of understanding of the systemic shifts that might occur. Secondary air pollutants are classic examples. These are pollutants that emerge only after primary air pollutants are released and then chemically react in the environment with naturally occurring gases to construct additional pollutants. Unintended consequences or feedbacks initially are not fully understood and often can long go unnoticed if not overtly evident. One has to have the ambition and focus (including sensors or equipment) to identify them. It is only after a period of time that the scientific evidence of unintended consequence becomes manifest. For example, it took decades of research in the mid twentieth century to finally determine how automobiles contributed to local air pollution.

Scientific uncertainty also significantly hampers response to environmental problems and their solutions. As issues emerge, there can be genuine failure to understand the processes at work and in turn recommendations for actions. The history of germ theory and urban settlement illustrates this point well. Knowledge deficits on how and why individuals became sick in settlements and cities are an important component of urban history. Various explanations were prevalent at various times – with explanations often being rejected as new narratives emerged. Miasma theory is a case in point. This long-accepted idea was centered on the notion that contagious diseases were from "bad air" or "night air" that rose up from rotting organic matter. The theory was accepted from ancient times in Europe and China and was only abandoned by scientists and physicians in the late nineteenth century when scientific evidence proved that specific germs cause specific diseases.

While germ theory signaled a revolution in urban public health, many other urban threats remained unexplained and relatively infrequent or required extended investigation. Conditions associated with extreme events are good examples. An early twentieth-century response to periodic urban flooding was the construction of built infrastructure such as levees and dikes to prevent such calamities. While in some cases these actions eventually worked or were successful, the solution was deemed faulty in many situations. It took decades for communities and investigators to recognize that these infrastructure solutions in many instances set the seeds for even more significant disaster. The infrastructure by providing a sense of security from flooding enabled or encouraged more development and construction to take place in at-risk locations and eventually extreme events occurred that overtopped the structures causing even greater loss and damage.

Another reason for solution failures relates to the definition of the problem time frame. Decisions are often motivated more by the need to address pressing immediate issues or concerns, rather than the longer-term issues. In addition, those who are acting are typically more focused on protection of self and their interests than those of future generations. The lack of intergenerational consciousness is a particularly significant deficit. At the same time, the strategic use of power and privilege by the elite further ensures that decisions are often directed at immediate and specific demand, and not the interests of the general populous.

Yet another reason that influences the likelihood of unintended consequences is how their repercussions are addressed and whether one individual or organization is defined as responsible and potentially held accountable for the impact. In the US and less so in other countries, legal action can be brought against agents responsible for unintended consequences, but they must be defined as negligent. If protections against these actions are not present, then they might continue to take place. In the US during the 1960s and 1970s, there was a rapid expansion of how environmental problems could be addressed within a legal framework. The growth of tort law, class action lawsuits, and the provision of legal rights to nonhuman entities provided a broader legal basis to address a wide spectrum of environmental problems. It became clear that legal action could be taken against those entities responsible for creating the problem.

Environmental historian Joel Tarr has been a leading proponent of the concept – the ultimate sink – that states that human action results in externalities that are cast off from the process, and that the environment provides the best and eventual place for them. Externalities in economic terms are costs that are not accounted for or formally incorporated, and in turn are expressed onto other systems or individuals. More broadly, externalities can be described as burdens that are expressed onto others whether they be part of the human society or the biosphere. Externalities are always present and result from the fact that systems always have waste and bi-products, but societies make decisions on how they are distributed, allocated, and managed. They are often distributed inequitably and illustrate well how inequity can be socially constructed.

The concept of the ultimate sink helps further reveal how and why urban environmental problems emerge. The ultimate sink brings up a range of drivers, including human behavior, economic efficiency, and limited governance capacity. The concept also highlights the notion that environmental problems typically occur in response to a complex interaction of biophysical limits and societal structures. Urban environmental histories are filled with narratives of use, overuse, or misuse and resolution and these conditions occur across many pathways and sequences and are a result of many mechanisms.

Other narratives of environmental problems speak to unexpected issues or concerns that become evident with an increase in knowledge and understanding. In these situations, the pathway by which the environmental problem becomes known is a big part of the story. These stories are often surprising if not jarring and provide opportunities for potentially sudden shifts in thinking and approach as the issue becomes fully revealed to the scientific and lay public. Perhaps the full-scale understanding of the ecological impacts of pesticides as illustrated in *Silent Spring* by Rachel Carson presents a high-profile case in point. In this example, an issue increasingly understood within the scientific community blossomed quickly within the popular conscientious with widespread readership of Carson's famous book published in 1962.

As environmental problems emerge over time, their process of development can be punctuated by system-level shifts that alter how basic environmental conditions operate. After an extreme event, a new major construction project, or a new policy or practice put into effect, environmental patterns of use can be redefined that can result in significant new environmental problems. For example, the construction of the Tamiami Trail highway in the 1920s across the southern end of Florida dramatically altered the pace and pattern of land development in the region, leading to a significant increase in hydrological and habitat changes that in the 1980s emerged as part of an ecological crisis in the Everglades.

These large-scale systematic shifts are often associated with inefficiencies and deficiencies that eventually result in environmental problems and challenges. In the case of the Florida Everglades and the impact of urban and agricultural expansion, these included lack of knowledge of how the systems function and respond to stress particularly associated with issues of deep uncertainty, and lack of efficient or inequitable distribution systems (e.g., water distribution pipes do not deliver water to areas of need). Underlying these issues are social inequities that also need to be investigated. These inequities reflect the presence of class systems and underlying uneven power relations, the presence of "others" or people seen as outsiders, undesirable, or less worthy, and the presence of external stresses that force interest groups to increasingly compete. This increased competition can occur when a natural system loses its capacity to respond to environmental pressures such as during chronic (e.g., drought) or abrupt shifts (e.g., extreme air pollution episode). These points and the basic narratives of how environmental stresses and crises emerge from everyday practices and are responded to are explored in greater detail in Chapter 3.

3

What about Cities Make Them Places for Environmental Problem-Solving?

> Nothing is talked of or thought of Croton in New York but Croton water; fountains, aqueducts, hydrants, and hose attract our attention and impede our progress through the streets. Political spouting has given place to water-spouts, and the free current of water has diverted the attention of the people from the vexed questions of the confused state of the national currency. It is astonishing how popular the introduction of water is among all classes of our citizens, and how cheerfully they acquiesce in the enormous expense which will burden them and their posterity with taxes to the latest generation. Water! Water! is the universal note which is sounded through every part of the city, and infuses joy and exultation into the masses, even though they are out of spirits (Diary entry of P. Hone October 12, 1842).

The city of New York's drinking water supply had been unstable and deficient for decades up through the opening of the Croton Reservoir system in 1842. For the first century and a half of New York City history, from the early 1600s to the 1770s, the colonial settlement managed the water supply with an ad-hoc set of private and public wells. Waste was disposed of locally, slowly diminishing the water potability and eventually fouling the local supply. The next half century, from roughly 1774 through 1830, was characterized by a series of failed private sector interventions to promote adequate water quantity and quality. What emerged de facto were two systems of water supply, one providing more expensive higher-quality water for elites through private carters and one of degraded quality for others. By the 1820s, New York was increasingly wracked by disease, fire, and commodity disruptions in part resulting from a lack of adequate and consistent supply of water. While the poor continued to suffer from disease outbreaks tied to the polluted drinking water, an emerging problem was the storage or availability of large volumes of water for firefighting (Burrows and Wallace 1998; Koeppel 2001).

Water shortages were an issue of concern, especially for the rapidly growing merchant class who began to lose a significant amount of merchandise in uncontrolled waterfront warehouse fires. This stress quickly became a crisis and demands for a solution rose significantly. The authorization, building, and the eventual opening of a new massive water supply system connecting the city to external resources was transformative. The celebration of the water's arrival brought days of celebration in New York with a five-mile parade on October 14, 1842 (Burrows and Wallace 1998; Koeppel 2001).

It is clear from this example that the building of cities causes change that can result in stresses and crises, which must be at least eventually recognized, and possibly even addressed. Cities once built out, also are exposed to environmental risks and hazards that result in shocks, stresses, and crises to which a response can be necessary as well. This chapter addresses the questions of how do cities become and then function as important sites for environmental problem-solving, what about the character of cities helps promote such problem-solving, and what are important exceptions to these conditions when cities do fail? Understanding when do these efforts occur and under what circumstances and why do some of these responses succeed or fail becomes an important part of a city's development history and affects local residents' quality of life. These processes can be found in all cities, but how they play out varies across a spectrum of different cities with respect to size (small, medium, or large) and level of wealth (low, moderate, or high) (e.g., Birkmann et al. 2016).

This work takes the position that the vast majority of urban environmental solutions are pushed forward in direct response to stresses and crises. The urban environmental history literature supports this assertion. However, there have been instances where cities have proactively diminished the likelihood of future stresses and crises. Forward-thinking individuals or collectives often promote action based on previous experience or observation from other sites. In this volume, both situations are reviewed, although most attention is given to the reactive character of problem-solving. Even with reactive problem-solving, one should focus on the intention of actors, or more specifically, in whose interest are they acting, and who benefits and who loses in the process.

Alternatively, numerous instances are present in which cities and their representatives have failed to act or were clearly unable to act, and the associated stresses and crises are left largely unattended. Sometimes these conditions remain in the short term to be eventually managed, but in other cases, the situation remains unaddressed. In these cases, the problem could press other broader systematic stresses and crises, leading to potential collapses (Solecki et al. 2017). In the worst cases, sustained habitation at the precrisis levels becomes untenable, and the cities decline or potentially fade into history (Woolf 2020).

3.1 Stress and Crisis in the Urban Environment

Urban environmental crises and their potential resolution bring forward several questions. When does a situation reach a crisis state? What are the metrics of a crisis (how can it be measured), and when is a situation considered to be in crisis? When does a condition become a stress, and when does a stress become a crisis? What conditions result in a significant response or not, and when is that response thought to be successful? The answers to these questions are often relative and context-specific and demand a systems perspective. Crises create conditions of uncertainty about how the current conditions will proceed, threaten the important goals of the entity affected by the crisis, and present a recognition that the existing system can no longer be maintained as currently organized.

The two terms – stress and crisis – seem relatively simple but in fact can have multiple meanings and interpretations. The concepts of stress and crisis have been long discussed in the research literature and relate to a variety of situations and contexts, including personal, social, economic, political, and environmental, among others. A stress can be defined as a change in a factor or quality that causes a process or system to alter how it functions or the rate at which it functions, while a crisis can be defined as a stress or set of stresses of such magnitude that the process or system might cease to function or cease to be able to function as it is currently. The notion of crisis is associated with a place, condition, or system that is potentially near collapse or at a state of collapse. By definition, a system in a state of collapse might be experiencing a magnitude of change that could be irreversible.

In a variety of professional fields and academic disciplines, different benchmarks and indicators exist to measure stress and crisis. Within medicine, for example, blood pressure, blood oxygen, and blood chemistry, indicative of trauma and infection, are such established metrics. With respect to stock markets, a 10% loss is described as a "correction," while a 20% drop can be classified as a result of a "recession." While agreed-upon metrics exist in a variety of settings, it is important to recognize that conditions of stress and crisis are relative and can differ vastly among those experiencing the crisis and be quite different for those experiencing it and those who are simply observing it. Crisis is often described as a lived experience and difficult to comprehend unless one is faced with the same or similar crisis.

Within the many fields associated with environmental sciences, a range of approaches are present to develop, validate, and use metrics or indicators of stress and crisis. This approach flourished in the 1970s, 1980s, and 1990s with the emergence of environmental impact assessment methods and the need to understand and document potential negative and positive effects of policy and regulation. In the 1990s, as the concepts of resilience and sustainability, and ecosystem health grew widely in the research literature and practice, so did the ambition to develop metrics and indicators of these conditions (Rapport et al. 1998). While debate continues regarding what are the most valid and reliable metrics, a parallel goal has emerged to develop indicators and metrics that could illustrate resilience qualities of communities, populations, cities, and other units of social organization and function.

As urban environmental management has developed in the past half century, public policy, regulation, and legal action have required the growth of a managerial and technocratic approach to environmental problem-solving. In the early 2000s, New York's Mayor Bloomberg helped crystallize this approach by popularizing the phrase, "if you can't measure it, you can't manage it." These empirical measures would help facilitate understanding of current conditions, the direction of change, and the relevant impact of specific policies or interventions. The rise of climate impact detection and attribution within climate-related litigation is a more recent illustration of the importance of empirical-based measures. Several cities in the United States joined into multi-party lawsuits against petroleum corporations seeking compensation for damages attributed to climate change and driven by greenhouse gas emissions (Gustafson et al. 2020).

These developments intensively discussed questions associated with crises, including who or what causes them or whose actions are driving them. Each crisis could have multiple narratives on how and why it came to be. These varying narratives can be highly contested with each leading to different potential responses and policy outcomes. The case of an acute large-scale industrial accident in an urban area, such as an explosion or other failure that causes damage, injury, or death beyond the facilities gates, provides an example of differing narratives and potential solution spaces. When such an event occurs and one looks for remedies or solutions to limit the future risk, many storylines can be present. Did the accident occur because of (1) deficient management and oversight at the plant, (2) lack of government hazardous facilities regulations to protect against such failures, (3) improper or deficient land use zoning that allowed for development to be located too close to a potential hazard site, or (4) even broader socio-economic factors that resulted in the development of facilities that produce or handle hazardous substances to such a degree that they represent a societal risk (e.g., the growth of the chemical fertilizer industry that promotes tremendous agricultural production increases but also a range of acute and chronic health exposure issues)? While crises often result from a variety of factors, analysis and the narrative of the crisis often tend to coalesce around specific reasons and possible solutions that are debated and often remain contested.

It is also understood that crisis narratives can change over time as new knowledge and interpretations are brought forward. In this way the story of a crisis can be seen as emergent and often iterative in that reconceptualization of the crisis narrative is an ongoing process. A critical facet of this understanding is how the crisis discourse is understood and presented when policy decisions and actions are taking place. The narrative will largely dictate the proposed action and the actions taken will transform the long-term narrative of the crisis, and understanding of its potential or actual solutions.

Issues of equity and justice are deeply embedded in the concepts of stress and crisis. For whom and by whom are fundamental questions to be asked about a crisis? While crises can be measured by agreed-upon standards or conventions, exposed individuals, groups, or communities can experience crises vastly differently. For example, in the 1980s, the AIDS crisis heavily affected specific populations, including gay men and intravenous drug users, but was essentially invisible to the larger society. Much like the crack cocaine epidemic of the late 1980s and early 1990s and the opioid epidemic of the late 2010s, although widespread nationally in the United States, most adversely impacted specific segments of the population and particular geographic areas.

The urban environmental realm is full of these examples. A recent high-profile example is the Flint, Michigan, water crisis of the late 2010s that directly impacted the users of the City of Flint water supply. While this crisis was of a limited spatial extent, the condition to resolve it was broader and has involved a larger territory and set of governance processes. This crisis alerted other older urban municipalities such as Detroit, MI, Milwaukee, WI, and Newark, NJ, to the possibility of similar lead or other toxic contamination in municipal drinking water. It is also understood that there can be spatial variation within individual cities and the recognition that particular communities or neighborhoods can be much more adversely affected than others. Concerns of over a variety of environmental threats such as urban heat island, air quality, water contamination, and flooding are typically spatially clustered and more often than not concentrated in communities of color or disadvantaged neighborhoods (e.g., low income, immigrant) (see Agyeman et al. 2003 as an early example).

The concept of environmental stress, its origin within cities, and its emergence are well described in Chapter 2. Here, we navigate the next crucial issue – how and when do stresses become crises for cities and their residents? Cities can face a range of different types of crises. The different classes of crises are, of course, often interlocked but also can be evaluated with respect to different stresses that are underpinned by system-level drivers and conditions. The interaction between stress and crisis is complex and often context specific. A fundamental question is how and when does a stress result in a crisis within a system. Stresses affect the operation of the system's operation and disrupt its ability to operate, function, and respond to shocks. In effect, stresses test the resilience of a system. As the stress increases, the system can enter into a crisis.

Homer et al. (2015) define a "stress" as a force that, if unopposed, will move a system away from its current state and that a "crisis," in turn, can be understood as a sudden event or a closely connected series of events within or across social–ecological–technological systems that result in the transition of that system from one equilibrium state to another, often during a period of suddenness and sharp nonlinearity. Crises in the context of cities are often associated with significant disruption or harm, in a relatively brief period, to the well-being of the city's residents. A benefit of a generic definition of crisis is that it is context neutral and allows for processes and conditions of crises to be compared.

While the concept of crisis is well understood, it is also clear that there are a multitude of metrics or descriptors to be used to illustrate a system being in a state of crisis. A key quality is an assessment of the system's resilience, particularly as it compares to the level of stress. If the level of stress exceeds the resilience of the system, the system can go into a crisis situation. Stress and resultant crises can be related to long-standing pressures and more acute and sudden pulses (Berkes et al. 2009). It is also clear that the occurrence of any one crisis can initiate cascading crises as one crisis can lead to or generate another crisis. At times, two or more high-stress conditions could occur simultaneously as a compound risk – potentially advancing the condition for a crisis.

The concept of crisis is deeply embedded in the urban narrative – the stories of how cities grow, decline, and often grow again. In the first half of the 20th century, extending a trend from the latter half of the nineteenth century, US cities and the pattern and pace of urbanization grew tremendously. In the second half of the twentieth century, a series of forces drove a shift in this pattern, especially in the country's older more industrial regions, such as the Northeast and Midwest. The notion of the "urban crisis" was prominent in scholarly literature and public policy debates about US cities. The concept of the urban crisis first emerged in the 1950s with the first waves of economic disinvestment and urban stagnation and decline (Weaver 2017). The urban crisis was layered onto by a range of other elements and interpretations in response to conditions of racial inequity, fiscal shortfalls, rising crime, and environmental pollution. The narrative of urban crisis was complex and interwoven by a range of drivers and the highlighted potential solutions. Five primary categories of urban crisis can be defined and include the following (derived from Solecki 2010):

- Ecological resource – for example, water, food, and energy supply shortages
- Urban spatial development – for example, congestion and mobility, sprawl, environmental pollution, and quality
- Socio-economic – for example, war, civil disturbance; gentrification and capital disinvestment and reinvestment
- Demographic – for example, in migration and out migration, ethnic and racial shifts, in the US "white flight" and demographic tipping points
- Extreme Events – for example, acute hazards and disasters

While it is simple to assume that many of these crises are driven by population growth, as discussed in Chapter 1, resting on population as influencing crises masks a series of critical elements that actually create the crises. Overall, some of the crises are primarily rooted in the physical qualities of the city, some include physical-societal system connections, and some are more explicitly societal in origin.

3.1.1 Ecosystem- and Resource-related Crises

Urban residents are dependent on the development, transport, and delivery of vast supplies of resources for their everyday life and well-being. When these networks are chaotically insufficient to meet these needs, fail or are otherwise disrupted, cities and their residents can enter conditions of stress and crisis. These crises have been described within physical terms as biophysical limits or ecological concepts of carrying capacity. The limits can be superseded by societal action, which promotes the acquisition of more distant or other previously unavailable resources (e.g., building of a water conveyance structure). Climate change can and already has in some cases significantly altered resource availability for cities. Shifts in rainfall and increased droughtiness, for example, are pressing on many cities located in semi-arid and arid locations.

3.1.2 Urban Spatial Development-related Crises

Urban growth and expansion also bring a variety of stresses and crises. While the sustainability of urban life is clearly dependent on the provision of basic everyday needs of residents, urban sustainability also is dependent on the ability to move goods and people around the city and live in an environment that is not a threat to one's physical, emotional, and mental health. Urban environmental crises related to congestion and pollution (e.g., water and air quality) are present throughout modern urban history.

3.1.3 Socio-Economic-related Crises

The social organization, structure, and conflict can create crises in cities. Cities are continuously being built and rebuilt. Patterns of capital investment, disinvestment, and reinvestment (including gentrification) can dramatically alter the everyday life of city residents and the structures they inhabit and use. Civil disturbances including mass riots, rebellions, uprisings, and open warfare also foster crisis conditions in cities. For example, the City of Newark, New Jersey, a once robust industrial city, experienced a racially charged mass rebellion or riot (depending on one's position and understanding of historical context) for many days in July 1967. The crisis tore apart the social and economic fabric of the city and in many ways it has still not recovered.

3.1.4 Demographic-related Crises

Rapid in migration and out migration of cities can change the dynamics and character of cities setting up conditions for significant stresses and crises. While it is clear these sorts of shifts are driven by systematic societal changes (e.g., forced relocation creating a refugee crisis), demographic changes can rapidly transform places. In the US, during the 1960s and 1970s, white flight was observed and studied as part of the ongoing debate on the urban crisis. Urban sociologists, demographers, and geographers attempted to define neighborhood scale tipping points where white residents, driven by racist fears and concern over potential declines in property value, would begin to rapidly leave neighborhoods as nonwhite residents moved into the neighborhoods.

3.1.5 Extreme Events-Related Crises

Extreme events by definition are often associated with significant disruption if not significant loss and damage and possibly loss of life. Extreme events in cities can in themselves cause a crisis or press underlying stresses into a crisis condition. Extreme events such as environmental disasters and technological failures are shocks to urban systems that might or might not provide early

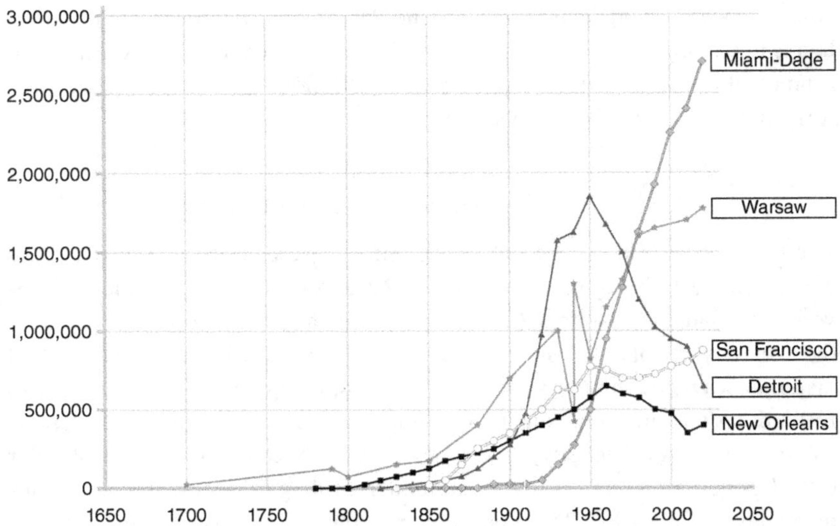

Figure 3.1 City Population Change over Time – 1700–2020. Source: Developed by the author from US Census data and Poland Census data.

warning signals. Hazard and disaster research literature is full of clear examples of how these events coupled with underlying social and environmental conditions can result in the sudden and dramatic transformation of cities and, in rare but documented cases, their substantial decline, the disintegration of everyday life for the city's residents, and population loss.

3.1.6 The History of Crisis in Cities

The population of cities can illustrate the varying impacts of crises on cities. In Figure 3.1, population shifts in cities that have experienced crises are compared. Each city has its unique story.[1] Warsaw was devastated by World War II and lost a significant percentage of its population. After a rapid increase in the late nineteenth century, San Francisco's population increase was slowed significantly during the aftermath of the 1906 earthquake and resulting fire. Detroit for much of the first half of the twentieth century was one of the United States' most rapidly growing cities. By 1950 it was approaching 2 million residents, but after experiencing multi-crises including social unrest, significant job loss

[1] It of course should be noted that the loss of population in a single jurisdiction does not mean that the larger metropolitan area population also loses population. For example, New York City during the 1950s and again in the 1970s lost population while the surrounding metropolitan region continued to grow.

and disinvestment, and financial collapse lost over 1 million in population by 2000 (with just 639,111 residents in 2020). New Orleans also has faced a series of urban crises but then also was dramatically affected by Hurricane Katrina in 2005. Between 2000 and 2010, the city lost almost 30% of its population. In comparison, Miami, a city that was founded in 1896, has continued to grow steadily through a series of major shocks, including several catastrophic hurricanes. The question remains whether it will be able to withstand accelerating sea level rise and more frequent flooding being driven by climate change.

The history of any city often includes many environmental crises; each emerging over time yet frequently conflated and disappearing into the background as other events pressing conditions take shape. The case of New York City's water supply is a good example. Few New Yorkers today know how challenging and contentious it was to bring a stable and sustainable supply of water to the city. Stresses build over time and occasionally are held back by partial solutions or solutions that work for a while but eventually fail. These stresses can lead to a crisis stage. Often a series of failed solutions occurs, and eventually, a crisis stage is reached. Things often get worse before effective action is possible or taken.

The story of Pittsburgh, Pennsylvania's air pollution problem is a case in point. The steel production history of Pittsburgh led to more than a century of complaints and concerns. During World War II, the massive wartime production of steel caused a spike in air pollution that eventually brought a fundamental solution to a stress smoldering for much of a century (Davidson 1979). James Parton, writing in a piece published for *The Atlantic Monthly in January 1868*, recounted his reflections on a visit to Pittsburgh. In what was essentially a causal piece of travel writing, his words had a profound impact on the city and its residents for generations to come.

> There is one evening scene in Pittsburg which no visitor should miss. Owing to the abruptness of the hill behind the town, there is a street along the edge of the bluff, from which you can look directly down upon the part of the city which lies low, near the level of the rivers. On the evening of this dark day, we were conducted to the edge of the abyss, and looked over the iron railing upon the most striking spectacle we ever beheld … It is an unprofitable business, view-hunting; but if anyone would enjoy a spectacle as striking as Niagara, he may do so by simply walking up a long hill to Cliff Street in Pittsburg, and **looking over into – hell with the lid taken off**.

By the 1840s, Pittsburgh was already a major industrial city with an international reputation for manufacturing and pollution on par with Birmingham, England, according to Charles Dickens when visiting the city in 1842 (Dickens 1913). The industrial prominence of the city only accelerated during the final third of the nineteenth century as did the degradation of the city's environment. The ongoing environmental crisis over Pittsburgh's air quality was connected to industrial production and economic growth and deftly used as a vehicle to prevent an aggressive pollution reduction proposal. The presence of the polluting facilities ensured steady employment for workers and the welfare of their families. Smoke and soot controls were presented as potentially limiting the profitability of the plants and potentially closing them. The air pollution problem in Pittsburgh remained fundamentally unresolved for decades, well into the middle of the twentieth century.

Environmental crises can eventually emerge as a threat to the very economic stability and continued growth of the locale, and in some cases, the viability and identity of the city itself. Water crises, either related to frequent flooding or droughts, are often associated with these conditions. Any water crisis, especially with drinking water systems, can have widespread effects. For example, the "Day Zero" water supply crisis in Cape Town, South Africa during the late 2010s, left a legacy of trauma and a call for action that can take decades to fully respond to (Taing et al. 2019). During these crises, tipping points are frequently passed, and transitions occur. These moments, variously described as inflexion points or phase changes, are where the system dynamics associated with the crisis might significantly change or not. Crises can lead to modifications or adjustments that resolve a portion of the issue but do not entirely become transformative.

Again, the Pittsburgh air quality challenge is illustrative. The intense pollution with World War II-era production and the catastrophic Donora, Pennsylvania (about 25 miles from Pittsburgh), smog incident of October 1948 that killed 20 residents and sickened 7,000 of the 14,000 residents helped peak concern about air quality. Local legislation to address the problem was only partially successful. To eventually, significantly address the issue required decades more of activism and federal legislation and regulation, and the steep decline of the steel industry as an economic driver in Pittsburgh.

It also should be remembered that crises and transitions happen all the time in cities yet are mostly limited with respect to spatial and temporal impact; and that, there can be additive effects eventually resulting in larger-scale transitions across a city. Crime rates in cities, which are typically very spatially heterogeneous, are good examples of these phenomena. In large US cities violent crime rates vary significantly from neighborhood to neighborhood and often is limited to disadvantaged communities. When crime as a social process increases in wealthy neighborhoods, it is often only then that dramatic action is taken to reduce crime.

Resolutions of these crises lead to the emergence of new conditions that contribute to future crises that can appear at similar or other spatial, temporal, and social scales. The concept of unintended consequences is significant here. The building of new highways throughout cities is an obvious example. The opening of new highways while initially seen as emancipating and modern eventually facilitated dramatic shifts in urban spatial development, land use/land cover change, and increased environmental pollution.

3.2 Linking Urban Environmental Crises and Transitions

Urban crises emerge from stresses that grow and deepen. The peak of the crisis can result in some fundamental shifts that force changes or system level transitions that can seem abrupt or sudden. In this way, crisis and transitions are coupled. Urban environmental transitions occur under a variety of conditions. Fundamental questions about transitions are (1) when and where do they occur, (2) what part of the affected systems under goes change, (3) what are the system connections within the site of crisis, and (4) whether the transition cascades to other systems or sites. The basic sequence of transition events can be described in four steps or stages. First, underlying or long-standing stresses intensify and become crises. These crises can promote system transitions that, in turn, are connected to a process of reorganization that result in transformation (see Figure 3.2). This general process is well documented in academic literature and the lived experience of individuals. For example, elements of these basic steps are highlighted in the adaptive cycle diagram promoted within the

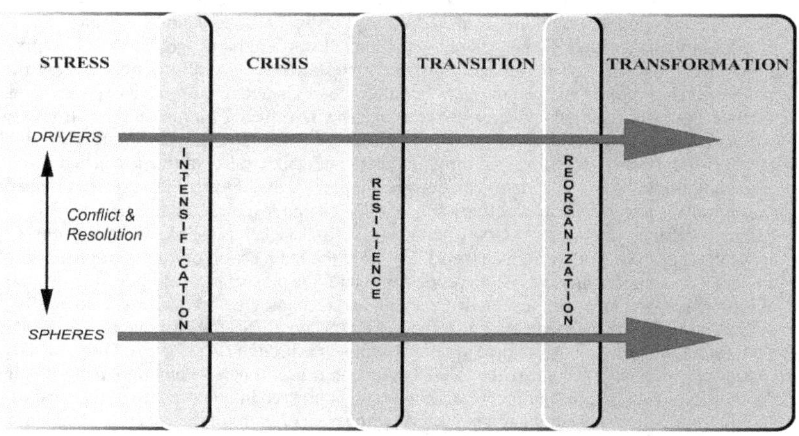

Figure 3.2 Connection between stress, crisis, transition, and transformation. These four phases and their overlap are derived from the research literature. Source: Author.

resilience research community (e.g., Gunderson et al. 1995) in which a disturbance results in a release of material/resources that facilitates a process of reorganization, then resource exploitation under these new conditions, and rapid growth to be followed by a period of slowing growth and senescence, and in turn priming the system for another period of release. One difference is the process outline employed here is not assumed to be circular or for that matter explicitly linear. Our focus is on specific moments of transition and not the legacy effects of such or how one transition might begat a subsequent transition. Another significant difference here is that the overlap between the phases becomes an important analytical component for understanding urban system resilience and transitions. The focus is on the conditions associated with the shift from one step to another as equal to the conditions of each step.

Within each phase, the conditions are manifested by interactions between the system drivers (root, context, and proximate) and the spheres of action (societal, environmental/ecological, and technological).[2] The movement from each phase to phase is associated with changes (e.g., intensification, resilience, and reorganization) which can be assessed and explained. This framing illustrates what we know and what part of the system needs further elaboration and explanation. The case studies in Chapters 5–10 and their analysis will address these knowledge needs. Questions to be examined include exactly

[2] The use of the phase "sphere of action" attempts to encompass two separate streams of thought within the urban research literature. Pelling and others (Pelling et al. 2014) develop a political ecology-framed concept of the adaptation activity space, which represents sites where the diverse components (i.e., individuals, technology, livelihoods, discourse, behavior, environment, and institutions) interact within coevolving social–ecological systems. This approach is derived from Harvey's political economy-framed "activity spheres" that help guide understanding of meta-systems through an analysis of interactions, flows, and blockages between system components. Activity spheres are places where contestations between power can be revealed and the reach of power mapped through the influence of change in one activity sphere upon another. Power is acquired and expressed through the movement of information, entropy, and influence between actors and spheres. The interaction between the spheres captures the ability of actors to influence structures and through this to maintain control of the decision-making process of others. Activity spheres can become places where contestations between competing sites of power and influence of activity sphere upon can be revealed and understood. The Pelling, O'Brien, Matyas, and Harvey approach spotlights a central space of interactions. Other approaches derived from resilience theory highlight the intersection of multiple spheres, each of which have complex internal system properties. Here, the presentation of three system spheres of interaction (social, ecological/environmental, and technological) reflects the elements of the Social-Ecological (Environmental) and Technology Systems (SETS) framework, designed as an elaboration of the social–ecological systems framework through its recognized importance of technology in the urban context. The SETS approach is useful here to highlight and investigate the development and propagation of crises that might emerge in one or more of the spheres, and how and where transitions might emerge within one or more of the spheres. The metrics of stress and crisis and measures of resilience will be different within each sphere, and as a result having the simultaneous internal functioning in a complex set of interactions across spheres is important to maintain and conceptually highlight.

(1) when do underlying stresses manifest as crises, (2) how do the transitions take place and how is resilience of the existing policy system overcome, and (3) how does the reorganization in the transformation phase take place. For each question, the relative roles of the drivers and spheres of action are to be assessed.

3.2.1 Crisis and Resilience

Two basic results of a crisis can occur. One can be a system transition, and the other can be an adjustment (or series of adjustments) that draws on the resilience and adaptive capacity of the system to allow for the crisis to be resolved, dampened, or delayed without requiring a transition at that moment. These adjustments can temporarily or possibly permanently forestall the need for transition. In the context of a crisis, the adjustments connect to the resilience and adaptive capacity of the system under stress (Hosseini et al. 2016; Ribeiro and Goncalves 2019). The drivers of this situation connect to the system's underlying resilience properties, including its capacity to entrain resources, ability to utilize new resources, and flexibility to reorganize its system level structures. While these adjustments might seem to reflect environmental problem-solving, in many cases, the underlying stress causing the crisis is likely not resolved and the stress and potential for crisis will be sustained.

In the example of the New York City water supply system, adjustments to the system for decades from the 1780s to the 1830s pushed back the need for a transformative change, stalling the system transition process. When the transition to a new water supply system eventually occurred in the 1830s, it happened manifestly because the situation had reached a breaking point and the system was failing to supply enough quality water to meet the rapidly growing demand. Described in the context of systems analysis, the resilience and adaptive capacity of the existing system were exceeded. The system had become brittle and unable to utilize new resources and make adjustments to current and emerging threats.

The concept of resilience is central to this discussion. Systems operate within a dynamic range of dynamic environmental conditions. The resilience of a system defines the capacity to withstand the stresses and shocks, embedded in these shifts, and continue to function and maintain its operation. An extensive literature has been developed in the past decade on the connection between cities, the systems within them, and resilience (Meerow et al. 2016; Leichenko 2011; Ribeiro and Goncalves 2019). It is important to remember at this point that the key unit of analysis in this book is truly not the city or the municipality but the system or systems that are present or operate in a city and provide or enable well-being for the city's residents. Therefore, it is also vital to analyze the relative role of different contested and highly contextualized parameters that can influence the resilience of urban systems. These parameters can be described within a set of short provocative questions: (1) resilience of what, (2) resilience at what scale, (3) resilience to what, (4) resilience for what purpose, and (5) resilience for whom; and the implications of the political choices involved in defining these parameters for resilience building or analysis (Dewulf et al. 2019).

Several factors can influence the resilience of an urban system, including diversity, redundancy, connectivity, feedback, slow variables (e.g., conditions that change but only over a long period), participation, learning capacity, adaptive management, and polycentric governance (see for more discussion González-Quintero and Avila-Foucat 2019). These factors can be extended into a set of broader factors that need to be considered when examining resilience and its connection to urban environmental crises and transitions. These include the following:

1. Unit of analysis – what is the system in crisis and what is the structure and character of the system in crisis? Is it extensive and integrated or is it small and discrete? The focus here is on an urban system in crisis. These could be a social, ecological, or technological system or confluences of several integrated systems. The smallest unit is the discrete urban system, and at the largest scale, the municipality or metropolitan scale.
2. Onset of the crisis – temporal and spatial – what is the relative speed of the crisis – rapid or slow and is it contained to one location or is it simultaneously in multiple locations? Furthermore, is the crisis set within other crises? Is it set off by itself or one of many – that are similar, or where the crisis in question is the most significant or prominent? What are the diffusion properties of the crisis, and how is it spreading – slowly, quickly, continuously, leapfrogging, or along particular pathways?
3. Drivers of the crisis – what factors create the conditions for the crisis, transition, and transformation to unfold? Here we focus on root (e.g., cultural, historical), context (e.g., policy, development context), or proximate (e.g., specific influential time and spatial factors). Several key narratives of urban environmental crises are defined later. Examples of drivers of urban environmental transitions are numerous and include the application of a new technology, population growth, poverty, environmental hazards, wealth accumulation, resource limitations, institutional capacity, and capability.

4. Spheres of action – urban systems are composed of three overarching components in which a large number of simultaneous interactions within and between the components take place. These spheres of action are societal, environmental/ecological, and technological in character.
5. Function of the systems – the interaction between the drivers and the spheres of action is where the debates, struggles, and contestations take place that define the character and practice of the system at each stage of stress–crisis–transition–transformation process.
6. Resource utilization – ability to reach and integrate resources endogenous to the systems; and ability to reach and integrate resources exogenous to the systems. Resource utilization can diminish the pressure or thwart the opportunity for a transition.
7. Measurement or description or understanding of the crisis and what is an effective response including that of a possible transition. This includes a description of the material reality, of the perceived reality – often cultural or socially defined and of the lived experience of those connected to the events directly.

How these components intersect will determine whether a system crisis will occur, whether the crisis will shift into a transition or not, and, if a transition does occur, what the reorganization associated with that transition and eventually longer-term transformation will look like. It is important to understand how a transition can be advanced or forestalled through the resilience of the system as well as the system-level drivers embedded within. The incorporation of the system-level drivers as part of the broader context of system resilience represents an intellectual advance in that it provides further insight into specifically how the resilience of the system could operate under stress and result in a crisis and eventual transition. Analyzing the resilience of the root, context, and proximate drivers as critical parts of the system resilience helps to theorize how urban system transitions take place.

3.2.2 Urban Environmental Transitions

Transitions often include a phase change described as a nonlinear adjustment associated with specific tipping points. Urban environmental transitions are significant shifts in the character and structure of nature–society relationships within cities and between cities and their hinterlands (Solecki 2010). Transitions are associated with dramatic reconfigurations of how the system undergoing change functions and result in a cascade of changes that affect interconnected systems and the people, places, and pulses associated with the transition. While transitions typically result from disruptions, they themselves also can be disruptive. Examples could include a specific policy decision that leads to the development of a new water supply system or a large-scale shift associated with numerous policy changes and broader societal turns that for example led to a new mode of production and social reproduction; for example, the change of a city from predominately a trading center to a manufacturing production center.

Transitions are described and analyzed within many disciplinary contexts, including political economy, political ecology, environmental history, and conservation biology, and have focused on issues of resilience, vulnerability, environmental transformation, sustainability, and adaptive management (Solecki 2010). Transition theory suggests that critical transitions or regime shifts, a precursor to a transformation, can be precipitated by a massive shock or series of shocks that expose system-level instabilities and diminish or overwhelm the resilience of the system. These shocks bring an increased risk of an transition of a single system or a sequence of transitions across interlocking systems and can be associated with opportunities for transformative change (Scheffer et al. 2012). The connections between system-level transitions and larger-scale societal transformations have not been yet fully specified, yet they provide an area ripe for additional research.

The connection between system resilience and system transition is illustrated by Figure 3.3. In each example (a–c), a different level of resilience is presented. In condition ***a***, a large force or shock will significantly degrade the system-level state (e.g., its productivity, its input and output functioning); however, the system itself has the resilience to eventually recover. In the setting illustrated by ***b***, the resilience of the system is lower such that even a moderate shock can result in a significant reduction in the system's operation and function, but again the system will be able to recover. In each case, the system does not go through a transition. In condition ***c***, the system has an even more reduced resilience and at such a low level that even when what

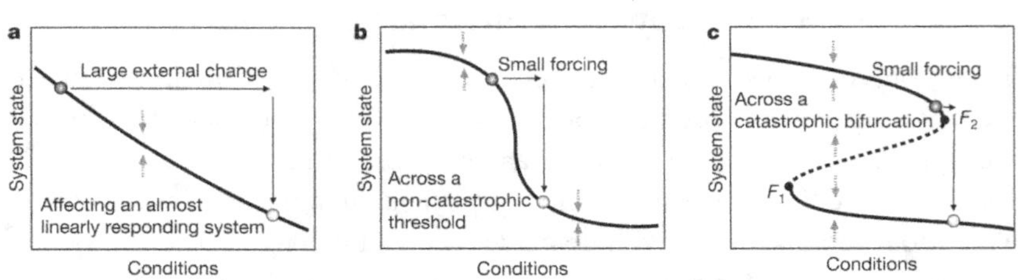

Figure 3.3 Connection between forcing (stress), system state, and transitions. Source: Scheffer (2009).

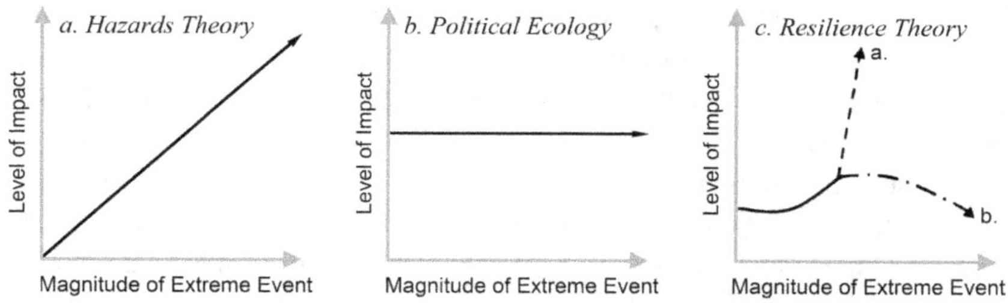

Figure 3.4 Association between the magnitude of extreme event(s) and level of impact in different theoretical frames. Source: Author.

objectively might seem like a minor shock results in a system-wide change in the system's function to such an extent that a new system state emerges. In this scenario, presented by Figure 3.3c, the system goes through a rapid transition or what Scheffer (2009) describes as a critical transition (or catastrophic bifurcation).

The size and frequency of the shocks are central to the discussion of how the resilience of a system connects to whether or not a transition will occur. The approach highlighted by Scheffer and other resilience researchers often makes the assumption that physical and social systems might operate in similar ways with respect to stress and crises. Within this framing of resilience theory, the magnitude of an extreme event(s) (encompassing both the size and frequency of the shock) as presented earlier in Figure 3.3 can result in widely varying impacts depending on the resilience of the impacted entity (whether it be a household, community, organization, or otherwise).

The relative influence of a shock is portrayed differently in varying scholarly literatures (Figure 3.4). The difference unpins basic assumptions regarding how social structures and agents (i.e., actors) can moderate (or not) the impact of external stresses and be responsive to them. In resilience theory, the response to a shock is dependent on the resilience of the system, and shocks led to two classes of outcomes – recovery, minimal long-term change, or a transition and fundamental change. In the hazards literature, there is an expectation that the greater the magnitude of the extreme event(s), the greater the impact will occur. Some variation in this relationship might come as the result of the differing vulnerability and/or resilience of the impacted entity, but the overall relationship is linear. Within a political ecology frame, the impact of the extreme event is socially constructed through a set of context-rich, social relations and physical conditions. As a result, the association between the magnitude of the event and its impact is not linear and highly specific to particular circumstances.

3.2.2.1 Understanding and Predicting Urban Environmental Transitions

Researchers have utilized a variety of perspectives to understand the link between extreme or shock events and resulting changes. In this volume, we investigate several perspectives including hazards theory, political ecology, and resilience theory. Each perspective offers a potential contribution to the understanding of how stress and crisis result in transition and the circumstances surrounding the transitions. The assessment enables a better understanding of how transitions occur under these conditions and the nature and character of what are defined here as transition variables (as opposed to system state variables that include extent, condition, and character of a system).

Transition variables help show the conditions or possibility of change in response to external and internal factors. For example, Benati and Guerriero (2021), in their analysis of climate change and state evolution, find evidence of the actions of elites as examples of transition variables. Solecki et al. (2017) define three generic transition variables within socio–ecological–technological systems. These include switching back and forth on decision-making, slowing the process of decision-making (i.e., taking longer to decide), and increasingly limited response capacity (i.e., less effective use of the resources for decision-making and decreased adaptive capacity as a result of less ability to activate resources for action). Three specific states of action during a crisis can be defined for each system; those that bounced back, bounced forward, or bounced away. The analysis of the transition case study narratives developed here attempt to determine the robustness of this framing and possible advancements. A qualitative assessment of transition variables and actions during a crisis will be employed.

This effort of theoretical integration is reflective of a broader approach that endeavors to connect a "hazard-in-context" approach with system-based resilience theory. It attempts to examine the processes of change in the earliest stages as they occur as opposed to resultant conditions that become evident long after the impact of the stress, crisis, and transition. The analysis focuses on the conditions of the transition – the when and how of the moment of change as well as transition variables, which would be especially useful to fully understand the stress/crisis – societal response interface. The analysis defines the relative role of root, contextual, and proximate transition variables as critical to understanding the process of societal-environmental change.

Research has begun to connect analysis of current drivers of change with the future conditions and in turn identify opportunities for transformative action (Wolfram et al. 2019). The work in this volume attempts to be innovative by setting current and future conditions within a longer temporal scale process, thereby promoting an understanding of past conditions and drivers of change and what they might reveal about current conditions of change and future opportunities, and by illustrating the connections between chronic stresses and episodic crises and the sequential process of change. Given this approach, the specific timing and structure of an environmental transition and transformation are critical to understand. A set of strategies and evaluative methods needs to be applied to understand if a transition is occurring, has occurred, and whether the transition can be predicted or even managed, and its potential effects understood. Several basic characteristics of transitions can be studied to evaluate their qualities. These include the speed of transition and whether and how the transition was accelerated, slowed, or stalled?; empirical measures of transition and to determine whether or not an environmental transition has occurred and when it might have occurred?; and observation and prediction of a transition, and how can one understand when transitions are occurring or be predicted. Investigators look for evidence that a transition has occurred. A variety of early warning signals have been identified including a slower recovery from perturbations, increasing autocorrelation, increasing variance, flickering and the appearance of alternate system states, and increased spatial coherence (Dakos et al. 2012; Scheffer et al. 2012).

Other important concerns are how does the process of transition and transformation propagate, and how does a transition or transformation at one scale manifest or add to the likelihood of a transformation at another scale? For example, it is also clear that individual, household decisions will be influenced by how these individuals observe or perceive the actions of their neighbors and the larger community. Simply put, people will be influenced by their neighbors and the trends that they see around. The connection between individual household behavior and neighborhood change is well documented in socio-demographic tipping points such as seen in the US during the 1960s and 1970s with white flight from inner-city neighborhoods. Conversely, how is a transformation that occurs at a "higher" scale, translated downscale to the household level. These upscale and downscale processes are highly relevant when applied to communities' transformation in response to accelerating climate change.

3.2.2.2 Urban Environmental Transitions and Reorganization: Collapse or Transformation

Transitions research illustrates potential linkages between system shifts, transitions, and broader-scale transformations (Solecki et al. 2017). It is clear from this research that not all urban environmental transitions are associated with transformative change. This in turn prompts two additional questions. What is the long-term result of an urban environmental transition; and what is the connection between different types of transitions and the system-level shifts or disturbances that follow? Transformative change occurs when the transition and early post-transition period root, context, and proximate drivers interact. The full spectrum of interactions within a specific transition and transformation are unique to each setting, but there are qualities that are comparable across cases. Furthermore, how these drivers interact influences the longer-term outcomes of the transitions. At least two general scenarios of these interactions have been presented and each results in a different narrative. One narrative is that transitions can lead to collapse (presented as a negative outcome), and the other is that transitions lead to transformation (presented as a positive outcome). In some ways this distinction is artificial because a transition by definition will result in a significant systemic change or what can be defined as a transformation.

The distinction between the scenarios is made when the interpretation of the implications of the changes takes place. For example, there is a robust collapse literature that highlights conditions following a transition or tipping point with different forms of societal breakdown or dissolution. Often anthropological or archeological in method and approach, these studies focus on the role of increased stress and crisis in the collapse of societies, cities, and cultures (Butzer and Enfield 2012). Analyses of Native American societal collapse, for example, the Mayan, Anasazi, and Cahokia cultures, are widely evident exemplars of this literature. A fundamental question in this literature is when does a crisis-induced transition lead to a collapse. Much of the early collapse literature focused on the significance of physical limits, exceedance of local environmental/ecological carrying capacities, and degradation of the resource base (e.g., soil erosion). More recent analyses have increasingly focused on societal conditions as critical mediating factors. The focus of analyses has shifted to how collapse is linked to an unsuccessful response and associated with lack of trust, uneven distribution of the costs and benefits (i.e., temporal, spatial, societal), lack of agreement on the solution, and lack of knowledge and scientific uncertainty.

Environmental transitions imply a process of reorganization. Within the collapse narrative, reorganization is associated with a breaking apart or breaking down but without a set of steps of recovery or building back up. Conditions where there is a construction of new order or pathway that is associated with a positive outcome can be broadly described as a transformation. A complex interplay between different elements of the root, context, and proximate drivers, in part influenced by the transition variables, is how this interaction manifests as a positive outcome associated with a "solution" to the originating environmental crisis. Transformational change and solution-oriented responses are related to a set of context and proximate drivers, including: (1) capacity to define the question/issue of concern; (2) condition of equity – question of fairness; (3) capacity to define solutions with sufficient science and information; (4) governance capacity; (5) alignment of interests across a spectrum of society; (6) capacity to integrate the diversity of opinion and defining solutions found through synthesis; and (7) material and visual implications of actions – witness the results of the action.

Root drivers influencing the transformation include a variety of cultural factors, such as the need and capacity for tolerance and acceptance; conditions that affect the everyday life of elites and the pressure on them that result from experiences in a public space; and the interactions between public space and private space. Political and economic factors include: existence of sites for new modes of capital (wealth) accumulation such as a second circuit of capital (i.e. real estate investment) and administrative control as well as governance opportunities for experimentation – that is, starting on a small scale; the need for a new social contract and commitment to some semblance of social order; and a place for both formal sector and informal experimentation.

This chapter illustrates the basic assertions regarding how environmental stresses and crises emerge from the urbanization process and what are the key considerations regarding how these crises led to transitions and reorganizations associated with environmental problem-solving. The discussion in the three chapters helps frame how we should analyze the case studies. Critical issues are how these processes interact – what are the linkages between the variables and components.

The discussion frames urban environmental transitions through a combination of political ecology and resilience theory that provides new insights into how these transitions can be understood and learned from and provides the groundwork for building new theory. The examination also helps reveal critical issues to make this investigation useful and germane to contemporary climate change challenges. These identified issues include the role of the state and private sector; and how to enhance equity and diminish inequity; drive transformation and accelerate change; manage uncertainty; deal with scale issues; make these processes transparent and enduring; and monitor and measure the transformations.

4

How Urban Systems Change

Cities, their change, and development have been the object of study for millennia. People have reflected on and theorized how and why cities change. This chapter frames these narratives and illustrates how the process of urban change can be understood, and what is the connection between these changes and urban environmental transitions. Change in cities happens as a result of human actions and intentions. Cities are in a state of becoming and as a result are unfinished (Bender 2002). Root, context, and proximate drivers of change and their interaction with three spheres of action create conditions for change in cities across several dimensions. These dimensions include the spatial development and spatial organization of cities as well as the social development and differentiation of cities and city life. These interactions and the resulting spatial and social organization of cities are critical to understand because they not only help provide the broad canvas from which urban crises in part originate but also the conditions into which crises are defined and responded to (or not) and from which transitions occur. Crises and transitions are both produced by and resolved within these conditions, and many crisis resolutions and transitions alter the construction and production of these underlying dimensions.

The overall structure of the chapter is organized around the theory of the social production of space. Advanced by Lefebvre (1991) and others, including Harvey (1990), Soja (1989), and Unwin (2000), the theory defines social space (as opposed to natural or absolute space) and its production. Space in this context is produced through the actions of a three-part dialectic (or conceptual triad) that includes three components: actual space (physical), discursive space (representational space), and lived space (via human experience). Space can be seen as a social product that is based on power relations, value, and the social production of meanings (Lefebvre 1991). Space, as such, in turn affects social practices and perceptions. This perspective allows for analysis of each dimension of space, as well as the space that is a product of the three components of space. The physical space (or actual space) is constructed by various actors or agents (e.g., developers, planners, and policymakers). Representations of space relate to discourses about a social space or what the space represents regardless of it being real or not. And third, the lived space is the experience of people who interact with the space. This triad, dialectical approach is useful for understanding urban space (Gottdiener 1985) as a product whose conditions, functions, and shifts are embedded in the articulation of competing power and agenda, and for the purpose of the investigation of crisis and response, vulnerability, and resilience.

Given this as framing, the chapter is divided into four sections. The first section focuses on the specifics of urban growth and development, and why cities grow and change with an examination of the role of drivers with specific attention to local contexts and interest coalitions. The second part focuses on cities as normative projects and is often designed and built to meet specific needs and objectives. Third, the chapter examines frameworks that illustrate and explain the urbanization process and their potential link to urban environmental transitions. Attention is given to how the urbanization process can be theorized as stages of development and how with each stage environmental transformations occur. The final section of the chapter attempts to synthesize some of the key findings of these first four chapters of the book and present a set of guiderails for understanding and assessing the application chapters' case study narratives and discussion. Overall, the discussion lays out the background needed to understand how environmental crises and transitions play out in cities.

4.1 Urban Growth and Development – The Material Reality of Cities

4.1.1 Spatial Development and Organization

The historiography of cities has evolved over time. As a result, a vast range of frameworks and theories exist to explain how and why cities develop and grow. A dominant and recurring theme in these histories is that cities have significant administrative, cultural, and economic roles. Cities function as central nodes for power and control, discourse and expression, and sites of exchange and of reproduction of social norms, traditions, and aspirations (Mumford 1961). Early observers of urban development focused on the two principal properties of cities. First, the more significant the role the city plays or the more roles it plays, the larger the city will become. The societal roles and services that towns and cities provide represent agglomeration factors that in turn drive the growth of the settlements. Furthermore, the more economically or politically significant the civilization or society, the larger the city could become. As an example, at the zenith of the ancient Roman Empire, the city of Rome might have upward of one million residents, making it the largest city in the world at that time by many-fold.

During the 1930s urban scholars defined other factors driving the conditions of urban growth and urbanization. This work was spearheaded by German urban spatial economists and geographers (particularly August Losch and Walter Christaller), who adapted the work of Von Thunen (described earlier in Chapter 2). In their reasoning, those locations that emerged as centrally located relative to other settlements were defined as likely to grow more rapidly and greater in size in comparison to other locations. In a spatial hierarchy of settlements, those most centrally located would be accessible to the largest number of potential clients and customers and therefore would have a greater amount of service roles and in turn be the greatest in size.

The internal structure or divisions within the cities is a second property of cities that urbanists historically have had interest in. Throughout much of the twentieth century, urban geographers and planners attempted to discern specific patterns of urban land use configuration and the factors behind them. Where specific urban land uses are located and whether or not they are typically coincident with other uses and the forces that drive these uses are key topics of research. This process of urban spatial organization was seen to reflect the needs of society and designate where the functions of manufacturing, administration, housing, transportation and mobility, and culture could take place within different spaces in cities. As the culture of a city changes, there is a possibility if not an expectation that the spatial arrangement of the city will change over time as well. For example, the modern cities of Beijing, London, and Paris have been built upon the ancient cities in those locations.

In these cities and others with moderate to well-developed market economies, urban land use patterns were theorized to be the result of different land values, competition for space, and policy interventions. The spatial differentiation of urban space in these analyses reflected the assertions of urban economics and land bid rent theory in which central locations with greater access and potential market demand have higher property value in turn necessitating more profitable land uses or land uses consistent with high costs. Central business districts often had the highest land value because they were highly accessible and were occupied by land use that could pay the commensurate higher rents. Moving from this urban core to other distant locations, less economically competitive land uses would take place. Using land rent as a basis, several different urban spatial organization theories were developed that include the definition of land use rings (e.g., Burgess and Park and Barrows), spatial sectors or wedges (e.g., Hoyt), or zones (e.g., Ullman and Harris).

Urban theorists also recognized that the processes of agglomeration and growth and the conditions that drive them, and the spatial differentiation and structure of urban space interact were seen as synergistic and reflexive. For example, cities grow because of a series of factors and this growth drives and connects with a set of dynamics within cities such as local site characteristics, social organization and norms, and cultural traditions and legacy that translate this growth into the building of specific districts and neighborhoods within cities. This pattern of urban spatial development can in turn further enhance or even slow the process of urbanization if the city becomes more or less attractive for investment or the siting of administrative headquarters.

It should be noted that the amount of urban development and its drivers vary significantly across the world's cities. While agglomeration factors (e.g., economic activities and employment) and pursuit of services (e.g., education, health care, security) incentivize rural to urban migration and the growth of cities globally, most cities are severely hampered by lack of governance and planning capacity and by the lack of poorly defined markets and modes of valuation and exchange. The result is that substantial proportions of urban economies are informal, as is the housing for a sizable proportion of the cities' residents. These conditions are found especially in the small- and medium-sized cities in low- and moderate-income countries. For example, 15% of residents in Brazilian cities live in informal or slum housing, while roughly one third of urban residents in India do the same, and more than half of Nigerian urban dwellers live that way (UNHS Programme 2024). In these contexts, spatial development and organization are defined as highly fragmented, heterogeneous, and disrupted (Inostroza 2017; Tellman et al. 2022). The urbanization process is patchy with subsistence farming taking place in urban areas and far-flung high-density urban settlements taking place in distant periurban locations. Transportation corridors play a critical role in linking the disparate pieces together.

4.1.2 Social Development and Differentiation

The process of urban development is interlinked with the process of social development and differentiation in cities. Different development contexts lead to varied social outcomes. While urban development is often associated with wealth generation and improvement of the overall quality of life, the distribution of these benefits is often uneven and inequitable. Significant debate exists as to the mechanisms that create these disparities. Structural conditions associated with racism, bias, bigotry, poverty, alienation, xenophobia, and lack of access to power are most often at fault. These inequities manifest as social and income segregation in cities, which also is often presented as a hierarchy of social or income groups and spatial segregation. Often those most vulnerable and least able to access resources are at greatest of environmental degradation and environmental risks (Kuddus et al. 2020). These types of structural inequities manifest as a process of economic differentiation and often tensions between the interests of owners and workers and between the wealthy elites, middle class, workers, and lower classes. Political differentiation also emerges to parallel these conditions, often reinforcing the social and economic differences between groups, communities, and spatially disparate parts of the city.

4.2 Cities as Normative Projects

Parallel to this work, yet another literature focused on more normative assertions of how cities could be shaped and organized around a specific goal or set of goals. These goals included making cities efficient and modern, equitable and just, or resilient and sustainable. The key assumption here is that cities should or could be planned and through planning they would be better. Contemporary notions of urban planning developed in the nineteenth century, as cities of Europe and much of the Americas grew very rapidly. This growth was often seen as uncontrolled and chaotic, resulting in cities that were crowded, dirty, and unsafe. The city of Chicago, for example, as an emergent central place on the American prairie, grew from a population of about 4,400 in 1840 to nearly 1.7 million in 1900. Other cities in North America and Europe had a similar history of rapid growth as the industrial revolution transformed cities within decades. As the concept of the modern city emerged in direct response to this haphazard urbanization of the nineteenth century, urban planners and visionaries promoted new designs for cities. As an example, Baron Hausman in the third quarter of the nineteenth century promoted a vision of Paris with grand boulevards to better control and orchestrate the movement of people and a geometric logic of the city's streets to more effectively move goods in and out and around the city (Harvey 2005). More modernist notions of efficiency and rationality were brought into urban design during the first half of the twentieth century (Ward and Zunz 1992). The French urban designer, Le Corbusier, promoted grand-scale urban development with tall residential towers surrounded by open space and connecting transport routes.

A parallel stream of urban planning at this time was on how to deconcentrate the congested urban cores and expand urbanization into surrounding hinterlands. The objective was to integrate urban life with natural features and to allow urban residents to separate themselves from the chaotic and polluted life of cities. Patrick Geddes, for example, advocated a garden city approach that promoted a more environmentally sensitive and more human scale of construction that influenced the work of later urbanists like Jane Jacob, Holly Whyte, and the New Urbanist movement more generally. While New Urbanists focused on the building or rebuilding of city centers, other urbanists explored opposite notions focused on the expansion of urbanization in hinterlands and in some ways borrowing the same logic of a settlement-natural area tapestry. Frank Lloyd Wright's *Broadacre City* concept was presented as the antithesis of the city with an automobile-dependent, single-family home settlement. When introduced in 1932, Wright's work added force behind the rapidly emerging concept of the suburb and suburbanization.

Modernist city builders and their visions for the city have had a profound impact on what cities should look like, how they should function, and how they should serve their residents. Their work spurred a profound break between the unplanned organic city and the planned city. Planning and design were present in the premodern city; however, most of the focus was on ceremonial grounds connected to residences of leaders (e.g., palaces, castles), religious practices, or administration. The age of contemporary city planning was signaled to begin with events like when the New York City commissioners in the early nineteenth century authorized the use of a geometric grid to rationalize development across Manhattan Island through a series of regularly spaced streets and avenues. The city's streets would not grow out as a warren of irregular passageways but as fixed grid that would provide maximum access to property as well as location coordinates that enhanced efficient navigation and wayfinding. Hausman's later work on Paris extended design into the realm of refitting existing cities in Modernist form (Harvey 2005).

The efforts to plan and modernize cities within what often seems like chaotic and uncontrolled growth highlight the inherent struggle over cities and the right to the city that is just below debates about urban planning and design. Planning and design force arguments over individual property rights, collective rights, the power of the political and economic elite, the rights of the disadvantaged, and the needs of the most vulnerable. Planning and design focus on specific questions and by definition include some interests and exclude others, and success at resolving some issues but also result in creating others.

The legacy of past efforts often leaves an indelible mark on cities that significantly impacts how environmental stresses and crises and the capacity of cities and residents to respond to them. Going back to the example of automobiles, they initially was often presented as a means to enhance mobility and enable people to live in communities of their choosing and make them less bound to high-density neighborhoods that often came with substandard housing and infrastructure. The Regional Plan Association efforts in the 1920s to detail the design for a Greater City of New York that would spread out over five counties (or boroughs) was presented as a great advance over the crowded, congested, and inefficient New York of the nineteenth century. By the 1960s, it was clear that the building of an increasingly automobile-dependent city had created a place where, evermore congested highways had destroyed neighborhoods through which they were built, cut off the city's residents from its prized amenity – the waterfront, and dramatically increased air pollution. The extensive conversion of farmland and open space for urban and suburban land uses also brought social alienation, loss of sense of community, and comparative disadvantage to large low-income populations and communities of color, as well as increased flooding and urban heating driven by the loss of pervious surfaces and urban vegetation and increase of heat-absorptive surfaces.

More generally, the work of urban planners and designers has been critical for the social construction of urban lifestyles and preferences, which in turn has driven resource consumption patterns. In the late nineteenth century and twentieth century, residents of cities had to be encouraged to live in high-rise apartments with electric elevators and other electric-powered devices. The social construction of urban life has been a significant factor in the development of consumption patterns of city residents. In the US, the emergence of the "American Dream" of suburban-style living has been one of the most significant drivers of increased rates of land conversion, and per capita resource consumption (Leichenko and Solecki 2005).

Suburban, nonurban core lifestyle is by far the most dominant in the United States with a similar pattern now emerging to a lesser or greater extent in many highly developed countries. Shifts in consumption patterns and demands typically emerge slowly, and no matter the speed, leave a built environment legacy on the landscape. Suburban landscapes encircling American cities, for example, are fixed in place and will remain the dominant metropolitan land use for the foreseeable future. Embedded in the question of lifestyle is a set of technology choices. How individuals move around, how they heat their homes, and what materials are used in construction are choices that have direct and cumulative effects on the local environmental conditions as well as more distant impacts through patterns of resource extraction. As discussed in Chapter 2, these individual and collective choices along with their capacity to afford them (i.e., their wealth) have significant implications on the overall rate of per capita.

The ambition for urban planning and design has emerged in cities throughout the world, yet by no means is uniform. Most of the world's cities, especially those that are small- and medium-sized, lack planning and zoning capacities. In many settings, especially where there is significant informality, formal planning methods and approaches are rarely present. In fact, tension often emerges in these cities between interests promoting, what has been described as western-style urban planning, planning approaches more Indigenous to specific regions and settings, and informal settlement patterns. It is important to recognize this highly heterogeneous context because it often presents as complex patterns of development with different modes and levels of development across the urban landscape, with highly distinct patterns often pressed up next to each other. This heterogeneity and the force behind it add to the explanation of how urban environmental crises emerge and transitions emerge and why their impacts could be so uneven and inequitable.

4.2.1 Urban Change, System Drivers, and Spheres of Action

Descriptive and normative statements on the patterns of urban spatial development provide opportunities for an initial understanding of how environmental change, stress, and crisis might emerge in cities. The interaction between urban change dynamics, system drivers, and spheres together helps illustrate more fully the processes through which one can understand and examine the broad process of urban environmental stress, crisis, transition, and transformation. In this regard, another theme of urban research focuses on why cities go through these changes and how societal drivers influence and control the pattern and pace of development inside cities. And more specifically, why are parts of the urban landscape used for different types of land uses, why are some areas poorer or wealthier, have fewer amenities than others, and why are some neighborhoods subject to disruption while others are protected. While the work of early and mid-twentieth century urban geographers incorporated neoclassical economics into their work on urban spatial development, urban regional economists (like Alonso, Fujita, and Isard) later significantly deepened these efforts by integrating abstract measures of normative economic rationality into the analysis of cities. This analysis helped to frame optimal conditions for spatial organization of cities. The locational decisions are described as a process of choice underpinned by assumptions of optimality.

Aspects of this approach are useful for understanding how urban environmental problems emerge and get resolved. The framing provides an explanation of how different urban land uses are promoted. Land uses that can provide the highest bid or rent occupy the most desirable places, typically those with high-utility (e.g., central locations) or high-amenity value. Such sites can develop agglomeration value through which other similar high-rent uses can be co-located, thereby providing synergies and the siting of uses with positive amenities. For instance, central, large parks in cities as high-amenity sites can attract high-rent residential properties and residents, which in turn can encourage the coincident location of high-rent businesses and enterprises that serve the professional and personal needs of wealthy citizens. Urban land economics also explain how and why specific properties because of their lack of desirability resulting from low amenity value or remoteness emerge as having comparatively low rent and as a result become locations of poorer and vulnerable at-risk populations and for locally unwanted land uses (LULUs), such as, for example, waste sites, polluting facilities, and noxious uses (e.g., airports). The close proximity of at-risk vulnerability and LULUs creates conditions for an extremely disadvantaged environmentally defined underclass in cities. The compounding of the processes creates, without state intervention, significant opportunities for spatial externality sinks to which these sites become further disadvantaged.

A broad range of other urban theorists emerged during the second half of the twentieth century – each connecting a different theoretical frame to the question of urban spatial development and the life of the city's residents and communities. For example, urban sociologists and urban anthropologists focused on how families and communities function within the space of cities and how social organization and interaction in cities are constructed and contested. From anthropology and sociology and other social sciences, there are a range of critical perspectives that focus on how power relations set in motion social and environmental inequities. Depending on their ontological and epistemological position, these perspectives incorporate Marxist, political economy, political ecology, poststructural, or postmodern framing into the analysis. Fundamental to their approach is that beyond the empirical reality, there are deeper structural arrangements and symbolic (i.e., representative) conditions that influence, explain, or are reflective of the mechanisms that organize everyday life in cities and privilege specific individuals, groups, or interests over others. The critical approaches also directly question the validity of the liberal notion of choice and whether it actually exists during decision-making processes and policy debates about urban structure and function. They instead present the notion that the decision-making process is controlled by elites, for the interests of elites against those of the working classes. Other social divisions within urban societies such as race, ethnicity, and gender also drive the urbanization processes. Race-based policies and actions in the United States including redlining areas and blighting them with reduced development prospects, siting polluting or other undesirable facilities in specific neighborhoods, white flight to the suburbs, and gentrification of old residential areas and the dislocation of lower-income predominantly communities of color have dramatically altered the city-building process for almost a century. Ghettoization of minority populations and slum development and clearance are also widely present throughout all continents and in most countries to varying degrees.

A key part of this examination was the description and analysis of the social production process and a recognition that while an empirical reality exists, its organization, structure, attributes, and meaning or value are socially constructed. To be socially constructed connotes that the social processes create physical manifestations that in turn illustrate and reveal how the underlying structural elements of societies are built and change. These power relations, inequities, and biases are defined along class, race/ethnicity, and other cultural differences and divisions. Through this framing, one can define the social construction of urban space and the social construction of nature in cities. From this perspective, societies are not organized by the collective actions of rational economic agents (as defined by neoclassical urban economics) but by structures that empower and disempower different segments of society.

The process of social construction is complex and multi-faceted. A robust theoretical literature has emerged in an attempt to explain these processes (Demeritt 2002). Specific to understanding the complexities of transition and transformation, three frames are particularly useful – political ecology theory, structuration theory, and regime theory. Political ecology theory first explicated in the late 1980s provides a framework to thoroughly integrate political economy assertions about the organization and function of structural tensions and conflicts as set within the context of ecological processes and human interaction within the physical environment. First widely used in the rural and developing country contexts, the approach also has been successfully applied to urban contexts (see Gandy 2003; Swyngedouw 2004; Heynen 2014; Kaika et al. 2023). Urban political ecology helps define the conditions for social production and contestation across a wide spectrum of application contexts, but especially with respect to water and land development conflicts. Implicit in urban political ecology are the notions of conflict and resolution (i.e., transitions). For example, a pathway or mode of urban water resource development emerges at a particular moment under specific circumstances to serve the interests of local elites.

In a similar way, urban regime theory presents a useful framing of how and under what conditions these moments of transition transpire generally, and how coalitions of interests are formed, how they act, the roles they play, and what occurs during the process of transformation following the transition. Urban regime theory has been most consistently applied to the process of urban development where interest groups, often operating collectively across numerous cases, form a coalition that actively pursues a specific agenda through self-interest (Mossberger and Stoker 2001). Development regimes are loose, often times informal assemblages of elites with other groups with parallel agendas that weld significant power but are most often not elected officials and outside the realm of the public eye. Implicit in urban regime theory is that key individuals and interest groups play a significant role within the transition decision-making process while bound by and reinforcing the underlying structures of society.

This interplay between structure and actors or agents is the focus of structuration theory (Stone 2017). Also first defined in the 1980s, and like political ecology, attempted to bridge a divide. Instead of linking social structure with the physical environment, structuration theory attempts to link behavioral approaches to human agency with social structures. Most fundamentally, structuration theory posits that humans as agents create structures and these structures in turn influence agents who continue to act within and without structures. The process of engagement is presented as iterative and reflexive. Although not typically applied in urban environmental contexts, structuration theory provides insight into how urban environmental coalitions could form to address an issue, create conditions of resolution during a transition, and then are further influenced by or bounded by the structures that emerge from the decisions.

These critical approaches provide opportunities to explore and attempt to explain how urban stresses and crises emerge (whether they are environmental in character or not) and how they are resolved. Central here is that stresses and crises do not emerge because of inefficiencies in the market but because of self-interest and the desire for comparative control and wealth. The tensions between different interests (e.g., economic classes, racial and ethnic groups, gender, residency status) drive the systems. In this context, stress and crises could be understood as a mode of control and not a deleterious result of the urbanization process. An urban environmental stress or crisis, such as extreme air pollution or traffic congestion, can become a mechanism for elites to define new pathways for capital accumulation. As an example, in US Midwest and Northeast cities, US declining quality of life in cities and racist responses to the in-migration of Blacks from the American South helped foster the dramatic increase in suburban development – simultaneously creating new and expanded opportunities for wealth generation among a suite of companies and investors.

These approaches also provide a critique of environmental and sustainability planning. The critique focuses on how environmental and sustainability planning does not necessarily bring forward new modes or processes of enlightened governance but enables the perpetuation of inequity and nonsustainable practices by either providing cover for harmful and dangerous practices (e.g., the true impact of the environmental and sustainability planning is minimal in comparison to other practices) or proving to be a vehicle for elites to further achieve their goals. For example, coastal resilience efforts increase the costs of residency in high-amenity yet highly vulnerable sites opening them up for green gentrification and dislocation of existing lower-income residents who cannot take on the extra expenses associated with resilience. At the same time, the cumulative result of these development trajectories is a lock-in of a specific built environment that both enables and constrains future planning efforts. This condition can further reify urban landscapes of inequity and extend patterns of environmental crisis in ways that further repress disadvantaged populations and heighten the advantage position of the wealthy elite.

4.3 Urban Environmental Transitions

Understanding of how cities develop became an important question of social science research in the early twentieth century. However, it was not until the later part of the twentieth century that a greater understanding of the connection between urban development theory and environmental change and crises emerged. Urban environmental histories focused on case study examinations of the connection between the growth of cities and the level and character of the resulting environmental burden. Within these stories, one emerging theme was the observed link between urban environmental burden and growing affluence (see examples Berry 1990; McGranahan and Songsore 1994).

4.3.1 Transition as Sequence

Emerging from this approach was urban environmental transition theory (McGranahan et al. 2001; Marcotullio and Lee 2003; Ernston et al. 2010). The framework argues that environmental stresses and crises change in cities as they become wealthier. In a basic way, the approach is similar to other transition expositions, such as the demographic transition that states that as a society becomes wealthier, its population growth rate shifts dramatically. With respect to environmental risk burdens (Smith and Ezzati 2005), urban

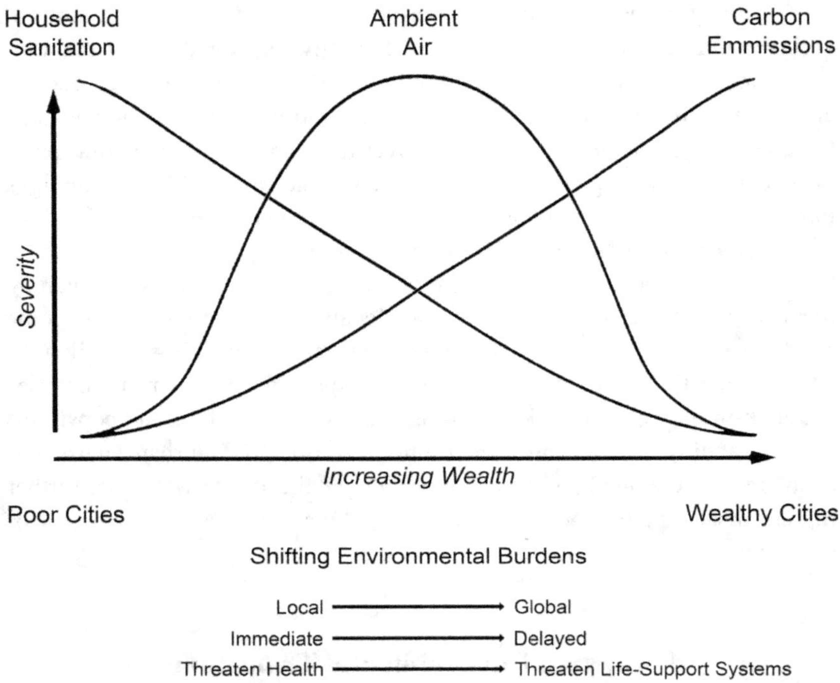

Figure 4.1 An urban environment transition: from sanitation to sustainability. Source: McGranahan et al. (2001).

environmental transition theory argues that as wealth accumulation occurs, environmental challenges become more dispersed, delayed, and shift in type. For lower-income cities in Global South contexts, environmental challenges are localized, immediate, and threatening to human health. In Global North cities, environmental risks are more often global, delayed (intergenerational), and ecosystem threatening. At the same time, the character of the stresses shifts from generally focused on issues of solid waste management and removal and land-based concerns (i.e., brown problems) to those emerging with rapid economic growth and industrialization that dramatically increase local air, water, and land pollution (i.e., gray problems). As these issues are resolved, the focus on the cities might turn to the broader and distant problems of climate change forcing emissions (e.g., CO_2) (see Figure 4.1 later).

Like the demographic transition (developed in the 1940s) and epidemiological transition (developed in the 1970s), the urban environmental transition can be seen as abstraction and point out potential futures but is not deterministic, recognizing that context is very important to understand the pattern and

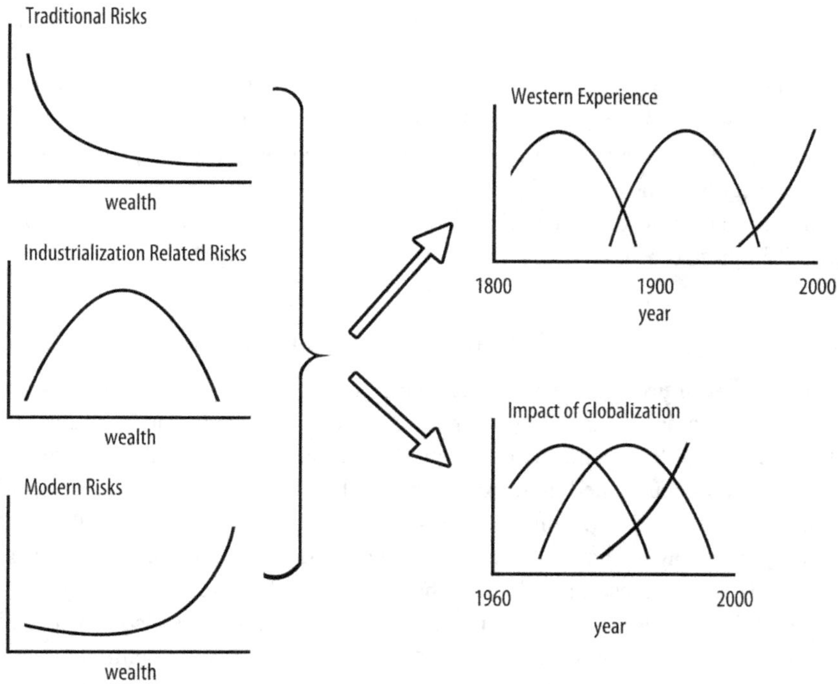

Figure 4.2 Schematic different urban environmental transition experiences – comparing the western experience (Western Europe and North America with rapidly urbanizing areas) in Marcotullio and Lee (2003).

pace of the transition present in any specific city (Marcotullio, Rothenberg, and Nakahari 2003). Further investigation of urban environmental transition defined regional differences between the pattern and pace of change. In western city contexts (e.g., Western Europe and North America), the speed of the transition in the nineteenth and early twentieth centuries was much slower than observed in East Asian cities during the latter part of the twentieth (Bai and Imura 2000); while in Global South contexts, transitions are presented as further conflated and not fully realized or achieved. In Western Europe and N. America (Melosi 1999), such transitions are described as occurring over a century or more of time, while, for East Asian cities, it occurred in decades. Urban environmental transitions in East Asian cities not only occurred faster but also overlapped (Marcotullio 2002; Marcotullio, Rothenberg, and Nakahari 2003). Marcotullio (2003) posits that accelerating globalization coupled with national and local contexts has compressed and telescoped urban environmental transitions (See Figure 4.2).

Underpinning the discussion of urban environmental transition theory is a recognition that urban stress and crises emerge and that solutions can be defined as well as sequences during which these conditions occur. Each has its own trajectory and pattern of change. Even though the overall pattern and sequence of environmental problems are presented as significant, the focus is not explicitly on how and why the transition process occurs or more explicitly what are the socio-cultural, economic, and political contexts and drivers that result in these changes.

4.3.2 Transition as Collapse

The process of urban environmental change can lead to multiple outcomes. In urban environmental transition theory, one mode of environmental pollution is replaced by another as the economy and society shift and grow. Another result of transition documented in the research literature is societal collapse. Societal collapse following environmental stress and crises has been documented in a variety of settings (Costanza et al. 2007; Diamond 2011; Scheffer et al. 2021).

While the collapse narrative has been particularly attractive as a mechanism to detail and illustrate the vulnerability of societies, there also has been a parallel debate regarding its use as a totalizing discourse and potentially oversimplifying (Middleton 2012). It is important to more fully critique the historiography of past crises. Most critical is the attempt to fully understand the crisis within the context of their day and not attempting to impose a story of collapse within the past. Rankin et al. (2021) state that historiography of the collapse of the massive Native American settlement site, the largest in the pre-Columbian North American period, which focuses on environmental misuse and decline of local wood supplies, does not match the record in the stratigraphy. The authors posit that the notion of collapse might not be valid and that there might be other nonenvironmental factors for people's eventual departure from the site.

The concept of collapse has been applied to the decline of ancient cities. In more recent history, the concept of collapse has been associated with the rapid decline of cities resulting from massive disruptions and disasters. The contemporary history of city collapse includes only a few well-documented examples, including sites of environmental devastation (such as from technological or other hazards), economic collapse (e.g., closing of a massive site of resource extraction), or social conflict or warfare. The most storied example in recent decades has been the massive radiation release from nuclear plant accidents. Most prominent is the Chernobyl disaster in 1985 that forced the evacuation of Pripyat, Ukraine, along with several other surrounding communities.

Most recently, a parallel narrative has emerged in which positive tipping points associated with disruptions can be incorporated into enhanced sustainability (Tabara et al. 2018; Scheffer et al. 2012). In specific urban settings, new and disruptive technologies can be understood as opportunities for innovation and advancement (Bai et al. 2018).

4.3.3 Transition as Advance

Transition in cities also has been described within the context of advance, improvement, or betterment. The aspiration to create the modern city was presented as an advance. Modernist urban design and planning opted for mechanization of the city, functionality, order, and zoning as ways to distance city life from the perceived chaos and inefficiencies of the premodern city. This approach has been roundly critiqued as dehumanizing and leading to a vast number of social and environmental ills of late twentieth-century cities. Even so, the notion of enhancing efficiency and modernist projects is still deeply embedded in the city planning discourse, as illustrated by the smart city concept that has focused on integrating a data-rich management regime into city operations and policies.

In the past two decades, a variety of additional normative urban transitions have emerged within the research literature and practice. The term transition used as a discursive device to present opportunities to advance cities and the lives of their residents has been entered into a range of domains. The focus on an urban sustainability transition emerged with the 1992 UN Conference on sustainability and accelerated in the early 2000s (Hansen and Coenen 2015). The goal was to integrate sustainability science into urban development, practice, and everyday life. This approach helped spawn a set of more targeted transitions. As an example, the socio-technical transitions grew as a framing to illustrate a co-evolution of social and technological relationships that can fundamentally change in a way to promote or enable sustainable consumption (Raven et al. 2012; Geels 2019). Attention is given to transitions as a broad, multi-faceted process, but the connection to system dynamics is typically not considered or, if so, described in a broad sense. Transitions are typically described in this approach as beginning in niche sites where experimentation can take place and once fully vetted, a process of diffusion, acceptance, and adoption takes place. This approach incorporates an earlier model of innovation adoption that references early adopters and late adopters, originally proposed by Rodgers in 1962. The concept of the s-shaped curve of adoption has been allied to a variety of urban issues associated with new technology use, new planning approach use, and other environmentally relevant applications.

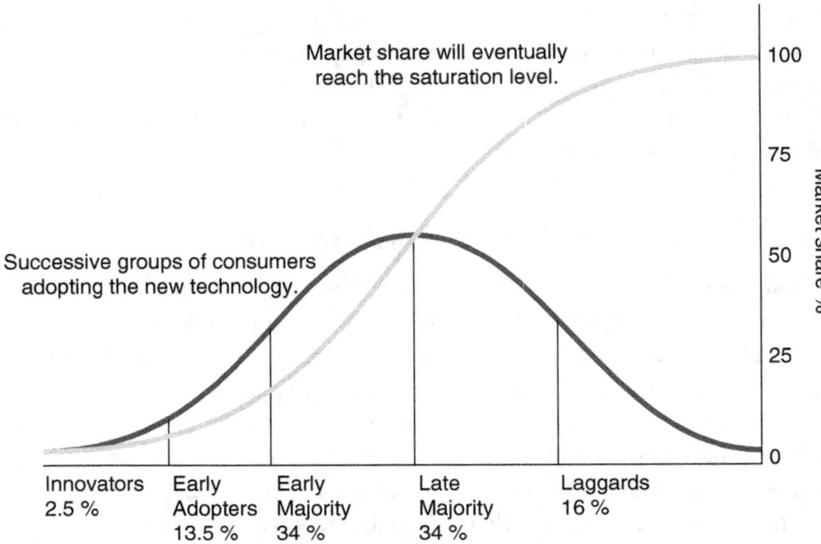

Figure 4.3 Diffusion of innovation across potential users. Source: Rogers and Williams (1983).

This approach though valuable is not directly used to explain how crises reduce or overwhelm the resilience of urban systems, resulting in transitions (Figure 4.3).

4.3.4 Transition as Future

Climate change is driving conditions for transition in cities throughout the world. Climate change is causing cities to respond either reactively or proactively. Extreme weather disasters such as Hurricane Ian in southwest Florida in September 2022 forced Fort Myers and the communities in the surrounding extended metropolitan area heavily damaged by the storm to rethink how they are going to occupy the coast.

Climate change is altering the environmental baseline of cities. Cities and the built environment that compose them were constructed with an understanding of what sort of weather extremes and climate variations they would face. Of course, adjustments to the base assumption were consistently made as the history of these cities expanded. New floods or droughts of record, or the strongest earthquake ever experienced, might have caused shifts and innovations in building design and infrastructure development. Now climate change is altering this environmental baseline and raising questions about whether or not a specific city is built for its emerging and future extremes. This condition has raised significant questions about how to help the city and its residents adapt to these shifts and become more resilient. This process can be broadly described as an adaptation transition. Adaptation transitions can be described as forced – for example, where action comes in response to a disaster event in a reactive fashion or planned and in proactive context.

At the same time, cities are increasingly being forced to address the issue of how to reduce their own carbon footprint and greenhouse gas (GHG) emissions. While cities and metropolitan regions make up about 54% of the world's 8.4 billion people, most estimates state that urban areas make up approximately 70% of global GHG emissions. Many cities in small and large ways have begun to develop plans and initiatives to take on this issue, while the implementation of the actions has been much more limited. International and national scientific assessments are increasingly focused on what sort of condition could promote this type of transition to low- or zero-carbon cities. The Intergovernmental Panel on Climate Change (IPCC)'s Special Report on 1.5°C describes the need for several global transitions that would be required to stay below the 2.0°C global climate warming limit and toward 1.5°C of warming. All of the transitions have a direct bearing on cities. In fact, cities are presented as a globally significant center of opportunity for climate action not only because they represent concentrations of vulnerable populations and GHG emissions but also more often sites of innovation, social change, and governance. In this context, cities could work proactively to foster climate transitions.

4.3.5 Transitions as Just (Sustainability) Transitions

A growing volume of research literature is focused on under what circumstances could society achieve substantial progress toward a more just and sustainable world (Markard et al. 2012; Heffron 2021; Wang and Lo 2021). This normative approach links together the notion of transition as social advancement and environmental advancement. Just transitions are most typically associated with a movement toward a low- or zero-carbon economy that will include significant social and technological shifts with complex and large-scale societal impacts. Within the literature, the just transition should occur in a way as to not reproduce or exacerbate existing social, economic, and environmental injustices. In more recent work, the focus has shifted from not only avoiding more injustice to ensuring that the transition process can enhance the opportunity for the conditions of justice. A key component of this is to ensure that those workers and industries negatively affected by the changes in the economy need to be recognized and aided to overcome these losses. For example, coal miners left out of work because the declining use of coal would be given retraining to help acquire new types of employment. Overall, these efforts must recognize distributional equity (impacts), procedural equity (ensuring that the process is transparent and accessible to all parties), and recognitional equity (ensuring that all groups and voices are included in the dialogue), as well as augment democratic governance, reduce poverty, and promote appropriate technological advancement among other social goals (Wang and Lo 2021). In all situations, sustainable transitions cannot be a success without social justice being a central concern (Bennett et al. 2019).

In recent scholarship and international climate negotiations, many elements of just sustainability transitions have been embedded within the concept of climate resilience development, which focuses on how to create the social conditions that connect climate adaptation and climate mitigation with development in a way that is sustainable for all. It was recognized that for this to happen, it must include methods that promote equity and justice.

4.4 Urban Environmental Transition Framework

Chapters 1–4 provide basic insights in how to understand and frame analysis of urban environmental transitions and how consideration of them might unlock insights that will help cities as they attempt to respond to climate change. The chapters reveal that fundamental to any investigation of environmental solutions and transitions in cities, four components of the transition process should be examined: stress, crisis, transition, and transformation. By using this four-component narrative of transitions, the book attempts to answer the crucial underlying question – how to examine the observed, empirically based environmental transitions and the resulting trajectory of change within specific cities in a way to meet the current needs of cities facing accelerating climate risks? More specifically, the ongoing demands of urban climate change force one to ask three questions: (1) How well do the past environmental solutions serve the current demands?; (2) How can the lessons from the past be realized in the present?; and (3) What are the gaps between these past solutions and the current needs and how can this solution gap be addressed?

Linking the narrative of urban environmental transition to the requirements of contemporary demands of climate change solutions will be provided through the application of an urban environmental transition framework and articulated through a series of application chapters with examples of how cities solved (or did not solve) environmental problems. The case studies are organized to examine the temporal and spatial sequence of stress, crisis, transition, and transformation.

4.4.1 Phases of the Transition Framework

A general description of each phase of the transition framework and the overall architecture of the framework are presented here.

4.4.1.1 Stress

An understanding of urban environmental stress includes an analysis of the patterns of use and the specific impacts and their overall pattern of equity. Root drivers of stress include physical limits and historical and cultural foundations that are associated with the patterns of resource use. Context drivers include those factors that caused stresses to emerge in specific locales as opposed to others and proximate drivers emerged from conditions that emerge from circumstances most directly associated with stress, for example, an acute and disruptive event.

4.4.1.2 Crisis

Environmental crises that emerge from stresses reveal the resilience and vulnerability of the social systems. A specific focus of crisis analysis is whether there is a decline or increase in the systems' resilience and vulnerability. Underlying stresses by definition are a key context in which drivers associated with the crisis will be examined. Equity and other distributional conditions are key context drivers.

4.4.1.3 Transition

Transitions are associated with key enabling conditions and catalysts that are employed to drive systematic change. The role of enabling conditions and catalysts that function as proximate drivers will be highlighted in the transitions. The presence or absence of early warning signals of transition and instability of the system function (i.e., switching back and forth in system function) and other characteristics of transitions will be documented and evaluated. Enabling conditions that could be potentially relevant include ecological and physical elements and technological, financial, institutional, and cultural elements.

4.4.1.4 Transformation

In addition to the structure of the transition, it will be critical also to evaluate the success and effectiveness of the transition and its legacy. The investigation will attempt to understand whether the transformation can be described as a success or failure, the equity implications of transformation, and whether it resulted in a relative decrease or increase in the system function and resilience.

4.4.2 Integrated Framework

The urban environmental transition framework is illustrated in Figure 4.4. The four phases (stress, crisis, transition, and transformation) are presented. Within each time phase, the interaction between the drivers and spheres of action is evident. Each moment brings forward specific processes and products that are simultaneously connected and are passed on to the next period.

The framework includes four stages or phases including stress, crisis, transition, and transformation. Within each time slice, the interaction between the drivers and spheres of action occur. Three types of drivers (root, context, and proximate) influence the conditions within each phase as their influence is mediated through and influenced by three spheres of action (social, ecological/environmental, and technological). Each phase results in specific products and processes that are transmitted or transferred to the next phase through specific shifts that occur within the phase (i.e., [A] intensification of the stress, [B] system resilience shifts, and [C] reorganization following the transition).

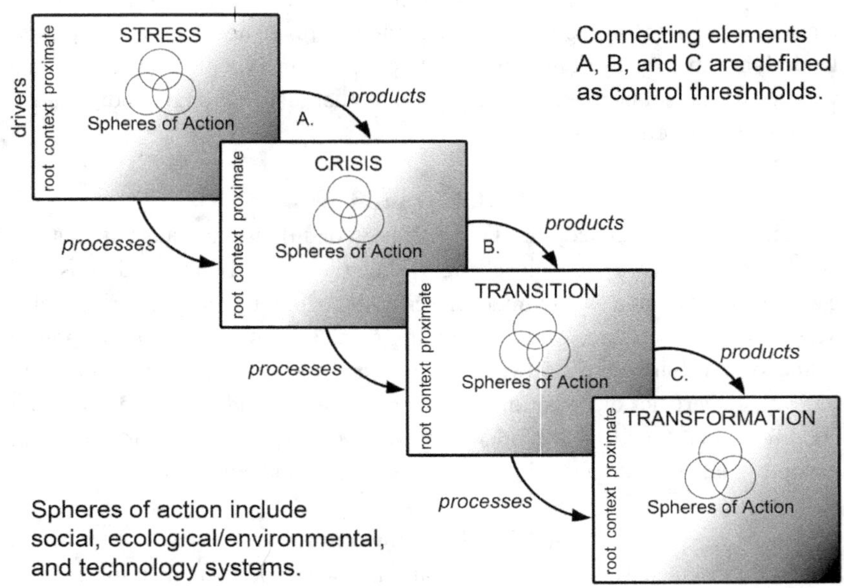

Figure 4.4 Key elements of the urban environmental transition framework. Source: Author.

Collectively, these products and processes that are passed from section to another are broadly described as legacy issues. Legacy issues can play a critical role in the transfer of norms, values, and behaviors, tools and resources, and assets (including financial, technological, and otherwise) from one phase (i.e., time period) to another. These conditions can be either constraining or enabling depending on the circumstances.

For each step or phase, the underlying root, context, and proximate drivers will be examined to understand how and why the transition was feasible and enabled across and within the three defined spheres of action (social, ecological/environmental, and technological). In each phase of the process, all three types of drivers are evident, yet it is clear that the relative significance of the drivers will vary within and across the phases and in fact differ from situation to situation. Furthermore, the conditions in one phase could become drivers in another phase. As an example, consistent resource shortage stress and how they are managed by cities will become an important root driver of an environmental crisis. The key driver of change in one phase can be associated with one or more control variable(s). Control variables are defined as those conditions that significantly drive the processes of the system in question and in turn will influence, along with the system's resilience level, whether or not a system is approaching or crosses a threshold or tipping point. As with drivers, it should be noted that some variables can operate as important control variables at one phase of the transition but are not as significant at other moments (Solecki et al. 2025).

The focus during each phase will be simultaneously on the process (i.e., how the conditions of change are emerging) and outcomes (i.e., products and results of the process). Key outcomes include the growth or diminishment of social and environmental equity, resiliency, and vulnerability. Central to the analysis will be circumstances within these conditions that have positively or negatively changed – for the better or the worse? For example, how might have the risk vulnerability of a city's population changed and to what extent was the vulnerability concentrated or widely spread? Interpretation and evaluation will provide insights in how to potentially transfer lessons of how to encourage positive outcomes and avoid negative outcomes.

The connection points between phases are of special importance since they define those processes where conditions drive dynamic shifts in the structure and capabilities of the environmental policy system. These connection points are defined here as control thresholds since their configuration and significance play a defining role in whether the transition proceeds to the next stage. The connections between the four phases of the framework are defined as: (1) *intensification* of the stress into a crisis, (2) *system resilience shifts* that result from a heightened state of crisis and how it connects with the existing policy regime, and (3) *reorganization* following the transition and emerging as a transformation.

One way to understand the connection between the transition phases is to consider the concept of legacy. Places are a layering of problems and conflicts as well as solutions. The influence of legacy on a contemporary transition moment can be manifold. One key way that legacy affects how societies face contemporary crises is how past crises and transitions left a physical, economic, or emotional impact on the city. Legacy also can play a role within any one transition – meaning that the nature of stress and crisis has an impact on how the transition is debated and emerges, and in turn the transition will frame the structure and character of the resulting transformation.

The concept of legacy effects is well used within disciplines that examine how past actions influence current and future actions. Legacy can be described as structural or physical/material things such as large-scale infrastructure systems that tend to "lock-in" patterns of development. For example, decisions to construct massive urban highway projects and construct low-density housing promote an approach to mobility and lifestyle that makes it difficult to implement the widespread use of mass transit. Even so, in transportation history, new economic realities and new policy have embedded the overlay of one type of transportation over another. In the northeast US, for example, the system of canals and dredged waterways for barge traffic was replaced by the railway, which was then replaced by the highway and truck. In each step, the pre-existing infrastructure, at least partially, could be described as a "stranded asset" – because it suffered from an unanticipated or premature write-down or devaluation of its worth. These types of legacy conditions can have significant long-term environmental ramifications since they set the patterns and processes of environmental change in cities – for example, concentrating population growth and land use conversion in some locales versus others.

While these are material examples of legacy, deep-seated social divisions and tensions also can have significant legacy within a place. In cities where traumatic events have occurred or where systematic and prolonged hostilities and frictions occurred across racial, ethnic, income, or other divisions, it will leave a mark on the residents' psyche and identity. For Warsaw, Poland, the legacy of the devastation and loss during World War II is still strongly felt by many. In many southern US cities, the legacy of slavery and continued racist policies have continuing implications for the everyday life of residents. These impacts are often pervasive, though often not directly or openly spoken about, but can bubble up in a variety of contested spaces such as housing, employment, and schooling.

Within a specific crisis to transition to a transformation episode, legacy can manifest in a variety of ways.

For example, the spread and intensity of the stress and crisis will influence the social pressure for a solution. The more a crisis causes hardship and suffering, the more likely different consistent groups will want to be involved in the solution.

The following application chapters will utilize the framework to analyze examples of past urban environmental transitions. The topics include environmental resource quantity with a focus on drinking water supply crises (Chapter 5). Next (Chapter 6) will be on urban pollution challenges as an environmental quality crisis and transition. Chapter 7 will investigate public health crises, specifically diseases and pandemics. While many of the crises and subsequent transitions emerge from chronic and long-term stresses, Chapter 8 will specifically focus on the role of extreme events and disasters as components of urban environmental transitions. The sustainable resource management crises will be explored through case examples of recycling and waste management (Chapter 9). The broader demands and conditions of transitions enhancing the livability and sustainability are examined in Chapter 10. The specific case studies in the application chapters are presented in Table 4.1 and Figure 4.5 later. An attempt was made to include significant geographic and temporal variation. Examples of crises in cities in all world regions are presented. The earliest is from the early 1800s, but the vast majority are from after 1900, and many occurred in the past 40 years. In most instances, the larger cities were chosen as case studies because more data and literature are available on these in comparison to smaller- or mid-sized cities. Application and reference to small- and mid-sized cities are made as appropriate in Chapters 11 and 12. The merits of the urban environmental transition framework are reviewed in Chapter 11, and direct application to cities and the climate crisis are examined in the final chapter (Chapter 12).

The case studies are built from a comprehensive review of the specific environmental problem of interest with a focus on the events and conditions present for each city and the role and significance of relevant individuals and institutions. Most of the literature reviewed included secondary data (e.g., journal articles and books) and included primary data (e.g., government reports) when available. All the source material was written in English originally or translated into English. Although the author was not able to access non-English references, the author has visited all the study sites and was able to incorporate field experience and knowledge into the analysis. Each application chapter is organized around an introductory section setting the tone and scientific background for the four case studies to follow. Each study is made up of five sections. First is introduction to the city, its environs, and the relevant development background. The bulk of the case study is comprised of four analytical sections describing and assessing the socio-environmental transition in

Table 4.1 *List of city case studies, the continent on which they are located and the time period during which the crisis reached a defined apex and when a policy transition was articulated and experienced. Source: Author.*

City	Global Region	Natural resource supply – Drinking water supply	Environment degradation and quality – air pollution	Disease and Pandemics	Environmental Risk and Hazards	The three R's and the triple bottom line	Mobility and Settlement
Atlanta, US	N. America	1960–ongoing					
Cairo, Egypt	Africa	Early to late 20th century					
New York, US	N. America	Early to late 19th century					
Tel Aviv, Israel	Southwest Asia	1980 to 2000s					
London, UK	Europe		1950s to 1990s				
Los Angeles, US	N. America		Early to late 20th century				
Ruhr Region, Germany	Europe		1970s to 2000				
Tokyo, Japan	E. Asia		1960s to 1990s				
Hong Kong, China	E. Asia			Late 19th to late 20th century			
Marseille, France	Europe			Early 19th century			
St. Louis	N. America			1918–1920			
Seoul, Korea	E. Asia			2020s			
Abu Dhabi, United Arab Emirates	Southwest Asia				2000s to present		

Kolkata, India	S. Asia	1850s to 1930s		
Cedar Rapids and New Orleans, US	N. America	1980s to present		
Rotterdam, Netherlands	Europe	1980s to 2010		
Buenos Aires, Argentina	Central and South America		1980s to 2000s	
Johannesburg, South Africa	Africa		1990 to 2000s	
Seattle, US	N. America		1980s to 2000s	
Taipei, Taiwan	E. Asia		1980s to 2000s	
Grenada, Grenada	Central and South America			2010s to current
Miami, US	N. America			1990s to current
Oslo, Norway	Europe			2000s to current
Shenzhen, China	E. Asia			2000s to current

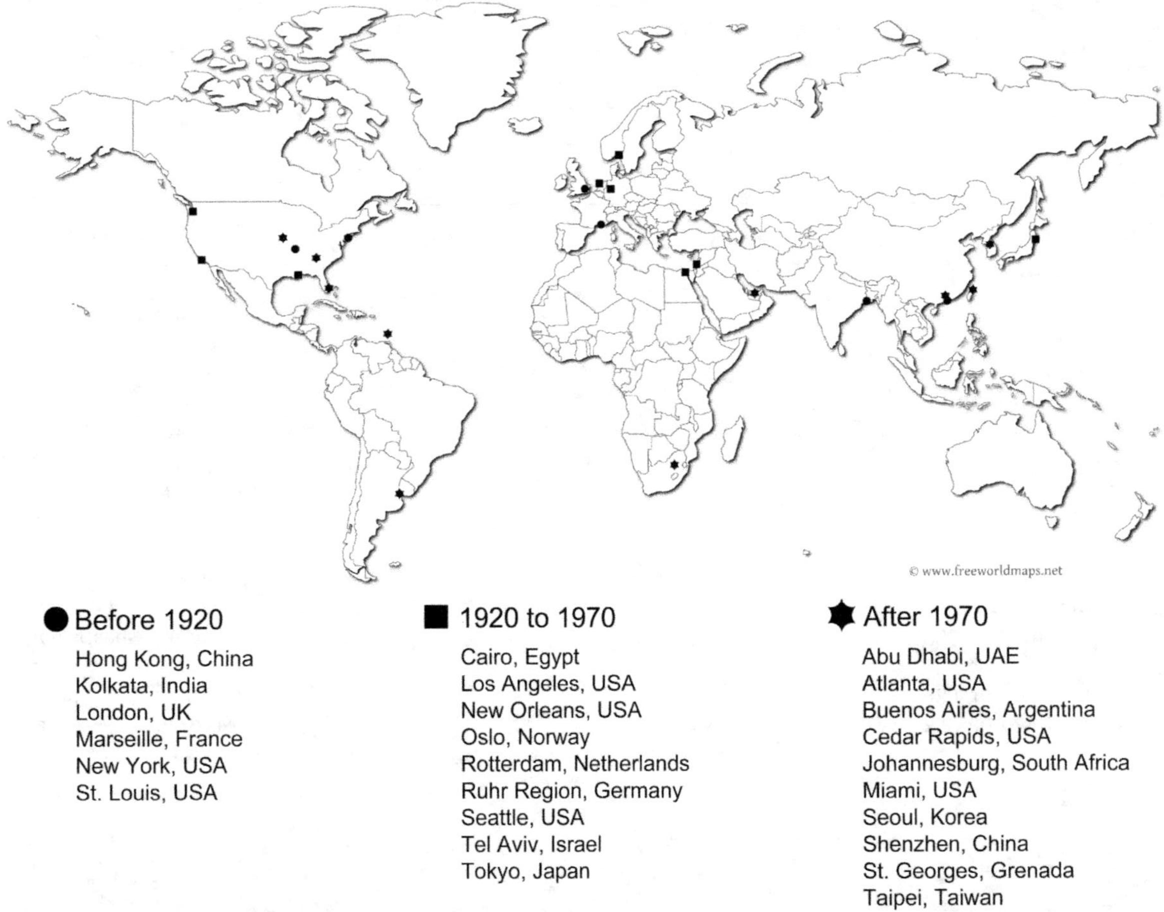

Figure 4.5 Map of case study locations with the time period when the crisis in question first emerged (dark circle – before 1920; diamond – from 1920 to 1970; open circle – after 1970). Source: Author.

question. The sections are defined by the four stages in the framework: stress, crisis, transition, and transformation.

The final section of the chapter is an integrated discussion that links the four narratives together and is composed of three subsections: conditions of crisis, drivers of transitions, and spheres of action and legacies. Together the three subsections assess the content of the case studies together vis-à-vis the framework for urban environment policy transitions. This assessment can lead to an evaluation of the robustness of the framework, its validity, and opportunities for tweaks and adjustments. The "conditions of crisis" subsection provides a synthesis of the circumstances surrounding the development of the crises presented within the chapter. The attention is on whether overarching statements regarding the stress and eventual crisis conditions can be defined. "Drivers of transition" discussion takes on a broader question of are there similar patterns regarding the relative role of root, context, and proximate drivers across the case studies and how they compare. The "spheres of action and legacy" write-up highlights key system-level interactions within each phase and the extent to which these carry over. The ambition in this discussion will be to identify common themes and threads. For example, points of focus could be whether aspects of the crisis conditions have implications for the transitions to follow or to what extent conditions of the transitions have implications for the resulting transformation.

The final section of each application chapter turns directly to the question of climate change. A brief discussion of how climate change is connecting with the urban environmental stress and crisis in question is followed by an assessment of how the results could inform city stakeholders who are attempting to address climate change now and in the near future. A set of specific recommendations is provided.

4.4.3 Thoughts on Framework Application

The framework makes a series of implicit assumptions about how urban societies operate and transform themselves. The framework is structured to recognize that cities are highly contested spaces where varying interests and agendas press for dominance and control. Critical urban political economy (ecology) research has well documented how elites either as individuals or as coalitions (sometimes described as regimes (Pierre 2014)) structure a city's economy to their advantage. These interests are often in opposite to or not in sync with those of other groups (other elites or other collectives including those of the disadvantaged and marginalized). The resulting contestation for space, resources, and the means of economic production results in a process of conflict that defines the urbanization process.

Urban environmental crises fit within this complex urban landscape. The debate and resolution of these crises will reflect these underlying tensions. It is assumed that they will be uncovered during the crisis–transition–transformation process. The framework does not explicitly assume or expect that the underlying socio-economic structures of the city will be changed or altered during the environmental transition process, but it does not rule out some type of evolution or convulsion. For example, it is expected that the resolution of some crises might be associated with a reorganization of the governance structure including the development of new government institutions and operations including new agencies and departments and expanded mandates. Transitions also could come with advances in the status and significance of civil society in the public policy discourse. Shi (2021), for example, documents how twentieth-century urban planning advances were often coupled with progressive changes in the role and capacity of civil society and increased consideration of equity.

Another assumption baked into the framework is that the environmental crises and other elements of the transition process are socially constructed. While it is obvious that cities exist in settings that include biophysical limits, the urbanization process has allowed urban societies to vastly exceed local limits. The framework is designed to be useful to understand for cities that are quite close to the local biophysical limits, and those for a variety of reasons (e.g., wealth, geopolitical position) have growth that vastly surpasses the local environmental limits (e.g., Abu Dhabi). The application analysis will attempt to illustrate in broad terms how the social production of crises and potential policy solutions emerged, and identify commonalities and differences across the sample of narratives. Space constraints would not allow for detailed examinations of the social production process, but certainly the broad structure of such will be illustrated.

The framework proposed here is general and therefore can be applied to a variety of settings. This flexibility reveals that the framework also does not reflect or define all the fine-scale conditions that influence how environmental crises emerge and what response takes place. For example, the framework does not directly speak to the economic differentiation of the different interests (e.g., workers vs. owners, poor and working class vs. middle class vs. wealth elites) connected to urban environmental issues. The framework also does not explicitly specify the roles of individuals versus collectives. That said, the case study narratives are designed to highlight when individuals and/or collectives play a large role in the definition of the crisis, proposal for its resolution, and articulation and implementation of potential policy transitions and large-scale transformations.

PART II

Application Case Chapters

5

Natural Resource Supply and Scarcity

Securing Urban Drinking Water

> Nothing is talked of or thought of Croton in New York but Croton water; fountains, aqueducts, hydrants, and hose attract our attention and impede our progress through the streets. Political spouting has given place to water-spouts, and the free current of water has diverted the attention of the people from the vexed questions of the confused state of the national currency. It is astonishing how popular the introduction of water is among all classes of our citizens, and how cheerfully they acquiesce in the enormous expense which will burden them and their posterity with taxes to the latest generation. Water! Water! is the universal note which is sounded through every part of the city, and infuses joy and exultation into the masses, even though they are out of spirits (Diary entry of P. Hone October 12, 1842 (Hone 1889)).

Cities have faced a wide variety of resource shortage issues. Perhaps none is as profound as water supply. Without water, a city won't be able to function. Every city now present has faced or continues to face a concern over a stable and sustainable drinking water supply, and has likely faced several moments of water stress if not full out crisis. The objective of this chapter is to present case studies about how urban drinking water supply provision is a story of significant failure and success, and associated policy experimentation and transition.

5.1 Basics of Urban Water Supply Shortage

The earth is dominated by water (about 71% of the earth is covered by water), but the supply of fresh, potable water is relatively small. Only about 3.0% of the world's water is fresh water, and the vast majority of that is frozen in glacial ice. The amount that is flowing surface or groundwater supplies is around 0.5% of all the water in the world. And then considering that a significant amount of this supply is either in rural areas, already environmentally degraded by pollution, or in groundwater sites that might be difficult to extract, the amount of water available for city life and business is relatively small. The statistics vary depending on how it is defined, but current estimates state that about 2.1 billion people (~29% of the global population) lack access to a safely managed drinking water service and 844 million people do not even have basic drinking water service (WWAP 2019).

Water is a fundamental requirement for life. Humans need regular inputs of water to sustain bodily function. Besides this, water is needed for a variety of daily uses in cooking and cleaning, and more broadly across a range of societal uses. Urban water supply requires consideration of both water quantity and quality. Water should be of sufficient quantity and quality to meet the variety of water demands in cities. Agreements regarding water supply including formal and informal arrangements, policy, and laws often involve conflicts and compromise across a variety of interest groups and demands. The potential areas of tension are varied and include over the water rights (especially regarding access), obligations and responsibilities of upstream users versus downstream users, residential versus nonresidential uses (i.e., agricultural, commercial, industrial, transportation), common property users (e.g., commercial fishers, recreational fishers, and boaters) versus private property users, Indigenous water rights versus private property users, and current users versus future users.

Embedded within urban water conflicts and solutions is the role of the state – and how governments manage and resolve (or fail to resolve) water supply stresses and crises. Resolutions often focus on two modes of problem-solving – supply driven or demand driven. Supply-driven solutions involve large-scale adjustments to water supply infrastructure to increase supply and as a result require significant social and economic commitment to development and implementation. Demand-driven solutions focus on strategies and tactics to reduce water requirements of a specific sector or across multiple sectors. Demand-driven solutions can be initiated without large-scale infrastructure development but also typically require compromise or shifts in the overall allocation of water supply and as a result produce policy winners and losers.

Throughout history, humans have worked very aggressively to provide water for their settlements. Two basic terms are associated with this process. Water withdrawal is defined by the amount of water removed from a source. By definition, withdrawal amounts always are greater than or equal to consumption given that there is water lost during transfer. The second term, water consumption, is the volume of water withdrawn but not eventually returned to the source and no longer available for other local uses. That said, there are often conditions where water could be used and then returned to another water body as in the case of groundwater being applied to an agricultural field and then any excess washing off as surface water into a nearby stream or other water body.

The capacity to withdraw and consume water has expanded dramatically over time. Ancient civilizations built complex irrigation and water conveyance systems. For example, early Rome had about 11 major aqueduct systems, which supplied freshwater to the city from sources as far as 92 kilometers away (*57 miles*) (Khan et al. 2022). In the contemporary era, constructed water distribution systems can supply cities hundreds of miles or more from their source. Most significant is the use of interbasin transfer in which the water available in one watershed is conveyed through tunnel, pipe, or channel into another watershed. All these are mechanisms to increase the supply of water and overcome the relative scarcity of the resource. More dramatic efforts to meet water supply scarcity have been developed. Deep groundwater withdrawal into ancient aquifers and the desalination plants (which convert salt water into fresh water) are the most prominent examples.

5.2 Case Studies

The case studies presented illustrate conditions present in a variety of cities. Examples include cities in relatively water-scarce regions or where accelerated demand dramatically exceeded local supply. The case studies include Atlanta and New York City in the United States and Cairo, Egypt, and Tel Aviv, Israel, both in North Africa and Southwest Asia, respectively. Each case study will include background discussion and then an examination of how water supply emerged as an issue of stress and crisis and under what conditions a policy or management transition occurred or not, and to what extent the transition results in a transformation. The concluding discussion in the chapter focuses on the relevant analysis and implication of the case studies.

5.2.1 Atlanta, US

Metropolitan Atlanta has grown tremendously in the past half century. In 1970, the metropolitan region population was about 1.1 million and by 2020 the population was hovering around 6 million. Almost all of this growth took place in the extended suburban areas of the region. In 1970, the city of Atlanta's population was approximately 497 thousand (after a long period of growth), or just below half of the region's total population. Federal mandated racial desegregation led to a significant white residential exodus from the city. By 1990, the city had lost more than 100 thousand residents. Finally in 2020, the city had again topped its previous record with 500 thousand residents. The far-flung suburbs and exurbs brought tremendous rates of population growth in previously highly rural counties. As an example, Forsyth County north of Atlanta grew from 17.3 thousand residents in 1970 to 251.0 thousand in 2020. With this expansion also came rapid growth in residential water demand as well as a massive increase in local industrial and commercial activities as the region became a major national hub for transportation, trade, and manufacturing. Together these factors dramatically increased local water demand. The original siting for Atlanta came in response to an early 1840s ambition to site a critical railroad junction and in many ways is described as an accidental city (Borden 2014). The city and later the metropolitan region expanded across the Piedmont Region of North Georgia, where groundwater is scarce and surface water is limited to small, headwater streams with highly variable flows. Unlike many other large US metropolitan regions, Atlanta does not have access to major river tributaries or other large water bodies (Feldman 2009; Borden 2014).

5.2.1.1 Stress

The city of Atlanta and the metropolitan region have a humid subtropical climate with hot, humid summer and cool winter. The region experiences ample rain (1320 mm [52 in.] per year on average) with a consistent amount throughout the year, although slightly more during the winter months. Atlanta water supply infrastructure has been constructed around the premise of controlling headwater water resources of two large regional watersheds – the Apalachicola–Chattahoochee–Flint (ACF) and Alabama–Coosa–Tallapoosa (ACT) watersheds (see Figure 5.1). As a result, Atlanta's water supply depends heavily on two large nearby storage reservoirs at the headwaters of these watersheds built by the US Army Corps of Engineers during the mid-twentieth century. These reservoirs, Lake Lanier and Allatoona Lake, together provide much of the metropolitan region's water supply. At certain times of the year, over 90% of the supply. No reasonable alternatives to these reservoirs exist, and as a result, the metropolitan Atlanta region remained highly dependent on them. The conditions of the water detention and control by metropolitan Atlanta, and increasing downstream uses within each watershed, created a condition of chronic resource stress (Borden 2014). Atlanta's water demand was increasingly in conflict also with downstream uses in nonmetropolitan Atlanta parts of Georgia, and in the states of Alabama and Florida.

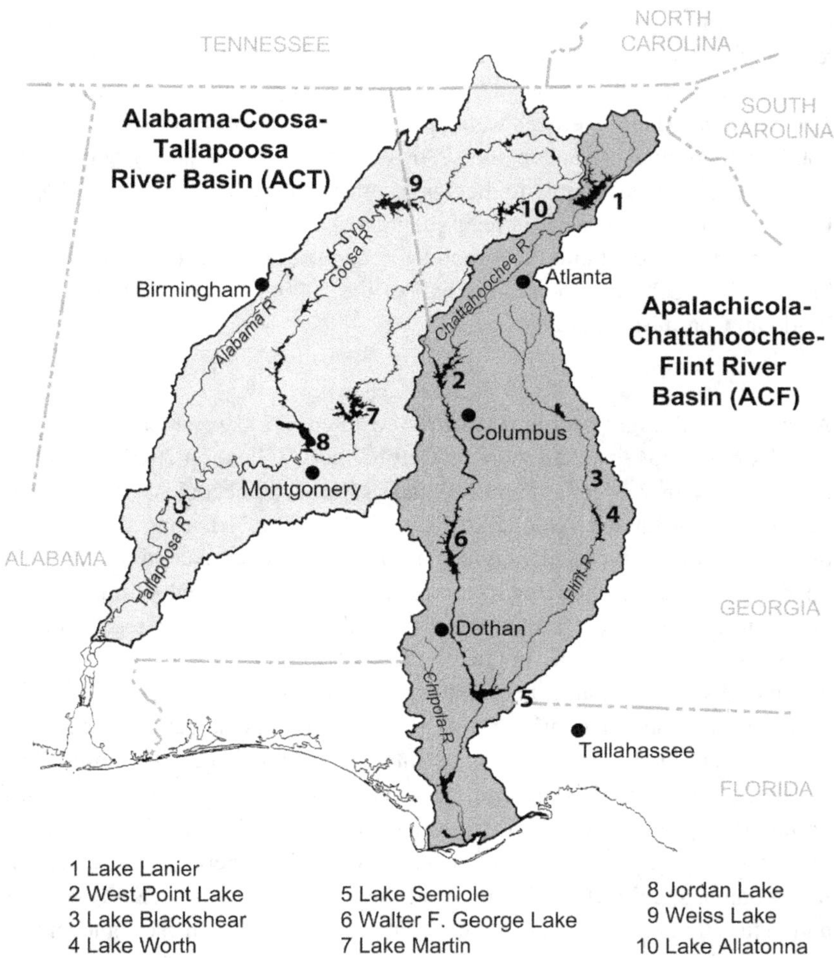

Figure 5.1 Map of ACF Basin and adjacent ACT Basin showing major urban areas and reservoirs. Source: Tri-State Water Commission

A drought in the 1980s alerted the region to the growing conflict over water and further highlighted the US Army Corps of Engineers' critical role in managing its reservoir function and meeting Atlanta's growing water supply demands. Beginning as early as 1983, the three states and the Army Corps took part in several collaborative forums in an attempt to forge a new water allocation agreement. The three states initially agreed to work together, but by 1990 Alabama filed litigation against Georgia (Ruhl 2005). Controlling the flow of water in Atlanta's reservoirs to quench its thirst meant less water for hydropower generation in Alabama, agricultural irrigation, and interrupted the natural flow regime critical for the Apalachicola River and Bay ecosystems and their oystering industry. By the late 1980s, these states and the Army Corps of Engineers became part of a growing litigation effort to challenge metropolitan Atlanta's efforts to impound and divert even more water (Ruhl 2005). Metropolitan Atlanta in the 1990s was able to further strengthen its policy of securing water supply to meet present and future demands (Ruhl 2005). During this decade, a series of legal judgments and agreements backed by the US Army Corps continued to support the competing allocation and riparian interests in check until the second half of the 2000s (Glennon 2010; Atlanta Regional Commission 2023).

5.2.1.2 Crisis

An extended drought beginning in 2004 resulted in Lake Lanier water levels to fall 4.6 m below its peak stage by October 2007 (Glennon 2010). Atlanta's need for ever-increasing amounts of water supply had become especially evident during an intense regional drought in 2006–2007. During this specific drought, local reservoirs already began to operate under exceptional drought operations. By 2007, the drought continued to worsen. The reduction of stored water in the reservoirs pushed the chronically stressed water region into a severe water crisis. It was predicted that Lake Lanier would go dry within 3–4 months (Corn et al. 2008). While the drought continued until 2008, its severity diminished by early 2009 as rainfall and lake stages returned, with more typical conditions returning by late 2009 (Figure 5.2). The immediate water shortage and crisis receded, but the events of the previous years set off an intense conflict in what has been defined as the "Tri-State Water Wars," pitting mostly Alabama and Florida against Georgia, generally, and metropolitan Atlanta, specifically. This reduced the release from upstream reservoirs and in turn threatened to damage the interests of downstream users and endangered species.

5.2.1.3 Transition

The crisis set off protracted additional legal battles between the three states. A central issue was that earlier legal settlements had put in place agreements that needed to be continually revaluated as Atlanta's dramatically increasing demands placed greater pressure on the system. At the same time, downstream users in Alabama and Florida argued that their water demands also needed to be met. This reevaluation and contestation led to a policy transition that was finally codified, more than four years after the end of the drought. Atlanta's right to fully utilize the Army Corps water supply and reservoir projects was not established until 2012, when the competing claims were finally formally

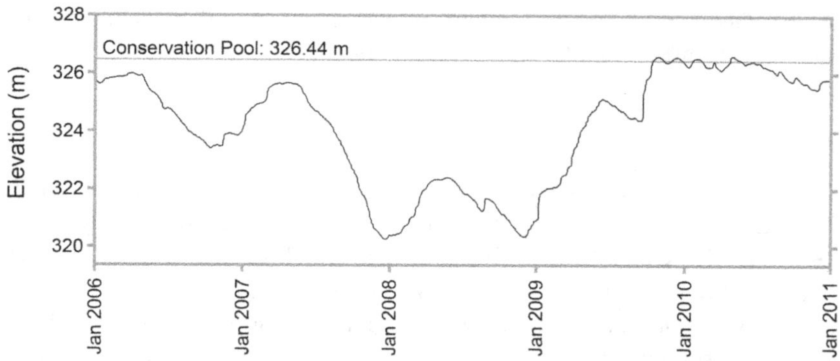

Figure 5.2 Diagram showing the stage variation of Lake Lanier from 2006 to 2011 (Anonymous 2013). Note the extremely low stage of the lake during the late 2007 and early 2008, and again at late 2008.

resolved. After a series of earlier cases, parties to the litigation against the state of Georgia appealed a lower court decision (i.e., US Court of Appeals for the Eleventh Circuit in *In re TriState Water Rights Litigation*) up to the US Supreme Court. On July 6, 2012, the Court declined to hear the appeal, thereby affirming the lower Circuit Court's decision (Tonsmeire 2012; Jones et al. 2013; Missimer et al. 2014). This, in effect, created a new policy precedent and provided Atlanta via the State of Georgia the capacity to meet its own water supply demands. On the very next day (July 7), the USACE then decided that it had jurisdiction in this situation to reallocate the reservoir water use without securing additional congressional authorization. Given this, the Corps could decide on a reallocation plan for water uses in each watershed basin and, in turn, ultimately how much water could be allocated for power production, recreational use, environmental flows and reservoir maintenance, and for water supply (Jones et al. 2013; Missimer et al. 2014).

5.2.1.4 Transformation

The droughts and 2012 judgment set in motion fundamental change in the region's water supply. In 2013, the state of Florida offered another lawsuit against Georgia to test the 2012 ruling. While elements of this suit remained unresolved, the conditions of the 2012 decision were upheld, and Atlanta continues through the action of the US Army Corps to maintain a steady supply of water. The region has not experienced any drought approaching the levels of the late 2000s. Even so, water conservation efforts were put in place and per capita water demand in Metropolitan Atlanta has declined by approximately 10% over the past decade and by more than a third since the early 2000s

(North Georgia Water 2021). This further diminishes the likelihood that Atlanta will suffer a similar water crisis in the future.

5.2.2 Cairo, Egypt

Cairo is an ancient city with settlements in the area going back several thousand years. The origin of contemporary Cairo began approximately 2,000 years ago. The city and development have always been tied to the Nile River as a site of transport and as a source of water in an otherwise desert environment in which it typically receives 25–50 mm of rain per year (1–2 inches). The city first grew on the east bank of the Nile, but soon thereafter the west bank was developed, and now new development has spread out in almost all directions. The metropolitan population was approximately 2.5 million in 1950; 13.6 million in 2000; and the 2020 population just under 21 million (UN – World Population Prospects).

5.2.2.1 Stress

In low- and middle-income countries such as Egypt, the formal water supply system infrastructure often cannot meet current and growing demands and can be understood as operating in an ongoing state of crisis in which flow interruptions, low water pressure, and other informal systems make up for the deficiencies. These systems resolutions put in place are implicit or explicit recognition that the system operates in a deficit state. The case of Cairo helps to illustrate how difficult it is for water systems to forestall critical transitions and in turn achieve positive transition after being positioned in a steady degraded state. For Cairo, Egypt, the main water supply system was originally built out to meet the demands of approximately 2 million people (El Araby 2002). Cairo's metropolitan population is now over 20 million, and the amount of water demand far exceeds the volume conveyed by the formally established system, even though the central Egyptian government and local government have made great strides to increase the amount of water supply delivery in the past several decades (Ashour et al. 2009; Mohamed and Jagannathan 2009).

Egypt and Cairo have both been described as "gifts of the Nile," and as a result, the supply of water has not been the limiting factor for city water managers – two chronic stresses have been building a robust system to convey drinking water to the city's residents while at the same time protecting the quality of water so that it maintains its potability. British engineers, in the early 20th century, were concerned about how to maintain water quality and enhance the water distribution system in Cairo (Anonymous 2008). The initial construction of the contemporary water supply system in Cairo took place during the latter part of the nineteenth and early twentieth centuries during the period of British colonial control.

5.2.2.2 Crisis

By mid-twentieth century, Egypt was going through a series of dynamic changes, including a post-World War II development boom, a political upheaval with a deeply involved socialist experiment, followed by an increased expanse of the capitalist economy. In the 1960s, the population of Cairo grew at its fastest rate at over 5% per year – equivalent to a doubling time of only 14 years. The significant population growth, largely uncontrolled urban expansion, and degraded river water quality set in motion a crisis associated with the structure and capacity of the Cairo water supply system (Raymond 2000; El Araby 2002; Sims 2003; Allen et al. 2006). In Egypt, much of the growth during this era took place without any formal planning effort or Cairo government oversight (Sims 2003). The system faced further pressure from the noted decline in the Nile River water quality and the recognition that the quality was being further compromised by uncontrolled sewer seepage into broken or otherwise deficit pipes and by the fact that many of the distribution pipes were made of or contained significant amounts of lead (Ashour et al. 2009; Mohamed and Jagannathan 2009). A late 1970s assessment of the Cairo water facilities found significant deficiencies in the water supply infrastructure and service provision. Much of the infrastructure was found to be in poor repair and lacking the necessary capacity to serve the population already connected to the networks (Hoehn and Krieger 2000).

5.2.2.3 Transition

Starting in the 1970s and accelerating into the 1980s and 1990s, the Cairo water supply system became the focus off huge capital expenditures largely coming from increased foreign aid (Hoehn and Krieger 2000). The expenditures brought a dramatic extension of the distribution infrastructure and construction and expansion of 13 water quality treatment facilities along with the building of many primary and secondary sewerage treatment plants. A master plan was presented to execute a phased-in implementation of a greater Cairo waterworks project, starting from 1977 to 2000 (ECG N.D.). The plan addressed domestic, industrial, and irrigation needs of the served areas. The effort included the development of high-priority projects that could be developed immediately to improve the existing conditions in parts of the city and region not adequately served by the existing water system.[1] The Greater Cairo

[1] The Cairo water supply system consisted of about 2,500 km of mains and branch lines (compared to New York City that had 10,950 km of water mains).

Waterworks Master Plan attempted to address several key areas of improvement, including a 24-hour flow measurement infrastructure, inspection and evaluation of the water meter infrastructure, a comprehensive leak survey program and water wastage survey program, and recommendations for a water conservation program. By 1996 about 80% of the residents had access to piped water (Attia 1999). At the same time, 56.4% of households lived in informal settlements on former agricultural or desert land (Sims 2003), indicating a continued pressure on existing and expanding water supply provision. By the latter part of the 2000s decade, the Cairo Water Authority officially cited that over 90% of the city's residents were connected to piped treated drinking water (Mohamed and Jagannathan 2009; Ashour et al. 2009). At the same time, other major problems persisted. The extension of the municipal water network was accompanied by a lack of maintenance, which resulted in 1995 high seepage losses reaching up to 40% of the delivered water (Attia 1999).

This period of dramatic build-up of the infrastructure directly responded to the crisis. The major investment in infrastructure could have promoted a positive transition (to significantly more robust access to useable water for Cairo residents), yet the rapid and largely uncontrolled urbanization process, coupled with the limited ability to develop and/or enforce planning and regulation, particularly in the dynamic periurban areas of the city, hampered the long-term robustness of the transition (Sutton and Fahmi 2001). Across the vast metropolitan region of Cairo, it is clear that the quality and quantity of piped water vary greatly. Some neighborhoods have relatively consistent flows and in fact could be considered as quite well advanced, while many other neighborhoods do not have consistent high-quality flow and more often than not go without any flow. For those without, intermittent and often lengthy periods of low pressure/no supply/varying quality push for consistent engagement with alternative informal sources of water.

5.2.2.4 Transformation

So while on paper, the period of water infrastructure expansion signified a transition, the actual situation for consumers is generally not so positive, and the period of transformation actually led to a different trajectory. Even with the expanded infrastructure, a large number of households lacked sufficient water pressure, water of quality to safely use, or even easy access to water (i.e., water might come to one central tap in a building). The poor, often in high-density neighborhoods, were particularly at risk to water shortages (Raymond 2000). In a survey of the Cairo slum neighborhood in the early 2000s (the Ezbet Bekhit neighborhood – an informal settlement of 37,000 residents) had roughly 60% of households connected to the public water system (Sims 2003). For those connected, the water costs were relatively inexpensive, but the water pressure was frequently zero and when flowing, the water quality was low. Forty-two percent of those connected households had no monthly cost for water – meaning that they received no water through their pipes. Households not connected had to rely on a variety of means to get water, including private caterers, informal networks, and quasi-legal/illegal appropriation of water with noninfrastructure-related water delivery processes (e.g., water trucks, bottled water). In many cases, these strategies provided water in an irregular fashion (i.e., limited time, low pressure) and often contaminated water that spread illness and disease. In Ezbet Bekhit, "borrowing" water from more fortunate neighbors or purchasing water from local vendors at rates up to 27 times the national rate for metered potable water was most typical. The situation was similar for the sewerage network. Sewerage was first introduced in the late 1970s and possibly 40% of households were initially connected. The population growth made even this minimal system completely inadequate and as of the early 2000s, most households relied on "soak-away pits" – equivalent to outdoor privies that needed regular emptying by cart or suction truck.

5.2.3 New York, US

New York City is a global center for commerce and financial services. Its history as a trading site stretches back to its origin as a Dutch colonial port in the early 1600s. The natural setting of New York City generally (the five boroughs or counties that comprise it) and Manhattan Island specifically (the island onto which the initial European settlement grew) provided abundant resources for its human inhabitants. Manhattan looked out onto one of the best natural harbors in the world and was rich with forests, wildlife, and freshwater. Sanderson (2009) in his masterful recreation of the 1609 landscape of the island writes that its biodiversity and natural beauty would make the setting one for a national park or conservation area.

By the end of the American War of Independence in 1783, the city had already emerged as the major port of the new country. Its status as significant was greatly accelerated with the opening of the Erie Canal through western New York State in 1825, which opened the interior of the rapidly growing country to Atlantic trading partners by way of the port of New York. From 1790 to 1830, the population of the city grew from 33,131 to 202,589. The city remained as a highly concentrated settlement at the southern end of Manhattan, only extending approximately eight kilometers north of the Battery, the extreme southern tip of the island. This growth and associated rapid economic expansion put tremendous pressure on the local resources of the city and its immediate environs.

5.2.3.1 Stress

The original source of drinking water for the city was local streams, ponds, and springs. The first one and a half centuries of the city's existence, water supply was provided by a largely ad-hoc system of first private wells, later supplemented by public wells. Locally disposed of waste eventually polluted many of these wells. By the late 1780s, many of the local wells in the city had become polluted and cumbersome water delivery systems became necessary (Galusha 1999; Koeppel 2001). Well-water shortage was a chronic problem.

The next half century, roughly from early post-US independence through 1830, was marked by a series of failed private sector interventions to address the chronic water quantity and quality concerns. More frequent and more intense waterborne disease outbreaks began to affect the city. The idea of bringing fresh water from great distances into the city was first proposed in the late 1790s. The Manhattan Water Company was established to supply the city with fresh water and was chartered to provide fresh water from the Bronx River, approximately 40 kilometers north of the city. Instead, the company opted for developing large wells within the city near the Collect Pond (Swaney et al. 2012). As one of the main sources of local surface water, the Collect Pond also experienced a decline in water quality with increased development and a lack of water supply protection. Attempts at increasing supply via private carters and companies proved ineffective, inefficient, or fraught with corruption. Access to fresh drinking water became increasingly an issue of inequity – the wealthy could afford the clean water brought into the city while the poor and immigrants often could not. The city developed a series of local-scale actions involving the modest expansion of existing water conveyance and storage capacity to resolve the issues, all of which failed to foster a large-scale system shift. The city's water supply was in a degraded state not unlike that of contemporary lower-income countries' city water supply systems.

5.2.3.2 Crisis

The water supply crisis of the city emerged steadily through the 1820s and into the 1830s. A series of significant disease outbreaks fed by the use of foul water and building fires that spread because of a lack of adequate supply for fire suppression racked the city on a regular basis (Solecki et al. 2025).

By the early 1830s the situation had become increasingly difficult and reached a heightened level of crisis. The system had become unable to meet the increasing demands for change. The rising international and national trade through the city accelerated with the opening of the Erie Canal brought a dramatic increase in the number of disease outbreaks often associated with infected cargo – for example, cholera outbreaks hit the city in 1832, 1833, and 1834. The demands for more sustained supplies of high-quality water further grew with rapid economic and demographic expansion at the same time. The circumstances became untenable with the additional burden of providing sustained supply for water for fire suppression for a city mostly built of wood structures. It was concern for fire losses that eventually brought a coalescence of support for a new path forward, especially through an alliance of the city's new and emergent wealthy entrepreneurial classes. The fires had been ravaging their neighborhoods and businesses and it became clear to them that large-scale transformative action needed to be taken (Burrows and Wallace 1998).

The lack of sewerage removal made the situation worse. By 1830, Tarr (1996) estimates that "human sewage was being generated in privies, cesspools, or open pits and migrating, untreated, into waterways at a rate of nearly 100 tons per day." The problem was exacerbated by the significant number of horses and other livestock in the city at that time and the associated large volume of manure that was deposited on the streets every day, very little of which was removed regularly and would accumulate along with other organic wastes. Swaney and others (2012) estimate that the horses in the city in 1825 created an estimated 270 tons of manure per day.

5.2.3.3 Transition

The failure of the early initiatives and impediment to large-scale water management shifts largely emerged from an entrenched alliance of the largest and highly dominant private water company (the Manhattan Company) and the northern Manhattan property owners (Burrows and Wallace 1998). The northern three quarters of the island remained farms, fields, and forests and ready for urban development. With fresh water piped to the city, they feared that development would continue to be clustered in lower Manhattan and demand would decline for their northern Manhattan homestead properties with ample water and other positive amenities – for example, relief from the disease, dirt, and congestion of the city.

The new coalition of business leaders recognized the need to fundamentally restructure the city's water supply system and create a new system. The resulting action was the wresting of control for water provision for the city from private to public hands and a public referendum that called for funds to be raised to construct a totally new and massive reservoir and water distribution system (i.e., the Croton system in remote rural highland areas approximately 40 kilometers north of the city) to bring abundant supplies of fresh water to the heart of the city by the early 1840s. When the water was officially turned on in 1842, a five-mile parade in celebration took place.

5.2.3.4 Transformation

A series of dynamic transformations occurred as a result of the city's new reservoir and long-distance water conveyance system (Gandy 2003; Solecki et al. 2025). Water consumption immediately increased and indoor plumbing was added to many buildings or at least water pumps outside of lower-income residences soon appeared. While disease outbreaks and large-scale fires remained an issue, their frequency and intensity began to diminish. One of the genius elements of the Croton system was that it was designed to be added onto, and within decades, planning began to significantly expand the city's water supply. Two additional reservoir systems (i.e., Catskill, completed in 1924, and Delaware, completed in 1954) were developed on lands further away from the city. The current system has a storage capacity of 2.1 trillion liters and provides over 4.5 billion liters per day of drinking water for approximately 9 million people as well as the business and commercial establishments in the city and in several outlying municipalities, which are connected to the system.

5.2.4 Tel Aviv, Israel

Tel Aviv, Israel's largest city, has a metropolitan area population (Tel Aviv-Jaffa in 2021) of 4,264,000. While Tel Aviv's origin is relatively recent (founded in 1909), the history of Jaffa, or Jafa in Arabic or Yafo in Hebrew, goes back almost 4,000 years. Tel Aviv grew quite dramatically in the twentieth century, during which it eclipsed Jaffa in population and economic significance. The current population of Tel Aviv is about 460 thousand with Jaffa and numerous substantial, adjoining suburban municipalities making up the rest of the metropolitan region. The metropolitan region serves as the economic and technological center of Israel. The history of water supply in Tel Aviv-Jaffa has been deeply connected to that of the country of Israel since its founding in 1948. Feitelson (2013) describes four phases of water supply policy in Israel – each one responding to different stresses. These include the hydraulic mission period (1948–1964); the wise management era (1959–1990); the reflexive deliberations era (1990–2005); and the desalination and privatization era from 2005 to the present. Each phase has been associated with crisis, and the last phase emerging from a profound transition.

5.2.4.1 Stress

Water supply and scarcity have long been issues of concern in the eastern Mediterranean region generally and for the city of Tel Aviv and the country of Israel (Tal 2017). Much of the country can be described as a desert and as such receives 250 mm (10 in) of precipitation per year or less. Tel Aviv has a climate more similar to a Mediterranean climate and receives about 580 millimeters (23 inches) per year with typically all of it occurring outside of the summer months and especially in the winter months. The north of the country typically receives more rain while the south receives less with the southernmost city of Eilat getting less than 50 mm (2 inches) per year.

The threat of water shortage presents an existential threat to the security of Israel and as a result has been deeply embedded within its national agenda. The focus on securing water supply has focused three broad strategies that have emerged sequentially. Each of the three broad strategies emerged as a result of policy debates and transitions. The initial focus was on securing the maximal amount of water supply from existing surface and groundwater supplies with specific attention to reducing water loss during the bulk infrastructure transfer to a minimal amount (~3% loss). The second was on recycling and reusing water as much as possible, and the third focused on expanding the supply of water – particularly through the use of desalinization.

With the country's founding, water supply in Israel was associated with a series of substantial stresses and national strategic plans focused on national resource development. It immediately became a high-priority national security issue and in turn established direct connections to the military establishment and as a resource that needed to be heavily protected. The focus on national security was heightened when Israel was prevented by United Nations action from extracting water from the upper Jordan River and instead was required to extract water from Lake Kinneret (Sea of Galilee). As early as the 1950s, Israel began an extensive water supply development project that would convey fresh water from the Sea of Galilee southward across the country to various demand sites, including Tel Aviv at some 150 kilometers distance (Thi Hoang Duong et al. 2011). This was also designed to overcome the wide disparities in the spatial and seasonal variability of rainfall. The innovative system allowed for the storage and conveyance of water from the wetter north to the drier center and south – the main agricultural areas. Since the country is relatively small, only about 22,140 sq km (8,630 sq mi.) and comparable to the size of the US state of New Jersey, the distances to move are significant but proved not to be insurmountable.

In this early formative era, the rapid and extensive expansion of water resource infrastructure was carried out by a small and cohesive policy community of experts. Water engineers, who were affiliated with the national labor movement and the agricultural sector, dominated this community. Within this technical elite, fierce struggles emerged that resulted in a shift of the dominant view of how water resources should be managed (Alatout 2008). Water was no longer seen as an abundant resource that could be exploited and utilized but as a limited and scarce resource that has to be carefully managed. The notion of scarcity emerged as the central narrative of the Israeli water development community (Feitelson 2013).

Starting around 1960, Israel began an aggressive water demand management strategy to use water more efficiently. The policies included pricing and economic policies, reuse of sewerage effluents, water conservation/improving efficiency of water use, agricultural water use innovations including drip irrigation, water markets and pricing strategies, virtual water policy including the importation of high water-demanding agricultural crops (that lowered the need for domestic use of water to produce those crops), and water metering and a national water licensing and allocation system (Arlosoroff 2003). This second phase of national water planning proved to be quite successful in forestalling radical water management transitions. By the late 1980s/early 1990, the volume of water use and Gross National Product per capita had increased dramatically in Israel, but the amount used per capita only slightly increased during the same time.

5.2.4.2 Crisis

Even with its sustained state of water resource stress, it took several large-scale droughts in Israel to foster the political will to take on even more ambitious water reforms that led to a realignment of water governance and illustrated the growing importance of nonagricultural water use sector, especially in urban areas of the country. Up through 1996, the water sector was managed by the national Ministry of Agriculture. The policy priority was to rely on natural surface and groundwater resources to meet all water demands (and over-pump as needed), with the agricultural sector remaining as the largest user. Shortages or deficits were handled by reducing water supply to farmers during droughty periods and expecting a following rainy period to refill water resources. Water supply was heavily subsidized, as example tariffs on water use were held very low for farmers. Domestic water supply and wastewater collection also were heavily subsidized. The consistent population growth and an increasing diversity of demands eventually showed an approach ever less sustainable. All these factors together meant that the Israeli water sector existed in a permanent state of heightened vulnerability (Marin et al. 2017).

Within this context, three periods of water crises eventually built the momentum for major demand and supply-side reforms in the 2000s. First, in 1986, a major drought for the first time caused a significant reduction in water allocations for agriculture (15%). This drought was soon followed by the even more significant 1989/1990 drought that required severe and widely unpopular water restrictions. These conditions were rapidly forgotten because, as had been the pattern, the drought was immediately followed by an extremely rainy winter in 1991–1992 (i.e., 1 in a 150-year event) that entirely replenished natural resources. A third even more severe drought happened soon after in 1998. During this event, water shortages affected not only agriculture but also municipal and industrial consumers, resulting in severe water shortages and even rationing in most cities in Israel. The 1998 drought and water crisis created a sense of urgency and a political window for action, eventually triggering far-reaching policy changes (Feitelson 2013).

5.2.4.3 Transition

In 2000, the Israeli national government changed the policy for water sector management. It adopted a more sustainable approach to help guarantee the country's water security. The policy shift included the creation of a special committee tasked with the responsibility to develop a plan to gradually establish over the next 15 years a new institutional framework for water management. Central to this new approach is the acceptance of a technological fix – the utilization of desalination plants and a set of policy reforms, which required years of implementation and refinement in order to optimize results. These actions required difficult political decisions, such as a steep increase in domestic use water tariffs, especially in response to another major drought, which took place in 2008. The policy shift also helped generate a series of innovations that eventually restored a sustainable water balance for the country and its rapidly growing urban areas such as Tel Aviv.

5.2.4.4 Transformation

To extend these supplies, Israel actively worked to recycle its water for secondary uses. In general, urban water is sent to wastewater plants and recycled for agricultural uses. In the last two decades, recognizing the potential for future water shortages Israel began an aggressive program building water desalination plans. The new National Water Carrier pipeline conveys desalinated potable water throughout the country from five plants along the Mediterranean coast. This transport represents approximately 75% of all the potable water transmitted by the national water company – Mekorot. Desalination is expected to help meet all future growth in domestic and industrial demand. This production would also generate a significant increase in the amount of reusable treated wastewater for the agricultural sector and public works. As of 2010, Israel was the global leader in the proportion of water it recycles. Israel treats 80% of its sewage (400 billion liters a year). From the Tel Aviv metropolitan area, 100% of the sewage is treated and reused (Figure 5.3).

Figure 5.3 Israel's national water infrastructure grid. Source: Tal (2006).

5.3 Discussion

Significant water scarcity is possibly the most important and fundamental crisis for cities. The case studies reveal how this stress and the resulting crisis can result in a policy transition and transformation. A striking thing about water crises in cities is that they have an ancient history and as a result it is an issue well understood and known to all segments of the population. It is comparative luxury of the current era that many urban residents throughout the world whose tap water is regularly supplied do not appreciate the widespread fragility of drinking water supply. The loss of sustained water supply for cities represents an existential threat, as opposed to a quality-of-life issue. In all the case studies, the response to the crisis and eventual transition was built on a series of responses to earlier stresses and pending crises. This pattern of flexible response and engagement emerged episodically in earlier moments as the situation neared an acute crisis. In these earlier moments, the solutions only partially resolved the issues, thereby requiring further future action as a new crisis, often more dire, emerged. It is interesting to note that earlier proposals to resolve the issues typically first solved by supply-side management options (i.e., focused on increasing water supply) while the eventual solutions also focused on demand-side management (i.e., reducing consumption demand).

5.3.1 Conditions of Crisis

While some crisis issues are specific to each case study, similar tendencies are present across the four city examples. For instance, all cases illustrate how the water supply issue is dynamic and requires consistent focus on it, especially as population expansion and resource demand increase take place. The studies provide evidence that stress is often not enough to motivate action and significant action occurs only with the onset of crisis. It should be recalled that in all cases, resource stress had a significant impact on a wide range of populations and interests, but neither the extent nor the intensity was enough to motivate a systemic response. The evolution from stress to crisis often was expressed as a shift from specific locations and moments of water shortage to more frequent and widespread shortages.

An interesting turn in focus also occurred during this shift from stress to crisis. In general, initial proposals and responses were more reactive during the stress and early crisis periods. The efforts became more proactive later as the crisis became more significant and the need and ambition for more larger-scale proposals emerged and were agreed to. The idea of making substantial and durable solutions became central to the transition and the evolution of the transformation. A consensus seemed to emerge that as long as change was occurring, it should be sizable enough that it would not have to be dealt with again anytime soon, given the effort and energy to create the conditions for transition in the first place.

Overall, the threat to economic development was a huge factor motivating action, in some ways more significant than health and safety concerns. Overall, business interests were significant in driving the stress to become a widespread crisis. The definition of the crisis was driven by the connection between the private sector and public sector, which typically involved the private sector seeking out the public sector to address their concerns, as especially evident in New York City. The crises were also sharpened by external factors, which became more important over time. In the case of Israel generally and Tel Aviv specifically, water was a critical security issue and any threat to it became an existential threat to the fledging nation. Cities such as Tel Aviv and also Cairo and New York benefited from their position within an extensive national and regional water supply infrastructure and from the intense concern regarding national development and stability.

5.3.2 Drivers of Transitions

In all cases, examples examined, it was eventually acknowledged that the scale of operation would have to be changed to address the crisis – that is, a need for a bigger and more extensive water supply system. The new policy regimes that emerged from the crises required the application of technology to change the scale of operation. New coalitions and governance structures were formed to address the emergent demands, and in this context, the capacity and engagement of the state (i.e., local, state/provincial, and often national government) were critical to the development and implementation of the new policy. A wide range of root, context, and proximate drivers were observed in the case studies (Table 5.1).

5.3.3 Spheres of Action and Legacies

All three types of systems – social, ecological/environmental, and technological/infrastructural – are present in the case studies and had critical roles to play in the crises and transitions. The three systems are tightly coupled with droughts playing a highly significant role in the emergence of the crisis. Given the central importance of the water storage via reservoirs and conveyance via aqueducts and piping, infrastructure systems have an oversized role to play in the case studies. The political ecology of how and under what circumstances

Table 5.1 *Key drivers observed in each case study. Source: Author.*

	DRIVERS		
Case Study	Root	Context	Proximate
Atlanta	Relative scarcity; lack of water at the Atlanta settlement site; transboundary conflicts between the states of Georgia, Alabama, and Florida	Competing economic interests; agricultural and fishing versus urbanization; legal precedent	Droughts
Cairo	Lack of governance capacity; water quality decline; rapid informal urbanization	Foreign aid, lack of adequate infrastructure	
New York	Water quality decline; failed private sector management; rapid urbanization and growth (with the Erie Canal opening)	Competition between real estate and merchant classes; economic inequity; lack of sewerage management	Inability to control urban fires; waterborne disease
Tel Aviv	Absolute water scarcity; transnational competition for water; national planning efforts to promote water supply	Shift from military control to civilian control of water; competing economic interests: agricultural versus urbanization; availability of new technology – desalination	Droughts

decisions were made to develop new infrastructure came as a result of shifts in power alliances backed by legal precedents. In all cases, the legacy of past decisions that legitimated longstanding water supply agreements played a significant role in forestalling resolutions before the widespread crises emerged. These agreements also had been directly connected to water supply infrastructure, which, as a fixed asset, also influenced how the initial stages of the crisis were understood. Thereby, the question was often asked, "Could the crisis be solved with the existing infrastructure or at most a minimal restructuring of it?" Here, the initial focus was on minimal adjustments and incremental fixes as a way of avoiding a massive restructuring of the system and equivalent investment and disruption. Once it was recognized that these steps would not be sufficient, the motivation for a larger, more substantive action and policy shift became evident.

5.3.3.1 Urban Water Supply and Climate Change

Climate change already is having observed impacts on urban water supply, and the projections are for increased impacts with more significant climate heating (Dodman et al. 2022). The physical changes include rainfall variability (more droughtiness; more extreme rainfall periods and events) as well as saltwater intrusion into coastal groundwater supplies. Vulnerability of urban water supply to climate change is dependent on existing deficiencies in the water supply infrastructure, the age of the infrastructure, the growth rate of water demand, and the response capacity of the city. Climate stresses are exacerbating existing urban water supply vulnerabilities and inequities (Dodman et al. 2022) and will continue to do more in the future.

The analysis of the urban supply crises examined here provides some insights that might be of interest for urban practitioners, managers, and other stakeholders. Specific recommendations include the following:

- Prepare local; plan regional – climate change-driven shortages often will be experienced in localized areas, either in specific neighborhoods or individual cities. While it will be important to recognize and prepare for immediate and site-specific crises, the case studies illustrate that solutions to these will be likely regional in nature. Collaborative region-scale solutions to urban water supply will be needed to resolve the chronic problem of water supply.
- Droughts and other related supply crises as windows of opportunities – water supply shocks can become powerful vehicles for the debate and progression of new policies and significant policy changes. Urban water scarcity is perceived as and remains an existential threat to city life.
- Need to focus on infrastructure – while demand-side management and reducing water consumption are important much of the attention among stakeholders and the general public during crises will be on the inadequacy and deficits of the water supply infrastructure.
- Legacy – the legacy of past decisions becomes very significant in the discussion and debate of new and emergent policies. This is especially critical for urban water supply systems that are dependent on capital- and labor-intensive projects that once built are difficult to alter or redesign. These features simply then become the foundation for future initiatives to be built on or connected to.
- Water shortages become existential – the actual or perceived water shortages will become portrayed as an existential threat to the city and broader region.

- Coalitions will form around urban water supply issues – the magnitude and importance of water supply deficits will bring together coalitions of interest groups and in some cases, these will be unusual groupings or groups that previously have not worked together. These coalitions can be quite politically powerful and collectively overturn longstanding water management regimes.
- Incremental adjustments preferred – the initial response to an emerging urban water supply crisis will focus on incremental adjustments to the existing systems. Coalition groups likely would not immediately go for large-scale, transformative changes and will try to avoid them because of the large-scale investment and other elements of disruption. Alternative options often have a difficult time gaining traction because of their novelty, uncertainty surrounding them, and massive capital expense.

6

Environment Degradation and Quality

Urban Air Pollution

> "*The sky over the Ruhr region must be blue again.*" Demand made by Willy Brandt as Governing Mayor of West Berlin during a speech on 28 April 1961 in the Bonn Beethoven Hall. The quote is seen as the start of environmentally conscious political thinking in Germany. (Brandt 1961)

Cities have faced a wide variety of environmental quality and pollution issues. Key pollution concerns have been water, land, and air pollution. This chapter addresses air pollution crises and their resolution. Air pollution concerns have been present throughout the history of cities. The air over a city and its smell can reveal a lot about a city's residents including how they heat their houses, cook their meals, how they move about the city, and even what kind of jobs they might have. For example, many a town has the sulfurous, rotten egg smell of an oil refinery or paper pulp mill signifying the presence of a major employer and polluter. Air pollution often becomes a more serious concern as cities grow in size and more local sources of pollution develop. The air pollution history of cities is reflective of significant switches and transformations that have taken place in the city. Pollution levels changed significantly with industrial development as well as with industrial decline and manufacturing plant closures. Air pollution shifts are also associated with switches from one type of fuel to another – for example, conversion from wood to coal, and then to oil or natural gas.

Urban air pollution becomes a crisis as it starts to impinge on human health and well-being and in turn on the livelihood of the residents and the economy of the city. Long-term exposure to air pollution causes a variety of negative health issues. The history of urban air pollution also is replete with incidents of acute exposure, resulting from industrial accidents and unusual weather conditions, that also cause significant public health hazards. Globally, air pollution is now regularly regarded as one of the most significant challenges facing cities and will increase in severity with climate heating (WHO 2016). Increased heating creates conditions for greater concentrations of air pollutants that emerge from atmospheric chemical reactions (described below as secondary air pollutants). The objective of this chapter is to present case studies about how urban air pollution is a story of grinding chronic exposure and devastating acute events, as well as spectacular, yet very context-specific, air pollution control policy successes. The discussion focuses on four case studies, including London, UK, Los Angeles, US, the Rhine-Rhur Region of northwest Germany, and Tokyo, Japan.

6.1 Basics of the Issue – Urban Air Pollution

While water noted in Chapter 5 is fundamental for life, air is a necessity. That said, the human body has an amazing ability to sustain itself on air of varying qualities.[1] People can live in highly polluted environments; however, air pollution imposes a significant burden on the human body, especially the respiratory and pulmonary systems, but also cancers and neurological impairment. Chronic exposure to air pollutants causes a wide range of damage to these systems, all of which can contribute to a diminished quality of life and early death (Cohen et al. 2004; World Health Organization 2016). In heavily air-polluted cities, typically residents take into their lungs the air pollution equivalent of a pack of 20 cigarettes or more.[2] Acute air pollution episodes are associated with high-concentrations of either primary or secondary pollutants that can be immediately negatively impactful on human health, including sudden death. The infamous London Smog Attack of December 1952 was linked with the deaths of approximately 12,000 people (Brimblecombe 2012).

Data on the extent of the public health threat and property damage from air pollution can vary depending on one's methodology. But overall, the numbers can be startling: 1.67 million lives were lost in India as a whole in 2019 due to chronic high levels of air pollution exposure, and resulted in a total annual

[1] This chapter focuses on ambient, outdoor air pollution issues and does not focus on indoor air pollution, which can be related to outdoor air pollution has a different history and set of impacts.

[2] Significant debate regarding air pollution-cigarette equivalency is present in the literature. The averages can vary widely. For example, in Beijing an average day worth of air pollution is equivalent to 4 cigarettes, but on a bad pollution day is would be 25 cigarettes. In Shenyang, a city of over 8 million in northeast China, researchers observed a day of 63 cigarettes equivalent – the worst the team recorded (Rohde and Muller 2015).

economic loss of approximately $36.8 billion, which was 1.36% of India's gross domestic product (GDP) (Pandey et al. 2021).

It has long been thought that significant air pollution only occurred with the modern industrial era. Recent research however has shown that Roman lead mining and smelting more than 2,000 years ago significantly polluted air throughout part of Europe (Preunkert et al. 2019). Furthermore, smoke and soot were prominent issues in cities throughout the ancient world (Gilgen et al. 2019). In 61 AD, the famous Roman philosopher Seneca wrote "as soon as I escaped from the oppressive atmosphere of the city [Rome], and from that awful odor of reeking kitchens which, when in use, pour forth a ruinous mess of steam and soot, I perceived at once that my health was mended" (Referenced in Heidorn 1978). Overall, the history of air pollution in cities extends through every region of the world and every time period, and up through the modern era.

Several qualities make air pollution particularly complex. Air pollution while most significant at its source areas by its very nature disperses via prevailing winds and can move across political boundaries complicating management and legal or policy action. For example, in the 1940s and 1950s, the neighboring states of New Jersey and New York had a series of disputes regarding transboundary air pollution, especially that originating in New Jersey and blown eastward toward New York City. The states' inability to resolve the conflicts drove some of the motivation for developing and implementing overarching US federal legislation that focused on universal standards for airborne pollution emissions.

Many types or categories of air pollution exist. Historically, urban residents were most concerned about air pollution that they could easily see like soot, smoke, and associated particulates. A range of other air pollutants also exist that are more difficult to see or smell, and are often associated with haze or discoloration of the sky. Two key distinctions exist that help define some of the variation among different types of air pollution – these categories include primary and secondary air pollutants and acute versus chronic exposures and impacts. All four conditions can significantly negatively impact human health.

Primary air pollutants are those that are emitted directly from the sources. Primary pollutants often discussed in association with cities and urbanization include particulates, carbon monoxide, sulfur oxide, and nitrogen oxide. Primary pollutants can chemically react with other pollutants or other gases in the atmosphere above cities and create what are defined as secondary pollutants. Particulate matter is a catch-all category of pollution and one of the most visible and historically significant forms of air pollution. It includes particles, such as dust, dirt, soot, or smoke, that are large or dark enough to be seen with the naked eye, although others can be much smaller. Particulate matter can be made up of hundreds of different chemicals and is emitted directly from many potential sources such as smokestacks or fires, construction sites, unpaved roads, and fields. Particles also can form as a result of chemical reactions in the atmosphere resulting from emissions from power plants, industries, and automobiles.

Classic examples of secondary air pollutants include photochemical, which is formed when hydrocarbons (HC) and nitrogen oxides (NOx) combine in the presence of sunlight to produce tropospheric ozone, peroxyacyl nitrates, and aldehydes. Another widely present secondary pollutant is nitrogen dioxide (NO_2), which is formed when nitrogen monoxide combines with oxygen in the air. Acid rain is associated with other secondary air pollutants that form when sulfur dioxide or NOx react with water molecules in the atmosphere and form acidic particulates that mix with precipitation. These acidic particulates can be deposited at some distance from the source location.

Smog as a type of air pollution has gained significant prominence since the great smog alerts of the mid-twentieth century. Smog, a combination of the words smoke and fog, is a type of visible air pollution composed of NOx, sulfur oxides, ozone, smoke, and particulate matter. Human-caused, smog can be derived from a range of sources including industrial emissions, forest and agricultural fires, coal combustion emissions, vehicular emissions, and photochemical reactions of these emissions. Two types of smog are often described: summer smog or winter smog. Summer smog is typically associated with the photochemical formation of ozone, as a secondary air pollutant. Winter smog occurs when thermal inversions cause ground-level emissions from the burning of coal or other carbon-based fuels to become trapped toward ground level and not dispersed. Both types of smog have deleterious human impacts, with winter smog at high concentration being especially harmful and in extreme cases deadly.

The distinction between chronic and acute exposure can be somewhat vague. The acute air pollution smog episodes in many twentieth-century European and North American cities and contemporary Asian cities and other developing country cities have been associated with immediate negative health consequences. Smog-related air pollutants much more typically occur at lower concentrations and manifest as long-term chronic exposures that result in a variety of illnesses and diseases that contribute to early death. These types of exposures continue to impact cities where acute smog attacks have not occurred for decades. While some progress has been made in New York City since the mid-twentieth century when the city's air was subject to numerous smog alerts, the city's air quality still does often exceed US federal air pollution standards (Slovic and Ribeiro 2018).

6.2 Case Studies of Air Quality Control Transformation

In this chapter, four case studies examine the process of urban air quality stress and crisis, and urban air pollution control policy transitions and resulting transformations. The case studies include London, UK, Los Angeles, US, the Ruhr River Valley Germany, and Tokyo, Japan. The case studies include cities and extended metropolitan regions that have gone through significant periods of air pollution and subsequent control resulting in a dramatic transformation with respect to air quality. Each case study includes background discussion and then an examination of resource stress and crisis, transition or not, and possible transformation. The concluding discussion in the chapter focuses on the relevant analysis and implications of the case studies.

6.2.1 London, UK

London is one of the world's most dominant global cities with a current population of the greater metropolitan area of just over 9 million. Founded by Roman invaders in 47 AD, a narrow point of the Thames River where a bridge could be put across, and just upstream from the river's estuary. The air quality of London has been associated with elaborate descriptions. The city throughout its history has been subject to dense fog episodes, and settlements along the river have been for a long time a source of wood and coal smoke. The history of air pollution in the region goes back centuries. Legislation that attempted to control air pollution was enacted as early as 1306, when the city already had a population of roughly 80,000 and was one of the largest in Europe. By 1661, when the population had reached approximately 350,000, famous English diarist John Evelyn presented King Charles II with evidence that smoke pollution could shorten the lives of people living in London. During the early part of the nineteenth century, when London had become the largest city in the world and growing incredibly fast, the amount of air pollution increased dramatically. The rapid population growth was coupled with a massive expansion of industrial and commercial activities, further driving an equally dramatic rise in pollution levels. Poet William Wordsworth described in 1850 London's air as "a solemn gray canopy of vapor was "sitting like an incubus" over the city" (p. 70, Hardy [2020] in Luckin and Thorsheim).

6.2.1.1 Stress

The extent of London's air pollution stresses continued to grow throughout the second half of the nineteenth century. The darkening, polluted skies led residents to ever more tightly close their doors and windows to keep the particulate matter that fell in "fat flakes" out of their homes (Hardy, p. 71). The combined color of the fog and smoke shifted from a dirty white brew of earlier in the century to a yellow-gray color or the "pea-soup" of Victorian England legend (Hardy 2020). At the same time, several attempts were made to try to control the pollution including the Smoke Nuisance Abatement Act of 1853 and smoke clauses in the Sanitary Acts of 1858 and 1866 and in the Public Health Act of 1875. Enforcement was initially done by the police, but powers were later transferred to the sanitary authorities that emerged with the professionalization of environmental protection. While they provided some control, it was also evident that their mandate and capacity were not sufficient to address the problems (Brimblecombe 2012). Pronounced air pollution episodes became increasingly deadly and in December 1873 one event resulted in a blacking and choking "crisis" that could kill even healthy individuals if overexposed, according to reports (Brimblecombe 2012).

6.2.1.2 Crisis

The next several decades brought hundreds of such episodes. In the peak years, 1886 and 1887, 86 and 83 episodes occurred, respectively. The death rates in London doubled during many of these events. At this time, the concentrations of particulate matter were on par with or greater than the amounts currently observed in highly polluted cities in Asia and other parts of the world. By the turn of the twentieth century, the number of extreme events started to decline as coal was replaced by other lower-polluting fuels and electricity became widely present, coupled with the observation that the humidity levels in the city (likely because of the filling of riverine wetlands and the increased amounts of impervious surfaces) and overall prevalence of fog had diminished resulting in more wind to disperse the pollutants. The burning of coal in houses for heat and hot water however remained a significant issue. Even so, overall levels of particulate matter continued to decline during the century, except for a slight rise during the depth of the Great Depression during which cheaper high-polluting fuels were burned (Figure 6.1).

The next significant crisis came in December 1952 (Brimblecombe 2012). During this time a series of drivers came together to cause one of the most significant acute pollution events in modern urban history. The Great Smog Attack occurred in London from December 5 to 9 of that year. During the post-World War II period, the United Kingdom was faced with financial hardship and a policy decision was made to locally burn cheaper high-sulfur bituminous coal or lignite while higher-quality anthracite coal was more likely to be exported to raise much needed capital. At the same time, increased private and

Figure 6.1 Average Suspended Particulate Matter (SPM) in London, England (measured in micrograms per cubic meters, developed by author from Fouquet (2011) (data accessed from https://ourworldindata.org/grapher/air-pollution-london-vs-delhi)

public vehicular use, especially recently introduced diesel buses and trains, introduced a range of additional air pollutants into the local environment. Early December 1952 turned relatively cold resulting in significantly increased coal burning for heating. On December 5, the situation was made grave by a weather pattern that created a significant thermal inversion in which relatively cool air is overlain by relatively warm air. The warm air serves as a blanket for the air closer to the ground, thereby reducing ground-level mixing winds and dispersion. As a result, the air over the city was stilled for the next four days and the concentration of the air pollution increased dramatically. Within a few days, the weather pattern shifted, the inversion broke apart, winds dispersed the pollutants, and the alert subsided. The acute conditions, however, had resulted in approximately 10–12 thousand deaths in greater London. It was later reported that the pollution levels during the London smog were as much as 5–19 times above current UK regulatory standards and guidelines and approximated or exceeded current levels in some rapidly developing country cities (Bell and Davis 2001).

6.2.1.3 Transition

The Great Smoke Attack created dramatic momentum for a significant new round of pollution control measures. Just months later, the UK Parliament in early 1953 recognized the need for significant action. The parliament authorized the development of a special report committee to provide insights on an appropriate response. By November 1954 the Committee issued its final report. Its most notable recommendations were a call for national clean air legislation that would include a move beyond just the control of industrial emission sources but to curtail and regulate domestic emissions as well. The report called for new controls that were more stringent than the recommendations envisioned by the London County Council, the local entity that had jurisdiction. The committee's work and recommendations eventually led to the authorization of the 1956 UK Clean Air Act (CAA).

The 1956 CAA dramatically expanded the scope of the earlier Public Health Act of 1936, increasing the number of specific legal clauses focused on air pollution control from 6 to 40. The CAA included a shift in tone toward a more modern contemporary approach to environmental protection that focused on reduced health impacts and a new attention to nonpoint household emitters and constraint of individual choice to enhance the common good. The CAA also provided encouragement to shift to lower-polluting fuels in addition to more traditional local smoke abatement clauses such as provisions on chimney heights, smoke control areas, and practices within industrial premises.

6.2.1.4 Transformation

While the 1956 CAA was a signature piece of UK environmental legislation, its full impact can be better understood as part of a larger transformation. The legislation has an important place within the longer history of air pollution control in London and the increased role of government in managing air quality. The CAA brought forward a broader set of "upstream" actions that transformed how the state could dictate (1) fuel choice, (2) fuel-burning practices, and (3) zoning and urban development, such as the relocation of industrial facilities out of central cities. Overall, the legislation and its subsequent updates (i.e., the CAA was extended in 1968 and both Acts were consolidated by the CAA 1993) had profound implications for how Britons heat their homes and what type of equipment they can use to generate heat. For example, the widespread construction of all-electric houses and gas-fired central heating made the switch in domestic energy sources desired by the Act, especially the reduction of coal burning, more palatable (Brimblecombe 2012). In subsequent decades, it also was recognized that the reduction of coal fuel smoke controlled the emissions of other pollutants such as particles, polycyclic aromatic HC, dioxins and furans, and sulfur dioxide. In smoke control areas designated within the 1993 CAA, local authorities were able to designate locations where smoke may not be emitted and the burned fuels could have a sulfur content of no more than 2% – making them effectively smokeless.

6.2.2 Los Angeles, US

Metropolitan Los Angeles is the largest metropolitan area in the United States, extending over 33,954 square miles (87,940 km^2), slightly larger than the country of Austria. The population of the region is approximately 19 million, making it among the most populous urban regions in the world. The population of the Los Angeles Basin grew very dramatically during the early decades of the twentieth century. The City of Los Angeles in 1880 had about 11,000 residents; by 1900 the population increased to 102,000; and by 1940 it was over 1.5 million. During this time, the population of the city comprised around 60% of Los Angeles County's population (in comparison to about 38% in 2020). Early in its history, Los Angeles was widely recognized as having exceptionally healthy air and attracted tuberculosis patients among others with similar ailments needing recuperation.

6.2.2.1 Stress

The physical landscape of the Los Angeles basin, which is ringed by high mountains, makes the region subject to thermal inversions where the warm air overlays colder surface air. It is with this "lid" that air pollution can become trapped close to the ground and not dispersed as much as it would be otherwise. Los Angeles throughout much of the early twentieth century had only small amounts of industry and was far less dependent on highly polluting coal burning because petroleum and gas were the key local energy sources, and large local coal deposits were not present. As a result, the air pollution problem remained relatively minimal, even though an ordinance as early as 1907 was passed to address smoke nuisance in the city. However, as the population growth of Los Angeles took off so did the automobile use in the region – which became the major source of air pollution. The City of Los Angeles and metropolitan region became an archetype of an automobile-dependent, lower-density, multi-nucleate conurbation. With increased traffic volume, the city began to experience occasional pollution-laden thermal inversions in the 1920s and 1930s. This haze was quite different from the well-recognized pollution associated with industrial activity and high-sulfur coal use (e.g., bituminous) like in heavily polluted cities like Pittsburgh and St. Louis.

6.2.2.2 Crisis

During the 1940s, Los Angeles continued to dramatically grow and became a critical wartime production hub resulting in rapid increases in pollution and in some circumstances a reduction or relaxation in controls. On July 26, 1943, Los Angeles experienced its first major smog attack shattering the Angelenos illusion of constant fresh and healthy air (Elkind 2011). The event occurred during a major heat wave, reduced visibility in the downtown to three blocks, caused extensive eye and throat discomfort, and robbed residents of their consistent sunny weather. Four other times that year through to November, major pollution episodes occurred resulting from what was understood to be a range of possible causes including industrial emissions, open pit burning of waste, and automobile exhaust. While it was widely agreed that a need for a policy response existed, a lack of scientific knowledge of how and why the episodes occurred stalled policy development. Initially, a lot of focus was on a large local gas plant that was producing butadiene as a potential key source of pollution. Soon after, public concern centered on a series of industrial point sources as the cause. Industrialists and lobbying groups argued that unfettered industrial production was necessary to promote the war effort. And in turn, local business leaders argued that regulators should turn their attention to nonindustrial pollution sources.

Air pollution at this time was increasingly seen as both a public health and business threat. While the air pollution had been seen as an irritant or nuisance for at least before the war, by 1950 local medical officials and other health experts more and more recognized that the smog presented more profound health risks (Uekoetter 2009). These concerns are connected with the worries emerging from the general public about the short- and long-term effects of air pollution exposure (Elkind 2011). At about the same time, the smog and pollution also were seen as a threat to business in the region with respect to business closures to reduce pollution, decline in tourism to the region, and most profoundly reduced migration from other parts of the country and subsequent drop in real estate development (Uekotter 2009). In this context, the Los Angeles Chamber of Commerce became an effective agent for increased air pollution controls (Elkind 2011). These three areas of concern coming together helped create the groundwork for air pollution control impetus not present at that time in the other parts of the US.

6.2.2.3 Transition

This confederation of interests fostered a series of developments to improve the air quality of the region. The ambition was initially focused on developing the science to understand how smog was formed and why it was a problem, create the necessary administrative apparatus to implement the new knowledge, and arrest the problem quickly. It was recognized that Los Angeles could not employ the 10-year plan recently promoted by Pittsburgh – but instead wanted the problem solved within a couple of years. A significant moment came with the establishment of a state law in June 1947 that set up air pollution control districts (APCDs). These districts could provide a more spatially integrated and coherent management structure to help coordinate action in politically fragmented Los Angeles County and the wider region. This fragmentation had limited the region's ability to coordinate air control policy in the past (Elkind 2011). The Los Angeles APCD was established a few months later and became one of the most powerful and well-funded public agencies in the country. By the late 1950s, the District employed almost 500 employees and accounted for almost 40% of the expenses of local air pollution control in the country (Uekotter 2009). While the focus on air pollution control had been heightened and institutionalized, the ability to make progress proved much more complicated. The transition had taken place – the focus on the issue dramatically increased and the policy agenda had shifted – but the full-scale transformation to dramatically address the air pollution problem in the region would take another couple of decades as the key focus of the problem finally turned toward the automobile, its use, and its emissions.

Confounding issues defined by critics also included an extended close relationship between government, private industry groups such as the Chamber of Commerce and industry that led to protracted voluntary arrangements to address air pollution as well as a shift toward controlling nonindustrial sources of pollution but without commensurate pollution controls. Another significant issue that needed to be resolved centered around the question of science. Historically, much of the focus of air pollution control policy centered around black or sooty air – pollution that could be seen. The condition of air pollution in Los Angeles centered around the development, acceptance, and implementation of a new science on invisible sources of pollution – the tail-pipe emissions from properly tuned cars and trucks that occurred at such volumes that through an atmospheric chemical process, the secondary pollutant of smog and haze was produced. Many including the general public were skeptical of this science because it ran counter to the history of air pollution control that focused on the obvious sources including black soot and smoke, and because the science was seen as biased since it shifted the focus from traditional polluters such as industry and illegal burning to automobile users and the general public.

6.2.2.4 Transformation

Nonetheless, increasing pollution levels and external stimuli for action – like the 1952 Great Smog Alert of London – continued to motivate Angelenos (Atwood 1997). The next several decades would see a series of actions to address the issue. While all sources of air pollution were investigated and addressed to a certain degree, eventually the focus moved toward automobile-related emissions. Gasoline storage facilities were secured to reduce emissions, but then more and more the attention shifted to the automobiles – and their combustion and emission process and their fuels. New administrative entities were created such as the California Motor Vehicle Pollution Control Board to implement the new policy agenda – the first such agency of this type in the country and likely the world (Uekoetter 2009). The Board brought forward the use of catalytic converters among other innovations to address air pollution and smog. Another transformative consequence was the direct engagement with the US automobile industry and its slowness in responding to the automobile emissions issue. The slow and steady developments in southern California generally and Los Angeles specifically led to significant changes in how the industry understood the issue of air pollution and how it dealt with it, which had national and international repercussions.

6.2.3 Rhine-Ruhr River Region, Germany

The Rhine-Ruhr metropolitan region is one of the largest metropolitan regions in Europe, with more than 10 million inhabitants. Named for the Rhine and Ruhr Rivers, the region is shaped through the integration of a set of large cities (including Cologne, Düsseldorf, and Essen, as well as numerous medium-sized and smaller cities). This polycentric conurbation covers an area of 7,268 square kilometers (2,806 sq. mi) and lies entirely within the German federal state of North Rhine-Westphalia. The region has long been a major economic and industrial region in Germany and Europe generally. The region, especially along the Ruhr River Valley, has long been recognized as one of the most important sites of industrialization. Large-scale industrial activity including early steel production began in the Ruhr Valley during the early nineteenth century. Later in the nineteenth century, industrial chemical production also expanded in the region. As a key industrial center for the Nazi German regime, the region was intensely bombed by Allied Forces during World War II. As a result, much of the industrial capacity had to be rebuilt following the war.

6.2.3.1 Stress

The Rhine-Ruhr Region became heavily industrialized by the early decades of the twentieth century. In a 1911 issue of the journal Gesundheit, it was described how a traveler "notices with some anxiety how much the appearance of the entire area, the vegetation, the houses, and the people is altered by chimney soot, and how oppressively the latter settles on the lung" (quoted in Uekoetter 2009, p. 188). While smoke and soot abatement programs were initiated during this time, unlike in the US, no strong ambition for comprehensive action was ever formulated. The momentum from civil society, industrialists, and the bureaucratic state never fully galvanized to promote aggressive action. This was coupled with the fact that Germany experienced a series of shocks throughout the first half of the twentieth century including the rapid military buildup and eventual collapse in 1945 with the defeat of Nazi Germany. According to Uekoetter (2009), members of the bureaucratic state buried deep under the demands of Nazi Germany recognized the need for more effective pollution control action but were unable to act until the 1950s.

6.2.3.2 Crisis

At the war's end, the German industrial economy generally, and in the Rhine-Ruhr region, specifically, was largely destroyed, and the immediate job rebuilding took place. The rapid reindustrialization brought a dramatic increase in the level of air pollution in the region. By the mid-1950s, increasing popular concern over air pollution became recognized. In 1954, the director of the Ruhr Area Federation for Regional Planning advised "that the wishers of the population are pushing more strongly than before toward the elimination of nuisances" (quote in Uekoetter 2009). Complaints about air pollution in the Ruhr region increased dramatically during the 1950s, although for the most part they were not connected to health concerns but to smell, dirt/soot issues, and ecological damage. While the public interest in pollution control was increasingly vocal, it was generally diffuse and did not promote immediate and clear guidelines for action. In addition to increased public attention, a coalition of authorities, industrialist, and researchers began to coalesce around the question of how to more forcefully address air pollution (Uekometter 2009). While these discussions continued, extreme air pollution continued to occur and reached a climax with a severe smog event occurring from December 3 to December 7, 1962. Daily sulfur dioxide means peaked at 5,000 micrograms/m^3 and total suspended particulates daily means reached 2,400 micrograms/m^3 – values comparable to recent extreme smog events in East and South Asian cities (Bruckmann et al. 2014).

6.2.3.3 Transition

As the 1950s continued, the public demand for more effective pollution control further increased. As industrial recovery and then expansion were achieved, the call for air pollution control grew louder. By 1960, the Ruhr region became the uncontested leader in federal German air pollution control. Willy Brandt, while campaigning to be German chancellor, introduced the notion of air pollution control as a political imperative in his "*The sky over the Ruhr region must be blue again.*" speech on April 28, 1961, his words were met with widespread disbelief or even sarcasm, given the amount of air pollution at that time. For example, observed dust deposition in the Ruhr Valley was up to 2 mg/(m^2day) (Der Spiegel No. 33, August 9, pp. 22–33, referenced in Bruckmann et al. 2014).

A range of factors contributed to this transition, many related to a series of conditions that were exogenous to the region. Together, the factors were similar to conditions found in other cases. Specifically, transitions occurred during a confluence of weakening opposition as well as the strengthening of the forces advocating for change. The factors included the creation of the North Rhine-Westphalia federal German state[3] that became more attuned to local interests and concerns, and the rise of an effective and more responsive state and federal bureaucracy that was better able to promote opportunities for reform. At the same time, leading industrialists and their companies lost significant amounts of political power following the war because of their connection with the Nazi government. Another significant factor promoting transition was the positive example of air pollution control emerging from Pittsburgh in the United States. While the methods and approach utilized in Pittsburgh would not work in Ruhr for the residents of the region, the US city was held up as a symbol of what could be done to improve urban air quality (Uekoetter 2009).

6.2.3.4 Transformation

From 1960 to 1980, the total suspended particulate emissions decreased by roughly 60% (Bruckmann et al. 2014) and by the mid-1990s, many of the key air pollutants in the region experienced a more than 75% reduction (Gladtke 1998). The air pollution control transformation that took place during this time was the result of a series of factors. Pollution control had become an important political issue and in response a sophisticated policy response had been built both locally and within the federal German government. Extreme events often helped push such measures forward. The policies put in place called for a gradual lowering of emissions levels over the decades. For example, the December 1962 severe smog episode triggered in December 1964 the first smog ordinance by the North Rhine-Westphalia state. The alert criteria were consistently lowered over the course of several revisions. Deeply connected to this process was a consistent advancement of the air pollution control technology and manufacturing design changes including more effective emission scrubbers, desulfurization units, and high smoke stacks to better disperse the pollutants (Bruckmann et al. 2014).

[3] Following World War II, the geography of several German states was redrawn and the North Rhine-Westphalia state emerged with the dissolution of the Prussian state.

6.2.4 Tokyo, Japan

Beginning as the small fishing village of Edo in 1603, Tokyo grew to a great imperial city and then a modern megacity by the late twentieth century. Its population grew steadily from the late nineteenth century (1900 population was 1.58 million) through to 1970 (11.4 million); however, it has grown much more slowly since. The city currently has a population of approximately 14 million, while the greater metropolitan region is the largest urban conglomeration in the world with a population of roughly 38 million. Tokyo functions as the administrative and economic capital of Japan and is organized as the Tokyo Metropolis, which includes a set of wards, cities, towns, and villages and is administered by the Tokyo Metropolitan Government.

6.2.4.1 Stress

Urban growth and expansion brought environmental concerns generally and air pollution concerns specifically to the city. As early as 1877, the Tokyo police began to regulate boilers for smoke emissions. After sustained local lobbying, the local government in 1912 enacted a law (i.e., the Factory Law) that enabled government personnel to inspect factories for a variety of issues, including noxious emissions, as part of its mandate to protect the public. By 1927 the City of Tokyo began to measure air particulate matter concentration as a mechanism of air quality monitoring. At the same time, air pollution in Japanese cities had become a chronic issue. This accelerated with the increased use of coal as a fuel and the rapid industrialization as part of the buildup to World War II (Fujikura et al. 2005). Dustfall in Tokyo's downtown areas was recorded as 18 tons per square kilometer per month in 1927, illustrating how the household use of coal for heating had emerged as a significant pollution source (Hishida 1974 in Fujikura et al. 2005). Local residents regularly petitioned the local governments to take measures to improve the situation, but air quality continued to decline. It should be noted at this time that other communities welcomed the black smoke of pollution because it represented signs of successful modernization (Fujikura et al. 2005).

6.2.4.2 Crisis

A significant proportion of the industrial base of the country was either destroyed or went out of production by World War Two's end and as a result concern about pollution subsided. But very soon after, the US-driven policy to rapidly rebuild Japan as a bulwark against instability and increasing communist strength in China, and the outbreak of the Korean War spurred rapid reconstruction. By the mid-1950s, the Japanese public was again increasingly concerned about urban air pollution. At the same time in 1949, the city of Tokyo issued an ordinance in response to growing public complaints about industrial air pollution. The ordinance, however, did not explicitly define the specific criteria for pollution control, and proved ineffective (Fujikura et al. 2005).

As part of its efforts to further increase national development, the Japanese government in 1960 proposed a massive additional industrialization effort such that the next decade would bring a doubling of the national economy (Aozora Foundation 2007). While this goal was met, the result was a dramatic surge of pollution problems facing the country's cities. As the main source of industrial fuel switched from coal to oil with the advent of cheaper international sources of petroleum imports, the main air pollutants shifted to include sulfur oxides (SO_x), NOx, and particulates associated with the burning of that type of fuel. In the worst air-polluted sites, visibility at times was limited to 50 meters (164 ft). Such pollution resulted in a rise of serious respiratory ailments being reported in many cities (Fujikura et al. 2005).

Industrial air pollution continued to increase and the meaningful management of it was largely thwarted by three main issues. These were the public's lack of awareness of how air pollution was a danger, inadequate technology and scientific knowledge to effectively manage the crisis, and the government's lack of commitment to pollution control. The factors were significantly diminished during the 1950s and 1960s. The rapid onset of widespread post-World War II industrialization brought a series of widely reported cases of devastating pollution, perhaps none more infamous than the acute mercury poisoning episodes known as Minamata disease (Aozora Foundation 2007; Tsuda et al. 2009). The neurological disease resulting in an array of disabling symptoms was first widely observed in the southern Japan city of Minamata in 1955. The disease was found to be caused by mercury-laden wastewater from industrial facilities. The Minamata disease victims contributed to the increasingly widespread notion of pollution victims that began to slowly permeate Japanese society at this time (Aozora Foundation 2007; Tsuda et al. 2009). Pollution in Japan was more and more associated with disease – a significant scientific and medical development. By 1962, Japan's national government established the Soot and Smoke Regulation Law. It was Japan's first pollution control law and imposed controls on emissions of SO_2, soot, and smoke. This new capacity to put forward emission controls on sulfur dioxide marked a significant policy shift.

6.2.4.3 Transition

By the end of the 1960s, the societal demand for an even more robust institutional bureaucracy to manage pollution was evident. Six years after the 1962

Soot and Smoke Regulation Law, Japan moved the pollution control agenda aggressively forward again with the passage of the 1968 Air Pollution Control Act. The 1968 Act represented a significant advance over the previous legislation, which it legally replaced. Most significantly, the new legislation was applied to areas not even yet polluted. It set stricter standards for emissions in areas that had not been previously polluted. Thus, the act enabled protection of locations not currently polluted and for the control of different types of industrial development. The 1968 act also replaced an ineffective earlier approach to SO_2 emission controls with an innovative index pollution value system that included the volume, speed, and temperature of the emission (Fujikura et al. 2005).

Air pollution in Japan, at this time, had become very much embedded in the national consciousness as a growing and substantial threat. The concern about pollution was even presented within the popular culture of the day. In the 1971 Japanese movie, *Godzilla vs. Hedorah* (aka. Smog Monster), Godzilla battles a bizarre and monstrous alien life form that arrives on earth via a comet. The monster, Hedorah, grows stronger and larger as it feeds off air and water pollution of Japanese cities. Hedorah, which is a Japanese word for sludge, slime, vomit, or chemical ooze, was a being that embodied Japan's broad concern for widespread smog and urban pollution and the challenges they represented. The movie is particularly interesting because Godzilla itself, a giant monster that destroyed Tokyo and other Japanese cities in previous films, now appears as a savior fighting against the evil of pollution.

The citizenry of Japan, in general, and Tokyo, specifically, were shocked by the pollution exposures that they faced. At the same time, the Japanese legal structure increasingly allowed for entities (e.g., individuals, communities) to sue for pollution exposure. In July 1970, Tokyo experienced intense episodes of photochemical (summertime) smog that reportedly caused partial suffocation and hospitalization of a number of school children (Hashimoto 1989). One year later in July 1971, the Japanese national government created the Environment Agency within the Prime Minister's office. The new agency was able to create and coordinate an expanding national pollution control policy and advance emissions reduction strategies. Soon thereafter and based on a major 1972 lawsuit victory for pollution victim rights, the Japanese government enacted the Pollution-Related Health Damage Compensation Law in 1973, which not only created a more robust institutional bureaucracy and capacity of citizens to sue, but also stated that those people certified as suffering from pollution-induced illness would not only receive medical cost assistance but also compensation for livelihood losses. A key critique of the law was that it did not directly focus on the responsibility of the corporations that caused the pollution and instead only focused on mitigating the impacts (Fujikura et al. 2005).

6.2.4.4 Transformation

This transition set the seeds for the development of an ever-broader national approach to air pollution that once developed could be transferred back to the local and even individual levels (Hashimoto 1989). As a result, several advances occurred over the next two decades including the increased number of citizens suing because of pollution exposure, increased monitoring and sensing infrastructure to trace and document pollution releases and exposure, and the increased diversification of the focus to other sources of pollution, especially automobiles. The Tokyo government was particularly aggressive against the automobile manufacturers' need to lessen air pollution from vehicular traffic (Bianchi et al. 2005). Japan's pollution reduction during this period was substantial and has been described as a "pollution miracle." For example, from 1970 to 1989, Japan's sulfur oxide emissions decreased by 82.4% from 1970 to 1989 (Fujikura et al. 2005). Highly significant was the engagement of the central government with new national policies in response to municipal early, yet largely limited, attempts to respond to local citizens' complaints about pollution.

6.3 Discussion

The four case studies reveal significant similarities regarding how the air pollution conditions emerged and the extent to which they were eventually acted upon. While air pollution is a longstanding problem in cities, the twentieth century brought a whole new scale to the problem and a much more significant threat. This new threat required the generation of vast amounts of cutting-edge science and knowledge as well as new types of government entities and legislations to tackle the growing risks and hazards.

6.3.1 Conditions of Crisis

The case studies illustrate a pattern similar to other urban hazards. Initially the significant air pollution events were seen as episodic, acute, and isolated and often in remote areas of the metropolitan region, those less politically or economically powerful, and/or disadvantaged and marginalized (i.e., communities of color, recent immigrants). Over time, the events morphed to being more frequent, widespread, and pervasive. It also became increasingly recognized that the pollution intensity and frequency occurred in part from the natural landscape in which the cities are located. This was especially the case with respect to cities (like Los Angeles) that are surrounded by mountainous terrain and associated smog-inducing thermal inversions. In all cases, the pattern and concentration of urban development influenced the local urban microclimates often making the pollution situation significantly worse. As the pollution levels escalated, the early policy actions in the case studies were targeted first to specific kinds of pollution or facilities or even to a specific facility that was considered to be to blame. Significant contestation over the extent and significance of the threat was evident. Arguments to take the threats as serious were supported by the growing empirical evidence that air pollution was an acute health risk and new science focused on how primary and secondary air pollutants could cause chronic exposure problems. Large-scale and sustained opposition, especially within the business community, regarding the impact of the pollution, the need for pollution control, and the potential negative economic impacts of the controls pushed back against the need for a substantive policy transition. They were often successful until a coalition of other interests including public health officials was able to force the crisis to a tipping point.

6.3.2 Drivers of Transitions

Urban air quality policy transitions are reflective of a rich variety of key drivers. While each case's history is full of significant extreme pollution events, their occurrence was directly connected back to the physical environment including specific meteorological and climatological conditions that were present for each city. Urban industrial development was obvious driver as well, even though the pattern and pace of this development varied widely with the Ruhr Valley being one of the cradles of industrialization in the early nineteenth century to the Los Angeles region rapidly industrializing with the demands of the World War II production and totally bypassing the highly polluting coal-burning phase of industrial development seen in the eastern US and Europe.

6.3.3 Spheres of Action and Legacies

The air pollution crises presented in these case examples illustrate the confluence of social, ecological/environmental, and infrastructure/technological systems. While the physical environment in these cases did play a significant role in the growing stress and crises, it was the interplay of the social and technological systems that really defined the conditions under which the

Table 6.1 *Key drivers observed in each case study. Source: Author.*

	DRIVERS		
Case Study	Root	Context	Proximate
London	Physical environment conducive to thermal inversions; industrialization; ineffective government efforts to control pollution; cultural identity of London Fog; "Peasouper"	Post-World War II economic hardship and use of high sulfur coal; dramatic national legislation response to 1952 pollution event	Dramatic thermal inversion in December 1952
Los Angeles	Physical environment conducive to thermal inversions; noncoal industrial economy	Dramatic increase in automobile traffic; growth in scientific understanding in photochemical smog and impacts; World War II dramatic increase in manufacturing	Dramatic pollution episodes; linkage of business (real estate development) and health interests; increased governance capacity to address air pollution issues quickly
Rhine-Ruhr Region	Industrialization	Rapid redevelopment post-World War II; increased frequent smog events; weakening opposition and strengthening interest for pollution action; loss of political power of industrialists following the war given their Nazi links; positive example of pollution control in Pittsburgh; increased effective technology; pollution control is an important political issue of the postwar era	Extreme pollution events
Tokyo	Industrialization and build up for war effort	Rapid redevelopment post-World War II; US policy to rebuild Japan; continued massive industrialization in the 1960s; connection of pollution with disease; growth of national government engagement; growth of capacity of individuals to sue for loss and damage	Pollution episodes with significant health outcomes; Minamata disease

crises emerged and the transitions occurred. Of particular importance was the increased societal questioning within rapidly industrializing societies of how to balance the economic rewards and the health impacts associated with urban environmental pollution. In these developed/rapidly developing cities, acute pollution events and new science were drawing a stronger and more profound connection between urban environmental contamination and public health crises. This development eventually became part of a global environmental movement in which urban residents and public health officials allied with some business interests and increasingly pressed for an urban environmental policy change to eliminate or reduce air pollution. This movement broke the long-standing assumption that any economic growth, irrespective of the volume of the pollution, was beneficial and should not be questioned.

In many ways, initial resistance to aggressively responding to urban air pollution threats of the mid-twentieth century was aided by the long-term legacy of urban areas being associated with air pollution. It was understood that polluted air in cities was an expected component of city life and experience and thus dampened the concern about the growing stress and low-level crisis. When the pollution became spatially and temporally pervasive and when the scientific connection between exposure and health outcomes was proven, the perception of the crisis changed dramatically and the social demand for change increased accordingly. Another legacy factor, though not initially expected, was the sizable indirect impact of World War II in all cases. The actual warfare and devastation were not the drivers of the crises; it was the economic losses and disruption and attempt to recover in the 1950s that were the drivers and could be seen as unintended consequences of attempting to respond to the impact of one crisis – World War II – and pushing forward another.

6.3.3.1 Urban Air Quality and Climate Change

Climate change will significantly exacerbate urban air quality problems through a variety of mechanisms, making acute and chronic air pollution episodes more frequent and often worse when they do occur. Specific pathways include exacerbating the production of secondary air pollutants, increasing the intensity of thermal inversions, increasing the frequency of wildfire smoke, and compounding the effects of extreme heat episodes with localized air quality issues (fumes from traffic). Air quality issues are especially significant in megacities or over large extended metropolitan areas where mixing with non-polluted air sources is more difficult (Dodman et al. 2022). Projections indicate that the intensity of acute episodes will increase and the frequency of chronic air pollution issues will be extended over longer periods of time.

Several specific recommendations can be derived from the case studies that would be helpful for urban practitioners, policymakers, and other stakeholders focused on urban air quality in the context of climate change.

- Significance of public health issues – acute and chronic air pollution exposure with advanced scientific and local knowledge have become highly significant environmental quality and public health concerns. Extensive evidence indicates that poor urban air quality causes widespread loss and damage to human well-being and urban infrastructure and assets. These impacts are well documented and widely perceived by urban populations.
- New governance institutions needed – addressing and mitigating urban air quality problems is complex and often requires advanced knowledge of the extent of the problem and new or revised governance structures to manage the issues. Regional cooperative agreements or institutions could be required to best tackle complex, transboundary air pollution issues.
- Air pollution and spread of concern – air pollution issues in cities begin as isolated episodes or sites within the city but can rapidly express themselves at a wider urban region scale. This spread can occur quickly and dramatically increase the number of city interests focused on the issue and demanding a policy response.
- Legacy of extreme air pollution episodes. Extreme air pollution episodes can be very significant benchmarks for action and catalyzing agents. Often when coupled with smaller precursor events, they can be seen as part of an emerging pattern that can galvanize the need for large-scale action.
- Air pollution and urban development – the connection between air pollution and urban development is complex. In the early twentieth century, air pollution was often seen as evidence of progress and development. More recently, it has been almost the opposite and the presence of extensive air pollution is seen as an indication of a city's inability to manage its environmental problems. The worsening and exacerbation of currently minimal air pollution issues in a city to moderate or even higher levels might cause renewed challenges for a city government. If these situations become a crisis, it will heighten or rekindle longstanding city-level debates and contestations over the sources of the pollution and potentially pit industrial versus residential versus transportation interests against each other.

7

Public Health

Disease and Epidemics

"*Without exaggeration, I may assert that, so far as trade and commerce are concerned the plague has assumed the importance of an unexampled calamity.*" Sir William Robinson, British Governor of Hong Kong describing the 1894 Bubonic plague outbreak in the city.

The spread of acute diseases, epidemics, and pandemics has been a significant component of urban history. Epidemics are defined as the widespread occurrence or presence of an infectious disease in a community at a particular time. Epidemics that spread over several countries or continents and affect many people can be defined as pandemics. They both have caused public health stresses and crises and significant debate and rethinking of city form and function. The COVID-19 pandemic has been only the most recent example of this since its initial outbreak in the early months of 2020. The virus spread rapidly around the world first impacting especially hard global urban transportation hubs and then urban areas generally. During the early days of the pandemic, the structure and social organization of cities were often described by experts as influencing both speeding up or slowing down the spread of the disease and capacity to effectively respond to it. In general, it is now clear that populations in heavily urbanized areas were no more at risk to COVID than those in rural areas and in many cases had greater capacity to respond than rural communities (Han et al. 2023; Wu, Wei, and Liu 2023).

7.1 Basic of Urban Disease and Epidemics

The earliest written account of a disease spread in a city comes from parts of Thucydides' *History of the Peloponnesian War*, during which the Spartan army invaded and devastated Athens in the year 430 BC. While the invasion led to significant losses for Athens, a simultaneous plague pandemic caused greater loss of human life. In the summer of 430 BC, plague killed nearly a third of the Athenian population and severely disrupted the social structure and governance capacity of Athens, leading to its eventual decline as a major power. In his account, Thucydides writes, [2.47.3] "Not many days after their [the Spartans] arrival in Attica the plague first began to show itself among the Athenians. It was said that it had broken out in many places previously in the neighborhood of Lemnos and elsewhere [including through Piraeus, the city's port and sole source of food and supplies]; but a pestilence of such extent and mortality was nowhere remembered."

The disease spread especially quickly because of a defense strategy pursued that included a policy of retreat within the Athens city walls. This policy resulted in the massive in-migration of the rural inhabitants into the already densely settled city, generating immediate heightened densities and resource shortages. Athens in turn became a breeding ground for disease as a result of the close quarters and poor hygiene. Debate still persists as to what pathogen caused the disease outbreak, and like many ancient events, lack of scientific knowledge hampers analysis of such moments.

As long as there has been illness and disease, there have been explanations regarding how and why people became ill and how the illness was spread. The historiography of disease is rich and varied. Disease trajectories, infections, and responses in human history have been associated with biological, cultural, historical, and socio-structural (e.g., class divisions) factors. Premodern or nonwestern societies used a wide diversity of disease explanations and methods to combat outbreaks. The science of disease has advanced significantly with the development and expansion of germ theory, transforming the understanding of diseases.

Germ theory states that affected individuals are exposed to a common pathogen agent. Illness emerges when germs (i.e., pathogens) invade a host and their growth and reproduction manifest as disease. Diseases caused by pathogens are defined as infectious diseases. A wide range of pathogens exist, including bacterium, protists (i.e., fungi), viruses, prions, and viroids. Several key pathways for transmission exist, including via airborne, water, animal hosts, surfaces, and person to person. Germ theory first proposed in the sixteenth century to describe the process of illness was not fully accepted in scientific and medical communities until the second half of the nineteenth century.

A wide range of other medical theories of disease predated the now widely accepted germ theory. The essence of these theories was that the disease took hold through the airborne transmissions emerging from contamination, rot, and decay. Before the advent of germ theory, miasma theory was dominant in western medicine. Miasma was associated with poisonous vapors or mists that presented as airborne particles that emerged from poor hygiene, foul air, and contaminated water. In general, under this approach, disease transmission was largely seen as limited to individual exposure to the environmental sources and not person-to-person transmission. Keeping clean, removing trash and other waste, and avoiding fouled water were significant modes for preventing disease.

The interconnection between disease outbreaks and prevention and urban form is complex. This interaction has had significant impacts on the construction and layout of cities and the everyday life of residents. The narrative that links population density and the increased likelihood of disease transmission is deeply embedded in the history of cities. When disease or illness strikes a locale, the tendency has been to move away or relocate to diminish exposure. In early New York, the wealthy of the city would regularly leave during the summer to avoid the heat and disease outbreaks that often struck the city during those months. With the occasional major disease outbreak, an even larger segment of the population would evacuate the city. In the early decades of the nineteenth century during especially harsh epidemics, nearly half of the city's population left the city for outlying rural areas (Thomas 2005). Mimicking past events, during the height of the initial COVID-19 wave in spring and summer 2020, hundreds of thousands of Manhattan residents, mostly wealthy, left their homes for exurban locations or more distant sites. A vast majority of commuters also stopped coming into Manhattan. By 2021, many residents relocated and the US Census Bureau estimated that between July 1, 2020, and July 1, 2021, Manhattan (New York County) saw a population decline of 6.9% (US Census Bureau).

Epidemic and pandemic outbreaks are associated with acute trauma in cities. The prospect of disease also has significant long-lasting impacts on cities and their form. For example, wealthy citizens of cities have long sought to separate themselves from the poor and underclasses in part to avoid exposure to disease and other risks. Early twentieth-century work by geographers and urban planners consistently highlighted the presence of high-income residential neighborhoods as a fixed element of contemporary urban form. The logic of suburban development in the same way was also a mechanism to distance wealthier or more advantaged residents from the congestion, pollution, crime, and risks associated with high-density urban life. White flight with its massive relocation of white urban residents to the suburbanizing edges of cities in the United States, while including a significant racist element, was largely framed around allowing these residents to avoid the ills of urban life (Frey 1979; Trounstine 2018).

The control of urban space to avoid illness also focused on removing "natural" sources of disease. The draining of swamps and removal of wetlands is the most storied example of this phenomenon. The connection between swamps and malaria goes back thousands of years. In ancient Rome, city planners and managers actively drained swamps to eliminate malaria (Sallares 2002). In Middle Age Europe, local rulers believed marshes to be source sites of plagues and incurable fevers, and that the marshes should be avoided or destroyed. Cities in nineteenth-century Europe and North America aggressively drained local wetlands and swamps, and increasingly so as scientific evidence in the late nineteenth century conclusively proved that mosquitoes, which breed in marshes, were the disease vector of malaria.

Another method to reduce the threat of disease comes in separating humans from animals. In many societies, animals have been seen as a source of disease. Across many US cities in the nineteenth century, municipal ordinances were put into place to remove farm animals from city limits. These actions connected the emerging planning profession with the growing understanding of the public health requirements for a hygienic and sanitary city. These efforts focused on disconnecting animal agriculture and husbandry from the urban food supply, waste management, and public space (Brinkley and Vitiello 2014). Charles Dickens visiting New York in 1842 was aghast by the number and size of pigs wandering the streets of the city (Muzzio 2018). As the connection between animals, especially mice and rats, and disease became better understood, the ambition to remove farm animals and eliminate rats, mice, and other vermin accelerated.

While disease outbreaks by definition cause significant social and personal hardship and loss, the short-term and long-term economic impacts of disease have also been extremely significant. Epidemics and pandemics force the everyday rhythm of life to be interrupted. The typical modes of economic exchange are significantly altered and often can be literally shut down. As an example, during the periods of three well-documented plague pandemic outbreaks (centered around the years 541, 1347, and 1894), the businesses of cities were shut down, trade declined or stopped, workers died or fled, and the decision-making processes were disrupted. The significance of these events led to the collapse of economic activity, which often lasted for years. The recent COVID-19 pandemic is another illustration of these conditions.

Disease outbreaks can have even more profound and longer-lasting impacts as in the example of Athens, Greece, described earlier. The story of the 1793 yellow fever outbreak in Philadelphia – the US capital at the time – is particularly sobering. The outbreak started in early August and disappeared by November, but during that time approximately 5,000 people died (out of a population of about 50,000). Half of the population fled the city, most businesses were shut, and federal officials left the city virtually shutting down the US government. Though the city was able to recover quickly with the autumn frosts killing the mosquitoes, which were the disease vector, yellow fever outbreaks occurred again in 1794, 1796, 1797, and 1798. Each episode brought further economic trauma to the city and contributed to it giving up its status as the nation's financial capital to New York, a position it never regained. In general, the small, dense cities of the new country seemed to be incapable of stopping these recurring outbreaks. Politicians, reformers, and intellectuals, including ardent agrarian Thomas Jefferson, professed the benefits of healthier rural areas outside of cities and pushed to direct growth in these places and the new western lands of the country instead of arguing for the further development of seemingly fouled and contaminated cities (Langton 2022). Urban reformers wrote of the immediate need to create more open green space in cities to make them more livable and less prone to disease – an argument that was recalled with the recent actions during the COVID-19 outbreak. The COVID-19 response in cities included demands for increased indoor ventilation, promotion of outside dining and activities, and the creation of pedestrian-friendly streetscapes and the closing of selected streets to cars.

The inequity of epidemics and pandemics in cities can be quite stark. As with other urban stresses and crises, the poor and marginalized of the cities are often most vulnerable and impacted by widespread disease outbreaks. These populations typically live in areas with substandard, vermin-infested housing, less consistent access to potable water, less access to effective health care, and fewer financial resources to leave an infected area or stay out of situations where they might be infected. Again, the COVID-19 pandemic provides a good illustration. Ribeiro and others (2021) through an extensive epidemiological study of COVID mortality in Sao Paulo, Brazil, found that across a range of socio-economic variables, lower income, less education, more household crowding, and Black populations were all positively associated with higher rates of mortality. The analysis further concluded that not only did the impacts of COVID reveal inequity, but the pandemic effects also worsened inequities since the widespread illness and social and economic distributions were more likely to lead to greater relative loss of income and loss of socio-economic status among these populations that were more disadvantaged at the outset. Marginal populations and neighborhoods are further biased against by the fact that the disease outbreaks typically affect them more than other communities, and the health crisis occurrence can reinforce pre-existing prejudices and antipathies.

7.2 Case Studies

Disease and pandemic have impacted every city. The case studies presented illustrate a variety of contexts. The examples span across several centuries and three continents and include two plague outbreaks, one of influenza, and one of COVID-19. The case studies include Hong Kong, China, Marseille, France, St. Louis, US, and Seoul, South Korea. Although very different, each case illustrates the rapid onset of a disease outbreak and how fundamentally disruptive the surrounding events can be and how quickly a crisis and demand for policy transitions emerge. The transformative legacy of each event are profound.

7.2.1 Hong Kong, China

The history of Hong Kong as a city and relatively small territory is complex. The land area of the Hong Kong territory is roughly 1,100 km^2 (428 sq. mil) or about two-third the size of Greater Metropolitan London. A significant part of this more recent history has been defined by tension and conflicts between mainland China and foreign interests, especially the British. Hong Kong and its harbor were seen as a key gateway between China and the world. The harbor and associated in- and outflow of goods and people however also served as a key mechanism for disease transfer. Hong Kong was held as a British colony from 1842 to 1997 and during that time it grew dramatically both in population and importance. At the time of takeover by the British in 1842, the population was 7,450; in 1901, it had grown to 368,981, and after growing rapidly in the mid-twentieth century, its population in 2021 was estimated to be 7.4 million. In 1897, Hong Kong was one of the world's top five ports by tonnage with 15.94 million tons of cargo and 1,652,016 passengers and 77,293 port calls (*Report Harbour Master* 1897, 370–71 in S. Davies 2015). With its return to the People's Republic of China, its development trajectory was increasingly connected to the dramatic regional growth in the Pearl River Delta and the metropolitan regions of the expansive cities of Shenzhen and Guangdong.

The history of Hong Kong has been connected to a variety of acute stresses and crises. During its modern history, Hong Kong has been characterized by extremely high population densities, significant in- and outflows of people and goods, proximity to source areas of viral outbreaks, and intense social divisions and inequities. All these factors are associated with favorable conditions for reported disease outbreaks. Outbreaks of historical significance include the 1894 Bubonic Plague (part of the third plague pandemic that lasted from 1855 to 1945), the 1968 Hong Kong Flu, and the SARS (Severe Acute Respiratory Syndrome) outbreak in 2003. Here the focus is on the 1894 Bubonic Plague outbreak.

7.2.1.1 Stress

The Plague while continuously a global risk has caused three pandemics of devastating historical significance. These include the Justinian Plague of 541, which originated in central Africa and spread to the North African and Mediterranean Region, the infamous Black Death, which started in Asia in 1347 and spread to Crimea, Europe, and Russia and killed approximately 30–50% of Europe's population at the time, and the third pandemic, which originated in the Yunnan region of China. By January 1894 plague had been observed in Canton (now Guangdong) about 130 kilometers from the British territory of Hong Kong. The disease appeared soon after in the city, with it being declared an infected port on May 10 of that year and by July the disease had already claimed 2,442 lives (Pryor 1975).

Hong Kong had grown significantly in the latter decades of the nineteenth century and had become a major *entrepot*, linking western influences with mainland China. Tens of thousands of ethnic Chinese came to the colony as economic development created new employment opportunities. A formal census in 1865 illustrated a vast difference between the Chinese and non-Chinese residents. The population at the time was approximately 125,000 of which only about 2,000 were westerners. Just before the plague outbreak, the population in 1891 had reached 221,000 and was growing quite rapidly. Significant divisions were present between the ethnic Chinese population and the foreigners. Housing segregation and the extremely limited political role of the vastly dominant ethnic Chinese population carried out through British colonial policies created tensions. The vast majority of the Chinese population was squeezed into the Tai Ping Shan area, which was approximately 1.25 sq. km. While foreigners lived in comparative splendor in spacious communities a few kilometers away.

The outbreak both revealed these tensions and contributed to a more intense epidemic (Pryor 1975). The Chinese had great mistrust of the British and western medical practices and rumors were circulating of abuse by British doctors of Chinese women and children patients and mistreatment of dead bodies. These issues also fostered a lack of compliance by Chinese residents to report illness and to bring sick individuals to medical facilities. The Chinese community in Hong Kong became panic-stricken as the outbreak worsened. Chinese workers evacuated the colony in huge numbers leading to further and more significant trade and economic disruption. It is estimated that approximately 100,000 Chinese laborers and merchants, about half of the labor force, fled from the colony in an attempt to avoid the plague (Echenberg 2002). Large swaths of housing either left empty or evacuated in the Tai Ping Shan district were razed in an attempt to stamp out the plague (Lee 2013).

7.2.1.2 Crisis

While the outbreak of 1894 could be defined as a crisis, the problem continued and deepened in the years following a retreat of the plague in 1895. By 1896, the plague returned and killed another 1,078 residents, almost all those crammed into the ethnic Chinese residential districts. The plague was present annually between 1895 and 1929. During that time, it killed over 20,000 residents and had a fatality rate of more than 93%. The period from 1894 to 1901 was particularly intense because of the high numbers of illnesses and disparate explanations for the disease and lack of adequate medical capacity to deal with those who were ill. For much of this period, limited medical information was available on how the disease occurred and was transmitted. The British and western medical explanations differed widely from the perspectives of Chinese medical experts and community members. The western medical consensus was that human transmission was a key mechanism or that it was associated with rat droppings. The medical and popular debate raged for a decade. While others continued to cling to the miasmatic theory (i.e., airborne vapors), which attributed the disease to noxious poisonous gases emanating from infected soil or from the bodies of plague victims (Echenberg 2002). The outbreak led to a series of conjectures regarding how the plague spread – much of it associated with the Chinese and things Chinese – that is, their lifestyle and property (Peckham 2013). For example, one theory was that disease had spread from Canton to Hong Kong via bales of opium being shipped to the colony.

The crisis was fed by the fact that public health officials trying to cope with outbreaks were often no better prepared than those in premodern, pregerm theory times. The officials used plague control practices such as burning of homes and personal property of victims taken from old European practices. While the demographic impact of the plague was not as significant as in other British colonies, the psychological impact of the outbreak was highly significant since it brought into question the position of *entrepots* in the empire, and as described by Peckham (2013) – "possibility that the networks, which sustained the empire were also the very source of its weakness." The outbreak, while a medical crisis, exposed significant social divisions and severely disrupted trade and commerce, resulting in a more complex crisis.

7.2.1.3 Transition

The plague outbreak and its repercussions were a major turning point in the history of colonial Hong Kong. While the initial response to the disease in many ways exacerbated existing problems, the following years (in the late 1890s and early 1900s) brought a significant transition in the daily life of the city, and its long-term prospects for economic development and the betterment of its residents' lives. A critical element of the transition was the development, application, and widespread acceptance of new medical science regarding the origin and spread of plague. While a significant amount of anecdotal evidence existed that its spread was somehow related to rats, the medical and popular debate raged until 1905 when the source of the infection – fleas on rats – was confirmed by researchers in India (another hard-hit British colonial plague region) and translated to China.

During this latter part of the 1890s, significant dialogue took place between Chinese community representatives and British officials regarding disease theory, the cause of the plague, and more broadly the merits of western as opposed to Chinese-style medicine. A significant breakthrough occurred when a Chinese, western-trained physician was put in charge of a local hospital used by Chinese residents. The appointment of the new head signified a compromise between the colonial government and the Chinese elites, thereby removing a significant amount of suspicion between British colonial power and the general Chinese population (Lee 2013). The outbreak also forced a stark reevaluation of Chinese residents' living conditions. Germ theory helped define connections between Chinese housing, trade, and the spread of the disease and how a reorganization of urban space could eliminate or significantly decrease the spread of the disease. For example, the first floors of many buildings, where Chinese lived in upper floors, were used as storehouses for cargo, and it was recognized that this cargo was often infested with rats (Peckham 2013). Eliminating this co-mingling of building uses would reduce opportunities for disease exposure. It was also acknowledged as important that sections of Chinese residential districts initially razed to eradicate disease should be rebuilt with better drainage and more ventilation to reduce the spread of future disease outbreaks.

7.2.1.4 Transformation

The late nineteenth-century plague in Hong Kong is well recognized as a major turning point in its colonial history. The trauma of the outbreak forced the British colonial government to dramatically reconsider the policies that dealt with the Chinese community and to increase the focus on the Chinese residents' well-being and forge a partnership with the community that enabled a reorganization of the social and economic order of the city. One of the numerous aftereffects of the Hong Kong Plague was the questioning of the merits of rapid economic globalization that emerged with colonialization (Peckham 2013). In addition, a series of reforms took place including new cargo protections to reduce the risk of disease introduction. New controls on immigration and residential overcrowding were also imposed. The district that was most heavily impacted by the disease outbreak and subject to razing by the colonial authorities – Taipingshan area – was rebuilt with the addition of new medical facilities that became the nucleus of one of the colony's hospital centers.

7.2.2 Marseille, France

The Mediterranean port city of Marseille in southern France is one of the oldest cities in western Europe. It was founded by Greek traders about 2,600 years ago. The current population of Marseille and its extended metropolitan region, which includes portions of the Provence region, is almost 2 million making it the third largest population center in France. The economy of the region has traditionally been focused on agriculture and trading. The Mediterranean region, long a site of civilization, has experienced an extensive record of disease outbreaks. Given that, Marseille's history reflects extensive experience with the diagnosis, prevention, and action against epidemics. Marseille pioneered the development and implementation of quarantine practices, a city-wide sanitary board, and hospital facilities specializing in contagious diseases (Barbieri and Drancourt 2018). Twenty-two significant plague outbreaks have occurred in Marseille in recorded history, the most recorded for any Mediterranean city, with the earliest documented in 49 BC. The outbreak in 1720 was especially impactful, and was the last major outbreak of plague in western Europe (Ermus 2021). The outbreak killed half of the city's population (about 85–95 thousand at the time) and upward of 125 thousand in the city and surrounding Provence region and caused massive social and economic disruption.

7.2.2.1 Stress

Following a plague in Marseille during 1580, the city's leaders worked to develop new measures to limit the spread of future outbreaks (Barbieri and Drancourt 2018). The city council created a sanitation board composed of local doctors. The board facilitated the construction of the first public hospital and accreditation procedures for medical staff. The board also helped organize a robust quarantine system that included several tiers of cargo and crew review and isolation in lazarettos/lazarets (stations for maritime travelers). By the time the 1720 plague struck, Marseille had then a long-established and sophisticated quarantine protocol and a range of well-tested sanitary cordons that had prevented any plague outbreaks for almost three-quarters of a century (since 1649). However, on May 25, 1720, a ship named the Grand Saint-Antoine returned back to Marseille with a variety of goods it had purchased across the Mediterranean. It was the practice that all ships would be subject to extended quarantine before the cargo and crew could be disembarked at the port. That was not to be the case with the Grand Saint-Antoine. A wealthy municipal official who owned part of the ship and its valuable cargo pressed to have the goods off-loaded to the city's warehouses so they could be quickly sold at a soon-to-occur annual fair (Ermus 2015, 2021).

7.2.2.2 Crisis

Soon thereafter, disease broke out in the city and within months the quickly spreading disease grew to become a crisis. Officials initially tried to hide the fact that the disease was in fact the plague. Hospitals rapidly were overwhelmed and it was widely recognized that plague was once more in the region. Mass graves were dug and then quickly filled, and residents panicked and started to leave the city. The local public health system collapsed and later in the summer, thousands of corpses lay scattered throughout the city. Squads of volunteers and prisoners were sent to the city to remove and dispose of bodies and also perished. The overall death rate in the city and outlying area ranged from 25 to 50%. Even though Marseilles had extensive local expertise in responding to pandemics – the 1720 outbreak devastated the city. Over the next two years, the plague would take 50,000 of Marseille's total population of 90,000. At its height, the plague killed up to 1,000 per day. The social and economic disruption was extensive.

7.2.2.3 Transition

As the initial phase of the outbreak started to ebb, it became clear that other forms of response were needed. In addition, it had become evident that the disease outbreak not only had significant local economic impact but also was having larger-scale, ripple effects throughout France's national economy, which had become increasingly integrated in the 1600s and early 1700s. The situation was seen to require a new large-scale integrated approach. In order to address the risk, a series of proposals were put forward and implemented that created for the first time in modern history a comprehensive central government disaster response to the emergency situation (Ermus 2015; Barbieri and Drancourt 2018).

Most significant was the transition that had to do with the role of the external state during a local/regional crisis – that is, the governance beyond Marseille and Provence. The plague outbreak was a disaster of enormous proportions. The governance capacity of the city and region collapsed and it became clear that outside governance capacity needed to engage to control the situation on the ground and limit the further spread of the disease. At this time, the central royal government of France became much more engaged in disaster management and illustrated an early example of the state-centralized crisis management that is widely evident today globally (Ermus 2015). This moment also marked a moment of increased concentration of central government state oversight that became increasingly emblematic of French state actions moving forward.

The new pandemic response came with a series of steps to minimize the spread of the illness, minimize the extent of the broader economic impacts, and help support the local governance and public health capacity of the heavily impacted sites. Officials within Marseille and outside the city were enlisted to help coordinate the response to the outbreak. For example, a General Commissioner was put in place to manage the plague response in one of the worst-hit Marseille port neighborhoods. The individual and their office established a land-based quarantine by setting up checkpoints, protected unattended properties against looters, established field hospitals, and organized the distribution of humanitarian supplies for the neighborhood and the city itself. Fundamentally, the General Commissioner was given absolute power in matters having to do with policing and administration of the city or imposition of de facto martial law. This type of authorization during a major disaster or crisis is another protocol that remains a critical component of most national emergency response strategies.

Another innovation was the policy to control the spread of the disease. It normally had been the case that with an outbreak of disease, residents would flee often resulting in these individuals further spreading the disease to previously uninfected areas. As an attempt to stop this mechanism of spread, an act was initiated by the Provence parliament that imposed the death penalty for any commerce, communication, or movement between Marseille and the rest of Provence. A regular army, military cordon was put in place to control movement. A plague wall, or *mur de la peste*, was rapidly erected across the countryside around Marseille to enforce this separation. The wall was built of stone and was about 2 m (6 ft 7 in) tall and 70 cm (28 in) thick. To further prevent escape, guard posts were incorporated into the wall construction. After the plague subsided, the central government further strengthened the port's plague defenses by building a larger waterside containment area with 15-foot walls for crew and cargo to be quarantined. Furthermore, crew and cargo were required to pass initial inspection at an island further out in the harbor.

7.2.2.4 Transformation

The transformation resulting from the plague outbreak and exertion of state power was both consistent with the growing governance capacity of a centralized French state that was taking place during the sixteenth and seventeenth centuries as well as a new context to express this authority. During the late seventeenth and early eighteenth centuries, the French royal government transitioned from a limited and undeveloped state to a more mature monarchical state (Ermus 2015). The state and its bureaucracy became better able to yield its power in more professional and expansive ways during this period. Ermus (2015) makes the case that during the plague of Provence, the French government took advantage of the circumstance to demonstrate the integrity, usefulness, and value of the state by extending its activities into what up to that point had been typically seen as a local matter. The model of central state engagement with crisis and disaster management became the approach of other emerging nation-states including Britain, Portugal, and Spain, in Europe. They would go on to soon institute or further develop a variety of similar measures to advance the administrative centralization and control processes.

7.2.3 St. Louis, US

St. Louis is a regionally significant city in the Midwest of the United States. The city grew tremendously from the mid-nineteenth to the early twentieth century, and during the early decades of this period was in competition with Chicago to become the great city of the country's interior (Cronon 1991). In 1850 the population of St. Louis was almost 78,000 and it was the eighth largest city in the country and by 1910 it had almost 680,000 residents and was the fourth largest in the country. Known as both the gateway to the American West and the largest city along the Mississippi River, it first became a trading and distribution site and then later an industrial center. The manufacturing generated great wealth and employment opportunities yet made the city one of the most polluted places in the US, along with Pittsburgh, during the early twentieth century. In 1900, Union Station in St. Louis was the busiest station in the country and 22 railroad lines converged at the city. In 1904, the city hosted both a World's Fair and the Olympics placing it as a focal point on the world's stage. At the same time, St. Louis' history is riven with racism.

In 1916, St. Louis voters, who were mostly white, voted by a two-thirds majority to legally mandate racial housing segregation, thereby becoming the first city in the country to do so.

7.2.3.1 Stress

In March 1918, the first known case of what became widely known as the Spanish Flu[1] was recorded in Fort Riley, Kansas, about 600 kilometers west of St. Louis. The presence of the disease expanded and spread to the eastern US and Europe most directly via US Army troop deployments to the European battlefronts of The Great War (World War I). By late summer the flu cases had begun to occur throughout the US and by early September it was front-page national news. During the latter days of September, Dr. Max C. Starkloff, the long-serving St. Louis Health Commissioner, was actively monitoring the westward spread of the disease from Boston, the initial large-scale epicenter in the US. To prepare for the flu's arrival in St. Louis, Starkloff first asked that all doctors voluntarily report any cases of influenza to his office. He also wrote an article for the *St. Louis Post-Dispatch* about how to avoid the flu. Then on October 5, a family with seven cases of influenza became the first reported incidences in the city. On the next day, 50 cases in the city were reported (UM Center for the History of Medicine ND).

7.2.3.2 Crisis

Realizing the possibility of a health crisis, Starkloff within days asked the city's Board of Alderman (an elected legislative body in St. Louis that acts to create, pass, and amend laws, as well as approving the city's annual budget) to pass an emergency law declaring influenza a contagious disease, thereby giving the city's mayor legal authority to declare a public health emergency (Kalnins 2006; Belshe 2012) and also provide for stiff fines for physicians who did not report cases of the disease. Starkloff, becoming increasingly alarmed by the rapidly growing number of disease cases, quickly went further and asserted the need for a sweeping closure order and a ban of public or private gatherings. Within days there had been 100 cases in the city and 900 at the nearby army facility, Jefferson Barracks, only 15 kilometers from downtown St. Louis.

On October 7, Starkloff brought together a meeting that included St. Louis Mayor and members of the US Public Health Service, the Red Cross, the St. Louis medical community, city business interests, local hospitals,

[1] It is widely recognized in the influenza pandemic of 1918–1919 originated in the United States.

and the public school system to confer on the most effective ways to fight the city's emerging health crisis. Many participants were against a policy of mass closures of public spaces and large private spaces. Starkloff, however, argued for the need for extreme action to disrupt the disease spread. After extended debate during the meeting, the group agreed to a sweeping closure order. Starkloff also was conferred by the mayor legal authority to make further public health edicts. It should be noted that five years earlier, Starkloff had run and was defeated in a bid to be the city's mayor. He lost to fellow Republican Henry Kiel, the very mayor he was now to work with so closely.

7.2.3.3 Transition

The meeting and the resulting action led to a dramatic transition in public health policy during the epidemic. Very soon after the meeting, the city's health department put forward an order to close schools, theaters, and other public places in an attempt to reduce the transmission of the disease. The proclamation went on to state that all public meeting places would be closed until further notice. The city's Catholic Archbishop also announced that churches similarly would be closed. The Department of Health provided this additional strong advice for those that became sick.

> Go to bed and place yourself under a physician's care. If you must go about, avoid gatherings of persons, crowded streetcars, elevators, etc. Do not sneeze, cough or spit unless you protect nose or mouth with a handkerchief. Remember your cold, under other conditions is a trivial matter, is now a public menace. Well persons are advised to avoid crowds, to sleep in well-ventilated rooms, to avoid using common cups and towels, and to wash the hands frequently (Belshe 2012, p. 121).

By October 13, the Health Department felt that closures and restrictions would keep the situation well in hand and prevent further substantial spread. But just five days later, on October 18, 559 cases and 32 deaths per day were recorded in the city. Even though the numbers started to decline by November 1, Starkloff remained committed to the closures and against the pressure by Mayor Keil and businesses who argued that the ban on public gatherings be lifted. Within the weeks, a decline in the number of cases and persistent interest in ending the closures led to the reopening of theaters, churches, and soon thereafter, schools. Again, within days the number of cases started to increase again, especially among the young, and by late November, schools were closed again and children were banned from stores and theaters. On December 3, the number of cases per day peaked with 1,467 cases, and a week later the peak in the number of deaths occurred with 58 deaths per day. The number of cases quickly declined thereafter and by the end of the year, all bans were lifted (Belshe 2012).

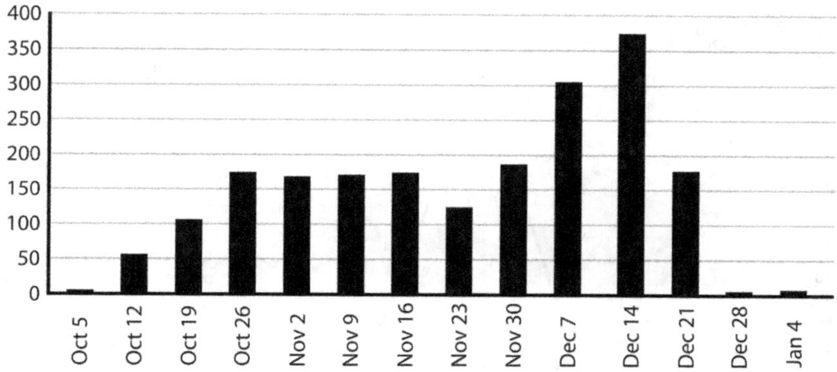

Figure 7.1 Deaths in St. Louis from influenza by week from October 1 to early 1919. Source: Belshe (2012).

7.2.3.4 Transformation

The influenza deaths by week are summarized in Figure 7.1. Two peaks in the curve are a direct reflection of the influence of the closure and the temporary reopening of schools in November.

The strict measures advocated by Dr. Starkloff and enforced by Mayor Kiel were thought to be largely responsible for dampening the general impact of the flu pandemic in St. Louis. In turn, St. Louis had the lowest number of influenza cases and influenza-related deaths of any of the ten largest cities in the United States (Belshe 2012; Navarro 2019). The infection curve of St. Louis (death rate of 352 per 100,000 in population) is often compared to that of Philadelphia on the east coast of the US, which did not enact significant restrictions and in fact went on with a massive parade during the early days of its outbreak (see Figure 7.2). Philadelphia's highest death rate was more than double that of St. Louis at 748 per 100,000 in population.

The case of St. Louis was transformative with respect to presenting a model of how a large city could respond to a disease outbreak. The case illustrates the value of a strong-willed policy innovator such as Starkloff who acted quickly and decisively but was also flexible as the latest medical information became available. Operationally, two other innovations were recognized in the city's response. The usefulness of a dedicated official to focus on risk communication between the health officers and the advisory committee and the public and different segments of the public (i.e., age-appropriate restrictions for children) was noted. The translation of medical science to public policy in a meaningful and transparent fashion was highly significant. And probably most important, the city's policies showcased the value of social distancing strategies to flatten the epidemic case load curve.

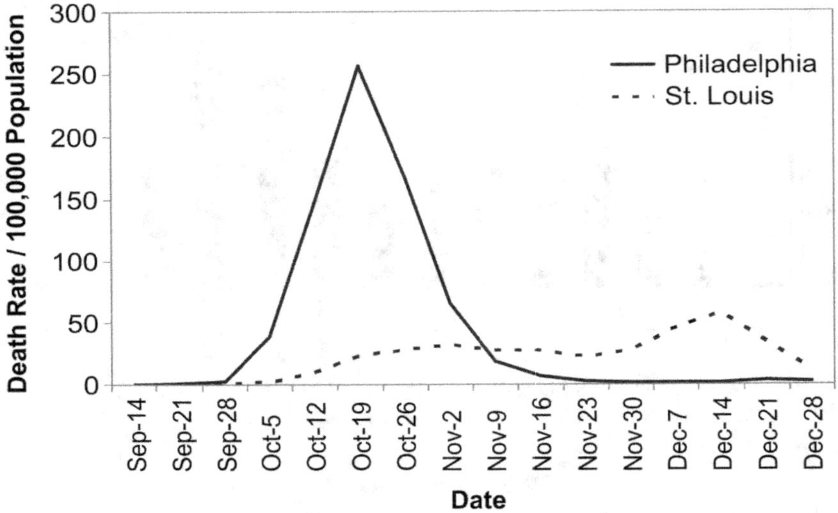

Figure 7.2 Excess pneumonia and influenza mortality over 1913–1917 baseline in Philadelphia and St. Louis, September 8 to December 28, 1918. Source: Hatchett et al. (2007).

7.2.4 Seoul, South Korea

Seoul, South Korea, is a major global city. Its current metropolitan population is just under 10 million, and the extended metropolitan region including Seoul, Incheon, and Gyeonggi Provinces accounts for approximately 42% of the country's population (in 2021, 51.7 million). More importantly, it is ranked as the fourth largest metropolitan economy in the world behind New York, Tokyo, and Los Angeles. Human settlement in the region stretches back at least 6,000 years. The history of the city is full of periods of rapid growth and decline or destruction. The city was heavily damaged during the Korean War (1950–1953) but started to grow dramatically in population and economic power during the mid-1950s. The rapid growth continued through the next several decades. It is currently home to several of the largest corporations in the world. The city is often rated as one of the most livable and technologically savvy cities in East Asia and globally.

7.2.4.1 Stress

East Asian countries have had significant experiences with disease. South Korea has had extensive experience with disease outbreaks that emerged during periods of occupation and warfare in the first half of the twentieth century. Japan brutally occupied Korea from 1910 to 1945 during which the medical capacity of the region was hindered and could not effectively respond to disease outbreaks. The Korean War was by itself much more disruptive. Significant outbreaks of a wide variety of diseases occurred including smallpox, typhoid, and typhus. A false alarm about a potential plague outbreak also occurred during the war (Sames et al. 2008).

In 2015, South Korea experienced an outbreak of the Middle East Respiratory Syndrome coronavirus (MERS). The outbreak was started when a 68-year-old Korean businessperson returned from travel in the Middle East. The individual visited four hospitals in Korea before he was diagnosed. The failure to detect the early case led to a substantial spread of the disease to other individuals. The Korean MERS outbreak involved a total of 186 cases, including 38 fatalities. Eighty-three percent of transmissions were the result of five super-spreader events. The epidemic persisted for two months and the government quarantined 16,993 individuals for two weeks to control the outbreak (Oh et al. 2018). While the initial outbreak was not in Seoul, the vast majority of the cases occurred in the Seoul metropolitan region. The MERS outbreak caused $18 billion USD in gross domestic product (GDP) losses, equivalent to 1.31% of South Korea's annual average GDP (Park 2019).

The MERS experience provided the South Korean government with important cutting-edge evidence regarding the challenges that a country faces when responding to a disease outbreak. To facilitate testing and response during the outbreak, the Korean Society for Laboratory Medicine (KSLM) launched a MERS response task force. The South Korean public and commentators harshly criticized the government and hospitals response. It was argued that they had failed to detect the first case and did not conduct as thorough an initial epidemiologic investigation as possible, allowing the cases to increase. Once the government realized the significance of the threat, a set of MERS control and intervention strategies was put into place by central and local governments, nongovernment organizations (NGOs), and schools. These included an aggressive quarantine and isolation system, temporarily closing schools, and canceling public events, and sharing fully vetted information and data from trusted entities (Park 2019).

As the MERS outbreak was controlled, the South Korean medical community reflected on what lessons could be learned from the event and what recommendations should be made for future outbreaks. Five key recommendations were presented (Park 2019): (1) Develop a traveler tracking system utilizing information and communication technology, (2) strengthen the health care delivery system, (3) strengthen the country's infectious disease prevention legislations (e.g., South Korea's Infectious Disease

Prevention Act of 2015 amended the procedures on how to regulate and implement quarantine measures more effectively), (4) create greater risk communication capacity between the medical community and government, establishing bioethics standards for quarantine and isolation policies, and (5) more closely engage with the World Health Organization's guidelines and updates.

7.2.4.2 Crisis

South Korea recorded its first case of COVID-19 on January 19, 2020. The disease started to spread rapidly and by early March it became the second most infected country after China. A sudden jump in the number of cases was attributed to Patient 31, who while ill participated in a large-scale church gathering resulting in a super-spreader event. The church in question insisted on in-person meetings, banned health masks, prayed while touching others, and initially refused to turn over its membership list to health officials wanting to do contact tracing (Wildman et al. 2020). This occurrence became a warning signal to the world regarding the failure to practice social distancing and self-isolation (Cha and Kim 2020). By early March, the number of confirmed daily cases in Korea was approaching 1,000 per day.

7.2.4.3 Transition

In response to the rapidly accelerating crisis, the South Korean government quickly moved into action. The early super-spreader event also helped to alert local and national responders about the potential need for an aggressive response that followed a 3T (Trace, Test, Treat) strategy (Kim 2020; Anttiroiko 2021). This approach involved proactive, widespread, and free screening of symptomatic individuals and their contacts. The flexible adaptation approach including a policy of enhanced transparency of data gathering, analysis, and decision-making proved to be very successful. While schools were closed, working remotely was recommended, and large gatherings were banned, lockdowns and the restriction of movement were not instituted. Specific action in Seoul closely mirrored these actions (Park et al. 2020). Seoul was able to develop key strategies that interrupted the transmission chains of COVID-19 including such actions as preemptive testing, isolation of positive infected individuals, quarantine and strict restrictions of contacts, and provision of proper treatment (Park et al. 2020). The country also relied on open access health informatics such as disclosure of real-time information on COVID-19 by the government through websites, mass media, phone alerts and messages, and mobile phone apps. As a result of this preemptive action, South Korea was able to flatten the curve of disease outbreak during its early days without closing businesses, putting out mandatory stay-at-home orders, or other strict measures taken by high-income countries at that time.

7.2.4.4 Transformation

Built from its extensive response capacity during MERS outbreaks, South Korea's initial response to COVID-19 in 2020 was quite impressive. It achieved relative success during the early months by quickly developing clear public guidelines, conducting widespread testing, innovative and high-capacity screening facilities, contact-tracing program, and supporting individuals in quarantine to make compliance easier. The country successfully managed significant limited outbreaks in March and August 2020, and even a wider and dispersed outbreak in December 2020. Overall, South Korea showed significant success in what was seen as three phases of the epidemic preparedness and response process: detection, containment, and treatment (Kim et al. 2021). The country's screening facilities and collaboration with manufacturers to provide a sufficient supply of test kits became a model that other countries followed. Containment strategies also were quite successful. Epidemiological intelligence officers had significant power to utilize a variety of data sources to trace contacts. Perhaps most impressive was that the South Korean health system was able to surge to meet the rapidly increasing demand. Across the country, especially in high-cluster sites such as Seoul, governments were restructured to increase health care access. Temporary hospitals were built, and shortages in health care equipment including personal protective equipment (PPE) were rapidly met.

The government of South Korea learned from its flawed response to the 2015 MERS outbreak and benefited from the significant number of reforms that were made to boost the public health emergency preparedness and response including greater coordination with and across government agencies and departments. This coordination as in the St. Louis case study allowed for much more effective and timely decision-making. This coordination was especially meaningful for developing preemptive measures of COVID-19 transmission in highly dense settings like Seoul (Park et al. 2020).

By the end of 2020, the South Korea experience was heralded as the model for successful COVID-19 containment. In the following years, 2021 and 2022, it did experience further outbreaks and spikes in the number of cases, eventually significantly overtopping the numbers seen in March 2020. Persistent use of extensive testing, an advanced immunization program, and preventive care, especially with respect to at-risk patients, allowed the country to keep the number of severe cases and fatalities to a low level. In a spike early in early 2022, South Korea was able to maintain the mortality rate among cases to 0.14%, approximately one-tenth the rates in the US and UK at the same time (Cha 2022).

7.3 Discussion

Like water scarcity, disease and epidemics represent an existential risk for urban populations. Not only is there the real risk of illness, incapacity, and even death associated with disease, but there is also the perception of risk that also significantly impacts communities. Given that it is understood that health risks associated with dread and the unknown generate heightened perceptions of risk (Siegrist and Arvai 2020), acute disease outbreaks often result in strong reactions that drive evacuation and relocation, prejudice against potentially exposed populations, and a break with typical norms of behavior. In the case studies, the risk response became significant as the outbreaks not only caused illness and death, they severely disrupted everyday life in the cities as laborers left their jobs, business and commerce collapsed, and governance systems ceased to function.

7.3.1 Conditions of Crisis

The examples highlight that once an outbreak is identified, it is mostly going to get a lot worse, especially as these moments typically set off a cascade of other events. Another significant dimension common to the case studies was that the crises came on very quickly. It was just a few days to a few weeks from the first local case to a large-scale public health emergency, and it was just as quick to direct significant impacts on the social and economic realms of the city. In all of the cases, the concern over illness drove people to leave the city further spreading the disease and in turn creating more illness and additional fear. This rapid out-migration caused additional disruption and the closing of business and economic activity because of a lack of customers and employees.

7.3.2 Drivers of Transitions

While the disease presence was the ultimate driver, how this driver interacted within the social context became the most important component of how the crises developed and how the eventual transition pathway formed. The past history of the disease in the cities also played a pivotal role in the crisis and transition. The exact function varied a bit; in some cases prior experience gave the city what proved to be a false sense of security (i.e., Marseille), while in other cases it seemed to afford the city with the prior experience needed to understand how best to act in the wake of the new outbreak (i.e., Seoul). In either situation, prior experience provided the citizenry of the city with either confidence that the city would be able to respond to the threat, and if not to their satisfaction, it would result in panic, fear, and outrage. In several cases, the development of new knowledge was critical in driving the transitions since it allowed the local managers and residents to redefine the hazard more clinically and eliminate or dampen the public reactions to the perceived threat. The new knowledge allowed the residents to better understand the risks and how best to reduce the risks. Shifts or reforms in social structures also were significant drivers in how the transitions emerged. New social arrangements were forged (i.e., some progressive reforms against the harshness of British

Table 7.1 *Key drivers observed in each case study. Source: Author.*

	Drivers		
Case Study	Root	Context	Proximate
Hong Kong	Colonialism; anti-Chinese bias; port facilitating spread of disease	Conflict between Chinese and Western medical science; advance of science and cause of the plague	Acceptance of germ theory; and appointment of Chinese, western-trained doctor – connection between colonial power and Chinese elite
Marseille	History as a port city; history of plague; significant history of plague prevention; strong state control	Massive plague outbreak; collapse of public systems and commerce; assertion of central state control; creation of disaster response	Breaking of quarantine rules
St. Louis	City as crossroads in rapidly developing region of the country;	Spread of Spanish flu via World War I military; capacity to coordinate local government response; strong public, private, and medical coordination	Emergence of strong policy entrepreneur
Seoul	History of disease, especially in twentieth century with military and political conflict	MERS response failure and detailed response and self-evaluation; highly coordinated and integrated public and medical response	Super-spreader event – Patient 31; proactive medical surveillance and rapid science-to-policy action

colonial rule) and scales of governance developed (i.e., the growth of the central national authority in France) that had immediate impacts on the policy response to the outbreaks and also long-term ramifications on governance and the structure of civil society.

7.3.3 Spheres of Action and Legacies

Considering disease pathogens as elements of the physical systems, they significantly defined the operations of the socio-economic systems and infrastructure during the crisis and transition phases. The positive feedback effects within the social systems dramatically accelerated the crisis and became the centerpiece of the events that took place during the crisis and were the core of the debate during the transition period. Technological systems often embodied by transport facilities or modes of transport, whether they be ships, ports, or planes, acted as mechanisms through which the disease vectors were transferred and spread. The process of isolation and quarantine became a mechanism to utilize physical barriers to break the cycle of infection and disease spread.

The legacy of prior events and underlying social conditions played a significant role in how the crises and transitions played out. An outbreak of a highly contagious deadly disease is a cathartic crisis for any city. As such, these events unmask and reveal all underlying tensions and inequities present within the city. These then become woven into the fabric of the crisis and the foundations of the underlying prospects for a successful transition. The legacy of mistrust and lack of faith in local government action was widely present across the cases, with the possible exception of St. Louis, where confidence in local government was pivotal to the success of the aggressive action implemented to control the flu outbreak.

7.3.3.1 Urban Public Health and Climate Change

Climate change is impacting urban public health issues generally (IPCC WG2 SPM 2022). Excluding extreme heat issues discussed elsewhere (in Chapter 8), observed evidence and projections indicate that climate change will bring more outbreaks of disease, more unexpected outbreaks, and global shifts in the pattern of disease outbreaks with polar movement of many disease vectors (Dodman et al. 2022). Hotter annual and seasonal temps will bring increased spread of waterborne and vectorborne diseases, and longer exposure seasons and declines in winter cold temperatures (that could kill or diminish the number of vectorborne diseases). Extreme flooding events will cause more disease spread through waterborne diseases. Extreme events also could significantly disrupt the health services provision in cities (IPCC WG2 SPM 2022).

The case studies reveal several important considerations for a variety of interested city stakeholders. These include the following.

- Expect the unexpected – disease outbreaks, such as flu, in some ways are expected as an annual event. It is the outbreak that is less typical that could become a crisis. The evidence seems to indicate that unexpected outbreaks can onset quite fast and that it is hard to avoid these episodes from becoming a crisis. Planning and preparedness for such events are crucial as is having a variety of proposals for potential action. Understanding how climate change could drive disease outbreaks in a specific city will be critical for advanced preparedness.
- Trust in government is critical – trust in government is a critical asset during crisis-related disease outbreaks given their rapid onset and the amount of unease and confusion they generate among local populations. Such trust can help facilitate rapid uptake of initiatives to slow the spread of the disease and mitigate its impacts. Conversely, the case studies show when the opposite is the case – when trust is not present – further disruption and devastation can occur. Effective and consistent communication between the government and residents and businesses could help to build the level of trust needed when such crises occur.
- Access to the latest information and data are invaluable – climate change has started to create very dynamic situations with respect to disease outbreaks. The pathways for increased exposure have increased and there is a need to acquire and develop the latest knowledge regarding disease and to gather monitoring data on disease presence and outbreak.
- Avoiding lapses of policy – the case studies illustrate several examples where a lapse of policy (i.e., absence or significantly flawed) can have significant implications and potentially result in a much wider population exposure to disease. Given the dynamic nature of disease outbreaks under conditions of climate change, it will be important to test the robustness of the policy through proactive monitoring, planning, and preparing.
- Value prior experience – previous experience with disease outbreaks provides a significant foundation for learning and enhancing future practice. As the prospect for an unexpected outbreak increases, it will be important for cities and their residents to maintain the memory of recent prior outbreaks and lessons learned.

- Avoid scapegoats – the disease outbreaks can be so intense and disruptive that scapegoat issues typically emerge as individuals and institutions look for easy answers to explain what has befallen their city. Often these reflect underlying prejudices and other biases (i.e., overcrowding, immigrants/recent migrants, poverty, racism) rather than what the empirical evidence is showing. It is important to look underneath and work to identify the prejudices and biases and keep pursuing the genuine reasons for the disease spread.

8

Environmental Risk and Hazards

Acute and Chronic Events

"The construction of the Publick Drains and the Water-Courses of the Town is extremely defective ... neither answer the purpose of cleansing the Town, nor of discharging the inundations occasioned by the rise of the River, or by the excessive fall of rain during the South-West Monsoon.... Experience has manifested that during the rainy season, when the River has attained its utmost height, the present drains become useless; at that season the rain continues to stagnate for many weeks in many parts of the Town, and the result necessarily endangers the lives of all Europeans residing in the Town, and greatly affects our Native Subjects." From Lord R.C. Wellesley (1803), the then-Governor General of British India published 1803 detailed minutes condemning the sad state of municipal affairs and flood management in Kolkata, India, published in *Goode, S. W. (1916). Municipal Calcutta: Its Institutions in Their Growth and Origin*; Kolkata: Corporation of Calcutta.

Cities are subject to environmental risks and hazards, both natural and technological. These events both as acute – low frequency/high consequence – and chronic events have played a significant role in the identity and structure of cities. For example, the San Francisco earthquake of 1906 fundamentally altered the development trajectory of the city as it took decades to fully recover during a time while Los Angeles and its own extended metropolitan region rapidly emerged as the primate Californian urban center. Environmental risks and hazards result in a variety of stresses to cities and their residents that can eventually manifest as crises and potential policy changes. Chronic risks, such as intense heat, as well as catastrophic events like a major hurricane/typhoon, steadily shape how the community manages and perceives their local environment. How cities respond to low-frequency/high-consequence events can be particularly complex. Urban risk management is mediated by several factors including scientific uncertainty and informal and formal management strategies. Risk and hazard policy transitions can result in fundamental new types of human–environment interactions and patterns of resource use (Solecki et al. 2017). Chronic and acute environmental risks and hazards are closely associated with how many perceive and experience the impacts of climate change. As a result, understanding how cities have been able to attend to and effectively respond to these events become key exemplars of how other cities might be able to respond to current and future climate change-related extreme events.

8.1 Environmental Hazards and Risks

An environmental hazard can be defined as a condition or phenomenon that causes disruption, damage, and/or harm, including death. The world is full of varying types of such extreme events. Events become a hazard when they interact with human systems or those ecological and physical systems on which humans are dependent. The term "risk" is most often associated with a combination of two concepts/terms – the likelihood or probability that a hazard will occur and the potential consequence or impact of the event. Each of these terms has a series of associated specific conditions and qualities that are often relative and context specific (e.g., what might be considered a significant risk in one location might not be considered so in another location). Another commonly used term in these discussions is disaster, which focuses a bit more on the impact of the event rather than the mechanism of the event itself. A disaster is defined as a "serious disruption of the functioning of a community or a society at any scale due to hazardous events interacting with conditions of exposure, vulnerability, and capacity, leading to one or more of the following: human, material, economic, and environmental losses and impacts" (UNGA, 2016).

What is seen as a hazard, like risk, is often defined within the context in which the event takes place. Extreme hazard events, or events significantly outside of the norm, can occur within any system. Extreme events that cause significant damage, disruption, or worse – injury and death – can be described as a hazard. Often times hazards that result in catastrophic loss and damage can be also described as a disaster, even though, the boundary between what is a hazard and what is a disaster does not have prescribed and accepted dividing line.

With respect to the term hazard specifically, varying descriptors can be used to illustrate the differences between its frequency, size, and relative impact. Acute hazards are defined as those that represent a single massive shock. A large-scale and damaging earthquake or flood is defined as an acute hazard. A chronic hazard could either be expressed as a slow onset event with a significantly long presence, such as a multi-year drought, or as a situation that is endemic to the site or occurs on a regular basis. The frequent landslides in the poor *favelas* on the hill slopes around Rio de Janeiro, Brazil, and mean monthly high tide flooding (King Tides) in Miami, Florida, are chronic hazards.

Some hazards in specific locations can represent both acute and chronic risks. For example, flooding in certain communities can occur regularly, such as with spring flooding following snow melt, or in cases with climate change-accelerated sea level rise, mean monthly high tide flooding can occur as a chronic risk. At the same time, these same communities also can face acute flooding from an extreme rain event or storm. Urban heat is also seen as both a chronic risk and increasingly an acute risk that emerges from an extreme heat event such as what happened in the Pacific Northwest coast of North America, especially in the US states of Oregon, Seattle, and Canada province of British Columbia where maximum temperatures were recorded 11–19°C (20–35°F) above normal during an extended heat wave lasting from late June to early July 2021. The event shattered all-time temperature throughout the region and resulted in at least 1,400 related deaths (White et al. 2023).

Another significant distinction when discussing hazards is whether their origin emerges from natural phenomena or human-developed technologies. So-called natural hazards have been traditionally associated with extreme events that occur within physical systems, such as climate-related hazards including typhoons (hurricanes), extreme rain events, tornadoes, blizzards, droughts, and heat waves, and geological-related hazards including earthquakes, landslides, tsunamis, and sinkholes. One of the significant advances within hazards theory during the past several decades is the recognition that the concept of natural hazards is misleading. In reality, while the origin of some extreme can be "natural", their impact and amount of damage and loss are socially constructed. Many scholars have argued that there are no "natural hazards" (Steinberg 2000; Blaikie et al. 2014).

While research on the societal dimensions of extreme natural events has significantly advanced our understanding of hazards and risks, another branch of hazards literature has emerged to investigate the risks that directly result from the development, use, and disposal of hazardous materials, infrastructure, and technologies. These circumstances and conditions are defined as technological hazards. Chemical, biological, and radiological/nuclear hazards are all types of technological hazards, as are industrial pollution, toxic waste, factory explosions, chemical spills, and dam failures. Technological hazards can also result from natural hazard events, where, for example, an earthquake in a city can result in a fire outbreak when gas lines are ruptured – such was the case for the 1906 San Francisco earthquake. Most technological hazards are limited in extent; however, large-scale technological disasters have occurred. In 1984, for example, a massive chemical release at a Union Carbide plant in Bhopal, India, resulted in the immediate and soon thereafter deaths of more than 10,000 people and the injury to more than 500,000 residents in the immediate area. The Soviet Union, Chernobyl nuclear power plant disaster in 1986 similarly caused intense nearby as well as widespread impacts, including being a contributing factor in the collapse of the Soviet Union some five years later.

Within hazards research, the connection between the magnitude of the extreme event and the loss and damage that result has emerged as a quite significant factor in understanding how risks could be managed and why there are vast differences between the level of impacts from place to place. Several relevant terms, including exposure, vulnerability, and resilience, help define these connections. Extreme events are described by measures that illustrate their properties (e.g., mm of rain, km per hour wind, meters of storm surge). How these event properties interact with the surroundings, including people and their interests and assets and the pathways between the event and loss and damage, becomes important considerations.

Exposure is a broad term that describes "the presence of people, livelihoods, services, resources, infrastructure and economic, social or cultural assets in places and settings that could be adversely affected by an extreme event" (IPCC 2022). Vulnerability, another broad term, has been recently defined as the "propensity or predisposition to be adversely affected by the hazard, and encompasses a variety of concepts and elements, including sensitivity or susceptibility to harm and lack of capacity to cope and adapt" (IPCC 2022). The socially defined or socially constructed aspects of vulnerability are of particular concern in densely settled areas like cities where often large concentrations of highly vulnerable populations reside and critical infrastructure assets are present. The concept of resilience is also widely used within risk and hazard literature. Here, resilience is applied to describe or illustrate the ability of entities (e.g., individuals, communities, institutions) to withstand the shock of a hazard and fully recover, often in a way to make them more resilient and less vulnerable in the future.

How individuals and institutions respond to risk and hazards is mediated by a wide range of factors, including their (1) understanding of the risk including the level of uncertainty regarding the risk, (2) perception of the risk including specific cultural and historical factors, and (3) access to resources including knowledge, financing, and decision-making capacity. Broadly defined, local contextual conditions are seen as playing a critical role in how these factors interact and result in risk and hazard response activities and strategies. That said, while risks, hazards, and disasters are associated with devastating damages and losses, they are also commonly presented as windows of opportunity and focusing events for transformational change.

8.2 Case Studies

The case studies examine the types of risks and hazards most often associated with climate change-driven shifts in the pattern of extreme events: fluvial and pluvial flooding, coastal storm surge flooding, and extreme heat episodes. A total of five sites are reviewed. Two, Cedar Rapids, Iowa, and New Orleans, Louisiana, both in the US, are located within the greater Mississippi-Missouri watershed – one of the largest watersheds in the world. Cedar Rapids is highly vulnerable to fluvial flooding, while New Orleans is vulnerable to fluvial and coastal storm flooding. The other three cities are Abu Dhabi, United Arab Emirates, highly heat exposed, and Kolkata, India, and Rotterdam, the Netherlands, subject to extreme coastal storm flooding.

8.2.1 Abu Dhabi, United Arab Emirates

The city of Abu Dhabi is the capital of the United Arab Emirates and is located in the southern end of the Persian Gulf. The city has grown tremendously with the development and export of the country's massive energy reserves. The emirate's oil reserves are estimated to be about one-tenth of the global total. In 1950, the city's population was just 4,000 and by 2020 the metropolitan population had grown to approximately 1.5 million. Approximately 80% of this population includes foreign workers who perform key labor roles within the growing city. The landscape of Abu Dhabi has been dramatically transformed during this growth. With an ambitious five-year development plan, started in 1968, the relatively small settlement was completely rebuilt and modernized. Modern water supply infrastructure, a robust electrical grid, and a central sewerage system were constructed, and new housing projects, government buildings, hotels, and a new port extension were built. As an important revenue-generating facility, a nearby oil refinery was put into operation in 1976. Abu Dhabi's revenue from its oil royalties and overseas investments has provided the emirate and city with some of the world's highest per capita incomes. This access to capital has led to a series of development initiatives that focus on large-scale construction projects and cultural advancement. Today, the city encompasses an area of 972 sq. km (375 sq. mi.); somewhat bigger than New York City at 793.1 sq. km (302.6 sq. mi.) but smaller than the Hong Kong Territory, which is 1,106 sq. km (427 sq. mi.).

8.2.1.1 Stress

Southwest Asia experiences some of the most extreme heat conditions in the world. Abu Dhabi has a desert climate and experiences almost no rainfall. The average annual temperature is 27.9°C (82.3°F), and the annual rainfall is 42 mm (1.7 inch). From March through November, the average daily high temperatures typically exceed 30°C. The summer temperatures are dampened by the high humidity with moisture coming off the waters of the Persian Gulf. The heat and humidity create extremely oppressive weather conditions. From June through to September, the nightly minimum temperatures are often 27°C (80.6°F) or above. In the Persian Gulf region, traditional clothing, housing design, and the pattern of daily life have been geared to manage the summer heat. With respect to dress, the long flowing robes of light cloth provide shading, air flow, and slow the rate of dehydration. Housing design in the region has included features to vent heat, avoid direct summer sunlight, and provide shade (St. Clair 2009). Avoidance of the heat of day with shops and commerce closing during the high heat of the afternoon and reopening in the evening are customary ways to manage the summer high temperatures.

Since the mid-twentieth century, much of the region has flourished and grown significantly with the exploitation and export of the vast energy reserves present, principally oil and natural gas deposits. The dramatic transformation of the city over the past 50 years has brought modern amenities, an impressive skyline of tall buildings and commercial centers, expansive residential areas, as well as watered green lawns, gardens, and golf courses with greens. This growth also has come with a huge application of air conditioning technology – often which residents might run 24/7/365. Cities such as Abu Dhabi have been built out significantly in the past half century with a recognition that the emerging urban form provided an opportunity to address the urban heat risk. As the city grew, there was a parallel increase in the number of academic and government studies and initiatives on how to promote heat reduction strategies and urban heat island mitigation (see Luomi 2009 for review), while the demand for air conditioning cooling continued to escalate (Pamuk 2011).

8.2.1.2 Crisis

The Persian Gulf Region generally, and cities such as Abu Dhabi, specifically, in many ways illustrate the tensions reflected in the impact and response to climate change. Energy exports have brought tremendous wealth and prosperity, but there also is increasing recognition that the cities and settlements of the region will face significant rise in annual and seasonal temperatures and extreme heating with climate change. Summer extreme heat of course has long been a well-understood component of life in the region. However, in the mid-2010s, several new research studies modeling projected temperature rise in the Persian Gulf changed the discourse surrounding heat and in some pushed cities like Abu Dhabi into a crisis. The studies illustrated how climate extremes in the region may by the end of this century more often reach deadly levels if significant greenhouse gas emissions reductions do not take place. Pal and Eltahir (2016) detail how the current combination of heat and humidity in the region makes it extremely susceptible to the dangers of increased temperatures and "a specific regional hotspot where climate change, in absence of significant mitigation, is likely to severely impact human habitability in the future." Several other well-publicized research articles confirmed this analysis and strengthened the argument (e.g., Schär, 2016).

8.2.1.3 Transition

Following these efforts and discussions with the UAE stakeholder community, the UAE sponsored a series of reports and efforts to examine the issue of climate risk, adaptation, and mitigation (see the report *UAE Climate Change Risks & Resilience: An Overview of Climate Change Risks to 12 Key Sectors* developed in collaboration with the Emirates Wildlife Society in association with the WWF and Acclimitise 2017). In 2020, the Abu Dhabi government created the Abu Dhabi Climate Change Initiative. His Excellency Dr. Thani bin Ahmed Al Zeyoudi, who is the UAE Minister of Climate Change and Environment, announced that "the Abu Dhabi Climate Initiative is the first platform in the region dedicated to accelerating the research and development of climate and water technologies and to support the shift towards a climate-resilient economy" (ADGM 2020). With a clear focus on linking capital investors with climate technology innovators, the ambition was to "work to ensure that climate action improves health and well-being while creating new jobs and industries."

Following up soon after, the Abu Dhabi Climate Resilience Initiative was launched (Peters 2021). It was a city-wide public program focused on a set of strategic and creative street and sidewalk-level heat mitigation interventions to improve the overall thermal comfort levels of pedestrians. The Initiative, which won several design awards, was based upon a broad range of international collaborations among urban designers, climate scientists, engineers, and landscape architects. The Initiative built on the understanding that such heat mitigation solutions would be most effective if they were designed for "hyper-local" and site-specific needs, rather than assume the posture that one-size-fits-all. The pilot projects put into place proposed a range of cooling strategies based on conditions of each particular location. Pilot projects were initially developed for three archetype locations: a pocket park, a public plaza (i.e., mosque entrance), and a road intersection.

8.2.1.4 Transformation

Abu Dhabi in the past several years has continued to evolve its approach to climate-resilient urbanism through a series of initiatives and engagement opportunities. The focus of new design increasingly is on blending new urban climate science, cutting-edge technology application, and traditional Middle Eastern design. These together focus on the role and significance of urban microclimates and conditions that promote cooling, airflow, and protection against the sun and heat at particular moments of the day and night. For example, some of the climate-resilient initiatives include design elements such as cantilevered shade structures and shaded seating to create a more comfortable setting when waiting at a bus stop or at a crosswalk waiting for the traffic light to change, or more traditional elements such as a "sikka" – a canopied or covered pathway between buildings that are oriented with the wind to maximize the breeze. In early 2020, the Abu Dhabi Department of Municipalities and Transport (DMT) launched the "Cool Abu Dhabi Challenge." The Challenge competition was an open invitation to architects, artists, designers, engineers, landscape architects, material fabricators, educators, researchers, students, and interdisciplinary teams to submit extreme heat mitigation plans. The contest attracted 1,570 participants from 67 countries (of which 338 entries met the criteria and were approved for consideration) (Abu Dhabi Media Office 2020). The 10 winning designs were selected based on their flexibility, forward-thinking, and practicality. The designs were to be placed across multiple sites in Abu Dhabi. Additional criteria were that the designs promote long-term sustainability to reduce the urban heat island effect while taking into consideration Abu Dhabi's socio-cultural context (DMT 2020).

8.2.2 Kolkata, India

The city of Kolkata is in easternmost India in the state of West Bengal. It has an urban core population of 4.5 million people with a metropolitan regional population of approximately 14.5 million. It is located on the east bank of the River Bhagirathi-Hooghly (Ganga) and is approximately 170 kilometers upriver from the Bay of Bengal. The whole metropolitan region is within the Ganges Delta and the city center is near sea level with an average elevation of approximately 5 meters. The site of Kolkata has had human settlements for at least two millennia. Its contemporary history began with the arrival of representatives of the British East India Trading Company in 1690. The company and then the British government wrested control of the city. The city grew rapidly as a trading port and was maintained as the capital of the British Indian Empire until 1911 (after which the capital was moved to Delhi). The city location next to several navigable rivers made it an ideal spot for commerce transport. The colonial period included significant dispossession and inequities imposed by the British rulers onto the local populations. Post-independence in 1947, the city emerged as a political and cultural hub of India and became well known for its progressive and leftist politics and movements. The climate of Kolkata is tropical with defined wet and dry seasons. The city receives approximately 1,800 mm (~71 in) of rain per year with almost all occurring in the summer monsoon season. The city also is subject to extreme storms – Indian Ocean typhoons – some of which have caused devastating flooding.

8.2.2.1 Stress

The natural setting for the city was a marshy wetland, and the earliest settlements in the area were fishing hamlets located on natural high levees and embankments along the Hooghly River and interspersed with forest and creeks and later canals that connected to the Hooghly River to the west and a system of lakes (i.e., the Salt Lakes) to the east, which were downslope of the settlements. The creeks and canals and numerous rain barrels in the hamlets were effective means to provide drainage and prevent large-scale flooding in most cases. In 1737 a massive cyclone struck the region. Known as the 1737 Calcutta cyclone, the Hooghly River cyclone of 1737, or the Great Bengal cyclone of 1737, the storm brought catastrophic flooding and devastation to Kolkata. The storm was the first "super" cyclone officially recorded in the North Indian Ocean. Historically observed as one of the worst natural disasters in India, it hit the coast near Kolkata and was reported to have killed over 300,000 people. The storm and other more typical and frequent flooding from

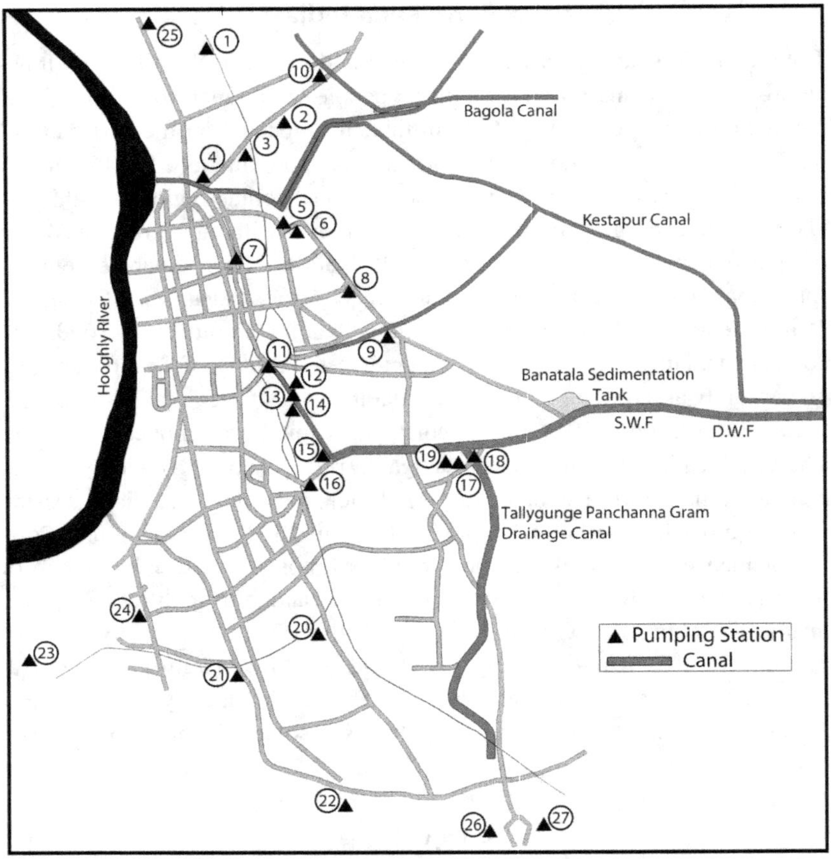

PUMPING STATIONS

1. Biarpara	10. Kashipur	19. 2nd Additional Chowbhaga
2. Laketown	11. Palmer Bazar	20. Jodhpur Park
3. Dutta Bagan	12. Pagladanga	21. Chetla Lock
4. Begachia	13. Chingrighata	22. Keorapukur
5. Ultadanga (old)	14. Kulia Tangri	23. Nimak Mahal
6. Ultadanga (new)	15. Topsia	24. Mominpur
7. Maniktalla Pump	16. Ballygunge	25. Barabagar Noapara
8. Maniktalla Pumping	17. Chowbhaga Old	26. Uttarbhag
9. Dhapa Lock	18. Additional Chowbhaga	27. Additional Uttarbhag

Figure 8.1 Canals and pumping stations of the Kolkata metropolitan region (Banerjee 2018).

monsoon rain illustrated the city's exposure and vulnerability. After the East India Company completed its takeover of the city in the mid-eighteenth century, rapid and unplanned or poorly planned growth took place resulting in the filling in of the creeks and closing of the water detention tanks. The result was increased waterlogging, flooding, and more frequent outbreaks of waterborne diseases. An initial response to these conditions was to excavate narrow sewers to drain rainwater and sewage west to the Hooghly River. The action exacerbated the problem because this flow was in opposition to the natural eastward slope of the city, leading to inflow from the Hooghly and more waterlogging and stagnation, especially during the monsoon season (Neogi 2018; Mukherjee et al. 2021).

8.2.2.2 Crisis

Subsequent attempts to address the flooding issues brought some limited success that was quickly overwhelmed by the continued population growth and expansion of settlement onto more marginal and flood-prone lands and relatively weak municipal governance capacity. Part of the challenge was to develop an effective water management system in a city where monthly rainfall is so variable. The canals and creeks would dry up during the dry season and fill, leading to clogged sections and stagnant water. Furthermore, they often would not be cleaned regularly. This led to pools of dirty water and putrefaction of human and animal fecal waste and other waste resulting in outbreaks of deadly disease. The problem became many times worse with the monsoon rains that brought water from all sources including the Hooghly River, canals and creeks, and the Salt Lakes to the west. The waterlogging and street-level flooding became a chronic problem, as many areas of the city simply lacked proper outlets for sewage and rainwater.

In the early nineteenth century, a series of British colonial government reports detailed the chronic waterlogging issue, poor drainage, regular flooding, and significant risk of catastrophic flooding. A decision was made to build a massive circular canal to the north and east to promote drainage through the dramatic expansion of the Beliaghata Canal (first a creek and opened as a smaller canal in the 1730s) and build other connecting canals. The expansion of the Beliaghata Canal was the single most important contribution of the colonial rulers appointed Improvement Committee – later Lottery Committee. The canal was cut across the northern edge of the city and simultaneously connected with several major drainage creeks and smaller canals as well as the Hooghly River and the Salt Lakes. The canal allowed for water to flow from west to east at times of high water – allowing for a reversal of the natural flow. The Beliaghata canal and other connecting canals still are in operation today (see Figure 8.1). While this effort was initially seen as quite ambitious, over the decades it has been recognized that a significant flood risk remains in the city. The canals proved not able to remedy the waterlogging and poor drainage problems of the city (Neogi 2018). The reasons for this were many of the same seen in earlier decades – wide variation in seasonal moisture levels, limited maintenance capacity, rapid urbanization, and lack of proper outlets for sewage and rainwater in several parts of the city. The waterlogging problems increased significantly during the monsoon season. With significant underground stormwater drainage and a depressed water table, large amounts of tidal water from the river and other water from the canal would fill the open drains. This enduring crisis brought forward a series of more comprehensive efforts being proposed including massive underground drains and canals. This pressure was combined with the fact that the city was becoming increasingly critical to British imperial expansion in South Asia. Kolkata became the second city to London in the Empire as free market reforms and the construction of major railroad and road connections from the city deep into the interior of the continent dramatically increased the city's economic and strategic importance to the British. The colonial districts within the city became fantastically wealthy and the city took on its reputation as the "City of Palaces."

8.2.2.3 Transition

In 1857, another major expansion plan was finally approved. It involved the building of a series of massive west-to-east flowing canals that would drain more water into the Salt Lakes district. This planning effort itself represented a significant transition in how the colonial rulers imagined the city and its flood risk. Unfortunately, on October 5, 1864, the city again was devastated by a tropical cyclone. Most of the city and critical port facilities were inundated and destroyed. An estimated 60,000 people died in its wake, from both the direct impact and the disruption, especially the disease outbreak that followed. Plans for the new bigger canal system were further adjusted as a result of the impacts, and progress was further hampered by limited funding and governance capacity as well as the rapidly growing population and urban footprint, both of which required adjustments to be made to the design. The revised plan was finally finished in the late 1890s and formed the basis of the modern drainage system of the city (Neogi 2018). With hubris, the British colonial rule had attempted to create a well-drained modern city with an elaborate system of canals and channels in a deltaic wetland region with limited site advantages for large-scale urban expansion. To a significant extent, this ambitious plan with associated effort did not achieve its goals.

8.2.2.4 Transformation

While the city had made a significant flood risk management transition and resulting transformation, the flooding problem persisted and continued throughout the twentieth century. The population and infrastructure of the city remain highly vulnerable to flooding (Mukherjee and Bardhan 2021). The population growth and urban expansion of the city during the twentieth century placed ever-increasing pressure on the overwhelmed and difficult-to-maintain drainage system. Another major planning effort to mitigate the flood risk in the early twentieth century was launched. The heavy siltation and inadequate maintenance of the water system continued to reduce the canal system's hydraulic capacity and value for flood control. Floods were a regular feature of twentieth-century Kolkata with significant, although not catastrophic, floods occurring many times per decade including in the last 50 years (i.e., 1970, 1978, 1984, 1999, 2007, 2016, and 2020) (Banerjee 2018; Mukherjee et al. 2021). Even with an intricate system of canals and pumps (see Figure 8.1), still today, an extreme rain event coinciding with high tide conditions will result in waterlogging and flooding in many parts of the city. In addition, Kolkata and its environs are undergoing land subsidence (Chatterjee 2010 in Dhiman et al. 2019), which will enhance the probability of future flooding. Presently the local population has been able to adapt to flooding events as long as they are not severe and lengthy in duration. The prospect of climate change presents the likelihood that future flooding will be worse and that local populations will be required to adjust and enhance their adaptation strategies. In many ways, the story of flooding in the city is still unfolding (Dhiman et al. 2019).

8.2.3 Mississippi River – New Orleans, Louisiana, and Cedar Rapids, Iowa, US

The Mississippi River comprises the world's third largest drainage system basin. It is exceeded in size only by the Amazon River and Congo River watersheds. The Mississippi system drains 41% of the 48 contiguous US states. The watershed is more than 3.22 million sq. km. (1.25 million sq. mi. and approximately the size of India) and includes all or parts of 31 US states and two Canadian provinces (see Figure 8.2). The basin is made up of hundreds of tributaries on which hundreds if not thousands of towns and cities are located. The recorded history of the river going back hundreds of years is full of flood disasters. While just a small proportion of the river basin, those low-lying sites are subject to flooding, it is often the case that these exposed and vulnerable sites are locations where shipping and trade can take place, river boat transit can take place, and adjacent areas make some of the best agricultural land – rich and fertile alluvial soils. The river towns and cities at these locations have all been founded and built up with flood risk as an important part of their development history. This includes major cities like Minneapolis and St. Paul, St. Louis, Pittsburgh, and New Orleans.

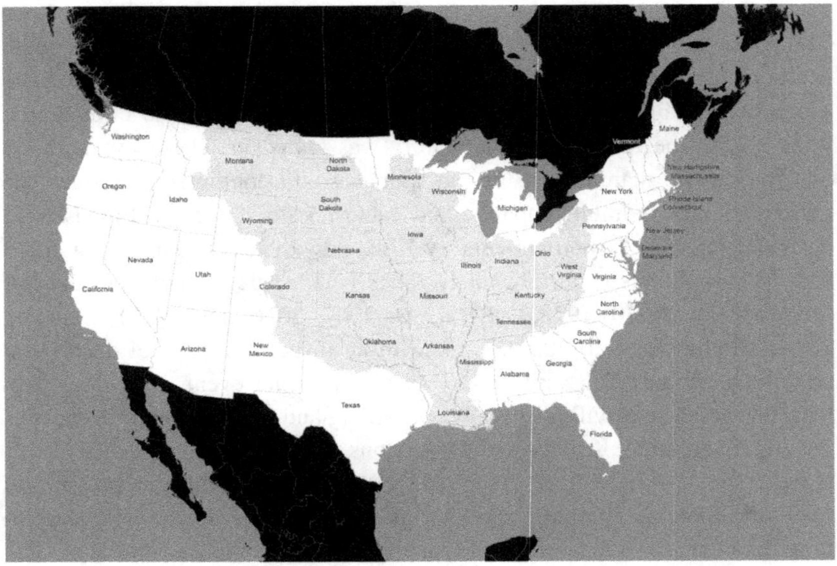

Figure 8.2 Mississippi river watershed. Source: World Atlas. www.worldatlas .com/rivers/the-mississippi-river.html

While many significant floods have taken place since 1900, two events shaped how people and communities respond to and manage the flood risk in the watershed. The two floods represent benchmarks in flood management policy. The first of these floods occurred in 1927 with heavy rains starting in late 1926 and flood waters lasting well into 1927. The Mississippi River remained above flood stage for a continuous stretch of 153 days at one point. The flood of 1927 was the most disastrous to occur in the Lower Mississippi Valley – covering the area below Cairo, Illinois, and extending southward through New Orleans to the Mississippi Delta region. During the flood, an area of about 70,000 sq. km (~27,000 sq. mi.) was inundated as existing levees were breached, flooding surrounding areas including cities, towns, and farmland. Local industries and transportation shut down and crops were destroyed. Upward of 500 people died and over 630,000 people were displaced, and possibly more than 1 million farm animals were killed. Poor African-Americans made up the vast majority of those permanently displaced. Most were placed in horrific tent confinements following the flood and eventually chose to leave the region – resulting in significant depopulation of Lower Mississippi Valley towns.

The prevailing strategy of flood control up to this moment was strictly focused on the construction of levees and other barriers to protect life and property. The 1927 Great Mississippi Flood drove the push for the federal

Flood Control Act of 1928, which authorized the federal government to take a leadership role in riverine flood management, as well as navigation (Pearcy 2002). While the attention was on how to promote flood control in the Lower Mississippi Valley, the area hardest hit by the 1927 flood, the bill helped the federal government more robustly engage throughout the Mississippi River basin and beyond. Another significant component of the bill was that the federal government was also authorized to assess in a scientific manner the merits of all flood control strategies including but not limited to levees, spillways, and channel improvements. Levee construction moving forward also would be regulated and controlled, as opposed to the haphazard and irregular methods used previously.

In 1993, another massive flood struck the Mississippi Basin and by many metrics, this event equaled or surpassed the events of 1927. The Great Flood of 1993 occurred from April to October 1993, with the most hard-hit areas in the northern half of the Mississippi-Missouri watershed. The total area flooded in the Mississippi River basin was approximately 78,000 sq. km (30,000 sq. mi.). Flood waters overwhelmed, breached, or were allowed to exceed in managed releases the intricate system of dykes and other water flow control structures that had been put into place. This led to the largest flood ever recorded on the Upper Mississippi River. The flooding overtopped and/or damaged 40 US federal levees and 1,043 nonfederal levees. Fifty people died during the flood, and the loss and damage was estimated to be \$15 billion (~\$30 billion in 2023) (Kondapalli and Sakamuri 2018). Approximately 100,000 homes were destroyed by the flood and vast areas of valuable farmland were left covered with silt and sand. The events had a series of long-term impacts on flood management in the region. First, the flood once again illustrated the importance of a flexible approach to flood control and not putting all focus on a single engineering fix – like levee construction. Second, it highlighted the importance of flood control maintenance, effective risk communication, and risk mapping.

The 1993 disaster was another turning point in how the federal and state governments approached flood control in the watershed. Most significant was the turning away from a single policy of hard infrastructure flood prevention. It was recognized that preventing this amount of damage from occurring again was excessively costly and unsustainable. The new approach focused on new construction of flood control structures only in critical areas, like major towns and cities. Since 1993, 72.5 sq. km (28 sq. mi.) of floodplain near St. Louis have been safeguarded by new or strengthened levees. Among these sites, the federal and state governments chose a policy of buyouts of highly flood-prone properties. Since the 1993 events, an estimated 14,000 properties have been bought by the US Federal Emergency Management Agency in nine states throughout the Mississippi watershed (Larson 2019). Another strategy included the purchase of agricultural acreage that was set aside as land that could be safely flooded during future events. The mixture of "soft" and "hard" flood control programs led to a decline in loss and damage in subsequent floods. As an example, the 1995 and 2002 floods, despite having similar intensities as the 1993 flood, caused significantly less loss and damage in riverside communities that were severely damaged in the earlier flood.

This history provides the background for a more detailed examination of how the acute and chronic risk of flooding have played out in two exemplar river cities in the Mississippi River basin. Through these cases, one can more fully understand how the flood crises translate in local urban environmental transitions and transformations.

8.2.3.1 New Orleans, Louisiana

The Crescent City is one of New Orleans' nicknames. It is named that because the original French settlement which became the City of New Orleans was built as a big crescent-shaped bend in the Mississippi River. It was built along this bend because it included some of the highest elevations in the area – the natural levee of the river. This condition illustrates well the intimate and tense relationship between the city and its river (Kelman 2006). Scholars have written about the "unnatural" quality of the city as it was wrested from a place largely unsustainable for large-scale urbanization (Colten 2005). Even with challenges, New Orleans had a robust history of growth – up through at least 2005 when Hurricane Katrina brought devastating impacts to the city.

The city of New Orleans was founded as a French colony in 1718 and in 1722 the settlement experienced its first hurricane. Through French and later Spanish control, until the US takeover at the end of 1803, the city grew as a rough and tumble port. With its first official US Census in 1810, the city had a population of 17,242 making it the seventh largest city in the country. It quickly became the largest port in the southern US. By 1900, its population was 287,104 and reached its greatest population in 1960 at 627,525 (with a 2020 population of 383,997). The metropolitan region has continued to grow to a 2020 population of 1.27 million residents. New Orleans is a city of significant levels of income disparity, poverty, and anti-Black racism that has defined much of its history. The median family income of the city is about $45,000, substantially below the US average of $67,000 in 2020, and it has a poverty rate of 23.8%, more than double the US average of 11.4% in 2020. New Orleans is a majority African American city (58.1%), which is significantly larger than the white population of 32.1% of the population.

Stress – Another nickname for New Orleans is the Big Easy, which honors the supposed easygoing, partying, laid-back attitude to life that local and visitors residents indulge in. While that is part of the reputation of New Orleans, the city also has faced multiple social, economic, political, and environmental stresses. The city struggled against racial strife, economic panics, civil unrest, military occupation and warfare, political conflicts, disease outbreaks, and perhaps most profoundly against flooding. Situated at the southern terminus of the Mississippi River, the city's commercial identity has been most connected to its function as a river and international trading port. This location and function put the city at risk for both riverine flooding from the Mississippi, flooding from extreme rain events, and storm surge flooding and related impacts from Gulf of Mexico hurricanes.

A central stress within the city has been the tensions between the flood risk and the history of urbanization. The growth of the city and its population has come with certain advancements in flood control and land reclamation and drainage. Innovative massive electric-powered pumping facilities dramatically expanded the amount of all-year dry land around the city for new development (Romagossa 2010). The increased importance of the city mandated that it be protected from flooding. During the Great Mississippi Flood of 1927, the City of New Orleans was threatened with devastating flooding. On April 29, 1927, engineers following the Louisiana Governor's order started a process of exploding 39 tons of dynamite to breach the levee upstream of the city to save the city from flooding. After the flood, the 1928 legislation created the Mississippi River & Tributaries (MR&T) Project that empowered the US Army Corps of Engineers to develop two key structures to protect New Orleans from a Mississippi River flood. The structures were focused on reducing the volume of flow that passes the city, and included the Bonnet Carré spillway bypass (about 40 kilometers upstream of the city) and Old River Control Structure (into the Atchafalaya Basin approximately 160 kilometers west of the city). Together both structures worked effectively at keeping substantial flood waters away from New Orleans for more than 60 years (Barry 1997; Rogers 2006).

Crisis – As Hurricane Katrina came north through the Gulf of Mexico, its strength grew from the gulf's warm waters and made landfall as a strong Category 3 storm on the Louisiana coast approximately 72 kilometers (45 miles) due east of New Orleans. The storm brought significant rain and wind to the city throughout the night of August 28 and into the morning of August 29. While the level of destruction was impressive with extensive damage to windows and street-level flooding, the loss was more catastrophic in coastal areas of the state of Mississippi east of New Orleans, which took the direct brunt with a nine-meter (28-foot) storm surge flood and winds over 192 km/h (120 mph). On the morning of August 29, New Orleans was battered and not significantly damaged, but the situation rapidly changed. Widespread and disastrous breaches of many levees and channels around the city (including those connected to the Bonnet Carré spillway) had taken place and water began to flood a large part of the city, with horrendous results. Within days 80% of the city was flooded. A humanitarian crisis of enormous proportions rapidly emerged, as the population of the metropolitan region was encouraged or mandated to evacuate. It is estimated that 1 million people evacuated, with a quarter million unable or unwilling to do so. The most heart-wrenching images of this evacuation were the loading of mostly poor African American residents of New Orleans onto buses to be taken to other cities throughout the south-central region of the United States without any clear pathway to return to the city. Approximately 1,500 people died in Louisiana, the vast majority in metropolitan New Orleans, and the estimate of the damage (both direct and indirect) was between $40–50 billion (Kates et al. 2006). In Orleans Parish (the City of New Orleans), the mortality rate for the Black population was 1.7–4 times higher than among Whites, for all individuals 18 years old and older (Brunkard et al. 2008). Overall, the African American residents of the city were most adversely affected across a range of metrics (e.g., mortality, dislocation, relative property loss) (Morse 2008).

Transition – Hurricane Katrina was an extreme shock to the New Orleans metropolitan region. Following the flooding, loss, and devastation, the daily life of the city was at a standstill. In the months that followed, a bitter struggle emerged regarding how to move the city and its residents forward. This debate immediately brought up and was defined by the deeply rooted drivers of the city – its history of racism, violence, and poverty juxtaposed to its easygoing, neighborly, artful self. Some argued for a traditional disaster recovery process where resources are made available to rebuild and replace what was lost (regardless of the equity implications), while others promoted the ambition to use the disaster as an opportunity for growth to make a new more resilient, equitable, and just New Orleans (Kates et al. 2006). An initial blue ribbon panel report advocated the notion that the city could not be made safe and secure from future flooding and that a process of degrowth should reduce the population and footprint of the city to be more similar to that of the early twentieth century, before the MR&T Project and other improvements. Members of the African American community immediately identified the racial bias that would be evident in this action. After significant public debate and outrage, the mayor and others embraced the notion that every neighborhood – whether they be Black or White majority – should be rebuilt. The overt policy adjustment was to ensure that the metropolitan region and every household would be protected from all future flooding scenarios up through a Category 5 hurricane.

The opportunity to drive the transition was vested with the federal government and its support of a massive upgrade in flood protection.

Transformation – Sufficient time has passed to understand the full transformative impact of Hurricane Katrina on New Orleans. By simple basic statistics, the city has been significantly changed. In 2005 just before Katrina, the population of the city was roughly 455 thousand, and in the early recovery phase in 2006, it was 209 thousand, and by 2021, the population was estimated to be 379 thousand. The population of the metropolitan region in 2020 was 1.27 million, which was almost a hundred thousand more than in 2010 but still below the 2000 level of 1.33 million. The city demographics also shifted along racial and ethnic lines. The city became slightly more White and slightly less Black and more Hispanic during the time since Katrina, although African Americans still constituted the largest single group with just 53% of the total population. The social transformation hoped for by many did not materialize. The poverty rate and murder rate in New Orleans continued to rank among the highest or at the highest level among large US metropolitan regions. With respect to flood protection, the debate at the federal level consistently diminished the level of approved funding. The promise of funding for flood protection against a Category 5 storm (~0.02% storm or 500-year storm) drifted away (Horowitz 2020). In 2007, Congress lowered the standard of protection again to one providing protection against a 1% probability (or a 1 in 100-year storm), largely abandoning the goal of making the city able to withstand another Katrina-type storm (Horowitz 2020).

8.2.3.2 Cedar Rapids, Iowa

The city of Cedar Rapids (population 137,710 and metropolitan area population of ~276,520 in 2020) is the second largest population center in the midwestern US state of Iowa. The city and state are crisscrossed by the drainage of the Missouri and Mississippi Rivers and so have a long history of flooding preparedness and response. The Cedar and Iowa Rivers, the most significant rivers passing through the Cedar Rapids Metropolitan Region (see Figure 8.3), flow into the Mississippi River. The land of Cedar River Valley was wrested from the Native American tribes who lived on the land up through the early decades of the nineteenth century. The first permanent White settlers occupied the area in the late 1830s/early 1840s and the city itself was incorporated in 1849. The city continued to grow steadily through the decades. It had a population of 25,656 in 1900, 72,296 in 1950, and 120,758 in 2000. The city prides itself on maintaining a high quality of life and tightly integrated communities and neighborhoods. Cedar Rapids nickname is the "City of Five Seasons," for the so-called fifth season, which is time to enjoy the

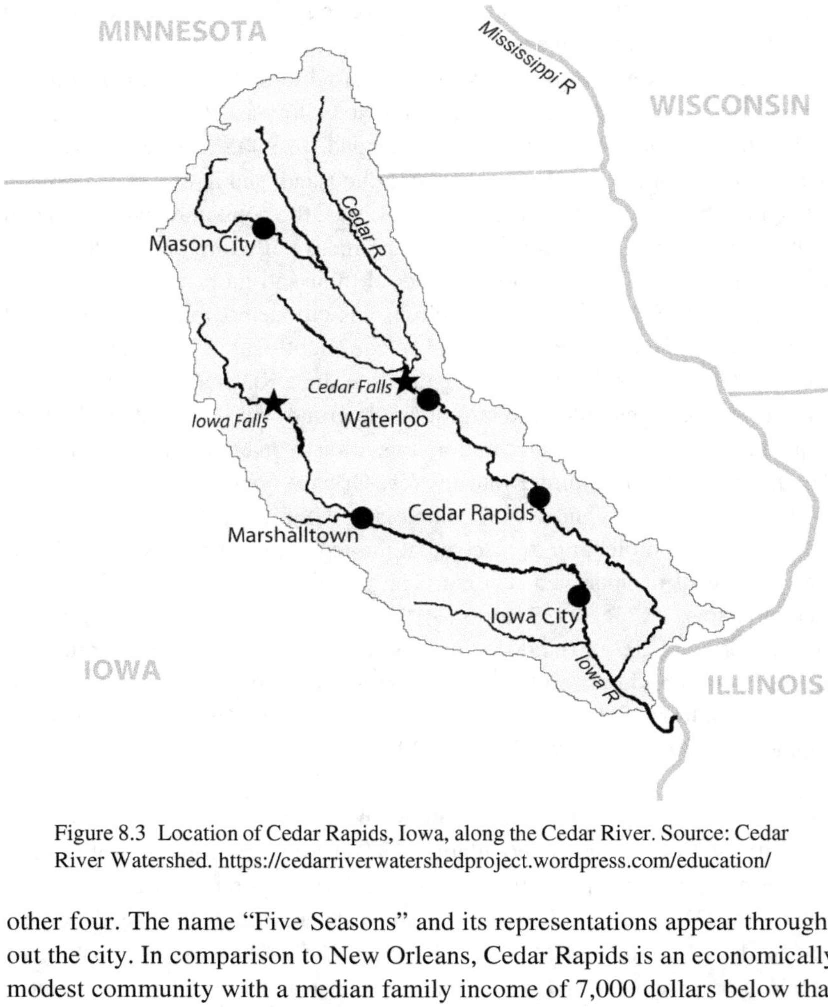

Figure 8.3 Location of Cedar Rapids, Iowa, along the Cedar River. Source: Cedar River Watershed. https://cedarriverwatershedproject.wordpress.com/education/

other four. The name "Five Seasons" and its representations appear throughout the city. In comparison to New Orleans, Cedar Rapids is an economically modest community with a median family income of 7,000 dollars below that of the US average (~67 thousand vs. 60 thousand in 2020) and a poverty rate at about the same as the US average of 11.4% in 2020. Cedar Rapids is an overwhelmingly white city with non-Hispanic Whites making up 80.1% of the population.

Stress – Cedar Rapids like all river front cities in the Mississippi Basin grew up on the river even though they faced the constant risk of floods. Before a massive flood in 2008, significant floods had occurred in Cedar Rapids, with 1851, 1929, 1955, 1966, and 1993 being especially significant. These floods crested at about 6 meters (20 feet), about 2.4 meters (8 feet) above flood stage. The connections between Cedar Rapids and the Cedar River are manifold.

The first non-native American settlement in the area was located on the east bank of the Cedar River and soon thereafter another settlement began on the west bank, and just after that on a small island (Mays Island) between the two was settled. As a compromise to boosterism interests on both the east and west banks, the island was designated as a site for government offices, even though the island and surrounding banks were known to be quite flood-prone. The river was used for steamboat transportation and the movement of cargo, but by the last quarter of the nineteenth century, the rail became the key mode of transport. The city and region continued to grow steadily during the twentieth century, as a variety of flood control levees were built along the river. The Great Flood of 1993, a key benchmark flood in the broader watershed, signaled a shift to more impactful floods (i.e., higher levels of loss and damage) in the state, and at that time became the worst flood in Iowa's recorded history. The Cedar River crested at 6 meters (19.83 feet) and significantly flooded some parts of downtown Cedar Rapids.

Crisis – Even as significant as the Great Flood of 1993 was, the 2008 Iowa flood blew past its record just 15 years later. The flood which began June 8 and continued until July 1 grew to take in most of the rivers in eastern Iowa. Critical levees were completely overtopped for the first time. The Cedar River reached a record high of 9.49 meters (31.12 feet) on June 13 surpassing the 500-year flood plain and more than 3 meters above the previous record. The flooding in the city was unprecedented as much of the downtown and surrounding residential areas on both sides of the river were impacted. More than 26 sq. km. (10 sq. miles) were flooded (14% of the city's total area), this included 1,126 city blocks of which 561 were severely damaged. Around 7,749 properties were flooded and had to be evacuated, including 5,900 homes. The government buildings on Mays Island (including the Cedar Rapids city hall, the local county and federal courthouses, and the local jail) were flooded up to the second-floor level. Water, electricity, natural gas, and telecommunications services were also disrupted.

Transition – The 2008 flood was a significant shock to the residents of Cedar Rapids. The Cedar River flooding shattered the previous record flood and many more areas of the city were flooded than ever before. Like New Orleans following Hurricane Katrina, the City of Cedar Rapids began an aggressive process of recovery. Just four days after the river crested on 17 June, the city government with an outside urban design consulting firm engaged the public (i.e., business and commerce, homeowners, and civil society) regarding possible recovery pathways through three public open house discussions attended by a total of 2,680 people. The discussions resulted in the development of a Framework for Reinvestment and Revitalization. The framework not only focused on recovery but also toward a vision of a "vibrant urban hometown – a beacon for people and businesses invested in building a greater community for the next generation." The approach was to link flood control with the creation of sustainable neighborhoods. In the first part of 2009, a massive public engagement, the Neighborhood Planning Process, was undertaken for ten separate neighborhoods. The Process was structured to ensure transparency and secure broad public participation. By mid-2009, the Cedar Rapids community created the framework of an action plan to mitigate future flooding and spur reinvestment, as well as a series of steps to implement the plan over the next 10 to 15 years. The final plan was defined as the River Corridor Redevelopment Plan (Jacob 2018; Tate et al. 2016). Nonlocal experts including folks from the Urban Land Institute (like in New Orleans) reviewed the efforts and made their own recommendations (Urban Land Institute 2009).

Transformation – One of the key elements of the Plan was the redevelopment of the city's river front. The efforts focused on encouraging retreat from at-risk residences and businesses through a buyout program (Smith 2014). In the summer of 2009, a coordinated buyout program funded by the US Housing and Urban Development began. The buyout program, although it had to be tweaked and adjusted, eventually enabled more than 1,300 properties to sell their properties. This flexible response and the presentation of opportunities for property owners to appeal both the purchase price and the property value appraisal were significant in fostering decisions to sell. The city government and local community-based organizations (CBOs) also developed a program to help homeowners and businessowners relocate within the community. Another key element of the plan was to rebuild and strengthen existing flood protection barriers or build new ones – although the construction as in New Orleans was pegged at the 1% flood and not the 0.02% (500-year flood), which the 2008 plan sought. This fact encouraged property owners in Cedar Rapids to relocate with the recognition that they would not be protected against future catastrophic floods, even though another flood in 2016 illustrated some positive benefits of the 2008 flood control actions were already being observed (Jacobs 2018).

8.2.4 Rotterdam, the Netherlands

Most of the city of Rotterdam in the Netherlands is either at or below sea level. The city specifically and the Netherlands generally have engaged in a multi-century struggle to both protect itself from the storm-related flooding while also attempting to wrest land for agricultural development and settlement from the tidal flats that defined the natural shoreline of the region (Corporaal and Jensen 2022). Even the name of the city speaks to this engagement with water.

Rotterdam in Dutch translates to the Dam on the River Rotte. In 2020, the population of the city was 651,446, while the larger Rotterdam-The Hauge metropolitan area has a population of approximately 2.7 million, making it the EU's 10th most populous. The city is a globally significant logistics and economic center and is Europe's most significant seaport and nicknamed the "Gateway to Europe" or the "Gateway to the World." Its strategic importance led to the city being significantly damaged during World War II – first by the Germans in the 1940s and intermittently by US and UK aerial bombardment over the next several years as the city remained in German control from May 1940 until the latter part of 1944. After the war, Rotterdam was able to engage in a process of rebuilding the city and expanding settlement and economic activity.

8.2.4.1 Stress

The city is subject to flooding from both coastal storms, often powerful remnants of tropical cyclones that move west to east across the North Atlantic, as well as inland rain events that bring riverine flooding. The history of the Netherlands and Rotterdam specifically is complete with numerous significant storm events that frequently killed 10,000s each, including the St. Felix's flood of 1530 that cost more than 100,000 lives and the Christmas flood of 1717 that resulted in approximately 15,000 deaths. The city of Rotterdam was built upon a complex delta geography in a highly exposed location. Some 30 kilometers (19 miles) from the North Sea, it lies along the banks of the New Meuse (Nieuwe Maas) River, which functions as the Rhine River's northern distributary. The city of Rotterdam was built out across two distinct zones. The historic urban center of the city was built on a slightly elevated peatland area that was surrounded by dikes as early as the thirteenth century. Just to the south of this site were a series of deltaic lowland islands on which the port facilities were first constructed. Up through the mid-nineteenth century, the bulk of the city was located on the north bank of the New Meuse River and protected by an extended dike and the area around the port was built on raised areas outside of the dikes. In 1863, a series of comprehensive dredging and dike building projects were begun that enabled the construction of the modern deep-water port of Rotterdam and opened new areas for urban development. This part of the city was the one heavily damaged by World War II and became the center of plans for rebuilding following the war (Meyer et al. 2012).

8.2.4.2 Crisis

In 1946, planners ambitious to rebuild the city developed the *Basic Scheme* for the reconstruction of the City of Rotterdam, then often referred to as the *Basic Plan*. The focus of the effort was the reconstruction and expansion of the port, which was the center of economic activity and growth. The postwar redevelopment trajectory was fundamentally redirected on February 1, 1953, with the onset of another catastrophic flooding disaster called the Great North Sea flood.

The flooding was caused by a dramatic storm surge that resulted from a severe windstorm combined with low barometric air pressure that occurred just at a high spring tide. The storm surge flooded lands up to 5.6 meters (18.4 feet) above mean sea level. The storm surge overwhelmed many of the sea defenses and the dikes in the Zeeland area just south of Rotterdam were breached in 67 separate locations (Meyer et al. 2012). The urban core of the city was lightly impacted in comparison to the areas to the immediate south and near the port area. Most of the communities affected were just above, at, or below sea level. The worst of the flooding occurred late on a Saturday evening and was associated with a limited warning response capacity – that is, local radio stations did not operate late in the evening and many meteorological offices were closed for the weekend. The flooding killed 1,835 people, forced the emergency evacuation of approximately 70,000 more, 30,000 animals were killed, 47,300 buildings damaged, 160,000 ha of polderland (~9% of Dutch farmland) flooded. The total damage was estimated to be 1–1.5 billion Dutch Guilders (~3–4.5 billion USD today) and shocked the nation.

8.2.4.3 Transition

The flood helped crystallize several significant sentiments regarding future flood control efforts. The dike and polder system had been weakened during the preceding decades by inadequate maintenance and management that was significantly made worse by the wartime occupation. The Germans built defensive structures into the dykes. Animals digging barrows further compromised their integrity (Gerritsen 2005; Weesjes 2015). Immediately following the floods, thousands of residents began the work of reconstructing and repairing the dikes. Aware of the complexity and often conflicting local-level decisions being made, the process was quickly centralized signaling a significant shift in management protocol from local community repair and maintenance that had been the norm for centuries. The Rijkswaterstaat, the Directorate-General of the Netherlands Ministry of Infrastructure and Water Management, founded in 1798 as the Burea voor den Waterstaat, took over control. By November of 1953, all the dike breaches were closed (Gerritsen, 2005).

The centralization of authority was further advanced by the blending of several planning efforts already underway within a renewed focus on flood control. Just 20 days after the flood, national officials, significantly shaken by the flood effects, appointed the Delta Works committee to research the causes of the disaster and develop measures to eliminate, as much as possible, future risk (Weesjes 2015). The committee took on the task to revise the pre-flood projects and formulate what became known as the Delta Plan. The plan included an extensive series of dams and storm surge barriers with corresponding sluices and locks, as well as an upgrading of the dike system that included heightening and strengthening (Meyer et al. 2012). The Delta Plan was very significant to the development of the city and expansion of the port, which helped make Rotterdam the largest port in the world by the early 1960s.

8.2.4.4 Transformation

The full implementation of the Delta Plan from the late 1950s through its completion in the late 1990s has led to a transformation of Rotterdam, its port, and the surrounding region. The plans were designed to protect areas around the estuaries of the Rhine, Scheldt, and Meuse Rivers. The 40-year building effort was capped off with the 1998 completion of a massive storm surge barrier near Rotterdam. The Delta Plan brought substantial expansion of the lands protected by flood barriers as well as new lands that could be opened for new urban development. Overlaying on these changes has come the increased recognition that the Delta Plan led to the massive loss of coastal wetlands and ecosystems that are critical to long-term ecological sustainability and the provision of nature-based, resilience-focused solutions. The city administration of Rotterdam became quite aware of the need to blend the demands of port operations, urban development and enhanced quality of life, flood control and sustainability, and in turn, created the Rotterdam Climate Initiative in 2008 to make the city a global model of sustainability and climate proofing (Meyer et al. 2012).

An innovative part of the Delta Plan was the ambition to define long-term solutions and not just responses to past disasters but also against future floods. A key objective was to develop plans to enhance resilience against very low probability yet high consequence events – like catastrophic flooding. The efforts included a series of rational planning methods[1] including the use of statistically based risk models and loss and damage cost estimates. Acceptable risk levels were determined for areas of the coasts and built to the standard of 1 in a 10,000-year event. These acceptable risks were put into the Delta Law (Dutch: *Deltawet*). The Law required the government to maintain risks of catastrophic flooding at or below these limits and to upgrade defenses as new insights and knowledge of these risks emerge. At the same time, all other existing defenses had to be upgraded to meet the new norm.

[1] A model of the planning process involving a number of rational actions or steps.

8.3 Discussion

The role of risk and hazards as drivers in environmental policy transitions is complicated. A common understanding is that such conditions, especially a disastrous extreme event, result in a shift or transition in policy. The observed conditions illustrate that the situation is much more nuanced. In some circumstances extreme events do lead to significant shifts, but in many others they do not, while in other situations a sequence of events or even a minor isolated event is associated with major policy changes. A fundamental question is why are there such differences?

8.3.1 Conditions of Crisis

It is well understood that some places in the world are climatologically and meteorologically more variable than others and therefore more subject to climate extremes. That said, all sites even those without a lot of weather variation are subject to relative extremes when the temperature, precipitation, or other conditions vary significantly from the norm and become what would be statistically described as low-probability weather events. Whether a specific extreme event becomes a hazardous event for a city is then directly related to the exposure and vulnerability of the location's population, infrastructure, and other critical systems. Each of the case study sites is subject to climate extremes, but the conditions of the risk and hazard have been made worse by the level and pattern of economic development and urban land use. The interconnection between the extreme event(s) and the physical and cultural conditions of the sites resulted in increased stress and eventual crisis. Of critical importance to the characterization of a risk and hazard-related crisis was that in some cases the crisis was fomented through a set of compound or closely sequential events – where one significant disaster followed close in time after another event. In other situations, the crisis was set off not only by the current conditions but also projections of future climate change and the likelihood of more frequent or more intense extremes.

8.3.2 Drivers of Transitions

The drivers of the risk management policy transitions are varied but typically center on (1) a confluence of loss and damage and the potential for more (and via climate change a lot more), (2) significant and well-understood vulnerability, and (3) most importantly a functioning governance structure and the financial resources to respond. In one case – Kolkata – the process

Table 8.1 *Key drivers observed in each case study. Source: Author.*

	Drivers		
Case Study	Root	Context	Proximate
Abu Dhabi	Intense summer heat and humidity; rapid urbanization and growth from oil and natural gas wealth; traditional designs to mitigate heat – cultural factors	Increased heating because of climate change and prospects for significantly more heating; extensive financial resources to mitigate urban heat conditions; planning and design	Very alarming scientific reports from the late 2010s about extreme heat projections
Kolkata	Water-dominated site for a city; colonial history of exploitation; British engineering tradition of hubris; flooding and typhoon history; rapid population growth and inequities	Series of failed hydrological projects; lack of governance capacity to maintain flood control facilities	
Mississippi River Basin – Cedar Rapids and New Orleans	Massive flood-prone water system; historical connection between waterways and transport and commerce; cities built in a highly vulnerable locations. History of social cohesion in Cedar Rapids – not so in NOLA – inequity and wide poverty rate differences and racism	Highly varying social response. Unity and harmony in Cedar Rapids; not so in NOLA. Pull back of federal commitment to protection against 1 in 500-year event in both cases	Key flooding events – Hurricane Katrina and the 2008 flood
Rotterdam	Massive flood-prone water system; historical connection between waterways and transport and commerce; city built in a highly vulnerable location. History of centralized, regional, and rational planning; extensive history of flooding	Loss of flood infrastructure because of World War II damage and occupation; comprehensive planning effort at the national level; planning to address low probability–high consequence events	The 1953 flood, particularly acute because of weekend timing

of transition and transformation was not fully completed – largely because of a lack of governance capacity and financial resources. This left the city in a continued state of heightened flood hazard stress if not crisis. A key question remains why did this lack of capacity and limiting enabling conditions persist in Kolkata, and not as much in the three other cases. One can point to conditions such as contextual factors such as uncontrolled land use/land cover change, congestion, and decay of drainage channels but also more culpable factors, such as the root drivers of the failed British colonial flood protection projects.

8.3.3 Spheres of Action and Legacies

Interlocking patterns and trajectories of social organization and structure set in motion conditions that persistently influence the prospects for hazard management and hazard management transitions. Complex system interactions were widely evident throughout each of the cases, leading to varying outcomes and limits and barriers to risk management transitions. Underlying social conditions were perhaps the most consistently powerful throughout the case studies. In the case of Kolkata, underlying social tensions and the political economy of urban development have led to vast differences in risk and hazards vulnerability with the creation of highly marginalized at-risk populations (Rumbach 2017). The opposite is the case in Rotterdam where extensive social programs and integration have created a landscape where large-scale regional flood control programs have long been accepted and integrated into the fabric of daily life. The influence of different drivers is quite evident in the comparison of the New Orleans and Cedar Rapids case examples. Both communities, though quite different in size, face significant flood risk and are located along sites of the same river system. Socio-economically, they are vastly different, however. The entrenched poverty, vast social and economic inequities, systemic racism, and divisive politics in New Orleans disrupted the development of progressive policy shifts and transformation following Hurricane Katrina in 2005. The community context of Cedar Rapids was vastly different with greater equity and less poverty. In comparison, the Cedar Rapids community context was built on a history of social cohesion and ability to work collectively in response to extreme events. Does this cohesion result from the reduced level of poverty and socio-economic inequity or from other factors embedded within the city? This is an issue that merits more investigation.

Legacy plays a significant role in connecting hazard stress to crisis and crisis to transition. How past events are understood, the narratives regarding why there was loss and damage, and the effectiveness of past responses all play a large role in the shaping of the transition process. In all four cases, the lived experience of past extremes and implications for everyday life had long-lasting consequences for how the cities socially constructed hazard risk and the extent to which this became a factor in the policy transition. Flooding became part of the cultural identity of each city, and how it responded to the threat was seen as saying something significant about the city – either good or bad. As expected, infrastructure systems and technology choice also had significant legacy effects. Decisions to build and locate physical structures including flood control features had significant impacts on the debates and character of the policy transitions that took place. Perhaps none more explicit than the case of Cedar Rapids, where the decision was made to locate key government buildings on a small highly vulnerable island in the middle of the two settlements growing on either bank of the Cedar River.

8.3.3.1 Urban Risks and Hazards and Climate Change

Is it well understood that climate change will result in more frequent and more intense extreme weather events? Urban populations and infrastructure will be exposed to a greater probability of loss and damage associated with these events. Urban climates have become more dynamic and have entered into a state of flux – meaning that stakeholders and managers are less able to predict the upper bounds on what types of weather and climate conditions could occur. Extreme flooding, from fluvial, pluvial, and storm surge events, and extreme heat are the climate change-driven extremes for cities most well-documented. Of course, cities have long experienced these types of hazards, the likelihood of a city experiencing them in conditions not previously recorded has become an increasing concern for city managers, stakeholders, and residents. As evidenced globally, cities already have begun to experience record heat waves and flooding events (Dodman et al. 2022). Other extreme risks associated with climate change include drought, landslides, dust storms, heavy snow episodes, salt water intrusion, as well as a series of compound risks (when two or more hazards occur simultaneously) and cascade risks (when one hazard event results in a second occurring and possibly others) scenarios.

The case studies provide the basis for several recommendations for those focused on urban hazards and risks in the context of climate change.

- Trust in government – governments should work consistently to develop trust with the communities in which they operate. This trust was incredibly important for cities when addressing urban hazards and risks. Risk and hazard mitigation advances require full community and stakeholder engagement in meaningful large-scale solutions. Climate change will expand the range of hazard impacts in a way that may severely test or exceed the current risk management capacity in many cities. As a result, it is not unlikely that climate change will result in a renewed sense of hazard crisis in locations where hazard risk has been reduced and elevate the risk level in cities where significant risk is still present. In both situations, climate change will likely force calls for extensions or reevaluations of existing risk and hazard control features and strategies.

- Hazard crisis focus – cities typically focus on one key hazard risk. In fact, one hazard type often can define the identity of the city, as seen in the case studies. New Orleans is known for flooding and Abu Dhabi for extreme heat. The pattern of crisis and adjustment typically defines the social history of hazard management in the city. The hazard management focus moving forward in a climate change-altered world will likely demand that this focus be continued. The lessons learned will provide the basis for growth and extension as the risk profile of the city is altered more with climate change. It is clear some cities might have to add a second or third major hazard risk to their identity. As noted later in Chapter 10, Miami, known for its hurricane and flooding risks, also will have to face the increased frequency of extreme heat.
- Opportunity of defining extreme event – extreme hazard events are defining events in cities and allow the city to profoundly connect with root and proximate drivers of hazard and risk policy transitions. Cities should be as ready as possible to take advantage of future-defining extreme events and facilitate accelerated movement from the crisis stage to opportunities for transition. Cities should not only develop robust emergency preparedness and response protocols; they also should be ready to meaningfully learn from the event and identify significant policy adjustments or transformations.
- Significance of legacy – the legacy of past crises and proposed management transitions are highly significant in urban risk and hazard management work. These histories are deeply ingrained in the city, as are the public programs and engineering infrastructure developed to respond to these past crises. It will be important for current and future managers and stakeholders to study this history, understand its significance for the city and its residents and businesses, and as possible use to their advantage.

- Avoiding hurry up and wait – debates about what to do about risks and hazards simmer for a long time and often are not advanced because they typically involve significant investment of expensive social and political capital. In the context of climate change and the onrush of exacerbated risk from hazards long thought largely subdued or still present, or even new hazards, there will be demand for innovative mechanisms to assess risk and new strategies to respond to emerging crises as quickly as possible.

9

Resource Use Efficiency and Pathways to Environmental Sustainability

The Three Rs (Reduce, Reuse, Recycle)

> "*For a policy like this to work, you have to make each one responsible for his personal consumption. You need waste disposal to sit firmly in the public consciousness…It's what makes [a] circular economy actually happen.*" Lai Ying-ying, Head of the Taiwan Environmental Protection Administration's (EPA's) waste management department describing the fines or public shaming that are part of the nation's aggressive trash recycling program (Lai 2019).

Environmental sustainability is one of the grand challenges of our day. The question of environmental sustainability was first widely recognized within the Brundtland report (i.e., *Our Common Future*), published in 1987 by the World Commission on Environment and Development. The report framed the concept of sustainable development and described how it could be achieved. Fundamental to sustainable development is the concept of the triple bottom line that requires the integration of economic sustainability, social sustainability, and environmental sustainability. Environmental sustainability is also associated with pathways to promote resource use efficiency that promote the three Rs (reduce, reuse, recycle). In the context of cities, environmental sustainability has been interpreted in a variety of ways, including promoting shifts in business and consumer natural resource decision-making and use patterns, greenhouse gas (GHG) carbon equivalent emission reductions, reducing air, water, and land pollution, and the promotion of ecosystem services. Among these varying facets of environmental sustainability, the focus of this chapter is how cities have addressed solid waste crises.

The question of how cities can manage their waste produced within their borders has been a constant challenge, stress, and crisis throughout history. Waste management is crucial for the protection of local public health and everyday quality of life for residents. Cities with rapid population growth and increased resource use are especially at risk to have a waste management crisis. Solid waste management (SWM) is a quickly growing issue for the world's developing countries, which are typically experiencing significant urban population growth coupled with growing economies and wealth along with growing income disparities, as well as insufficient public resources and capacity to manage the mounting waste. Coupled with the growing social and economic demands of the urban poor and their quest for a viable livelihood and work, and the aspirations for environmental sustainability, SWM systems have grown in significance and importance across the world's cities. In this chapter, several-city specific transformations are presented that illustrate how the crisis of waste management became a mechanism for resolving this ancient question of how to manage a city's waste while also advancing broader-scale sustainability efforts within the community.

9.1 Waste Management as an Urban Crisis

As soon as settlements began, the question of where to deposit their waste started as well. In ancient Jerusalem, the Dung Gate[1] was the doorway in the walled city through which residents would remove ash, dung, and other waste from the city's temples, residences, and streets and dispose of it in the Kidron Valley, just outside the gate. The Kidron Valley is a downwind location from the city so that the smells of refuse would dissipate away from the locations where it was generated. Like in ancient Jerusalem, how to manage waste generated in contemporary cities requires a significant understanding of how everyday life takes place, the structure and organization of society, and the connection between humans and their environment.

Solid waste management is much more than just an issue of nuisance and noxious smells, it is clearly a significant public health issue. Solid waste when not properly managed can easily cause a variety of environmental and public health crises including the pollution of critical surface and groundwater supplies or serve as a breeding ground for disease and infection. Waterborne diseases that heavily impacted urban water supplies include cholera, diarrhea, dysentery, hepatitis A, typhoid, and polio. The World Health Organization estimates that at least 2 billion people use a feces-contaminated drinking water source (WHO 2022). When solid waste is left on city streets, back alleys, and

[1] The origin of the gate's name dates back some 2,500 years as it is mentioned as one of the city's gates during the times of the Return to Zion (538 BCE) and noted in the Book of Nehemiah.

empty lots, it can become a haven for urban pests such as rats, cockroaches, and other animals typically described as vermin. The presence of rats feeding on discarded waste was and continues to be associated with disease and pestilence. Most infamously, rats were associated with the Black Death outbreak of bubonic plague that struck the world in the fourteenth century, and the imagery of rats as an urban scourge continues today (Sullivan 2005). Overall, the presence of solid waste piling up in the streets of a city is often presented as a failure, disarray, and illustration of underlying or looming stress, if not crisis (Melosi 2005).

A wide variety of solid waste is generated in cities. The most basic category of waste is the excrement or feces generated by humans and animals living in cities. Human excrement in cities and towns before modern sanitation was removed from households and buildings by local carters or collectors who often came in the evening or night – hence the name "night soil" for these collections. Depending on the traditions and norms of the society, human waste was used as fertilizer or otherwise disposed of. Animal waste similarly had to be regularly removed from cities often crammed with all types of animals. Before the widespread advent of automobiles and trucks, horses and other animals used for transport and work crowded city streets.

Environmental historians McShane and Tarr (2011) estimated how much horse manure would have been produced by the 100,000–200,000 horses that were estimated to be on the streets of New York City in the late nineteenth century. With each horse producing approximately 6.8–13.6 kg (15–30 lbs.) of waste per day, this would result in a range of 680,000 kg to 2.7 million kg (1.5–6.0 million lbs.) of fecal waste needing to be managed every day. In addition, typically more than 10,000 horses died per year in the city, many expiring on the streets and as a result also had to be removed. As an example, in 1880, 15,000 dead horses had to be lifted from New York City's streets. Dead horses were especially challenging given their weight to remove, and often were left to decay until the bodies could be more easily dismembered (McShane and Tarr 2011).

In other circumstances, animals in cities were not only a source of labor, transport, or nutrients (such as pigs, chickens, and cows), but they also helped to resolve some of the waste issues in cities. Before New York City developed an aggressive waste removal system in the late nineteenth century, the city streets were often clogged with waste of all kinds. The private carters that were hired to remove waste typically only did so in wealthy neighborhoods whose residents could pay the fees. In many parts of the city, hogs roamed the city eating from the waste piles and debris found on the streets. The hogs, while producing significant quantities of waste themselves (~5 kg [11lbs.] per day), did eat and remove waste, and also when slaughtered served as a crucial nutrient source for the city's large poor population (McNeur 2014).

A variety of other wastes also are generated in cities. The most significant sources are residences, industrial and manufacturing facilities, commercial establishments, construction and demolition, and institutions including schools, hospitals, and other government services. The World Bank estimates that the amount of waste generated globally is approximately 2.01 billion tonnes (2.22 billion tons) (year 2016), of which 33% is poorly managed through open dumping or burning (Kaza et al. 2018). The volume and composition of commercial and consumer waste have varied widely across time and space. In the US, the volume of solid municipal waste has increased from 79.9 million tonnes (88.1 million tons) per year in 1960 to 265.3 million tonnes (292.4 million tons) in 2018, while the volume of waste generated per capita has increased but at a slower rate, from 1.22 kg (2.68 lbs) per day to 2.22 kg (4.9.lbs) per day (US EPA 2025). In the UK, from the mid-1930s to the mid-1980s, the volume of waste from ash reduced dramatically, mostly from the reduction of coal use for heating and uses, while the amount of paper and plastics rose significantly with a parallel but slower rise in organic matter (Bridgewater 1986). In many developing countries, cities in the past half century have seen tremendous population growth and increased resource consumption that have resulted in a rapid rise in the volume of waste generation and often a limited governance capacity to manage the volume of waste. This condition has accelerated the SWM crisis in these settings. In low-income countries, the issue is especially acute since slightly less than half (48%) of the waste generated in cities is collected and managed (Kaza et al. 2018).

Like the time of the Dung Gate in ancient Jerusalem, throughout much of the modern era, urban commercial and household waste typically was either dumped in nearby sites or burned in open pits. As these practices were increasingly seen as noxious, undesirable, or more difficult to do because of limited space available for dumping, more distant locations or locations less able to protest (e.g., economically, racially, or ethnically marginal communities) became more widely used. Construction debris and demolition waste and other large-scale landscape transformations produce a lot of waste, especially in concert with rapid urban development. Waste of this sort because of its massive volume and weight was often dumped locally as fill into wetlands, marshes, open water, or other low-elevation sites. The remains of demolished buildings and structures also often become the foundation for new construction. The Citadel within the city of Erbil in northern Iraq has taken shape over thousands of years of human occupation partially on the remains of demolished or destroyed buildings at the site. As another example, the extensive wetlands that ringed much of the City of New York's shoreline were almost completely filled in by dumping of construction debris, demolition waste, coal, and wood ash. More recently, the rapid growth of Chinese cities over the past three decades has generated massive volumes of material to dispose. Lu et al. (2017) estimated that approximately 1.03 billion tonnes (1.13 billion tons) of construction and demolition materials were generated in China during 2014 alone.

While the issue of how to manage urban waste has vexed cities for millennia, significant progress has been made in the past 150 years in many cities as new modes of waste management techniques and systems have been developed including the engineering of sewerage treatment facilities, the professionalization of the public sanitation departments and agencies, and the removal of animals from city streets. The pigs that roamed New York City's streets at numbers up to 20,000 (estimated in the 1820s) were driven north out of what constituted the city in 1859 and out into the upper half of Manhattan Island (McNeur 2014). While the rise of the sanitary city in late nineteenth century and early twentieth Europe and North America can be heralded (Melosi 1999), many cities in developing countries are still making these transitions. Even with these advances, the challenge of urban commercial and household waste management has remained in many Global North cities as local landfills have filled and closed, and open burning of garbage banned. Long-distance dumping and ocean or lake dumping for coastal cities also had clear limits associated with legal constraints, ecological or natural resource implications, and increasing costs of waste disposal.

Solid waste management was further advanced as a important component of environmental sustainability with the promulgation of the United Nations Sustainable Development Goals generally, and Goal 12 more specifically, which focused on responsible consumption and production. A primary focus in the SDG process has been on how to enhance the reuse of items and recycling in a way that they can be used as materials for other production processes leading toward a condition known as zero waste, where no material is landfilled or otherwise disposed of. In less developed countries, waste management has become especially complicated because rapid population growth in many such countries has generated a significant increase in local waste generation overwhelming the capacity of municipal authorities to provide basic services. The deterioration of the solid waste infrastructure in such settings is coupled with economic stagnation in many cities, which further worsens the ability of urban managers to provide services. This condition coupled with unsanitary waste management has resulted in widespread health hazards and urban environmental degradation (Simatele et al. 2017).

Solid waste management, in many ways, has become a touchstone for a set of larger questions regarding environmental sustainability. While it does not encompass the risks associated with water scarcity or extreme urban pollution, SWM directly connects to fundamental questions of lessening or altering patterns of resource consumption and the function of urban society. The Zero Waste movement, which significantly advanced in the early 2000s, focuses "on the conservation of all resources by means of responsible production, consumption, reuse, and recovery of products, packaging, and materials without burning and with no discharges to land, water, or air that threaten the environment or human health" (see https://zwia.org/). The concept of Zero Waste has been adopted by hundreds of cities globally. At the same time, the notion of a closed city (as opposed to an open city) that adheres to a circular economy paradigm that can be more fully self-sustaining through local food and energy production and enhanced recycling and reuse also has gained traction among urbanists focused on sustainability, industrial ecology, and equity (Zeller et al. 2019; Lakatos et al. 2021).

9.2 Case Studies

To examine these intersecting issues, the chapter focuses on four city-level case studies in waste management and the three Rs (reduce, reuse, recycle). The case studies present illustration of the integration of environmental sustainability concepts into everyday practice within municipal government, businesses, and households, and the connection between the cities waste management crises and eventual policy transitions. The case studies include Buenos Aires, Argentina, Johannesburg, South Africa, Seattle, USA, and Taipei, Taiwan.

9.2.1 Buenos Aires, Argentina

Buenos Aires, the capital city of Argentina, is often described as the second largest city in South America (with Sao Paulo, Brazil, being the largest). While the city's population has remained steady since the 1940s – about 3 million – the surrounding metropolitan region has grown significantly with a total metropolitan population, including the city, now approximately 15 million. Buenos Aires historically has been the primate city in the country with the metropolitan region often accounting for nearly half of Argentina's gross national product. With respect to solid waste, it is estimated that the metropolitan region currently generates approximately 5,443 tonnes (6,000 tons) of waste daily (Sequeira 2015). SWM in the city is intimately connected to a series of complex socio-economic changes over the past 50 plus years within Buenos Aires and the country itself.

A period of economic and political instability in Argentina starting in the 1970s set off a series of national turns that brought significant shifts to Buenos Aires and everyday life in the city. Buenos Aires' population experienced widening income disparities during this period. The purchasing power of most households, except for those wealthier families, declined significantly from 1974 to 1990 and remained at low levels throughout the early 2000s. Poverty levels also increased dramatically. In 1974, fewer than 5% of households in the city lived below the poverty line, but by 1990 approximately 25% lived in poverty (Altimir 2002). Simultaneous to these shifts and associated tensions came foreign interest-driven, neoliberal reforms instituted especially in the 1990s as part of an effort to privatize many of the city services including waste management. The result was that the management of the city's environmental concerns and problems changed significantly with increased service deficiencies and inequities, and a rising informal sector to fill service gaps. Simultaneously, the city attempted to recognize and respond to a series of social, economic, political, and environmental challenges (e.g., increasing social fragmentation, economic deprivation, the end of military rule and return of democracy, and environmental sustainability demands) that resulted in a series of shifts in local waste management resulting in a complex layering process and limited solution spaces.

9.2.1.1 Stress

In Buenos Aires, local SWM has been a consistent challenge and stress. The stresses emerged from a triad of pressures associated with the constraints on dumping practice, external policy pressures, and grinding poverty and underemployment. For decades, the official method of disposal was sanitary landfills by waste treatment companies hired by local governments. Unofficially, a number of the mechanisms have operated including illegal open dumps and a large informal carting economy. Dumping of waste in sanitary landfills can be expensive and is not sustainable over the long run. Waste incineration was made illegal in Buenos Aires Province (the larger political unit in which the city of Buenos Aires is located) in 1978 (Schamber 2010). In response to decreasing viability of landfill dumping and an emerging environmental agenda against illegal burning and dumping, an aggressive waste recycling effort was launched. At the same time, cities such as Buenos Aires faced the implementation of a series of economic and administrative reform efforts that emerged during the 1960s as part of an international development agenda.

Since the 1960s, a wide range of engineering models and system strategies had been applied to less developed country cities to promote what was described as formal and rational decision-making processes and planning to in part optimize existing SWM systems. What was absent from these models were socio-cultural conditions and structures and the role of stakeholders in the SWM systems (Nilsson 2016). SWM stakeholders missing from the analysis were government officials, local communities, industrial interests and other formal private sector service providers, as well as the informal sectors especially the litter pickers (Marshall and Farahbakhsh 2013). Since the models failed to take local contextual conditions under consideration, the new strategies developed from them often were disconnected from how SWM was actually happening and how it could be advanced. For example, it is typically the case in less developed country cities that the public service institutions to manage waste are not present while at the same time high poverty rates and limited employment opportunities push a large number of residents to depend on collecting and selling recyclable materials for livelihoods. Informal litter pickers or *carteneros* (in Buenos Aires) play a large often unrecognized role yet in most developing country cities' recycling systems. The informal recycling sector can reduce the collection and disposal needs for local governments (Velis 2012).

9.2.1.2 Crisis

The crisis in Buenos Aires waste management strategy occurred in a stair-step fashion as much of the advance of neoliberal adjustments had run its course, and as the significant limitations of the then current approach to waste management began to emerge. The neoliberal reform-driven privatization effort led to widely diverse outcomes and different rates of waste management success (Altimir et al. 2002; Bonelli 2018). In poorer neighborhoods, private waste removal had been less successful. This lack of services, coupled with the absence of opportunity in these same marginalized neighborhoods, led to the rapid development of an informal waste management economy and associated management regime. In the early 2000s, a large number of poorer Buenos Aires residents were being pushed into litter picking because of the economic collapse, structural unemployment, and increased poverty. The Argentinian economy collapsed at the end of 2001 with its GDP severely declining from \$268.7 billion USD in 2001 to \$97.7 billion USD in the next year. The percent of the national workforce making less than \$5.5 per day skyrocketed to almost 50% (49.9% in 2002 from 31.5% in 2000) (World Bank data – https://datatopics.worldbank.org/world-development-indicators/). At the same time, the movement to integrated SWM had stalled and the price for raw materials spiked further driving more people into the informal garbage market – leading to increased competition between the formal economy carters and waste haulers and the *carteneros* (Schamber 2010). Simultaneously, the drive to promote sustainability reforms created and spurred an ambition to develop a decentralized and sustainable waste management process that provides jobs for individuals in poorer Buenos Aires neighborhoods but also recognizes the value of recycling (Carenzo et al. 2022).

9.2.1.3 Transition

In the 2000s then, waste management in Buenos Aires became tied to the growing social tensions, environmental requirements for enhanced recycling and waste reduction, and the need to respond to the growing significance of the informal economy, and the dependence on it of the city's poorer residents. Structural adjustments, including a transition in the waste management structure, were required to respond to the crisis. A key transition moment was the making of litter picking legal in 2002 (Balch 2016). The moment became a touchstone as a series of other advances that promoted the informal picker economy as part of the formal economy and utilized it to fill the existing solid waste management gaps and enhance prospects for sustainability. In 2005, a zero-waste law was implemented in the city that had four goals. The ultimate goal was to reduce to zero the amount of recyclable material entered in landfills by 2020. At the same time, Buenos Aires reached its landfill peak in 2012 and no more land to create new landfills was available locally.

9.2.1.4 Transformation

In the late 2000s and early 2010s, the Buenos Aires city government promoted a Ciudad Verde (Green City) project in an effort to reduce the amounts of generated waste and waste sent to landfills and to increase the levels of recycling. While the city was able to achieve some aspects of these goals, the full range of goals remained to be met and the actual amounts of waste deposited in landfills increased and continued to rise (Nilsson 2016). The landfill crisis that reached another peak in 2012, when Buenos Aires' surrounding provinces started to reject the city's trash.

To further accelerate recycling, the city struck a deal with the *carteneros* with the help of the Argentine Federation of Litter Pickers and Recyclers. The Federation represents about a dozen recycling cooperatives that operate in central Buenos Aires and have connections with the politically left-wing *Movimiento de Trabajadores Excluidos* (Movement of Excluded Workers). Under the city government's plan, more than 5,000 people would collect a base salary (as a subsidy) with state-sponsored minimal social security benefits and a small pension for emptying recycling bins that began to appear on the city streets in the early and mid-2010s (more than seven years after the zero-waste law was put into effect). The agreement created an opportunity to see the litter pickers as workers providing a valuable public service for the city (Balch 2016). That said, the process of transformation is still far from complete as still only about a third of *carteneros* were employed, competition with formal private recycling has increased, and limited government investment in areas away from the business districts reduced opportunities to expand the recycling efforts.

9.2.2 Johannesburg, South Africa

Johannesburg is one of the largest cities in Sub-Saharan Africa with a population of approximately 5.8 million as of 2020 and a metropolitan regional population of 10.5 (estimated). Several million additional people also might live in the region on an undocumented basis, and so the total population could be significantly higher. The racist policy of apartheid, which ended in the early 1990s, left the city highly segregated and largely divided along racial and economic lines (Ballard and Hamann 2021). In general, the core of the metropolitan region remains whiter and significantly wealthier than the surrounding expansive townships. Beyond this legacy, increased consumerism and sustained economic growth as well as population growth have resulted in a significant increase in waste generation during the past 30 years as well. For the city of Johannesburg itself, the population more than doubled from the period 1990 to 2010 increasing by 2.4 million. During the same time, the economy of the region grew at a rate of approximately 3.7% per year, higher than the national rate of 2.7% at the same time.[2]

9.2.2.1 Stress

As in most developing countries, waste management in South Africa only started being seriously addressed in the mid to late 1980s (Thomas-Hope 1998). The country has had the additional burden of the apartheid policy and immediate post-apartheid policy reforms adjustments, both of which had an additional profound impact on the country's SWM structure. During the apartheid era in South Africa from 1948 to the early 1990s, SWM was significantly underfunded and uncoordinated. This resulted in inadequate waste collection service, illegal dumping, too few permitted landfills, insufficient waste reduction and recycling initiatives, an absence of comprehensive regulation

[2] Source: www.commonwealthofnations.org/partner/city-of-johannesburg-metropolitan-municipality/#).

and enforcement of legislation, and in fact very limited waste-related legislation at all. South Africa's first law that required waste disposal sites to be permitted was only passed in 1989 (The Environment Conservation Act of 1989 – Act No. 73 of 1989). Furthermore, the implementation of the law proved to be a significant challenge. As of 2006, domestic waste in South Africa was dumped in approximately 1,203 landfills of which only 524 were actually permitted, meaning that the remaining continued to operate illegally (Greben and Oelofse 2009).

This widespread unlicensed and unpermitted disposal practices and facilities (Fiehn and Ball 2005; Nahman and Godfrey 2010) served as the foundation of stress on the SWM system in South African cities. Otherwise during the apartheid era, municipal solid waste in Johannesburg was traditionally most often either landfilled, dumped, or burned. Recycling at a minimal level was present as early as the mid-1970s in many South African cities, including Johannesburg. Most of the recycling was done by private carters and companies and specifically focused on commodities from which market value could be derived. Waste sorting facilities in major urban areas in Johannesburg and Pretoria, the adjacent national capital district, were already noted at this time. For one type of waste – paper – the recovery rate for South Africa was reported as 23% in 1973. In these early years, waste recycling in the country was most often driven by social needs and demands for resources that were scarce at that moment (Godfrey and Oelofse 2017). In this case, South Africa lacking extensive forest cover and associated paper production capacity made recycled paper important as a resource to compensate for this relative scarcity.

In the early post-apartheid era (mid-1990s and beyond), effective SWM in Johannesburg also has been hampered by the scale of population growth, the lack of capacity of national and local governmental institutions to respond to this rate of change, and the dramatic increase in the scale of waste production. The lack of financial and human resources and lack of knowledge regarding the scale of the problem not only limited government response to existing conditions but also hampered the capacity to plan for the current rate of change and projections of future growth. The situation has been further limited by the tradition of top-down, institutional siloing of city departments and significant corruption throughout the bureaucratic system (Serge and Simatele 2020). During the late 1990s and early 2000s, the country's and city's leaders worked to develop institutions of governance across a broad set of domains including environmental protection. While many new policies were developed and initiated, realization of their goals proved to be a significant and continuing challenge.

9.2.2.2 Crisis

In the late 2000s, a crisis in SWM was looming – while the country and city of Johannesburg had put forward new legislation regarding SWM, implementation and sustained funding proved to be significant problems. This was coupled with the fact that waste generation in the city was rapidly rising. In part driven by dramatic growth in the country's economy (measured as GDP, almost tripled between 2002 and 2007 – World Bank statistics). Surveys done at the time noted that waste generation in Johannesburg was increasing by 13% per year (Statistics SA 2007 quoted in Greben and Oelofse 2009). During the late 2000s and early 2010s, integrated waste management planning was introduced into South African governments with the policy goal of maximizing management efficiency while reducing costs and achieving the lowest environmental impact. The movement toward more effective and integrated waste management was associated with the promulgation of a series of new post-apartheid legislation and policies. For example, in the Waste Act, No. 59 of 2008, each municipality was required to develop an integrated Municipal Solid Waste Plan (IMWP) under the broader framework of the National Waste Management Strategy (Adeleke et al. 2021).

A set of key drivers for advancing SWM emerged at this time in South African cities. These included societal and biophysical limits such as increased demand for waste service provision and for waste minimization, recycling, and recovery, coupled with increased waste generation and limited sites for environmentally responsible land disposal of waste (Muzenda 2012). At the same time, the tradition of markets of recycled resources remained. The City of Johannesburg Integrated Waste Management Plan 2011 stated that "globally, human activities are depleting our natural 'capital' and the long-term capacity of our ecosystems to sustain future generations. As nonrenewable resources become scarcer, supplies become less reliable and prices increase. If the City of Johannesburg is able to do more with fewer nonrenewable resources, it will be better prepared for future declines in resources – in contrast with cities that are more resource-driven."

9.2.2.3 Transition

The waste management system went through a fundamental reorganization in the 2010s as the limits and challenges of the early post-apartheid policy were better realized when coupled with the persistent and in some cases growing income disparities and inequities that created more demands for a transition in the city's SWM approach. These conditions were made more intense as the great rush of economic growth in the previous decade faded revealing the need for substantive reform.[3] These conditions in Johannesburg were translated into another generation of waste management policy goals of advancing social equity, environmental sustainability, and increased resource efficiency (through recycling). The city planners attempted to encourage residents to recognize that it can no longer manage the local natural environment as a pristine resource to be exploited without consequence, and the need to minimize all residents' impact provided a vehicle to promote efforts for a more sustainable, resilient, and livable Johannesburg (Anonymous 2016). The ambitions were significant and attempted to tie improved environmental management with increased resource production capacity while attempting to address the persistent social and economic divisions in the country. For example, it was documented that in 2012 two significant Johannesburg landfills (i.e., Robinson Deep and Marie Louise) were recovering and flaring GHG at a rate of 7,449 m^3/h (Baker and Letsoela 2016). The landfill recovery system in the city has proved useful to address the local SWM crisis and also generate electricity and contribute to GHG emission reduction, although much more effort needs to take place (Baker and Letsoela 2016; Dlamini et al. 2019; Adeleke et al. 2021).

9.2.2.4 Transformation

Johannesburg, like other cities in South Africa, still had to respond to multiple and significant equity- and sustainability-based developmental challenges. The priorities of environmental sustainability and more recently also a focus on tackling climate change call for advancing toward the simultaneous goal of a more sustainable, resilient, and livable city. In an attempt to achieve this, Johannesburg has promoted the reduction of natural resource consumption and GHG emissions, the minimization of environmental pollution – air, water, and waste to land – and protect the city's natural environment. One of the most significant elements of the transformation has been the recognition that waste should be considered as a resource and a source of employment. Waste reclaimers also have been encouraged and assisted in the formation of co-operatives to promote employment and reduce poverty levels. As early as 2011, the City of Johannesburg developed a new program known as Jozi@ Work that was designed to direct the city's contracting service to support an estimated 1,750 new environmental sustainability-oriented and existing community-level co-operatives and enterprises and eventually support the creation of 40,000 new jobs servicing the city's sustainability needs.

[3] The country's GNP per capita sank from $8,737 per capita in 2011 to $5,735 per capita in 2016 – World Bank statistics.

Johannesburg's Mayor Park Tau highlighted the multi-faceted and interconnected policy approach stated when stating that

> They [the new jobs] will be servicing needs as diverse as de-sludging of chemical toilets, separating and recycling waste as it arrives at our dumps, providing food to our nutrition programs, resurfacing and maintaining our roads and providing frontline support to our water and power infrastructure. Our residents will be our suppliers as well as our customers – and transacting locally will make them better at being both. It will mean better value for money paid to the city and faster, more attentive service in return for money paid into the city through rates and service charges. (City of Johannesburg 2011).

With the close of the 2010s, SWM had shown institutional advancement but still is significantly challenged by a lack of governance capacity and persistent other problems such as underemployment and unemployment, and, like in Buenos Aires – a thriving informal market of pickers has emerged, although the social reforms seen in Buenos Aires have not taken place.

9.2.3 Seattle, US

Seattle, Washington, in the Northwest of the United States, is nicknamed the *Emerald City* because of its lush natural setting promoted by the region's modest marine west climate, which includes pleasantly dry and warm summers and moderately cool and rainy winter months. The city experiences typically 150 days of precipitation often with a drizzle or light rain for a period of the day. The climate is conducive to the luxurious growth of vegetation including the great coniferous forests in the surrounding mountain ranges. The city's history has been deeply connected to the local environment and resources. Settled by Europeans and other non-Indigenous groups only in the mid-nineteenth century, the city developed as a port for the shipment of timbers, minerals, and other resources and as a staging area for exploration and resource extraction from the interior of the US Northwest and Alaska, and parts of Canada. Up through the 1960s, the city and region were described as a regional port town and natural resource market and export center – including the export of timber, fisheries, and agricultural products. The city itself lost population in the 1960s and 1970s, as the larger region grew and started to restructure itself (Sanders 2011). As the host of the 1962 World's Fair and the construction of the now iconic Seattle Space Needle, a civic struggle was emerging to redefine the region and move beyond its provincial background. New and dramatic economic growth was spirited by the significant development of the local airplane manufacturing and later the birth and rapid rise of the computer software industry. The city has a population of about 737,015 as of 2020 with a metropolitan area population of approximately 4 million. Today, the city and the broader region are recognized globally as one of the most eco-friendly urban areas of the world. The city is seen as a capital city of ecotopia – a region first defined in Ernest Callenbach's 1975 novel, *Ecotopia: The Notebooks and Reports of William Weston*. The book describes a world of 1999 in which the society of a breakaway region is focused on ecotopian principles including a respect for nature, low environmental impact, and what would be later described as sustainability. The novel became very influential for the countercultural and back-to-nature movement as well as what would become the green movement. The image of ecotopia also became a point of reference for Seattle and its greater region. A central question is how and why was Seattle transformed from a resource port and gritty industrial town to a city highlighting an international reputation as a postindustrial green city? This question is examined here.

9.2.3.1 Stress

Post-World War II Seattle was fraught with social and economic stresses that divided the city and its region across income, racial, and political lines. The city began to face a series of development tensions and decline as the surrounding suburban areas were growing rapidly with the dramatic rise of the postwar Boeing Corporation airplane production center. Across the metropolitan region, the central city – Seattle – was seen as troubled, corrupt, and a hotbed of political radicalism and social unrest. The residents of the new suburban communities were quite wary of the city and the ambition for regional governance. Seattle's 1962 World's Fair was held on cleared land near downtown and was seen to illustrate the possibility of a new and modern city. Its siting was part of an active debate regarding how to re-envision the city.

A strong pro-redevelopment coalition in Seattle promoted a large-scale urban renewal program and slum clearance. One of the key sites of action involved the transformation of some of the most iconic downtown neighborhoods and features including the famous Pike Place Market. The market, opened in 1907, was a massive public farmer's market located in the downtown area of the city overlooking the Elliott Bay waterfront on Puget Sound. The farmer stalls were occupied by small-scale farmers, and local craftspeople and merchants.

9.2.3.2 Crisis

The 1963 proposal to demolish and replace the market and build up extensive projects in adjoining areas was backed by the Seattle mayor and city council. The proposal sparked a series of opposition efforts that resulted in the preservation of the market but also laid the groundwork for community engagement

(Sanders 2011). The grassroots movement that rose up to oppose the developers saw the fight to save the Pike Place Market as a flashpoint for a set of larger issues focused on what type of city Seattle would be and how to promote quality of life and environmental protection. While on the surface, the protests seemed to focus on a demand for protecting a piece of architectural and community history, the underlying issues focused on a broader crisis over place identity, environmental integrity, citizenship, social justice, and consumption. At the same time, elements of these groups bemoaned the rapid loss of farmland around the city via suburbanization and the growing sense of increasing environmental degradation and pollution – especially wastewater and sewerage – and the lack of capacity to respond to these new threats (Klingle 2008). The conflicts revealed underlying tensions that then became pivotal as the early outlines of a public debate about the character of a "sustainable city" (Sanders 2011).

Similar questions and crises flared up in many localities in the US during the 1960s and early 1970s and resulted in the birth of an environmental movement as well as a countercultural movement, which focused in part on the high consumptive lifestyle emerging in the United States. Collectively this questioning of society and its direction brought about an ambition for societal and environmental change. Within Seattle, the debate over the future of the city, its neighborhoods, and the larger region continued to be waged. By the late 1960s, the city had become one of the early recipients of US government urban renewal funding (Model City Program). As the mid-1970s wore on, several factors came together that forged the new environmental ethos of the city. The deficits of some of the urban renewal efforts were better and more widely understood, the bioregionalism of the Ecotopia concept was emerging making the Seattle region a hotbed of ecological thinking, and the 1960s environmental movement activists were finding ways to put their ideals into practice. This confluence allowed for the increasing application of ecological principles to society and the development of holistic, integrative, and more environmentally benign approaches and a new identity of the city itself.

9.2.3.3 Transition

This transition was fully articulated when the broad policy shift was made to incorporate these ideals more fully into the city's public policy. The implication for the city's SWM regime was profound. In the 1980s, Seattle environmental waste policy began to be fully restructured to translate ecological principles in practice. For example, Seattle's City Council Resolution 27871 adopted the City's 1988 Integrated Solid Waste Management Plan that established a goal of recycling 60% of the waste generated in the city. By 1990, the City of Seattle had rates of recycling and composting several times the values of cities of comparative size (US EPA 1994). Furthermore, in 1991, Sustainable Seattle (S2) – a dedicated group of local community members – emerged from a community forum hosted by the Seattle by Global Tomorrow Coalition. S2 then convened its first Civic Panel and hosted community participatory research sessions and workshops. S2 laid out an approach for communities to take part in ensuring environmental quality and access through an emphasis on local action and advocacy.

By the end of the next decade, the focus on sustainability had been immersed throughout a wider range of applications including a transformation in waste management. The 1998 Seattle Solid Waste Comprehensive Plan, *On the Path to Sustainability*, presented a suite of advances including a sustainability and stewardship policy framework, that positioned "zero waste" as a guiding principle, and the identification of programmatic goals. Under the plan, program goals were to be achieved in an approach that would balance cost-effectiveness and system efficiency and the interests of public and environmental health, as well as customer and community needs (Seattle City Council and Seattle Public Utilities 2007).

While the ambitions of transferring ecological premises into practice were yielding results, it was also creating tensions within other facets of everyday life and conflict within Seattle. Since the Pike Place Market protest and the civic struggle over the redevelopment of downtown Seattle, an undercurrent theme had been tension regarding the siting of noxious or controversial facilities associated with more traditional modes of urban planning. At the same time, alternative planning narratives focused on creating a more holistic household-centered approach within the ecotopia ethos (Sander 2011) pushed for even more dramatic environmental ambitions. To resolve the siting conflict issue, a decision was made to promote more transformational goals. As noted by Murdoch (2010), a waste transfer station battle and similar contestations in Seattle proved to be a catalyst for a more aggressive recycling policy and other waste reduction policies. Under the umbrella of sustainability, the tension brought together a coalition of interests including a variety of private citizens, who were worried about waste and the prospect of living next to a garbage dump, and local government representatives, who were in charge of collecting, sorting, and hauling that waste to a landfill. This coalition proved to be transformative.

9.2.3.4 Transformation

In latter 2000s, the Seattle Public Utilities (SPU) began to follow a practice of "Zero Waste," taking on the approach first defined in 2004 by the Zero Waste International Alliance. The Alliance defined "Zero Waste as a goal that is ethical, economical, efficient and visionary and guides people in changing their lifestyles and practices to emulate sustainable natural cycles, where all discarded materials are designed to become resources for others to use."[4] On July 16, 2007, Seattle's full City Council passed a resolution (The Zero Waste Resolution [30990]) that established new recycling goals for the City of Seattle. The resolution defined the focus of the city's waste-reduction programs and solid waste facilities including a Zero Waste Strategy that offered a new waste management philosophy. The philosophy was focused on the conception of waste as a resource, waste prevention and recycling as natural resource conservation, new jobs and products could be created from translating discarded trash into resources, that products should be durable and recyclable, and products and materials that become trash after one use should be discouraged (Conlin 2010).

9.2.4 Taipei, Taiwan

The city of Taipei is the capital of Taiwan. The city proper has a population of about 2.7 million residents with the greater metropolitan region having a total of 7.0 million. With the rapid economic growth during the latter decades of the twentieth century, Taipei developed into a major East Asian hub for business and commerce. This growth took place as the government of Taiwan also was transformed. Taiwan, officially known as the Republic of China, became the remaining center of authority of the Republic of China government, which lost its hold on mainland China to communist forces during the civil war in the second half of the 1940s. The country was under martial law from May 1949 until July 1987 and led by one-party rule – the Kuomintang (KMT). With the end of the martial law, Taiwan experienced a flowering of democratic practice, a dramatic expansion of public policy and engagement, and significant growth in the GDP per capita. The GDP per capita basically tripled between 1987 and 2000 and more than doubled between 2000 and 2020,[5] and as of 2021 has a GDP per capita only about 17% less than that of Japan ($39,246 vs. $33,143). With respect to the environment, Taiwan is subject to a wide range of challenges and threats including a significant natural hazard risk, especially typhoons and earthquakes. While Taiwan, generally, and Taipei, specifically, have made significant progress addressing these environmental risks, its transformation

[4] Additionally, Zero Waste means designing and managing products and processes to systematically avoid and eliminate the volume and toxicity of waste and materials, conserve and recover all resources, and not burn or bury them. Implementing Zero Waste will eliminate all discharges to land, water, or air that are a threat to planetary, human, animal, or plant health (City of Seattle – www.seattle.gov/utilities/about/plans/solid-waste/zero-waste).

[5] Data from the International Monetary Fund, https://statisticstimes.com/economy/country/taiwan-gdp-per-capita.php.

regarding waste management has brought it international acclaim. In recent years, Taiwan has had the highest rate of recycling of a developed nation at ~55% and continues to increase this rate (Ensia 2019). It has not always been the case as the case study attempts to reveal.

9.2.4.1 Stress

The economy of Taiwan rapidly developed starting in the 1970s, especially with respect to exports, and was heralded as the *Taiwan Miracle*. During the 1970s, residents of communities where new large-scale polluting industrial facilities were being built would celebrate as the new plants started operation (Shen and Yu 1997). The rapid economic expansion and parallel dramatic rise in the standard of living brought a significant increase in pollution and solid waste production from the 1980s to the mid-1990s. For example, the average daily production of municipal solid waste per capita grew from 0.63 kg in 1981 to 1.14 kg in 1997 (Lu et al. 2006). Already by the early 1980s, increasing social unrest and stress about the rising level of pollution started to emerge (Tang and Tang [1997]). Most of this protest was small and directed at local governments and not the central government, which continued to operate under martial law. Numerous civic-minded organizations made up of everyday residents formed during this time. The members, including those of the nationally famous Homemakers United Foundation (HUF) founded in 1989, advocated for a variety of environmental issues including green consumption and advanced SWM (Liao 2003).

In 1986, an event occurred that signaled a significant shift in the environmental agenda and broader politics of Taiwan. The Dupont chemical company had proposed the construction of a massive petrochemical facility in the city of Lukang, an old port city about 190 kilometers south of Taipei. Widespread protest against the plant construction quickly emerged and was directed at the company, the local officials, and the central government. The company eventually pulled back and decided against the construction, and the central government was somewhat mute in their response, providing incentive for further citizen-led environmental action. These events were part of a larger democratization movement that was rapidly growing during this time, contributing to the end of the martial law the next year and the collapse of one-party rule to a two-party-dominated system with the Kuomintang (KMT) and Democratic Progressive Party (DPP) (Tang and Tang 1997).

9.2.4.2 Crisis

The main island of Taiwan is not large – slightly smaller than the Netherlands or Switzerland, yet several times the population. Given the highly rugged terrain, most of the population is pressed into the few relatively small coastal plains. This in turn has created significant competition among various urban-dominated land uses. The lack of space for siting new landfills resulted in what is described starting in the 1980s as the "garbage wars" with significant conflicts regarding illegal dumping. In 1993, Taiwan collected only 70% of its waste with the remaining cast out as litter or burned in open pits, and virtually no waste was recycled. By the mid-1990s, approximately 70% of the landfills on the island were full or almost full. In the mid-1990s, the country was given the moniker of "garbage island" to illustrate its inability to manage its SWM crisis (Yoshida 2022). The first substantive response of the central government was the adoption of a comprehensive waste incineration policy. The initiative included the siting, construction, and operation of three dozen incinerator projects (Hsu 2006); 21 of which were to be managed by the public utilities and 15 by private companies. While the policy of incinerating trash was not widely countered, significant opposition to the siting of facilities did emerge. The Not in My Backyard (NIMBY) response further accelerated civic engagement in environmental issues. The growing and ever more intense opposition to the siting of incinerators forced the new government now led by the DPP to back away from the massive siting plan. This in turn forced the question of how to manage solid waste in cities like Taipei.

9.2.4.3 Transition

The partial collapse of the waste incineration scheme, rising environmentalism and demands for civic engagement, and concern for the DPP's ability to illustrate country-wide leadership all lead to the dramatic reappraisal of the Taiwan solid waste policy starting in 1997. The creation of an extensive SWM recycling economy was fundamental to this policy transition. This took place during a multi-step process. First, the government created a manufacturer-paid disposal fee thereby creating a revenue stream to develop a more robust recycling and waste reduction scheme as well as incentives to reduce waste. Next year in 1998, a series of other regulatory steps were taken countrywide that had already been first applied in Taipei in 1996. These included mandatory participation of local government waste collection crews in recycling, required waste recycling, and a stipulation that all citizens will place their recycling waste and other waste directly into the municipal trucks at designated locations at specific times. The added costs for the recycling included the purchase of additional municipal trucks to be used for recycling and as a source deduction strategy, costs associated with reduced use of disposal products, which were promoted and paid for by the central government. The results of the program were dramatic. As a result, the amount of recycled waste more than doubled over four years (1998–2001) and the per capita amount of waste generation declined by approximately 20% (Lu et al. 2006).

9.2.4.4 Transformation

The process of transformation in Taipei has continued over the past two decades. Additional recycling and waste reduction strategies have been put into practice through the promotion of recycling education, restriction on the use of plastic bags, economic incentives, and promotion of recycled materials (Lu et al. 2006). As cited in Fang et al. (2021), the resource recovery rate in Taipei improved significantly from 1998 to 2015 – from 5.88% (1.11 kg/day) to 55.23% (0.37 kg/day), respectively. The structure to collect, manage, and process the material has been well developed with maps and schedules of recycling and waste pickup widely distributed. As of 2020, recycling as a social norm has been fully developed within the Taipei citizenry and integrated into the everyday life experience (Fang et al. 2021).

9.3 Discussion

The case studies reveal how cities solved or attempted to solve their solid waste problem. The path a toward solution came through a set of complex links that connected both to everyday planning efforts and broader issues associated with the identity of the cities and their position vis-à-vis a comprehensive sustainability agenda. A critical component of each case study was the redefinition or reinterpretation of waste as a resource to be utilized, and that could allow larger goals to be achieved. The focus was not as much on competing interests or demands but on utilizing the resource of waste to address other needs. The use and incorporation of the informal (e.g., pickers and local residents) into a model of integrated management was evident. This approach enabled the solution space to be flexible and include some conditions for structural adjustment while not having to rely on large-scale infrastructure, such as the failure of the waste incinerators in Taiwan. Overall, the focus and rhetoric of sustainability and on the long-term time horizon became useful vehicles to address short-term policy and practice needs.

9.3.1 Conditions of Crisis

The conditions of crisis emerged from a chronic problem of not being able to manage the solid waste problem in the city. Waste management crises resulted from a lack of waste sites or lack of incinerating capacity. The crises did not emerge suddenly but rather reflected larger governance challenges, which eventually manifested as an existential test of identity – that is, what kind of city did it want to be. Cities attempted to resolve the SWM issues they were facing through a variety of solutions, each failing to a lesser or greater extent before the shift to more expansive initiatives emerged – for example, large-scale city-level recycling was brought into practice.

9.3.2 Drivers of Transitions

A rich set of drivers were responsible for the transitions, with proximate drivers less important than root and context drivers. The crisis of urban waste management is deeply set within the structure of urban society, urban governance capacity, and the notion of progress. As the drivers of the waste management crisis developed over time, they became intertwined with larger questions of democratization, equity, and sustainability. In many ways the transitions associated with waste management and the underlying transformative societal changes are not unlike the level of shifts that have been associated with the ambition for large-scale transformations needed to initiate and foster accelerated urban climate action. The link between local action and global scale or international conditions (including neoliberalism, a world's fair, growth after apartheid, and conflicts with a regional antagonist) is also a particular element of these drivers.

9.3.3 Spheres of Action and Legacies

The social systems are the most critical sphere of action within the waste management crises. The question of waste management in some ways becomes a parable for a broader city-wide discussion of the constitution of society and aspirations for improvement and advancement, including how to make the society stronger and more equitable. The issue of infrastructure and engineering also emerged with respect to waste management strategies and techniques. Although debate around these was significant for a while in Taipei because of the strong opposition to the waste incinerator program, it otherwise was mostly not consistently critical to the evolution of the crisis and the eventual policy transitions. What was significant is that the focus on waste management policy transitions initially was on technological approaches and land use decisions (e.g., waste dump siting) as ways to increase the waste handling capacity, but the decision space eventually moved toward socially oriented policies of increasing recycling and reuse. Much of the attention of the policy transitions eventually concentrated on the consumer and their waste generating and how that waste could be recycled and reused and who would do the recycling.

Table 9.1 *Key drivers observed in each case study. Source: Author.*

	DRIVERS		
Case Study	Root	Context	Proximate
Buenos Aires	Population growth; history of income inequities	Neoliberalism and international lending constraints; growing deprivation of the underclass; closing of provincial landfills and restriction of burning and open pit dumping	National economic collapse; collapse of employment and rapid growth of pickers
Johannesburg	Population growth; apartheid policies – inequities but also lack of governance; tradition of resource development from waste	Attempt at developing new post-apartheid governance, scarcity of local waste sites; aspiration to include sustainability practice as part of the new governance capacity and identity; waste a source of employment	N/A
Seattle	Urban-suburban tension; struggle over identity; rise of environmentalism and ecological – Ecotopia; racial/ethnic divisions; rise of the sustainability ideal	Slum clearance policies; World's Fair; development of new sustainability and zero waste policies	Pike Place Market planned destruction;
Taipei	Slow growth of democratic institutions; decline of available waste sites; economic development and expansion of waste	End of martial law; "garbage island" nickname; rising environmentalism and demand for civic engagement	Opposition to and failure of major incinerator program

The urban waste management crises were deeply imbued with the legacy of titanic global and regional policies, traumas, and conflicts. The transition policy debates were developed in reaction to these circumstances and/or as an assertion that the new government was able to move beyond these past limitations, constraints, and inequities. In this way, sustainable waste management strategy in response to the solid waste crisis became a way for governments and civil society to express and realize the opportunity for advancement and the capacity to problem-solve.

9.3.3.1 Urban Waste Management and Climate Change

Climate change is connected to urban waste management in a myriad of ways. While climate change will not directly significantly increase the amount of waste generated, the amount of waste generated per capita does shift in specific climate contexts. For example, extreme events could generate more waste from damaged property and goods, and increased waste generation from rapid urban energy transitions including the disposal of outdated technology and equipment. Furthermore, climate change also can disrupt urban metabolism and hinder the process of waste management collection and disposal systems (Dodman et al. 2022). Increased extreme heat directly exposes waste pickers to significant heat exposure illnesses including heatstroke, dehydration, headache, fatigue, and heat rashes (Chu and Michael 2019).

As noted in the case examples, waste management crises are profound because they bring into question fundamental issues regarding how everyday life should function and they directly connect the city's citizens to the demands and promise of environmental sustainability. The case studies provide some insights that could be relevant for how the societal transitions needed to achieve multi-dimensional climate action such as climate-resilient development (where adaptation, mitigation, and development are linked in a sustainable and just manner) can take place. Specific insights include:

- Engaging people in the everyday – the case studies well document how people when meaningfully engaged can be very responsive to the ambitions of environmental sustainability. This connection to problem-solving and solutions can be both empowering and satisfying for residents because they feel that their actions can directly link to answering environmental problems and that their individual actions make a difference.
- Connecting the particular to the general – the waste management crises and solutions illustrate how specific issues can be connected to larger questions of urban environmental sustainability. The focus on waste management as a crisis both accelerated wider city discussion of how other aspects of urban life can be made more sustainable, and in a positive feedback fashion, this broader dialogue on sustainability also promoted an increased focus on waste management. Advanced waste management, furthermore, was presented as a way to illustrate governance capacity and to provide evidence that the government could manage and solve problems.

- The value of a systems perspective – the case studies illustrate how a systems perspective that includes an implicit understanding of open and closed urban systems provides a viable mechanism to define and manage urban sustainability challenges that is useful and understandable for urban managers, policy-makers, and residents alike.
- Co-benefits – waste management solutions were successfully connected to other problem solution opportunities. Most obvious and important were mechanisms to turn waste products into a recycled valued commodity and, of equal importance, to provide regular and sustained formal employment opportunities for the urban poor.
- Value of networking – the early efforts in sustainable waste management connected to an early international wave in the urban sustainability movement. City networking and learning from others about innovative practice, and providing individual cities with a benchmark of achievement and strategies to better advance local waste management practices, all the while having healthy competition with other network cities.

10

Mobility, Livability, and Sustainability

Balancing Economics, Ecology, and Equity

The UN General Assembly voted overwhelmingly in July 2022 to declare that the ability to live in "a clean, healthy and sustainable environment" is a universal human right. Although cities or settlements were not mentioned in the declaration, it is clear that cities must play a central role in this process. The declaration strikes at the heart of what cities hope to provide but often fail to do so. Among the great challenges of urban development and city building is to create opportunities and conditions such that residents can live in a home within a clean and healthy environment and allow them and the goods on which they depend to move about the city in a way that promotes economic advancement and equitable well-being, while also being resilient to environmental and economic shocks. And now in the context of the climate crisis, promote low- to zero-carbon lifestyles. These conditions in the past decade have been linked together under the rubric of urban sustainability.

Central to this ambition is a balance of factors that simultaneously (1) enhance mobility and limit congestion, (2) promote densities where healthy environments are maintained yet also restrain urban sprawl, (3) utilize, maintain, and enhance ecosystem services, and (4) allow all residents to at least live in affordable and accessible housing. This requires action to address several of the prominent problems that befall cities. Promoting these conditions forces cities to integrate axioms of urban sustainability that include social and environmental equity, economic development, and ecosystem integrity. This chapter is focused on examining how cities have dealt (or not) with this simultaneity of urban sustainability stresses and crises and the extent to which solutions presented have led to significant transitions and transformations.

10.1 Background

Urban settlement has long been associated with the great tension between convenience and congestion, quality of life and environmental degradation, and access and exclusion. The focus of urban sustainability has been to define those qualities that promote well-being and livability while creating conditions for equity, economic development, and environmental enhancement for all. Urban sustainability can be promoted through shifts in how cities are built and rebuilt, how they are governed, and how their residents make everyday decisions on how they live their lives and the choices open to them.

As the form and shape of cities have been reimagined and reengineered in the past 150 years, there also has come fantastic urban growth. In 1900, approximately 300 million people lived in cities (~15% of the global population then 1.6 billion), and in the year 2000, the global urban population was estimated to be 2.9 billion, or almost 50% of the global population. By the year 2050, the United Nations currently estimates that the number of urban inhabitants will be between 6 and 7 billion. The urban transition and urbanization process have spread around the world. Coupled with this process has come terrible inequities in living standards and housing. Substandard housing is often described by the broad term of "slum". Policies that promote and sustain the world's slums are embedded in economic and political marginalization and racial and ethnic prejudice. How to address substandard housing in cities is one of the most significant stresses and crises facing cities. Currently, approximately 1 billion or ~23.9% of all city dwellers globally live in slums.[1]

Cities are places of high population density and as a result are often places that are difficult to move around in. Transiting to the central areas of a city can be time-consuming and when extremely difficult will limit commerce and diminish the quality of life for residents. In the nineteenth century, several solutions were presented as ways to address the problem. These solutions centered around restructuring urban form and promoting more effective modes of

[1] The UN-HABITAT defines

> a slum household as a group of individuals living under the same roof in an urban area who lack one or more of the following: (1) Durable housing of a permanent nature that protects against extreme climate conditions. (2) Sufficient living space which means not more than three people sharing the same room. (3) Easy access to safe water in sufficient amounts at an affordable price. (4) Access to adequate sanitation in the form of a private or public toilet shared by a reasonable number of people. (5) Security of tenure that prevents forced evictions.

It also should be recognized that by this definition, substandard housing present in wealthier regions of world is not included this definition. The marginal housing present in and around many US cities and other similar wealthy countries is included in these numbers.

movement. The new urban forms and modes of transit worked synergistically. Starting in the mid-nineteenth century, new modes of urban transport to supplement locomotion by foot or horse began to appear. The trolley car, street car, railroad, and eventually the automobile in the early twentieth century transformed the urban form, and especially in the United States, Australia, and a few other countries. These modes of transit allowed residents and goods to travel greater distances, enabling movement out to the hinterlands at the cities' edge. At the same time, cities were restructured with straight broad boulevards and grid street patterns to promote mobility and commerce. In these situations, highly dense pockets were cut through by new transport corridors and often lost population as the city edges were urbanized and cities became more widespread and sprawling. By the late twentieth century, this type of urban sprawl had brought a series of negative environmental consequences and a variety of stresses for cities to face including increased air and water pollution and loss of nearby farmland and natural areas that provided food stuffs and ecosystem services.

As cities grapple with the demands of promoting mobility, avoiding wasteful and inefficient sprawl, and fulfilling the right to adequate housing, they also attempt to ensure that they do not destroy or so diminish the local agricultural resources and ecosystem services. Ecosystem services, including those that provide drinking water, construction material, other natural resources such as fishery products, and recreation, are critical to the function and sustainability of a city. Their importance is highlighted in Von Thunen's nineteenth-century model of land uses in and around a city (see Chapter 3). The abstract model presents rings of economic activity with each successive ring associated with a different uses and processes. The second ring just beyond the intensive farming and dairy ring is dedicated to forests as a critical source of fuel and other products. While the development of extensive supply chains and regional and global trade networks has replaced local resource requirements, the importance of locally produced materials and urban-based circular economies in recent years has spotlighted the importance of local ecosystem services and agricultural production.

While the concept of urban sustainability focuses on achieving and growing the integration between environmental quality, economic growth, and social equity, the implications of its implementation and practice force a series of additional challenges associated with the structure of cities, their function, and the interaction between cities and their residents and between the residents themselves. A key facet of this is the appreciation of cities as interlocking and codependent systems and the definition of comprehensive and coherent system-level function metrics. Widely agreed-upon metrics are critical for the civil discourse and managerial aspects of urban sustainability. For example, the UN promulgated Sustainable Development Goals, generally, and with its Urban Goal, #11 includes a series of now-established metrics for urban sustainability.[2]

The transition to urban sustainability involves the adjustment of the city's systems and of those that are external on which they depend. The sequences of steps to move toward greater or lesser sustainability are often described through the narrative of pathways. The term pathways can be defined in a myriad of ways and is heavily utilized in the international environmental assessment process, specifically within the Intergovernmental Panel on Climate Change (IPCC). The IPCC 1.5°C Special Report, which heavily focuses on sustainability pathways, defines them as: "the temporal evolution of natural and/or *human systems* toward a future state. Pathway concepts range from sets of quantitative and qualitative *scenarios* or *narratives* of potential futures to solution-oriented decision-making processes to achieve desirable societal goals. Pathway approaches typically focus on biophysical, techno-economic, and/or socio-behavioral trajectories and involve various dynamics, goals and actors across different scales" (IPCC 2018).

Sustainability pathways by definition involve recommendations and adjustments to the pattern of resource demand, use, and production. These shifts can be instituted through policy adjustments and associated market forces and can include incentives as well as disincentives or penalties, or outright restrictions. Urban sustainability actions have experienced a wide range of support from strong to minimal or none. In many cases, environmental sustainability efforts have been controversial and often opposed, such as in the case of eliminating the use of plastic bags at stores and congestion price surcharges for those bringing private automobiles into downtown areas. The question of how to implement sustainable development practice into a city or neighborhood speaks to the question of the "right to city" and what power residents have to define their own everyday life and what they consider important to their quality of life (Merrifield 2011). The transition to urban sustainability will be uneven and not without conflict. It is increasingly recognized that if the practice and movement are to be successful, it will need to be based on the conditions of equity, transparency, and co-production.

10.2 Case Studies

The chapter includes an examination of four cities that have struggled with these challenges and to one degree or another have addressed them. These cities

[2] See https://sdgs.un.org/goals/goal11 for more discussion of UN SDG11.

highlight the process of integrating mobility and settlement within the broader frame of urban sustainability. The cities include Miami, US; Oslo, Norway; St. Georges, Grenada; and Shenzhen, China.

10.2.1 Miami, US

The city of Miami's short history is one of massive urban growth, pressing environmental challenges, and harsh social and economic divisions and inequities. The city's nickname is the "Magic City" because even with all these issues, it seems to grow, like magic. The city was founded in 1896 with the advent of a railroad built by a northern industrialist focused on building a railway from north Florida to Key West, which then was a strategic but remote US outpost 265 kilometers (165 miles) southwest of Miami at the southern end of the islands that make up the Florida Keys. In 1900, the population of the city was approximately 1,681; by 1960, 291,688; and by 2020, 442,241. The city of Miami since 1957 has been administratively linked to Dade County in a two-tier governance system. The Miami-Dade County population is just over 2.7 million (in 2020), while the US Census-designated Miami Metropolitan Region, which includes Dade, Broward, and Palm Beach counties, known as the Gold Coast, had a 2020 population of approximately 6.2 million residents.

The landscape of the region is almost without any relief and very low lying, with about 25% of the county's land less than 1 meter above sea level (Molinaroli et al. 2019). The settlement of Miami began on the slightly elevated ridgelines and barrier islands at the ocean front.

The city of Miami and surrounding urbanized land area grew rapidly in the twentieth century through the dramatic transformation of the local environment by converting "land into water and land into water."[3] A complex and integrated set of canals and water impoundments allowed land to be drained for settlement and contained water for agricultural use and flood control. The advent of inexpensive automobile travel in the first half of the twentieth century and then airplanes in the second half of the century made the southern peninsula of Florida much more accessible to the population centers of the US. The development of effective and inexpensive air conditioning also made the region much more habitable, where the humid subtropical climate can make the summer nighttime temperatures especially uncomfortable. The application of these strategies opened the area for the rapid increase in the number of permanent residents and vacationers.

[3] First part of the title of Blake's (1980) seminal work on the history of water management in Florida.

10.2.1.1 Stress

The glittering skyline of Miami masks a series of profound stresses that underlie the city's past, present, and future. The last several decades have brought these stresses to exposure as the pressure of dramatic and rapid development is revealed and recognized. By the early 1990s, the narrative of the region was one of unsustainability. The 1970s and 1980s had evolved with significant ethnic tensions and racial strife, often becoming widespread and tragic with massive police intervention. A series of urban riots and uprisings took place in the city from the late 1960s through the 1980s. An especially devastating multi-day rebellion with extensive looting and arson followed the trial of white police officers found nonguilty of murdering a local Black motorist (Grove et al. 2020). The case was widely recognized as a miscarriage of justice and abetting the racism and abuse of the local police. The immense water control projects and agricultural and urban water withdrawals caused large-scale ecological disruption to the region's Everglades – a site of globally significant biodiversity. Rapid urbanization brought mobility congestion and environmental quality declines and enormous income inequities that added to social strife and racial conflict and tensions (Grove et al. 2020). Local newspaper columnist and author, Carl Hiaasen, in a series of popular satirical books, presented the region and its residents as often unhinged and always heading toward crisis. Prominent social scientists described Miami as the "city on the edge" (Portes and Stepick 1993).

In response, stakeholders and reformers in the Miami region began a series of efforts to address these stresses. A comprehensive plan was put together to promote ecological sustainability in the Everglades (Harwell et al. 1996), elements of which were integrated into the Comprehensive Everglades Restoration Plan, which is a massive, several-decade, multi-agency effort led by the State of Florida and the US Army Corps of Engineers. Recognition of the social inequities and ethnic/racial divisions enabled more dialogue across the various communities. And even a free mass transit monorail system through downtown Miami, a stretch of just 7 kilometers, was started in 1986 and later expanded in 1994, in an attempt to promote mobility and reduce automobile dependency. The city and region also benefited from the long tradition of planning and regional management by the state, which was effective for formulating comprehensive regional water planning and land use policies as well as a regional consciousness. In the 1970s, the state of Florida was at the forefront of land use and environmental regional planning and management efforts. The legacy of these traditions has remained even though the politics in the state has become more conservative in the past several decades.

10.2.1.2 Crisis

Stark climate projections, increasingly evident climate change impacts in the region, and significant, yet not worse-case scenario near hurricane misses, (particularly in 2004), dramatically accelerated the narrative of how climate change was understood in 2000s metropolitan Miami. Political leadership in the region, bucking the trend of climate denialism in the state, formed the Southeast Florida Regional Climate Compact in 2010 as a partnership between Broward, Miami-Dade, Monroe, and Palm Beach Counties to work collaboratively through multi-level government partners, the private sector, community groups, and scientists to reduce regional greenhouse gas (GHG) emissions, implement adaptation strategies, and promote building in a climate-resilient fashion while ensuring that the region continued to grow economically. The Compact's work was designed to focus on three overarching objectives: (1) share regional tools and knowledge, (2) increase public support and political will, and (3) coordinate action. The threat of sea level rise (SLR) rose significantly during this time as advanced climate projections presented ever more concerning future flooding scenarios. In 2012, the Compact produced a Regional Climate Action Plan with 110 key action items related to climate action and urban sustainability more broadly. While ambitious, the early initiatives to address the crisis had begun at the city and county levels and had limited direct political or financial support at the state or national levels, except for extensive beach renourishment projects (Molinaroli et al. 2019).

It had become clear that Miami was among the world's leading cities, if not the lead city, with respect to assets exposed to SLR, and among the top 10 with respect to population at risk (Hallegatte 2013). By the end of the 2010s, climate change was increasingly being woven together with local stresses into a storm of interconnected problems. A recent round of research papers and reports has brought out a clear connection between the endemic social, economic, and environmental problems of Miami and climate change. The work highlights how climate change impacts whether it be increased flood potential (e.g., Czajkowski et al. 2018), SLR-driven relocation and gentrification (Keenan et al. 2018), or extreme heating will bring a series of first-order and second-order impacts. The intensity of discussion regarding climate change has further increased with more compelling evidence of and experience with sunny day (or nuisance) flooding coming with exceptionally high tides (i.e., King Tides), harsh projections of loss and damage estimates of a major direct hit hurricane,[4] and growing concern about summer extreme heat (First Street

[4] The 1926 hurricane is the storm of record in the Miami area. If that same intensity storm hit the region today, it could cause up to 500 billion USD of loss and damage (Molinaroli et al. 2019).

Foundation 2022). In late 2022, Miami-Dade launched an aggressive extreme heat action plan and mitigation effort (Miami-Dade 2022).

10.2.1.3 Transition

Taken together these threats have pressed the discourse of climate action and sustainability to heightened new levels by the end of the 2010s. Frequent public meetings, workshops, and media events have significantly raised these issues. Within the region generally and Miami-Dade specifically, initial activities have included setting a range of planning goals but with little tangible implementation. Much of the local response is dominated by a wait-and-see, low-regrets incremental approach. Local governments were and continue to be hesitant to "overadapt" because of the scientific uncertainties regarding future climate change and the effectiveness of adaptation strategies. An exception is the wealthy and progressive City of Miami Beach (separate from the City of Miami), which started efforts to elevate some of its streets, set up flood pump systems, and approve new flooding-relevant construction regulations.

The costs of climate action and sustainability efforts in Miami are massive. Adaptation costs for addressing SLR flooding and storm surge flooding alone could be $51 billion and $130 billion. The City of Miami voters approved a $400 million general obligation bond (the Miami Forever bond), of which half of it is earmarked for SLR mitigation and flood prevention projects. But this is a fraction of the total resources needed. Without direct support from state or federal sources, any meaningful progress toward the broader climate action goals will be impossible.

10.2.1.4 Transformation

The multiple strands of growing concern about the sustainability of Southeast Florida coalesced in the 2010s and helped a broad coalition of stakeholders press for an integrated planning process to address the concurrent challenges. While this transition has taken place, any prospect of extensive or long-term action is limited. This transition in the Miami metropolitan region can be described as incomplete and the transformation that could emerge from it is not possible at this time. The broad goal of this transformation would be to link together climate mitigation, climate adaptation, and development goals within a framework of sustainability for all residents and interests in the region. Right now, the key limiting factor is financing; however, the debate during these early phases of the transition has revealed several other structural impediments to a broader transformation. These restructuring of the tax regimes in the region to promote more sustainable development; adjustment of the existing water control infrastructure to be more sensitive to climate change conditions;

and perhaps most profound, meaningfully attempt to address the underlying racial and social inequities that consistently disrupt opportunities for profound social and environmental change.

Part of the financing challenge revolves around the fact that local municipalities have extremely limited revenue-generating capacity coupled with the condition that the state of Florida does not have an income tax. Because the state lacks this basic source of tax revenue, local municipalities are highly dependent on property taxes to finance government services and as a result are reliant on continued large-scale development of high-value properties, which are most often in high-value and highly vulnerable sites near or at the water edge (Conyers et al. 2019).

South Florida is a human-dominated and constructed landscape. How to connect with this legacy and the ongoing demands that the present structures embody (e.g., complex water management regimes) to the new pressing demands of urban sustainability is quite difficult operationally and managerially, and in the broader and long-term context of public policy. For example, when faced with growing flooding concerns in mid-twentieth century, South Florida opted to pursue structural, hard infrastructure engineering solutions (typical for the day). In the 1990s, it became clear that flood control solutions had begun to cause significant environmental damage in the region. Furthermore, it is now understood that the flood control infrastructure also reduced the potential of nature-based solutions to climate change. To make matters worse, the comprehensive package of ecological restoration projects proposed in the early 2000s and now partially implemented did not take into consideration climate change and SLR (Molinaroli et al. 2019).

How best to adjust and link the ongoing Everglades restoration efforts with pressing coastal resilience efforts is still to be debated. While the ambition and opportunity to connect them provide an excellent opportunity for innovation, it also requires dynamic and aggressive communication and outreach strategies to bring together the variety of constituent groups and stakeholders. The conversation and debate center around the innovative use of nature-based solutions and resilient building design. It also has brought up difficult questions regarding where and how to implement these strategies, recognizing that some sites and communities might be more at risk and less able to be maintained in their current form.

The added challenge for southeast Florida, generally, and Miami, specifically, is the deep underlying racial and ethnic tensions that have defined their history. During the past decade, local civic leaders celebrated the rise of regional resilience initiatives as a mechanism to improve the everyday lives of long-marginalized communities. This ambition was especially forwarded by the application of the Rockefeller Foundation 100 Resilient Cities (100RC) planning process that frontloaded social and environmental equity as core planning issues. While on the face of it this represented a significant advance, the planning process, as Grove and others (2020, p. 135), write hit an impasse as "the inclusion of equity concerns in Miami's resilience planning fails to address the wider structural and material 'environment' that absorbs racialized violence, abandonment and deprivations in the rhythms of everyday life."

10.2.2 Oslo, Norway

Oslo is the capital of Norway and has the country's largest population at 700 thousand and has a metropolitan population of slightly more than double that. Today, Oslo is often described as a global leader in urban sustainability with a wide variety of progressive environmental policies and well-structured and endowed welfare programs. It is well underway to implementing a series of comprehensive plans and strategies to become one of the first major cities to be genuinely low carbon and sustainable. The question to be addressed is how and why did the city of Oslo embrace this policy. Under what context did this transition take place?

Oslo was first marked as a city in 1050 and remained relatively small until the nineteenth century when its increasing trade and integration into the European economy promoted growth. Located at the head of a fjord, the development and history of the city have been closely connected to the sea and trade. Mobility around the metropolitan region and to areas outside has been stymied by the irregular terrain with deep bays and inlets and substantial hills extending down to the waters' edge. The country has grown immensely wealthy with the development of its vast oil and natural gas reserves. Norway, by many measures, is among the top 10 oil and natural gas producers in the world, and given its relatively small population (5.4 million), it is also one of the largest exporters. Even though Norway's economy has flourished in the past several decades, the display of wealth and prosperity is relatively recent. While the streets and buildings in nearby Copenhagen, Denmark, and Stockholm, Sweden, illustrate past imperial greatness, Oslo is a much smaller city with a relatively fragmented layout and few monumental structures and edifices. Until the mid-1900s, Norway was largely perceived to be on the edge of Europe, relatively poor, and without a grand history. The Norwegian welfare state was planned and built in the years following World War II, and was not until the mid-1970s and beyond that the oil economy began to infuse the system with abundant resources and enable a significant change in Norwegian society generally and Oslo, specifically. Besides being regularly ranked as one of the most livable sustainable cities, Oslo is listed as one of the most expensive.

10.2.2.1 Stress

The fjord location of Oslo can be broadly described as a bowl and includes a relatively small flat area close in around the main port facilities, then with small rising hills around reaching higher elevations the further one goes from the city. The history of Oslo's development can be divided into five periods (Nystad 2004). The two earliest periods include a small medieval settlement and later a small walled city. The industrial period starting in the nineteenth century is next. The population was centered in and around the downtown and near the port and associated shipping and ship-building industries. The wealthier residents moved to the west of the city into then-wooded hill lands. In many cases they also built summer homes in the extended metropolitan region. New factories and industries developed to the east of downtown and around them were constructed new neighborhoods for lower- and working-class residents, many of whom worked in the new facilities. While the new urban development continued to flow into ever more distant pockets of easily developable land, the 1930 general plan for the city reflected the planning profession's strong desire to control growth and consolidate the city into a "gesamtkunstverk," defined as a unified mosaic of neighborhoods and zones supported by ring roads and radial arteries. During this time, the single-family home was becoming increasingly popular and were built out along the rail lines up through the 1930s. At that time, Oslo was described as having completely filled in what a chief city planning officer at the time called the city's "natural body" of surrounding fjords and hills.

10.2.2.2 Crisis

After the end of World War II in 1945 to the 1980s, Oslo's built environment physical was impacted most significantly by concentric and relatively diffuse growth, consistent with patterns seen for other European cities. This decentralization was especially acute during the 1950s to the 1970s and exceeded the rate of population growth. In Oslo, the postwar period also came with a significant extension of the subway system – accelerating spatial growth, integration of modern spatial planning concepts in a state-controlled and state-subsidized housing program, and sprawling new manufacturing and transport areas. Within Oslo's continuous urban area, the population density declined by approximately 1.4% annually between 1955 and the early 1980s (Næss et al. 2011). This pattern of urban spatial development was driven by several underlying tensions including (1) the conflict between post-World War II pattern of urban decentralization in Europe and the growing role of all levels of government in urban planning coupled with the rise of the welfare state, (2) the rapid growth of Norwegian energy export wealth, and (3) the particular site characteristics of Oslo that, besides the relatively small coastal plain around the harbor, consisted of a few isolated pockets of low relief and easily buildable land.

It is during the 1980s that metropolitan Oslo experienced a policy "crisis" during which these tensions converged simultaneously. A key factor was the articulation and expansion of the Norwegian welfare state policies. After World War II, the policies of the Norwegian welfare state were rapidly expanded. Access to adequate housing became one of the foundations of the state and as such integral to planning efforts (Bojer 2011, referenced in Forsberg 2016). These policies are driven by the broader and system-level understanding that one's residence is not just an atomized good consumed individually; it and one's experience living in it are also affected by the local environment and in turn affect the same environment. As such, access to decent housing for urban residents became not only a political debate around access and just distribution. It also was a debate focused on how planning can achieve good and improved living conditions for the entire neighborhood that in turn will provide benefits back to the residents. This approach fed into other government planning policies focused on ensuring good and better health for residents. The municipalities and counties in Norway also were regarded as responsible for safeguarding and promoting the health of their inhabitants via progressive social and land use policies. For example, residential access to outdoor recreational land and associated activity opportunities was seen as very important in spatial planning and land use designation in the country (Forsberg 2016). This agenda translated into urban policies and resulted in significant impacts on the urban form of cities. The ambition of the new regime went beyond the regulation of the physical surroundings of the city, it extended to multiple aspects of community planning including architecture and aesthetics of the city, building strategies, and linking national social and economic goals to local landscapes (Nystad 2004). Urban densification was presented as preferable to outward urban expansion if done so to enhance environmental protection of biodiversity natural landscapes and social equity by providing effective mass transit and accessibility and reducing the amount of car-dependent travel (Næss et al. 2011).

10.2.2.3 Transition

While the pillars of the welfare state were put together in the post-World War II era, the capacity of the national government and regional and local governments to implement the policies in full effect only came with the rapid rise of energy exports during the 1970s and overall growth of the Norwegian economy and access to capital resources.[5] Since the mid-1980s, Oslo followed and was able to enforce the urban containment policy agenda. By the 1990s, it was able to break the long-lasting trend of spatial expansion. The implementation of the urban land use reforms set in motion a series of immediate changes in the pattern and process of urban spatial development in Oslo. The shift in the pattern of urban spatial development from predominantly outward expansion to densification and re-urbanization started to take place in the early 1980s. In the period 1984–1992, the earlier recorded drop in population density almost came to a halt, with annual decline reduced to only 0.1%. Furthermore, the urban development that did take place during this period occurred largely as infill and occurred in locations considerably closer to the city's center than in previous decades. The stabilization of population density in the early 1980s was then followed in the early 1990s by a shift to population density increases, particularly within the borders of the city of Oslo itself. At the broader metropolitan scale, the trend of re-urbanization and density increase – or at least reduced sprawl – was also present even though some development took place outside the continuous urban areas of the region.

The process of densification continued into the next decade – the 2000s. The density of the urban population of Oslo grew from 2000 to 2009 by more than 11%. While the urban core population grew from 132,700 in 1989 to 180,400 in 2009, with an increase in population density by as much as 36% (Municipality of Oslo 2009). The municipality of Oslo found most of its opportunities for densification through the use of "brownfield" sites, as well as, in some cases, remaining pockets of green open space within the urbanized part of the city. These brownfield and open space sites provided locations for housing, new schools, and other structures needed with increased population density. Other important improvements occurred in the public transport sector including a new metropolitan ring rail link, new street car lines and bus lanes, and more frequent departures for street car and metropolitan region trains to specifically encourage automobile drivers to take public transit. The impact of the transition was dramatic. As a result of all these actions, the annual consumption of land for urban expansion of metropolitan Oslo declined from an average of 3.8 sq. km annually during the period 1955–1985 to just 0.7 sq. km from 1985 to 2015, despite a population growth that was more than double than during the earlier period (Næss et al. 2020).

[5] As an illustration, Norway's GDP per capita in 1970 was $3,306 in comparison to the US value of $5,234 and by 1980 Norway had $15,772, while the US number had only grown to $12,575.

10.2.2.4 Transformation

Overall, the population density in Oslo's continuous urban area increased by as much as 27% during the period 1985–2011 (Næss et al. 2011). The population density increase was particularly elevated in the central Inner Zone of the city. The number of residents in the zone grew from 132,700 in 1989 to 184,500 in 2010, with no increase in the urbanized land, yet a 39% increase in population density. Figure 10.1 illustrates the rebound of urban residential densities in Oslo.

The implementation of the welfare state policies on social and environmental conditions of Oslo urbanization set in motion a series of significant changes including a set of positive feedback effects. For example, urban densification has resulted in benefits for mass transit efficiencies (Næss et al. 2020). Since its initial successes in the 2000s, Oslo has been able to continuously innovate and bring forward other urban sustainability initiatives. In the 2010s, Oslo put forward very aggressive climate mitigation goals (i.e., 95% GHG reduction by 2030 from 2009 values) including policies to discourage automobile use in the downtown (i.e., a congestion charge with different rates for EV vs. gasoline vehicles) and further advance public transit (Hofstad and Torfing 2017).

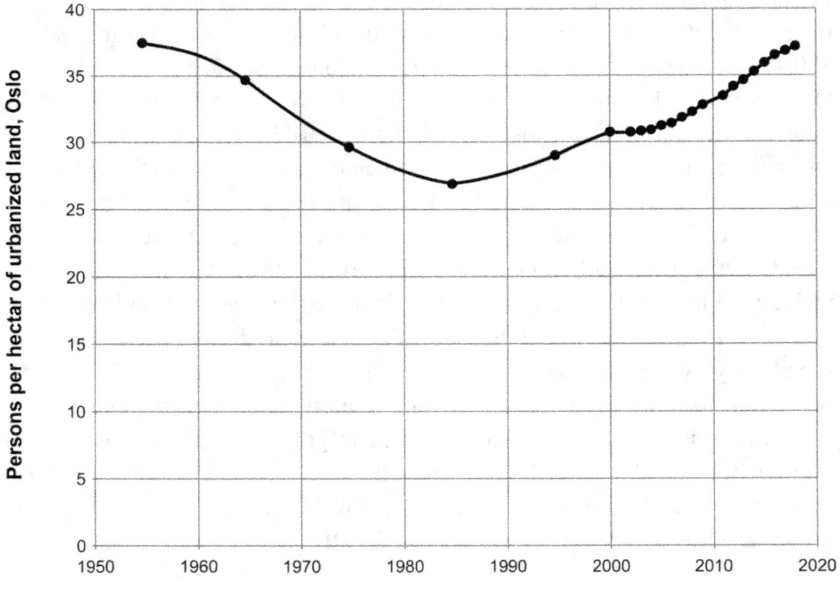

Figure 10.1 Population density within the continuous urban areas of Greater Oslo from the mid-1950s to 2009. Source: Næss et al. (2020).

At the same time, this transformation remains fraught with significant challenges and the process is far from complete. The ambition to move to and access the outlying areas remains strong. In the part of the Oslo metropolitan region beyond the continuous urbanized zone, low-density development took place for a longer time, with a high proportion of detached single-family houses among the new residences built (Næss et al. 2011). Moreover, a considerable expansion of the road capacity also has taken place – a condition responsible for some of the new land conversions present in the intra-urban green areas and periurban areas. The city of Oslo also has continued to build highways (often toll) that are especially technically complex with expensive tunnels to more effectively link together the far-flung parts of the metropolitan region. As in the 1980s, the fantastic wealth created by energy exports brought to Oslo the opportunity to both further its welfare society agenda while also providing amenities, access, and regional integration for the city's residents who are financially able and interested to use them.

10.2.3 St. Georges, Grenada

The island nation of Grenada is 348.5 sq. km (134.6 sq. mi) and has an estimated population of 112,523. Grenada is a member of a group of nations defined as small island developing states (or SIDS or simply small island states [SIS] or small islands). Almost one quarter of the United Nations member states are SIDS. The aggregate population of all the SIDS is roughly 65 million, slightly less than 1% of the world's population. One of the main concentrations of SIDS is in the Caribbean Basin. Grenada is located toward the southern end of an arc of islands called the Lesser Antilles that extend almost to the South American continent and form the border between the Caribbean Sea to the west and the Atlantic Ocean to the east. Most of the island's population is in the southwest around the capital of St. Georges, which itself has a population of approximately 34 thousand. Also located in the southwest is the country's international airport, a large private university with a major medical school (St. Georges University), and the numerous resorts and beach rental properties. Most of the 36% of the country's population that live in an urban area live in St. Georges. The country suffers from significant income inequities, with a poverty rate of 37% and another ~15% of the population at risk of falling into poverty (UN Office for the Coordination of Humanitarian Affairs 2020).

10.2.3.1 Stress

SIDS face a series of unique and significant social, economic, and environmental chronic stresses and vulnerabilities (Barrientos 2010). The economies of many SIDS are heavily dependent on the export of raw materials and/or agricultural products or tourism. They are typically dependent on the large-scale importation of food stuffs, equipment, and technology, and often essential resources such as energy and building supplies. Even fresh water resources are typically limited and need to be closely managed. Grenada is known as the Island of Spice because of its long history as a spice-exporting site. Its economy in recent decades while still including significant spice exports is mostly structured around beach and water sport tourism. Grenada is widely recognized as being located slightly to the south of the typical Atlantic hurricane (typhoon) tracks and as a result is a place where yacht owners like to harbor their boats. Grenada, similar to many other SIDS, faces a very heavy debt burden. In 2017, government debt service payments ran about 25% of total revenues, and in 2020 the debt was 71.4% of the nation's GDP. The economy was significantly negatively impacted by the COVID pandemic as that resulted in a collapse of the tourism economy. The airport was closed in March of 2020 and did not reopen until late October of that year, and even so almost no tourism took place until April of 2022 when many of the remaining travel restrictions to the island were lifted (Gregor 2022). Other stresses involve mobility and housing. Reflecting the extractive and export-oriented colonial economy, much of the transportation infrastructure is focused on the port facilities of St. Georges, limiting the internal development of the island and the mobility of the residents. Typical traffic time on the main coastal road to go from the south end of the Island to the north, a distance of 45 kilometers, could take 1.5 hours or more by vehicle. While only 6% of the housing is defined as slum housing by the World Bank, much of the local resident housing (nontourist) is quite modest and most often located near exposed coastlines, riverbanks and steephill slopes significantly increasing vulnerability.

10.2.3.2 Crisis

Although seen as too far south to get significantly impacted by hurricanes on a year-by-year basis, St. George's and the rest of Grenada were massively devastated by Hurricane Ivan in 2004. The storm caused widespread impact and crippled the island's infrastructure, with approximately 90% of the homes and buildings sustaining damage. St. Georges experienced significant destruction with many prominent and administrative buildings damaged or made useless, including the two largest hospitals in the country. Forty-one people were killed and the losses totaled $830.7 million (~$1.2 billion in current 2022 dollars), which represented almost twice the national GDP in 2004 (Asonuma et al. 2018). The following year, Hurricane Emily hit the island resulting in more but not as much damage as Ivan. These two storms significantly disrupted the agricultural export economy, making the country increasingly reliant on tourism for economic growth (Bhola-Paul 2015). The aftermath of the two storms and the growing global financial recession of the late 2000s manifested a national crisis in Grenada. The government debt crisis ballooned in the years following the storm and the national economy remained highly vulnerable to global economic crises and shocks. The national debt had been around 40% of the GDP in the 1990s and in 2001, it was still at 44.6%, but 10 years later, it was steadily at or slightly above 100% of the national GDP. While the international donor community did provide approximately $150 million in aid following the storms, there was a clear need to structure a new development pathway for the nation.

10.2.3.3 Transition

Prior to Hurricane Ivan, much of the development planning in Grenada was not reflective of sustainability principles even though in the late 1990s, the national government had already established a Sustainable Development Council, had developed sustainability practices in its forestry sector, and received support for sustainable development projects from several international development agencies and banks (Rosenberg 2010). In order to address the multiple crises spurred on by Ivan, the government began a process to outwardly reimagine itself and respond to the country's vulnerability to economic shocks and increasing climate change and associated climate disasters. Before the end of 2004, just a few months after the storm, the government of Grenada published a recovery plan that emphasized environmental sustainability practices and programming in all areas (Rosenberg 2010).

The country leaders put forward a set of interconnected efforts to promote sustainability and a green economy and promote itself as a SIDS leader in sustainability. In response to internal and external pressure from international development and loan entities (Rosenberg 2010), the national government of Grenada in 2007 put forward the National Development Strategy for Grenada. One of the main objectives of the Strategy was to promote and provide for disaster risk reduction and climate change adaptation. More specifically, the Strategy stated that climate change was among the main threats faced by Grenada, and defined a series of particular objectives. These included: "integrating environmental and physical development considerations into national development" (i.e., land planning, building renewal, disaster risk reduction, awareness raising, and education) and "an enhanced economic infrastructure sector supporting the country's development (i.e., exploration of alternative energy sources, increasing energy independence, addressing vulnerability of energy infrastructure to natural disasters)" (Grantham Research Institute ND).

10.2.3.4 Transformation

Over the past decade, Grenada has attempted to deepen and extend its sustainability ambitions through further efforts to develop green energy systems, enhance climate and economic resilience, improve mobility and housing quality, and promote ecotourism. To initiate the transition to a low-carbon economy and thereby hope to advance national economic development and improve the country's competitiveness, the government of Grenada approved a National Energy Policy in 2011. The new policy provided a framework to advance low-carbon energy technology and energy conservation and efficiency strategies. In 2012, the government went on to propose the Grenada Vision 2030 designed to enable Grenada to be "one of the first countries in the world to go virtually 100 percent green by 2030" (Emanuel and Gomes 2014). The Grenada Vision 2030 was composed of four major projects. Three of the projects concentrated on the growth of energy utility scale generation from geothermal, wind, and waste-to-energy sources, with the fourth focused on distributed solar. These projects were seen as quite feasible since they were expected to not require much capital investment, given the small size of the economy and energy demand (Roberts 2017). In addition to the national recovery plan and energy plan, the Grenada government during the decade also brought out several other high-profile sustainability plans and initiatives including the Grenada Strategic Program for Climate Resilience in 2011, the Grenada Disaster Vulnerability Reduction Project and Resettlement Policy Framework in 2011, the National Climate Change Policy in 2017, and the National Sustainable Development Plan 2020–2035 in 2019.

Grenada also attempted to more directly link sustainability and resilience goals with their growing economic focus on tourism, particularly via ecotourism. Ecotourism provided protection to the natural environment through designated entrance fees. These funds have enabled additional natural resource management work and the expansion of protected areas, such as some of Grenada's innovative underwater marine parks, Molinere and Dragon Bay (N. Joseph, personal communication, January 20, 2012, in Bhola-Paul 2015). An increased focus on ecotourism allowed the national economy to be less and less dependent on agricultural exports, which were seen as increasingly vulnerable to climate shocks such as hurricanes and droughts (which negatively impacted agricultural exports in 2018).

Even with the rhetorical and planning advances that the Grenadian government has made regarding sustainability, a large disconnect still exists between this progress and actual implementation. A wide set of institutional challenges such as lack of institutional capacity, a persistent focus on resilience to extreme events as opposed to long-term sustainability, continued funding deficits, and pursuing other priorities (Rosenberg 2010). With these limits, the opportunity for mainstreaming sustainability remained elusive, but Rosenberg (2010) defines elements in Grenada that provide optimism. These include an engaged and participatory democracy, advanced awareness and understanding of climate change risks, and meaningful connections and collaboration with international funders, such as the Green Climate Fund and the German Agency for International Cooperation (GIZ) that continue to encourage and promote socially and environmentally sustainable development.

10.2.4 Shenzhen, China

The story of Shenzhen is amazing and is much more than its fantastic recent history of rapid growth and industrialization over the past four decades. With respect to environmental protection and sustainability, the city also has been widely described as a forefront Chinese city over the last two-plus decades (Liu et al. 2007; Johnson and Weliwata 2019). While typically not ranked among the very top cities with respect to sustainability (i.e., not at a level of Oslo), Shenzhen has been increasingly recognized as a world leader in advancing urban sustainability practice. Shenzhen has been presented as a pioneer city and experimental in character, and paving the way for other places (Meng et al. 2020). At the same time, it has also been described as China's instant city (Du 2020), popping up from the mud flats of the Pearl River Delta in a matter of decades.

The land on which the City of Shenzhen was built is low-lying, well-drained land in a deltaic region intersected by numerous rivers and islands and situated between the historic city of Guangzhou and the global financial capital city of Hong Kong. Shenzhen's recent growth took off with its declaration by the central Chinese government as a Special Economic Zone (SEZ) for manufacturing, export, and trade in 1980. This initiative was part of China's ambitious "Open Door" policy to promote rapid economic development in the country. In 1979, 20 thousand engineers were brought to the city to start to plan the development of a great industrial and export center (UN Habitat 2019). Since that time the city has been completely metamorphosed from a small provincial city to one of the great economic engines of growth in China and the world. In 1979, the population of the city was approximately 20,000–30,000 (documented estimates vary).

By 1990, the population was 1.67 million, and by 2000, it was 7.0 million. The 2020 population is 17.56 million, of which 5.87 million are registered as local permanent residents (i.e., hukou holders), with the rest being non-permanent residents who work in the local manufacturing facilities and other businesses. The rate of economic growth in Shenzhen during the decades was fantastic, with values equal to or exceeding any recorded since the dawn of industrialization. In 1979, the level of added value from industrial production in the city was $3.37 million USD; in 1990 it had increased to $945.60 million USD, but by 2008 it was $53,054.55 million USD. The city's GDP grew at similar levels – from $0.04 billion in 1980 to $12.35 billion in 1990 and $114.47 billion in 2008 (Yuan et al. 2010). Yet as mentioned earlier, the story of incredible urban development and economic growth is only part of Shenzhen's contemporary legacy. In the early 2020s, the city also was recognized as a world leader in advanced urban sustainability practice. How a great ambition for urban sustainability was integrated into its amazing development trajectory provides a quite informative case study.

10.2.4.1 Stress

Historically, the Pearl River Delta was an important agricultural and fisheries region. Long-term human occupation and alteration of the landscape helped it become a regionally important site for food production (Shidong et al. 2001; Weng 2007). The designation of the SEZ status and the Open Door Policy fundamentally changed the delta's development path. The rate of growth picked up speed during the 1980s and really accelerated during the 1990s. It was already well understood that the pace and pattern of development were already profoundly altering the local environment and that a comprehensive system of environmental protection was needed to sustain the rate of population expansion and resource demand increase and also control the level of waste generation and pollution.

To help meet these great concurrent challenges, the Chinese Environmental Protection Agency in 1997 named the city as the first national model city for environmental protection (Liu et al. 2007). While the designation was significant, the pattern and pace of environmental transformation and degradation continued. By the early 2000s, urban planners began to call for a slowing of growth and a dramatic rethinking of the city (UN Habitat 2019). In 2002, Shenzhen was recognized as a United Nations Environment Programme (UNEP) Global 500 Roll of Honor city as a result of its efforts to simultaneously create both economic and environmental gains (UNEP, 2002). Shenzhen was seen as an attempt to rapidly develop an economy while not significantly damaging the environment, or what was described as a "win–win" strategy (Liu et al. 2007).

10.2.4.2 Crisis

In the mid-2000s, it was clear that the level of environmental degradation in Shenzhen had increased and had become a serious public policy question

(Liu et al. 2007; Shen 2008) and that prospects for a future environmental crisis at current growth rates were high (Güneralp and Seto 2008). Most standard environmental metrics showed the amount of change that occurred. The amount of arable land in the city declined from 35,000 hectares (532 thousand Mui – a Chinese unit of land) in 1979–1,900 hectares (29 thousand Mui) in 2006. Grain production almost ceased during this same time, declining from 132,584 tons in 1979 to 59 tons in 2006 (Shen 2008). The rate of rural to urban land conversion was dramatic as space was needed for factories, infrastructure, and migrant labor housing. The levels of water and air pollution, and waste generation recorded also showed significant changes, although not nearly as great as the rate of land conversion.

Most fundamentally, the settlement that was Shenzhen in 1979 no longer existed by the mid-2000s and at the same time, the city that was present was still in a state of becoming and from the perspective of Chinese urban planners, it was almost a *tabula rasa* – a blank slate to build on. Shenzhen's then-mayor Li Hongzhong in March of 2005 declared at a high-level gathering that the city's growth "speed" was unsustainable, particularly because of the rapid conversion of land for urban construction and development. It was clear that a new set of planning initiatives and technical measures needed to be taken to redevelop existing areas to use the land more efficiently, significantly increase focus on nature-based solutions, and create momentum for clever urbanization (Qi et al. 2020).

10.2.4.3 Transition

Creating a new identity and model sustainable city was now a central goal. The old settlement was gone, and the question was how to build a new city in the same place but without historical reference to the social and ecological systems that were there before, except at the most broad extent – the climate was still in a sub-tropical climate and the setting still a large-scale delta region with remnant beauty but also subject to high water tables and flooding. The ambition was to build a technologically smart city-driven, sustainable conurbation. Research literature was presented to illustrate how Shenzhen would be able to fundamentally link development and pollution reduction together in a way to overcome the urban environmental transition demands required by the Kuznets curves (Bao et al. 2023). Meaning that Shenzhen would not have to become highly polluted and environmentally degraded before it became wealthy enough to overcome it. Shenzhen could continue to rapidly develop economically while also becoming more sustainable and "green," and in effect pierce the curve. This policy transition was driven by a coordinated confederation of government officials, engineers, planning officials, technocrats, academics, and other interest groups. The efforts centered on promoting rapid urbanization and economic development in a way that promotes sustainability with a focus on mobility and quality of life in a very controlled, top-down governance structure. A strong link existed between the interests of the central Chinese state and the local pattern and pace of development.

10.2.4.4 Transformation

Shenzhen's sustainability efforts now connect with all aspects and sectors of the city – including its transportation system. The city by the late 2010s was the first in the world to ensure that almost all of the local taxis and buses were electric. This action reduced noise pollution and resulted in an significant drop in carbon dioxide emissions (Jiang et al.2022). Sustainability practice also has been closely integrated into the open space planning and management as well. The "basic ecological control line" policy (BECL) was implemented in Shenzhen to rezone the city to enhance ecology and reverse the environmental degradation and provide opportunities to enhance the local ecology in a way to reorder urban space to increase quality of life amenities and promote new economic development (Lin and While 2022). The massive land alteration of Shenzhen created a myriad of waterlogging, drainage, and flood issues. In response, Shenzhen was able to employ a sustainability-focused, sponge city program designed to manipulate and control the flow of rainwater through open green spaces and parks, sunken rain gardens, waterways, and other permeable surfaces (Wang et al. 2022). While creating striking urban landscapes, these approaches also have been associated with a broad suite of urban "ecological gentrification" and "environmental enclosure" through which environmental controls attract and retain wealthy residents and higher-value, nonpolluting, or low-polluting economic development (Lin and While 2022).

The connection between the central government and local transformation was further enforced with the application of the urban sustainability practice to Shenzhen. As an example, in February of 2018, the Chinese State Council issued the "Approval of Shenzhen City's Construction of the National Sustainable Development Agenda Innovation Demonstration Zone." The document stated that Shenzhen would take on a lead innovation role in the development of sustainable megacities. The Chinese State Council has the chief administrative authority of the Chinese government, and among its other duties, it directly oversees all actions of the provincial-level governments. The approval of this statement then required Shenzhen to focus aggressively on all aspects of urban sustainability with a clear focus on technical, engineering, and systems-based approaches, including optimization, efficiency, and carry capacity analysis (Zhang et al. 2021). This situation, as was the case for much of the past forty-plus years of Shenzhen development, highlighted the overwhelming authority and control of the central state to affect change in comparison to those abilities of local interests and the citizenry. In sum, the crises and transitions had been heavily mediated and orchestrated from afar.

10.3 Discussion

The case studies highlight the intricate process of building for urban sustainability that also enhances quality of life and livability of the everyday life for the city's residents. The set of cities shares a situational characteristic that provides perspective for those actors interested in re-imagining the cities. All located on an edge or a transitional space – Miami is the edge of North America and the Caribbean; Oslo is on the edge of Europe; St. Georges is on the edge of the Caribbean and South America; and Shenzhen is on the edge of China and the rest of the world. These vantage points gave the people guiding the growth of the cities some space – but literally and figuratively – to define innovative urban sustainability pathways. The analysis also shows that the cities' struggles with development and sustainability were both a very local and unique effort and one that was an archetype of what other cities will go through.

10.3.1 Conditions of Crisis

The press for sustainability in the cities emerged out of what was observed and perceived as a crisis of environmental degradation. These crises within the case studies came at different speeds depending on the rate of environmental change and resulting threats. At the extremes, the rate of change in Oslo was relatively slow and was first noticed and debated in the 1950s, while in comparison, the rate of transformation in Shenzhen was incredibly fast and took place within a very narrow window of time – from very late 1990s to the early 2000s. While different modes and speeds of environmental change took place, the residents and leaders of each of the four cities similarly felt that what they saw as the most important qualities of life in the city were in jeopardy and that the growing crisis required a comprehensive and innovative new approach to urbanism. In each case, this new urbanism needed to simultaneously reflect local traditions and lifestyles and widely accepted norms of sustainability practice (e.g., promote walkability, enhance urban greening, climate resilience).

10.3.2 Drivers of Transitions

The root, context, and proximate drivers each played significant roles in the development of the crises and the transitions that occurred. In each case, the physical landscape has a crucial influence on the patterns and process of urbanization. At a specific point in the development history of each city,

Table 10.1 *Key drivers observed in each case study. Source: Author.*

	DRIVERS		
Case Study	Root	Context	Proximate
Miami	Complex interdependent connection between the Everglades system and urban development; social and economic inequities; city on the edge	Regional planning tradition; tension between Everglades and flood protection strategy and climate adaptation strategies; financing and structural conditions of the tax policy make action difficult	Climate projections of SLR and ever-stronger storms
Oslo	Social progressive policies – connection between individuals and community; complex physical geography of Oslo; massive oil and natural gas revenue	Norwegian welfare state development and implementation; focus on urban densification	Concern over urban sprawl
St. Georges Grenada	Economic and environmental vulnerability as a SID	Ambition to create a sustainable and climate-resilient SID; interconnected development with climate resilience and sustainability; limited financial and institutional capacity to affect change	Hurricane Ivan
Shenzhen	Ambition by the Chinese government to create a demonstration city; deltaic landscape;	Special Economic Zone designation; ambition to create a sustainable city demonstration	Evidence of environmental decline and projected future further loss

questions about the long-term viability of these trends came into question. This narrative was then brought to a heightened state in response to a range of immediate concerns of environmental/ecological decline or of their projected decline. Similar to the solid waste discussion in Chapter 9, part of the pressure for environmental policy transitions rested on the commitment that the environmental trajectory of the city needed to be changed in part to illustrate how a more sustainable society could be built. In this way, the decisions to create what was seen as a more sustainable city would be reflective of broader and more fundamental city and national goals. For example, Norway was driven to illustrate how to apply on the urban landscape its social progressive policies, as was China interested in building a state-of-the-art sustainable city to show its engineering and planning sophistication and capacity, and the success of its own brand of governance. Miami wanted to show that it could wrest itself from the Everglades while protecting it and maintaining its connection to the amazing local environmental amenities. St. Georges and Grenada were driven to create a model sustainable small island developing state while enhancing its attractiveness to ecotourists.

10.3.3 Spheres of Action and Legacies

All spheres of action were heavily engaged in each phase of the environmental policy transition process; however, the complement of the three spheres varied significantly from case to case. Perhaps most variable was the technology/infrastructure. The massive application of infrastructure to basically enable the construction of the Miami metropolitan region has charted the entire history of the city. For Shenzhen, the enormous infusion of engineering and technology to create a new sustainable city was similarly transformative. Conversely, technology and infrastructure were less important in the sustainable transition of Oslo and St. Georges. Within the social sphere of action, financing and access to capital is of course critical to the transition process as well. While Oslo and Shenzhen had access to sizable reserves of capital, the lack of financial reserves in Miami and St. Georges has continuously limited the ambitious sustainability planning efforts.

Legacy as with the other comparisons across the cities varies widely. Miami and its metropolitan area, given its hydrologic history of transformation, in a way represent a massive fixed asset that was created by and dependent upon past planning and policy decisions. St. Georges, Grenada, and the countries of the Caribbean region live with the legacy of colonialism and with the present extractive and agricultural export/tourism-dependent economy. Legacy plays a fascinating role in the case of Shenzhen. At the broadest level, the city reflects the long-term ambition of China's drive for economic growth and expansion, but at the local level, the landscape of the Pearl River Delta was almost literally wiped clean to create the new city and with it all local legacy was largely eliminated.

10.3.3.1 Urban Sustainability and Climate Change

The connection between urban sustainability and climate change is central to the question of livability in future cities. Climate change will simultaneously alter the environmental baseline of cities making everyday life in the places more subject to climate disruptions and making the goal of urban sustainability harder to attain. Those residents and businesses most vulnerable and disadvantaged will be the most adversely affected. The equity implications of such challenges will be significant. Climate adaptation and mitigation strategies also can limit the effectiveness of urban sustainability efforts by initiating maladaptive strategies (i.e., air conditioning to limit extreme heat exposure that also increases the carbon emissions). So, while urban sustainability and urban climate efforts should be in sync and often are, in many circumstances this might not be the case.

The case studies reveal several conditions and lessons drawn from urban sustainability efforts that can be translated into climate action practices.

- Layering public policy – urban sustainability practice develops and broadens via a series of building blocks and takes place through a process of layering one initiative over another. Unlike urban water supply policy or air quality policy shifts that can occur in massive transformative steps, sustainability policy practice because of its deep and profound connection to society and its psyche seems to emerge in steps. These steps can be large and they can be closely spaced but do not come in one single swoop.
- Deep connections – urban sustainability practice must be by definition closely linked to multiple aspects of a place (i.e., its ecology, environment, and economics) and the identity that place as expressed by its history, cultural norms and traditions, and residents' life experiences. The case studies for example illustrate how sustainability practices are in part created in response to the physical site characteristics of the place. For example, two of the sites are harbors surrounded by rugged upland areas – a Nordic fjord and a small volcanic Caribbean island – and other two are largely former wetland sites (the Everglades and the Pearl River Delta) connected to broad deltaic expanses. This physical geography provides the basis onto which sustainable practices are built and have to conform and be responsive to. It also is understood that any sustainability practice needs to be connected to what works with respect to the trajectory of local economic development.

The climate action also should promote economic activity and be in keeping with the economic requirements of the city – for example, promote commerce and exchange, tourism, and industry.

- Crisis of identity and identity of crisis – the crises that brought on the sustainability transitions in the case study cities in large part were driven by a sense of loss of identity or placelessness, or a fear thereof. In each locale, current patterns of development were seen as a threat to the identity of the city as it was desired or perceived by the residents and counter to how they wanted their city to present to the outside word – as a tropical paradise (Miami and St. Georges), as a place of Nordic sensibilities and lifestyle (Oslo), as an expression of Chinese dynamism and innovation (Shenzhen). This dual yearning to express and build a place that meets the desires and aspirations of insiders and outsiders became key to the drive for sustainability. To recognize and incorporate this same response to increasing climate change threats to a place's identity could provide a useful vehicle for galvanizing broad support in a city for accelerated and transformative climate action.

PART III

Synthesis Chapters

11

Urban Environmental Crises and Policy Transitions

Few urban crises are as infamous as the Chicago fire of 1871 that killed approximately 300 people, destroyed an almost four-square-mile section or about one-third of the new city, destroyed about 17.5 thousand buildings, and made homeless nearly 100,000 (one-third of the total population at that time). The damage estimates were $200 million, roughly equivalent to $5 billion today. The event also is seen as spurring a period of great transformation as the city was rapidly rebuilt and continued its meteoric growth in population (in 1850 the population was 29,963 and by 1890 it was 1,099,850) and national prominence. A prominent quote by Chicago Tribune co-owner William Bross three days after the fire illustrates this point by declaring, *"Go to Chicago now! ... Young men, hurry there! Old men, send your sons! Women, send your husbands! You will never again have such a chance to make money!. CHEER UP. In the midst of a calamity without parallel in the world's history, looking upon the ashes of thirty years' accumulations, the people of this once beautiful city have resolved that CHICAGO SHALL RISE AGAIN."* (Bross quoted in Miller, 1997). This case dramatically makes the fact that cities are in a constant state of becoming and that urbanization and growth can be punctuated by significant moments of upheaval.

The 25 case studies in the preceding chapters (Chapters 5–10) reveal how the process of change can erupt from crises and related moments of transition. The goal of this chapter is to bring forward key results and insights from these case narratives. To do so, the chapter is structured around two objectives: (1) provide a general synthesis of the case study transitions and how the sequence of stress, crisis, transition, and transformation was expressed and (2) present and examine a set of insights revealed by the framework application. At the end of the chapter, some observations and suggestions on ways to advance the framework is also presented.

11.1 General Observations

What are some overall statements regarding how and why the transitions in the case studies took place? To address this question, attention is given to the connection between the underlying drivers (i.e., root, context, and proximate) and spheres of action (i.e., social, ecological/environmental, and technological/infrastructural) and the conditions of stress, crisis, and transition. The discussion will also focus on the connection between the pattern and pace of crisis and the resulting transition and transformation.

11.1.1 Connection between Stress, Crisis, and Transition

The case studies are rich with a variety of narratives regarding the conditions under which the crises emerged and transitions took place. Several different dimensions of the relationship between the crisis and transition can be considered. These include how pervasive the crisis became and to what extent did it affect the residents and economy of the city (i.e., was it completely widespread or held narrowly to a discrete set of interest groups), what length of time in years passed between the issue's emergence as a crisis to the time that the transition occurred, and what were the equity considerations that linked the crisis to the transition process. Of equal importance is the extent to which one can define or understand the motivation of the key players (either individuals, institutions, or interests) to act and to what extent they do so.

11.1.1.1 Character of Stress and Crisis

The growth of the environmental stresses documented in the case studies follows several different general patterns. In most cases, the stresses represented long-term underlying conditions the cities had to recognize and respond to, such as biophysical limits, including scarcities or excesses of water, and societal limits, such as widespread poverty, racism, and other social inequities. The daily life of the cities had adjusted to these stresses, and allowed for continued growth and viability of the cities. For example, the early twentieth-century city of Atlanta had already recognized their water supply limits and defined solutions to these challenges. The shift of these underlying stress situations to more significant crises was made worse either by a change in the underlying conditions or other factors such as increased rates of urbanization, political shifts or disruptions, or societal pressures (e.g., demand for greater equity). In most situations, the shifts that fomented a crisis that eventually led to the transition examined in the case studies were connected with societal pressures rather than biophysical ones. A relevant note regarding the challenge of climate change is that it is altering the basic biophysical limits of cities, most often causing them to be more significant.

The diffusion of the crisis throughout the city and extended region was another factor associated with the increased growth of the environmental crises. The early stresses typically largely affected specific segments of the society – being either socially or spatially limited to particular populations, sites, or sectors of the city. In some cases, the spatial or systemic diffusion of the crisis was limited such as in the case of flooding or solid waste management where the crisis was held to vulnerable locations or segments of the society. In other cases, the reach or extent of the crisis was widespread, where all components of society were connected to the crises, such as was the case for disease-focused case studies. Another dimension of diffusion in addition to the breadth of spread is the speed of the spread and how quickly the stress and resulting crisis became present within the community. For example, disease outbreaks spread incredibly fast in comparison to flooding hazards crises. These two factors together provide an illustration of the intensity of the crisis and extent to which it emerged within the city and region as a crisis that impacted the everyday experience of residents and businesses, and in turn could have required a public policy response.

Across the cases, one can observe a broad range of diffusion qualities. Figure 11.1 attempts to map the two diffusion dimensions (spread and speed). The rank order values are derived from the case study material. The rankings were organized from 1 (low) to 5 (high). The general trend is that spread/extent and speed increase somewhat proportionally, although the results illustrate some noticeable groupings and differences. For example, the risk and hazard cases had a slow diffusion process in comparison to the disease outbreak cases. The other groupings are situated in between these two, with the solid waste and recycling cases showing the most limited diffusion, and the mobility and sustainability and water scarcity cases possibly showing the most within-group variation.

11.1.1.2 Distribution of Crisis Experience

Another important characteristic of urban environmental crises is how they were faced and the extent to which they are concentrated either temporally, spatially, or societally. Of particular interest here are what can be termed as crisis sinks in which the crises were experienced as an acute phenomenon and the extent to which these situations became a significant motivation for action. The notion of the crisis sink[1] provides a heuristic framing to think about how

[1] Here the concept of a sink is appropriated from economics in which the term is used to describe locations or conditions that receive a disproportionate level of benefits or costs associated with a particular decision, policy, or outcome.

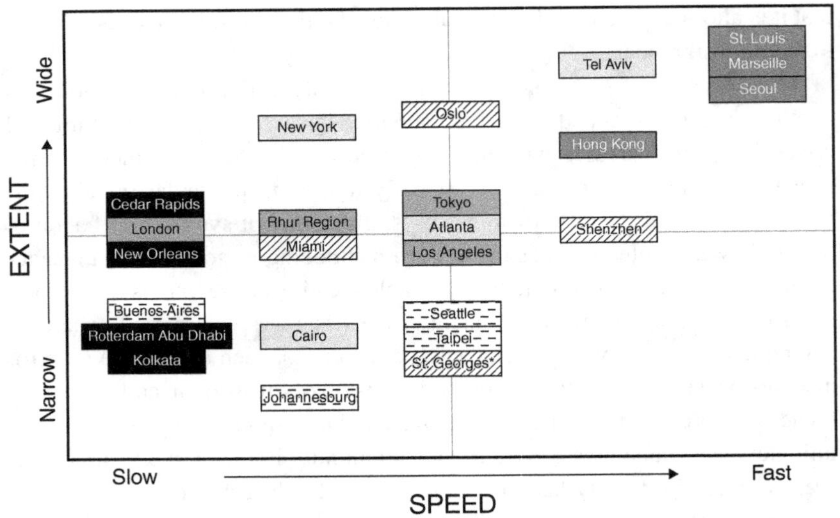

Figure 11.1 Diffusion of crisis – extent and speed. The figure presents an expert-judgment-derived assessment of the extent and speed at which the environmental stress within each case study emerged as a crisis requiring a possible public policy response. The city cases are color-coordinated (light gray – water resource scarcity; medium gray – air quality; dark gray – disease outbreak; black – risk and hazards; marble gray – solid waste and recycling; gray and white – mobility and sustainability). Source: Author.

the crises were lived experiences and what the implication of this collective understanding might be on how the crisis grew in importance, impacted the resilience of the existing policy and management regime, and eventually resulted in a tipping point or regime change associated with a transition. For example, in many situations, the crisis grew slowly at first and then grew to a point where it seemed to emerge very suddenly and pervasively (either in material terms or perception) to an extent that it would have been experienced as a great shock and in turn acted as a response catalyst. The cases of disease outbreaks serve as excellent examples of this condition. In this case the situation was even more accelerated because the emergent crisis was associated with an unknown health threat in which the dreaded health risk drove the need for an immediate response.

Another dimension of the crisis sink is connected to the uneven distribution of crisis effects and related equity and justice questions. Structural inequities of the crisis' impact at least to some extent were present in all the study cases. In many situations these inequities became a significant driver. It is important to state that while inequities and injustice were critical drivers, they were not by themselves sufficient to push for a transition. In fact, it was not the inequity or injustice as a moral or ethical issue that became the obvious component of the driver. Instead, the most consistent contribution to transition drivers was the civil protest and conflict and the political and economic instability that the inequity and injustice generated. The inequities were expressed via racial/ethnic, economic/poverty, and locational dimensions depending on the content. In many situations these were overlayed, such as during the plague outbreak in Hong Kong, the impacts of which were concentrated within the Chinese low-wage and marginalized worker residential districts.

11.1.1.3 From Crisis to Transition

How quickly did the policy transition occur after the stress emerged as a significant crisis provides additional insight into how the process of environmental policy change takes place. The growth of the stress and crisis varied across the set of case studies – in some situations the stress and crisis lingered for decades or more, while in other cases they manifested and reached a peak in weeks or months. Figure 11.2 highlights the time in years (derived from each narrative) between when the stress level associated with a particular issue began to be a consistent widespread concern and when a substantive transition occurred. The average number of years for the 25 cases was just under 33, and if one excludes disease outbreaks, which accelerated into a crisis extremely quickly, the average time increased to 38.6 years. Crises associated with risks and hazards took the longest to resolve – approximately 50.0 years, with water scarcity issues second longest at 42.5 years. The remaining three types of crises – air pollution, recycling, and sustainability – each took approximately the same time, 30 years. The observation that risks and hazards (e.g., flooding and extreme heat) and water scarcity took the longest is consistent with the reasoning that these stresses and crises typically could require the most amount of capital investment and large-scale projects or initiatives; often cities would try other methods and approaches that serve as partial solutions or require multiple jurisdictions to coordinate their actions, and therefore would require more time to resolve.

Other comparisons across the set of case studies have additional utility. For example, one could compare when the crises started to determine if more recent crises (those that occurred in more recent decades) resulted in a transition sooner than the earlier originating crises. For those that originated in the past 50 years (n = 10), 23.1 years on average eclipsed before a transition occurred, while in comparison those that occurred before 1970 (n = 15) took 39.4 years to result in a significant policy transition. Dividing the cases into three categories (originating in 1970 to present [n = 10]; 1920 to 1970 [n = 9];

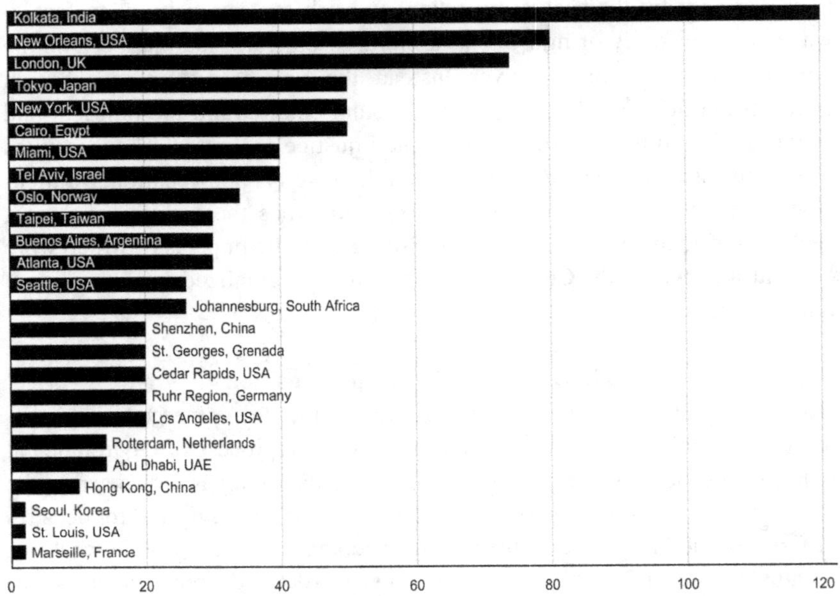

Figure 11.2 Time in years to environmental policy transition. The average number of years for the 25 cases is 32.9 years (38.6 years excluding the disease outbreaks and the number of years for each category of problems is 2.89 for disease outbreaks [light gray]; 27.5 recycling and reuse [slate gray]; 28.00 mobility and sustainability [black]; 33.00 air pollution [dark white/bone]; 42.5 water supply [white]; 50.0 risks and hazards [dark gray]). Source: Author.

before 1920 [n = 6]), the years to transition are 23.1, 31.7, and 42.8, respectively. This illustrates that the time to transition has possibly become shorter over time. A variety of potential explanations for this can be considered, but it is clear that the emergence of the crisis, the engagement of civil society, governance capacity, and the relevant science and knowledge have become more tightly coupled over time leading to the conditions for more rapid environmental policy transitions.

Other comparisons such as the connection between the development status of the city and the speed to transition or the difference between Global North and Global South cities could provide additional insights with the assumption that more developed cities might have the resources and capacity to promote transitions. The validity of this comparison is questionable since it is challenging to compare development conditions of cities over different times and contexts. For example, how was the development status of early nineteenth-century New York different from that of mid-twentieth -century Cairo? Mid-twentieth-century Cairo was much more advanced than that of early New York

City, but by what degree. Conversely, mid-twentieth-century Cairo was less developed than that of mid-twentieth-century London or Los Angeles.

11.1.2 Role of Drivers and Spheres of Action in Transitions

The case studies provide rich detail regarding the relative role of different drivers in the transition process and spheres of action in which they occurred. On a case-by-case basis, different drivers took on key roles. For example, policy entrepreneurs were critical in several situations, especially when the crisis seemed to be emerging rapidly, such as in St. Louis with the outbreak of the flu. Other instances where specific drivers were particularly important include the need for new knowledge and its acceptance (Los Angeles and smog, Hong Kong and the plague), sustained and growing economic pressure (NYC and water supply), emergence of new governance structures (e.g., shift in scale of governance from local to central/national government – Marseille and plague), and connecting with ongoing social tensions – poverty and systemic racism (Hong Kong and New Orleans).

Occasions where the stress and crisis narratives connect with ongoing and underlying social tensions are particularly meaningful. Cases with unresolved societal conflicts were more often associated with a lack of transition and unresolved crisis. This observation is consistent with more recent assessment work that shows that the greater the level of equity associated with an adaptation action, the more likely it would be effective (IPCC WG 2022). Underlying societal challenges played a significant driver role in Cairo, Hong Kong, Kolkata, Miami, New Orleans, and New York. The presence of these underlying issues also were associated with a much longer period of crisis to transition (58.4 years; n = 6), in comparison to other cases where such issues did not play as large a role (24.8 years; n = 19). By looking at all the cases together, a broad range of consistent drivers and action spheres can be associated with the observed transitions (Table 11.1).

Overall, ecological/environmental drivers and societal drivers were most significant. Physical environment conditions including site characteristics and to a lesser extent extreme events were highly significant. A wide variety of societal drivers were relevant across the case studies. The root societal conditions including cultural changes were especially profound. In some situations, the chronic stress and crisis conditions can tend to operate as a root driver (e.g., the NYC extended water supply crisis of the early 19th century). Overall, the root drivers often played an oversized role in the transition process especially those connected to social and economic inequities

Table 11.1 *Synthesis of key drivers and actions sphere presents across the case studies. The objective here is to highlight those conditions that appeared across multiple case studies. Source: Author.*

Action Spheres	Drivers Root	Contextual	Proximate
Ecological/ Environmental	(1) Physical site characteristics including exposure or scarcity; (2) location as transit and transport hub		(1) Extreme physical event (including biophysical) with economic, social, and health outcomes
Technological/ Infrastructure	(1) New technology/infrastructure – transportation; automobile; (2) industrialization	(1) New planning and design; (2) failed or ineffective projects; (3) constraints on application	
Societal	(1) Rapid urbanization including population growth; (2) lack of policy and governance; (3) growth in role and power of civic society (capacity for legal action and responsibility); (4) structural inequities including poverty, racism, and segregation; colonialism including divisions and tensions; (5) history of social cohesion including central planning; (6) struggle over societal and cultural identity	(1) Follow-on from war or other severe social disruption; (2) shift in governance from private or military control to public control; (3) local economic imperatives and competition; (4) shift in power from industrialists; (5) conflicts of science and policy; (6) emergence of new science; (7) access to massive financial resources; (8) growth in regional and central government planning; response; and capacity; (9) previous experiences with stress; (10) struggle over societal identity	(1) Policy entrepreneurs; (2) policy agreement (including over science/medicine); (3) new science projections; (4) economic collapse

generally and poverty, racism and bigotry, and colonialism. Cities often tried to address stresses and crises without addressing the underlying roots of the problems. In some instances, academic research contributed to this condition by just focusing on the surface problems without analyzing the underlying problems.

Comparing root, contextual, and proximate drivers, it is clear that all three played significant roles in the transition process. Local environmental scarcity (i.e., lack of water, lack of land, a high percent of at-risk land area) as a root driver consistently limited the extent to which a long-term solution or "easy" long-term solution was possible to achieve. The societal root drivers reflected core issues within the cities. In some examples, these drivers reflect a history of social cohesion and capacity to resolve issues (e.g., Cedar Rapids) and in other cases these emerged from deep-seated divisions within the local society (e.g. New Orleans). The drivers significantly impacted the extent to which equity and justice issues were considered (including procedural, representational, and process/product considerations).

With respect to contextual drivers, the drivers presented generally could be placed into the three primary categories of policy enabling conditions often present – governance, financing, and knowledge/information. A shift in governance control to the state (e.g., from the private sector, local informal interests, and military control) was present in transition examples. In many situations there was a growth in regional and central state authorities. Prior experience and new scientific knowledge were both essential in many cases. What is particularly interesting about the presence of these enabling conditions is not so much their presence, but the fact that in many instances, their presence or stock dramatically increased at the moment the crisis conditions were reached and potential transitions were being debated and considered (i.e., central state power legitimized the process). These increases were associated with disruptions or perturbations in the everyday or common practice, such as those resulting from warfare, social unrest, and economic imperatives driven by competition or failure of a massive development project.

Several categories of proximate drivers also were present. These of course included extreme events with a range of economic, social, and health outcomes. Societal proximate drivers were represented by policy entrepreneurs, policy agreements, economic collapse, and science breakthroughs. It is important to note that while proximate drivers were important and many cases necessary for the transition to take place, they were not sufficient. Thus, their presence facilitated transitions, but they themselves were not powerful enough to drive a management or policy regime to a significant change and transitions.

11.1.2.1 Legacy Effects

Each step in the stress–crisis–transition–transformation processes influences the next. These effects vary widely across the case studies in some situations constraining the transition process and in others facilitating it. Across the cases, legacy effects are clearly evident in response to past decisions. Agents including individuals and institutions made locational decisions, allocation decisions, and managerial and operational decisions that influenced the rate and condition of steps in the overall transition process. While it is relatively easy to identify these actions in hindsight (after the fact), it is important to recognize that some of these actions were taken in direct response to nascent stress associated with the environmental problem at hand, while others were seemingly unrelated and had implications on the conditions after the fact. In the case of the New York City water supply, the decades before the paradigm shift to a large-scale publicly held water supply system were punctuated by a series of adjustments that attempted to boost the operation of an increasingly brittle private water supply system. The legacy of these attempts to increase the resilience of the system was that when the system reached its limits, a crisis ensued as illustrated by a set of dramatic and very overt failures including poor water quality-related disease outbreaks and large-scale urban fires that could not be suppressed because of a lack of sufficient water for firefighting. The legacy example of Des Moines, Iowa, is quite different. In this case, the decision to put the key government buildings on the small island in between the two settlements on either side of the Cedar River was done to promote civic society and cooperation. The impact of this decision however was to place some of the most important public infrastructure in a highly flood-prone location, and one that eventually led to them being significantly damaged by a flood resulting in a crisis and helping push forward a transition. A central observation from these two examples and the numerous others within cases is that the legacy effects can emerge from a variety of decisions, some seemingly large or small and directly connected or not, and that within the topic at hand (be it either water supply, risk and hazards, or now climate change) need to be evaluated carefully.

11.1.3 Crisis and Resilience Interface

Environmental policy transitions can occur under a variety of conditions, but generally they take place under two conditions. First, when the magnitude and conditions of the crisis overwhelm the resilience of the existing management and policy system (described here as crisis-oriented transition context). In this case, the absolute level of resilience of the system, whether it be a formal management regime (e.g., a legislative policy regime) or an informal mechanism (e.g., collective action), might remain roughly the same, but its resilience relative to the rapidly growing size and scope of the crisis leads to a collapse. In a second scenario, the crisis could reveal a weakness in the system that results in a diminution of resilience to a sufficiently low level that the transition is then more likely to occur (described here as resilience-oriented). Sometimes both factors come into play and thereby both promoting the likelihood that a transition will take place.

A critical question is how does the interplay between the crisis level and policy regime resilience influence the likelihood of a transition? This question can be answered through the analysis of the case studies to describe what are key resilience and crisis properties that were associated with the resultant transitions. The role of drivers will be significant here since they are mechanisms through which the crises manifest and the resilience properties are expressed. The interaction between the crisis properties and system resilience can be broadly described as the push factors associated with transitions. Together, they push or provide pressure against the established regime increasing the probability of a transition.

While stress and crisis reduced the resilience of the existing system and are signature markers of a regime shift or transition, another feature of this process is the definition and momentary emergence of an alternative system state – a window into what the future policy would look like. For example, within physical systems, this alternative state and future conditions can pop up and emerge intermittently as the system becomes unstable and the possibility of transition increases. This process can be described as a flickering (Solecki et al. 2024) as it appears in multiple moments during a period of time. Within a social system regime shift, such as an urban environmental policy transition, an important additional element of the transition process is the emergence and definition of a coherent policy alternative, or in the terminology of system transition theory – a flicker. The case studies revealed a flickering process associated with an unstable regime. The flickering was manifest as interim alternative system structures that became momentarily evident but for a variety of reasons were not viable or sustainable.

The emergence of an alternative stable state seemed to have an important role to play in the eventual transition of the system. This is because the evidence and presence of this different state negatively impacted the resilience of the existing dominant system by illustrating that a different management regime was not only coalescing, but simply by its existence could be perceived as a viable alternative. With its continuing presence, the resilience of the new system state would be seen as promising and growing. At the same time, the current regime or state of affairs could be increasingly understood as possibly coming to an end, something often difficult to imagine. This interaction between the existing policy regime and the increasingly viable future regime and its influence on the probability of a transition can be described as transition pull factors. Without a viable alternative stable state, the likelihood of an environmental policy transition diminishes. This condition helps illustrate why some of the case studies included transitions that were significantly protracted or failed to fully take hold. In these situations, underlying and unresolved societal schisms and other divisions prevented or disrupted a viable alternative stable policy state from forming. In these cases, there was no transition pull factor, leading the system to either remain weakened and unable to resolve the crisis or possibly further degrade into a state of collapse.

The policy transitions documented in each of the case studies highlight a process of dramatic change. The conditions of this change vary across the case studies. In some cases, the transition is preceded by a drawn out series of policy adjustments and refinements that lead to what could be described as a limited policy transition (i.e., a system-level adjustment within a specific circumscribed institutional setting). This type of condition was present within water resources cases (Chapter 5) and risk and hazard cases (Chapter 8) where deliberation and debate regarding the crisis often lasted decades with many interim policy steps along the way. In these cases and others where the crises rapidly mushroomed (e.g., the disease and pandemic cases), an eventual large-scale transition moment was reached. Embedded within each of these, or what can be described as a catastrophic bifurcation or nonlinear system change, one was able to see characteristic elements of these types of transitions including early warning signals of a potential transition, flickering of current and alternate states illustrating the system's instability, recognizable tipping points, and the dramatic reorganization (i.e., transformation) with the emergence of a new policy regime.

The relative coarseness of the case studies in many instances does not provide the granularity to enable one to see specific examples across all cases. Examples of early warning signals involve situations where resilience of the existing management regime might temporarily collapse, significantly decline in a disproportionate way to the extent of the crisis, only to be recovered soon after, or in other cases, very slowly recover from a shock or perturbation. Specific early warning signals are illustrated in cases where there was mass protest or civil unrest demanding action be taken in the face of the gathering crisis. These events as presented in at least half of the cases signaled that the dominant governing structure and policy were coming under pressure to take direct and significant action, and it also provided evidence to competing interests and coalitions that a plausible alternative policy agenda could be taken seriously.

Similarly, in many cases, one can discern distinct tipping points when a new policy is ratified or agreed upon. It is evident that such policy regime switches involve or are the result of shifts in variables that often take time to change (e.g., public opinion, investment patterns, cultural norms). Such variables are described in the complex system literature as *slow variables*, as opposed to *fast variables*, which can change often and quickly.[2] Within the case studies, often subtle changes of slow variables make identification of well-defined tipping points much less likely than in physical systems, which typically have widely recognized, empirically based slow variables (e.g., changes in net primary productivity or biodiversity). In social systems the tipping points themselves might evolve over an extended period of months or longer. It should be recalled here that tipping points in the case studies are not the nadir of the crisis by itself but when this intense condition is coupled with evidence of a system-level change/possible alternative system. In this way, extreme events including massive floods, extreme air pollution episodes, or solid waste management emergencies are not the tipping points but need to be connected with direct and overt policy regime reconfiguration. Within the case studies, some of the policy tipping points occurred at specific moments that were not associated with specific extreme events, but when a confluence of enabling factors and drivers emerged. The tipping points had complex location and temporal qualities as well. In some cases, understanding that a tipping point had been passed only occurred until after the fact, such as was the case in the solid waste management shift in Seattle or water policy changes in Tel Aviv, while in other examples, the tipping point was very high profile and immediately understood by all – such as the decision to build a massive drinking water reservoir system for the city of New York.

One of the more important messages from this analysis is that there is significant evidence that the observed policy system transitions reflect some of the patterns defined within the complex system transition literature. One can discern system early warning signals, flickering, and tipping points. If this is so, one could expect future urban environmental crises and resulting policy transitions to operate in similar ways, and, therefore, their potential action could be predicted. The application to understand and assert future urban climate policy transitions is valid. The implications of this are explored in Chapter 12.

[2] See for more discussion on slow and fast variables – Walker, B. H., Carpenter, S. R., Rockstrom, J., Crépin, A.-S., & Peterson, G. D. (2012). Drivers, "Slow" Variables, "Fast" Variables, Shocks, and Resilience. *Ecology and Society*, *17*(3). www.jstor.org/stable/26269094.

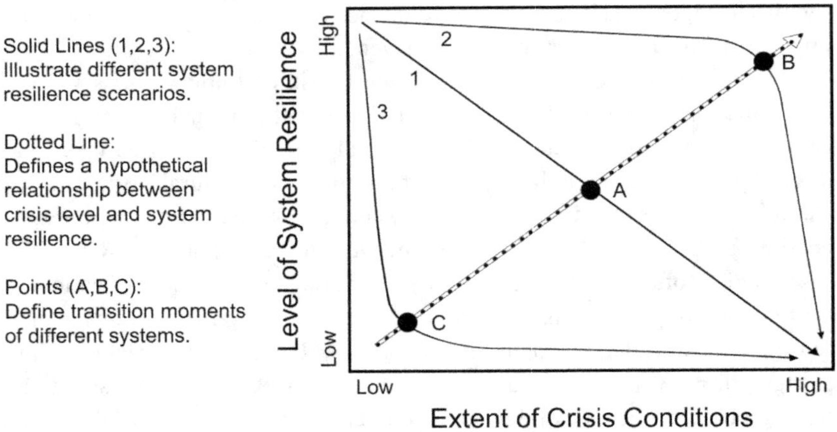

Figure 11.3 Connection between crisis conditions and system resilience. The likelihood of a transition is inversely associated with the level of system resilience and the crisis conditions. The decline in the system's resilience and the growth of the crisis conditions are influenced by root, context, and proximate drivers. System resilience is a function of endogenous and exogenous factors. Source: Author.

The association between the resilience of the system and the crisis level and likelihood of a policy transition is presented in Figure 11.3, which defines three exemplar transition scenarios (on lines 1, 2, and 3). The y-axis shows the level of system resilience and the x-axis shows the intensity of crisis. The graphic highlights two assertions: (1) As the level of crisis increases, so does the pressure on the resilience of the policy system and (2) a policy transition would occur when the level of crisis is equal to or exceeding the level of resilience of the system. In one scenario, the resilience of the system might decline proportionately to the increase of the crisis, and at some point, the level of crisis pressure could result in a policy transition. This relationship is presented by the dashed line on the graph, and a specific case – point A on the middle line – highlights the correlation between the two variables.

In a crisis-oriented transition, the collective impacts of the crisis eventually overwhelm the resilience of the specific governance system associated with the issue. The resilience of the management or policy regime could be quite high, but after a protracted period, the level of crisis becomes so significant that the crisis "exceeds" the resilience of the system. This hypothetical condition is highlighted at point B on the graphic – on the upper line. The risk and hazard cases are reflective of this scenario – given the generally long time before the transition occurs in these cases.

A resilience-oriented crisis would be the case when even a small or limited crisis results in a steep decline of the existing management or policy system resilience resulting in a transition (as noted by Point C in the figure). The public health and disease-focused case studies are examples of crises and transitions more consistent with this scenario.

While Figure 11.3 presents these hypothetical transition conditions, it should be remembered that system resilience and the crisis conditions do vary over time and do not follow a linear pattern. A crucial question is how and why the resilience of the existing management or policy system declines and whether and to what extent the crisis conditions reduce the resilience of the system. A range of indicators can be used to evaluate the relative decline or possible increase of a governance system's resilience. Often used indicators include decision-making structure, transparency and accountability, responsiveness and flexibility, participation and inclusivity and experience and support (Li et al. 2020; Tariq 2021).

11.1.3.1 Observed Crisis and Resilience Indicators

The conditions of crisis and resilience can be defined for the set of 25 case studies. The research literature is complete with a great number of particular indicators that could be applicable to urban environmental crises and the associated shocks that dominant management and policy regimes might face. Here, six crisis indicators and seven system resilience indicators are defined (see Tables 11.2 and 11.3). The fundamental assertion here is that with an increase of crisis indicators and a decrease in the resilience of the established management regime taking place, as well as the emergence of a viable alternative stable state management/policy regime occurring, the greater the likelihood that a policy transition will take place.

The case study narratives provide an illustration of the extent to which the crisis conditions varied. In Figure 11.4, general estimates of the relative strength of different crisis indicators within each set of case studies are presented. The graduated circles define the strength of each of the crisis indicator conditions. In the exercise, an attempt was made to provide a qualitative best estimate of the composite crisis indicator metric for each separate group of case studies (i.e., values for the resource scarcity cases, for the environmental quality). The values illustrate the wide intragroup and intergroup variation in the crisis indicators.

The three crisis indicators that are most present and most consistently at a high or moderate amount are the level of economic impact, deep-seated societal issues, and existential threats.

Several other interesting observations can be made from this assessment. As expected, the disease and pandemic cases were connected to the broadest

Table 11.2 *Crisis Indicators. Features of urban environmental crises have been defined within human–environment coupled systems. The set of key composite indicators expresses conditions that will put pressure on the existing management and policy regime. Source: Author.*

Crisis indicator	Description
Dread	Potential for immediate and unpredictable loss; lack of control
Unknown risk	New or emergent; unfamiliar, limited knowledge
Level of economic impact	Known potential for economic loss and damage
Cascading – compounding risk	Systematic losses and damage that grow and become more impactful; not fixed
Deep-seated societal issue	Connects to and lays bare foundational schisms, ruptures, and unresolved issues
Existential threat to way of life	Left unchecked can make nonviable the daily activities of community and commerce

Table 11.3 *Resilience Indicators. Features of urban environmental management regime system resilience have been defined. The set of key composite indicators expresses conditions that illustrate the extent to which a regime system's resilience will increase or decline. If the attitudes increase, the resilience of the system will increase and vice versa. Source: Author.*

Resilience indicator	Description
Trusted entity	Extent to which the regime was trusted by the various groups
Capacity to engage resources	Ability to bring in and manipulate the necessary resources including financial and labor
Legitimacy	Having the political authority; seen as the legitimate decision-maker, the attributor of the situation
Capacity to meet demands	Actual and perceived ability to meet demands of the various groups
Control of narrative and knowledge	Ability to manage, dictate, and produce a dominant stream of information and data
Networks in/across scales (coalitions)	Links with other institutions and groups within and across scales
Learning/Flexibility	Ability to integrate new knowledge and respond reflexively to new situations

set of crisis indicators given the nature of this type of crisis. The case studies of recycling and reuse, and mobility and settlement have very similar characteristics, again which could be expected because they connect with wide-ranging

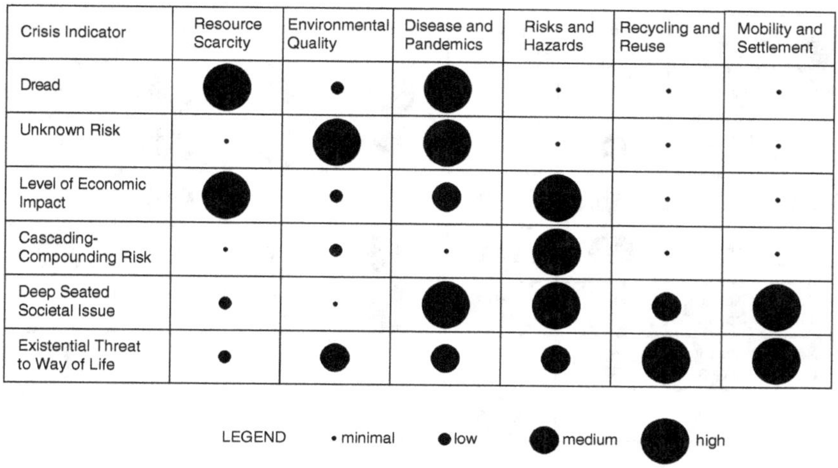

Figure 11.4 Crisis Indicators. The extent to which key crisis indicators were present with each case study category. The larger the cycle, the more significant the factor was in driving the crisis. Source: Author.

sustainability issues and the root-level nature-society connections within each city. It is interesting to further note that the risks and hazard cases were less associated with dreaded or unknown crises, which seems to illustrate the reason why they might have taken on average the longest time to result in a transition. In these situations, the crises were familiar and understandable, and perhaps generally seen as broadly acceptable, although it would certainly be the case that their impacts were distributed unevenly and many populations remained highly at risk.

Figure 11.5 illustrates the relative role of different factors that could influence the relative resilience of management and policy regimes as the crisis conditions developed. A total of seven different composite resilience indicators were evaluated and ranked according to their relative importance. In this analysis, the ranking illustrated how important the indicator was in lowering or diminishing the resilience of the regime. From this assessment, one can define several key observations from this ranking. For example, the resilience indicators that were consistently highly impactful on the regimes' resilience were the capacity to meet demands – meaning that in all cases the crisis increased when there was a decline in the dominant policy system's capacity to meet the demands of the citizenry. Disease and pandemic outbreaks seemed to be the crisis that represented the most significant challenge to a regime's resilience. This condition reflects that observation that the public health crises developed most rapidly and overwhelmed the existing medical care system within each

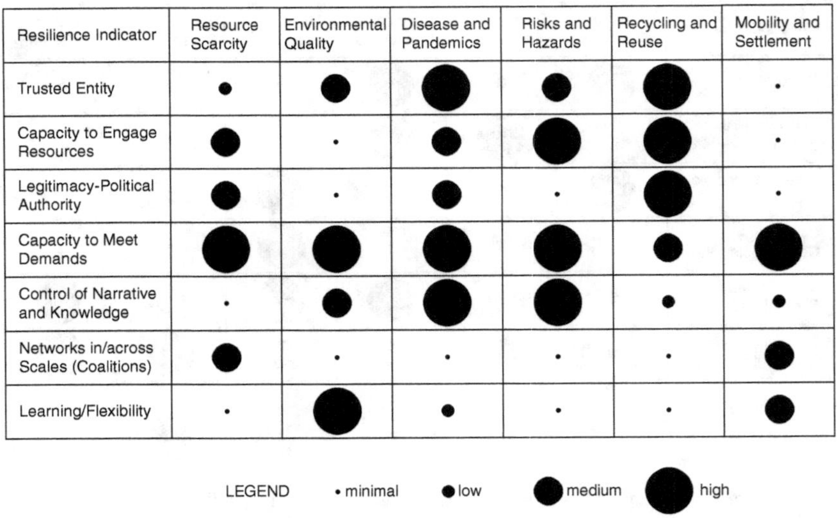

Figure 11.5 Resilience indicators. The extent to which key resilience indicators were present. In the presentation, indicators were included if they were present and were negatively stressing the existing management and policy regime. The larger the circle, the greater the impact of the regime's resilience. The estimates are provided for each case study category. Source: Author.

case study. It is interesting to compare the situation of the public health crises with that of the environmental quality and risk and hazards crises, which took the longest time to result in a transition. A notable difference between them is that in the two latter situations the management and policy regimes did not experience a legitimation crisis. This might have been a factor in why the crises in these cases were allowed to linger so long before there was a policy transition. Another interesting comparison is between the recycling and reuse cases and the mobility and settlement cases. The comparative crisis indicator analysis (Figure 11.4) showed them as having similar qualities, but with respect to resilience indicators, they seemed to follow a divergent pattern, with little overlap in the factors that impinged on the resilience of the policy regime.

11.2 Insights Revealed by the Framework Application

The framework application helps to reveal several key insights on what conditions influence or can influence the urban environmental policy transition process. These include a new understanding of the (1) length of time associated with the rise of a crisis and resulting transition, (2) interconnections between the transition process and the urbanization process, and enabling conditions, including the new governance structures; and (3) how the transition process and immediate aftermath in large part defined the transformation to follow.

11.2.1 Resilience and the Social Production of Transitions

The length of time between the emergence of the crisis and the associated transition or speed of transition reveals several interesting phenomena. Overall, the time from crisis to transition seems to be becoming shorter (i.e., reducing almost half the number of years), while some types of problems consistently take longer than others to resolve (e.g., flooding-related transitions that are multi-decadal vs. disease outbreaks that evolve to that same state in a year are extreme opposites). A possible answer for the added length of time for the hazards-related crises is that the existing management regimes were highly resilient and as a result were able to sustain their mode of operation for an extended period. Conversely, a range of factors appears to accelerate the speed at which transitions can take place. For example, evidence within the case studies illustrates how policy transitions were sped up when private sector interests joined forces with a broad coalition of government and reform-minded interests – as was the case with the New York City water supply system transition in the 1830s. Other examples: the advent of new science and new knowledge had dramatic impacts on several crises leading to an acceleration of the transition (e.g., Abu Dhabi – extreme heat, Hong Kong – disease, Los Angeles – air pollution, and Miami – sustainability).

A systematic review of the case studies shows that in most circumstances the resilience of the policy systems declined as the crises emerged. The policy systems came under increased pressure from a variety of internal and external sources, which are often associated with a legitimation crisis (i.e., calls that the system is broken and is no longer effective or able to respond to the current situation). An advance here is that the case studies reveal that a critical factor associated with this steep decline of policy system resilience is the linkage of different elements or facets of the crisis and that the confluence of these conditions can significantly change the relationship of the resilience and crisis conditions.

The case studies revealed an important distinction regarding how the crises are understood and described and how they could result in a policy transition. This approach brings forward a new understanding of how a crisis can be considered. The most typical consideration is that as the crisis grows, interested parties form a coalition and rush forward to address the crisis. The suggestion is that crises typically emerge from actual or perceived limits (e.g., scarcity), threats (e.g., hazardous observed conditions), or risks (e.g., possibility of experiencing harm or loss). The case studies highlight that crises are much more complex and are reflective of multiple perspectives and interests that coalesce and can be described as additive or synergistic, as illustrated in Figure 11.4 and 11.5.

The analysis of variable conditions that influence the intensity of the crisis and the shift in resilience also provides a window into how the various factors associated with each can be described and whether any specific alignments either enhance or detract from the likelihood of a transition. One issue that was particularly evident in the case studies is that there are different facets of the crisis that seem to influence the likelihood that a transition would occur. The work of French philosopher Henri Lefebvre's classic statements on the social production of space (Lefebvre 1991) can be helpful here to understand these different facets of crisis and how they might associate with the probability of a transition. Lefebvre argued that the social production of space (Lefebvre 1991) took place as part of a set of complex interactions between material reality, a perceived reality, and lived experience. The material reality includes things that are observed and measured. The perceived or discursive reality is one that can include the meanings and significance of the space – what it represents. This also includes planning and policymaking, which can (re)imagine space to meet current and future demands. A third component of space includes how it is lived in, or how people act or respond, and how they find themselves enabled or constrained by it. Lefebvre's project goal and for others who pick up on it (e.g., Gottdiener 1985), was to examine how the struggle over space and its construction takes place.

One can use a similar triad to understand the different dimensions of crises and their collective role in the process of urban environmental policy transitions. In the case here, crises also can be presented as having three elements – an objective crisis (i.e., the biophysical and societal drivers), a perceived or discursive crisis (i.e., how the crisis is understood and represented), and a lived experience crisis (i.e., how it impacts the everyday well-being and quality of life of residents, businesses, and other interests). Using this framing, one further understands how urban environmental crises emerge and coalesce. Through a review of the case studies, it seems evident that the occurrence of a transition is significantly increased with the occurrence of these three elements. The crisis-to-transition process then can be described as associated with the development of a physical limit, threat, or risk, as well as a contestation over its meaning and its control, and the experiences of individuals facing the peril on an everyday basis.

Returning to the case studies to further illustrate these three crisis elements, it is clear that a significant part of the narrative was about what the topics/issues/resources associated with the crises do and represent (their utility – social, economic, and otherwise) and less about what they are (i.e., what are their natural properties, how they are structured, or function). While the objective crisis was important (i.e., what was scarce/absent or overly abundant), overall what was most important about the crises was what they represented and how they impacted the lived experience. Most significant was how do the crises disrupt daily life and are a threat to well-being (i.e., life, family, and wealth) or a threat to the promise of well-being (i.e., will diminish future economic activity, future generations). It should be noted that different crises have varying connections to different components of the Lefebvre triad. For example, the solid waste crisis is more associated with meaning and identity, which has a lot of relevance to climate mitigation, while extreme events are much more connected to material conditions that are more relevant to climate adaptation.

Overall, a very limited amount of the crisis narratives was focused on the property or character of the crisis subject and on the larger-scale systemic questions and issues at work. Although when a systems perspective entered into the discussion, it was often quite central and useful (for example, when there were new scientific projections of future stresses and risks). Even so, much more of the discussion was on what the crisis caused or provided and what it might mean to the city than anything else. If one considers two factors – (1) threat to life and well-being and (2) opportunity for betterment – the discussion and focus on driving a transition forward occurred when both conditions were greatest.

11.2.2 Transitions in Context

The specifics of how the crisis results in a policy transition are connected to a variety of contextual variables and conditions that significantly influence the conditions of the transition. For example, in several cases, the lack of coalitions and governance structures was identified during the crisis period. Their eventual formation provided new state engagement and support to address the underlying issues and new capacity that was critical to the development and implementation of the new policy transition. In this section, the role of six key contextual conditions is assessed. Four involve enabling conditions often highlighted in the research literature: governance, financing, knowledge, and technology. Two other key compound factors emerged from a review of the case studies themselves – urbanization and warfare/social disruption.

11.2.2.1 Importance of Enabling Conditions

Several enabling conditions played key roles as the possibility of a transition increased. Enabling conditions, in this context, can be defined as those circumstances that increase the feasibility of a transition. Several key enabling conditions have been identified and include governance capacity, finance, knowledge, and access to technology. Throughout the case studies, these enabling conditions emerge time and time again as critical to the transition process. In some cases, all these enabling conditions were present and just needed to be redirected to the crisis (e.g., addressing heat in Abu Dhabi). For the vast majority of examples, one or more enabling conditions were enhanced or restructured as part of the transition process. In most cases, new government agencies or institutions were required as part of the transition. Several of which were associated with a shift from private to public control of the issue or a shift in the scale of governance from local to state or provincial to central government (e.g., Buenos Aires, Los Angeles, Marseilles). Financing of course was critical in all instances but became particularly important in cases when a massive infusion of capital was required for large-scale investments associated with the development and implementation of new infrastructure, such as in the building of new urban water drinking supply systems (e.g., New York, Cairo). Access to relevant and new knowledge was especially critical with the emergence and response to new and not well understood crises, especially related to public health issues (e.g., secondary air pollution in Los Angeles, plague in Hong Kong, and COVID in Seoul). Access to technology proved instrumental in promoting a transition across a wide diversity of situations, especially those with risks and hazards-related crises and those related to mobility and settlement.

11.2.2.2 Moderating Influence of City Building and Urbanization

The crisis development and transition process are also significantly influenced by the urbanization process. The role and outcome of urbanization can both have a negative and positive influence on the environmental policy system's resilience as well as a negative or positive influence on the conditions of crisis. Urbanization drives a variety of conditions that have implications for the development of crises and the circumstance, under which transitions can be considered. For example, urbanization in several of the sites was associated with the emergence of environmental constraints, the pace and pattern of urban environmental change, and the revealing of institutional limits, barriers, and demands.

11.2.2.3 Warfare and Disruption

The threat or reality of warfare and social disruption also played a significant role in many of the crises and transitions. Interestingly, the connection was not direct as one might expect – warfare did not immediately precipitate a transition in policy, but instead the profound impacts of warfare percolated through the social–ecological–technological systems to become a root and contextual driver of change. Only in one case, did it approach being a proximate driver of change. For example, in the case of the deadly flu outbreak in St. Louis during World War I troop movements led to the dramatic spread of the disease locally (and nationally as well). In Rotterdam, the use of the city's surrounding dikes for German army fortifications and general deferred maintenance during World War II lead to weaknesses in the structures' foundations and then significant failure of the flood control barriers during the massive 1953 storm. The economic hardship faced by Britain following World War II pressured the country and the city of London to burn domestically produced and less expensive high-sulfur coal. The resulting increased pollution load became a significant factor in the deadliness of the December 1952 air pollution episode. In yet another example, the China Civil War and eventual retreat of the nationalist army to Taiwan led to an extended period of martial law that finally ended after almost 40 years in 1987. This end brought a flowering of public policy engagement and with it, new policies to address a set of pressing environmental issues including solid waste.

11.2.3 Transitions and Transformations

The case studies illustrate how transitions set in motion transformations. An important question to ask is what is the connection between the character of the transition and the resulting transformation? More specifically, how does the quality and character of the transition influence the transformation process to follow? Is a narrow transition focused on a specific policy regime shift associated with a similarly narrow transformation, and conversely, does a broad transition, involving a massive switch in environmental management philosophy, result in a wide transformation?

The nature of transitions can be quite varied as evidenced by the case studies. Policy transitions, for example, can differ widely with respect to their level of societal impact or effect. When describing the role of different drivers of the transitions, they were described by the terms root, context, and proximate. These provided insights into how the transitions occurred. Here one can use a set of descriptors to illustrate the different foci of the transitions. For example, root transitions are those focused on or engaged with a broad policy agenda connected with multiple social, ecological/environmental, and technological/infrastructure spheres of action. A context driven transition has a narrow policy focus, while proximate transitions are narrower still. In turn, one might assume that there is an equivalence between the type of transition and the level or scale of the resulting transformation. For example, root transitions are more likely to result in broad-scale societal transformations. This was the case for the Seattle and Oslo transitions and to a lesser extent the Miami transitions that focused on a set of broad-scale changes to the city's society including a refashioning of the city's identity and relationship with its local environment and ecology. Conversely, the Atlanta water supply transition was fairly focused and could be described as either contextual or even proximate as it resulted in significant shifts in regional water supply but relatively little else.

The question remains as to whether proximate transitions can eventually lead to or be coupled with larger-scale transformations. The case study material seems to indicate that this is possible. For instance, the targeted policy shift in Hong Kong during the plague outbreak was part of a much broader reappraisal of the British–Chinese relationship and its movement toward a greater role for Chinese interests and residents in colonial management and affairs and some increased justice for the majority Chinese population. Similarly, wider transformative shifts developed from rather specific policy adjustments in Taipei's waste management policy, London and Tokyo's air pollution policy, and Rotterdam's flood control policy. The converse also seems to have occurred. A few of the transitions were part of attempts to implement larger-scale reformulations of urban life via root-level transitions (such as in Cairo, Kolkata, and to a lesser extent New Orleans and Miami) but were shown to be only partially successful and lead to what could be described as a limited transformation. As discussed, these transitions proved to be incomplete because of the cities' inability to reconcile underlying root-level societal divisions, including poverty, racism, and ethnic divisions.

11.3 Advancing the Analysis and Framework

While the framework proved to be useful for understanding and analyzing urban environmental crises and transitions, several potential enhancements could be made to advance the framework. The framework provides a way to understand the broad arc of the crises and transitions, but it is clear that more detailed analysis is needed within each case study to determine specific reasons for the relative decline of the management regime's resilience in the face of pressure for change. More detailed analysis of system-specific shifts would help in the identification of early warning signals, system flickering associated with instability and transitions, and tipping points.

What can one say with the case studies? One can define how the key structures and actors influence the transitions, and one can state what they do and what their outward objective and motivation are but not their deeper motivation. One can't plumb into and know about the deeper psychological motivation of the transition. An extended framework to investigate psychological issues would be an advance.

The case studies in many respects are just scratching the surface both with respect to the deep complexity of the issues and the variety of crises and city contexts. At the simplest level, it would be useful to develop more case studies, especially on small and medium-sized cities. Of course, the caveat when attempting to study small and medium-sized cities is that there is often a paucity of data and existing assessments and research to review and synthesize. Analysis of these cities would require more in-depth primary research. The advantage of primary research is that it enables one to examine the case studies in greater detail to define the role of specific actors and drivers in the transition process. This process would also allow for a more focused examination of the role of structural elements including economic inequities, racism, among others. Collectively, these advancements also allow for a more extended analysis of the connections between transitions and transformations and whether or not transformations forged from the transitions are sustained or not.

Perhaps one of the most significant potential advances of the framework and its application would be to better understand its utility for understanding climate change-related urban environmental transitions. That is the focus on the next and final chapter.

12

Opportunities to Advance Environmental Policy Transitions and Transformative Climate Action

Cities around the world are responding to the increasingly dynamic shifts set off by the deepening climate crisis. Climate change impacts have begun to press against the capacity of cities to meet the daily demands of their citizenry and are generating conditions of growing environmental stress and crisis. A pressing need exists to understand how, when, and why to adjust policies that influence a city's capacity to foster and enact climate adaptation and mitigation. The objective of this book has been to define what we can learn from past urban environmental crises and resulting policy transitions that might be applicable to understand how climate change will manifest as crises in cities and what can be done to help accelerate urban climate action. The case studies provide understanding of how existing urban environmental practices can be adjusted and enhanced. In this chapter, we turn our attention more directly to define ways in which learning from the book's case studies can translate into meaningful urban climate action.

The results of the case study analyses provide potentially significant insights for cities attempting to grapple with the challenges of climate change. In some ways, the findings reinforce our understanding of how cities could enhance and accelerate their own climate action. The analysis also provides the groundwork for a set of innovative recommendations on how to conceive the urban climate crisis and how to consider new urban climate change policy.

12.1 Understanding the Urban Climate Crisis

The case study analysis points out the importance of several known conditions regarding how climate crises can emerge in cities and what might be the implications for the subsequent pursuit of city-scale climate policy transitions.

12.1.1 Tackling Root Drivers

Underlying deep, embedded poverty, racism, and other social divisions and inequities and injustices limited the potential for a policy transition and/or decreased the effectiveness of the resulting transformations, resulting in a continued crisis. Overall, the opportunities for positive outcomes were diminished if problematic root drivers were left unsolved. The effectiveness of climate policies in cities would be increased if the policy environment could include actions to address existing tensions and divisions within the city's social structure. Of course, it should be recognized that root drivers are built and emerge over time and therefore can require a long time to address. In addition, many root drivers, especially those more explicitly socially derived, most often serve the elite interests. As a result, resistance among these interests might be present since they could potentially lose power or advantage if the power structures that created the root drivers are upset or dismantled.

Of the three main categories of drivers, ecological/environmental and societal drivers consistently are more important than technology and infrastructure drivers in defining the patterns and processes of urban environmental policy transitions. While technology and infrastructure are often generated as part of the transformation following the policy transitions (i.e., the new policy dictated the construction of physical infrastructure), these features themselves were consistently not central to the transition process, somewhat counter to what might have been expected.

12.1.2 Crises as Lived Experiences

The narratives of crises exposed in the case studies focus more on what effects the crises had/might have had on people and on the economy, rather than on how the crises operate. Therefore, to engender strong climate change policy debate and potential innovation, it would be appropriate to focus less on the climate change process itself and the mechanisms of climate change and more on the impacts on the everyday and lived experience, including asking people how climate change is affecting their daily lives. These latter elements will be of more interest to the city's stakeholder community.

The case study evidence also shows that different types of crises lead to varying levels of community concern, engagement, and action. From the climate change literature, it is clear that distinct aspects of climate change and associated risks and hazards (e.g., extreme heat, coastal flooding, sea level rise) will be understood and perceived differently because they manifest as distinctive types of crises, each of which are felt in a variety of ways. *Therefore, climate change is not one crisis point but is expressed and experienced as multiple crisis points.* This understanding represents both a potential challenge and opportunity for those promoting climate action. Some aspects of the urban climate crisis might require immediate action and have properties like a pandemic crisis, while others could be more like an isolated acute hazard (e.g., large-scale coastal flood inundation) that are typically associated with a slower protracted policy response, following the immediate shock of the event.

A key point is that while the multiple facets of the climate change impacts present a looming crisis, most city residents experience only a few of these aspects. Therefore, the impulse behind the phrases of "climate crisis" or "climate emergency" as expressed by organizations and institutions does not reflect how many urban interest groups experience climate change. As a result, it is important to understand that the use of these tropes might have unintended negative consequences of not connecting with or not making sense for urban stakeholder groups; potential pushing some groups away to become oppositional to the proposed climate policy transitions. That said, if there was a way to present climate change as a disease or pandemic, it will likely result in the most aggressive action response and transitions.

12.2 Important Circumstances for Urban Climate Policy

The case study analysis helps identify several circumstances associated with the policy context present in urban environmental transitions that have relevance to climate policy transitions.

Some of the findings support current knowledge of how specific factors contribute to policy transitions. For example, the city cases illustrate how enabling conditions could enhance the opportunities for climate adaptation and even potentially transformative adaptation. These key enabling conditions are: (1) transparent and effective governance; (2) financing and capital resources (including technology and infrastructure; (3) knowledge as well as the role of new knowledge; and (4) an equitable decision-making process.

Other insights are more nuanced or less well understood. For instance, the case studies illustrated that enabling conditions are necessary for making a transition feasible, but they by themselves are not sufficient. A complex of drivers plays a critical function in creating the setting for a policy transition. While some of the drivers remained fairly static during the crises and transition, such as biophysical drivers, other drivers were linked with more dynamic elements causing their significance to increase over time. The condition, extent, and rate of urbanization and other types of social disruption, including the legacy of warfare, for example, played consistently important roles. It is critical for urban environmental policymakers to understand how change in the different drivers might affect the crisis and transition process and be responsive and flexible to shifts and, where possible, take advantage of them. In a related finding, the case studies demonstrate that policy diversity and flexibility are especially valuable when the conditions are highly dynamic, such as with rapid urban development and rapid local environmental change. Such conditions can create challenges and opportunities with respect to initiating and carrying out urban environmental transitions and in turn require in-depth and rapid trial and error, evaluation, and adjustment to determine which approach works best.

The cases also illuminate how the need for policy transitions can develop over a short period of time, and it is important for urban stakeholders and policymakers to be ready to take advantage of the opportunities for transformation. This would be especially true during the current moment when seemingly each month creates new climate-related risk understanding. Evaluation of ongoing crises and noting possible early warning signals of conditions for a possible policy transition will be important to identify during this time. Abrupt changes can often be brought on by extreme events such as floods, extreme air pollution episodes, and pandemics. Extreme events of this type often played a significant role as proximate drivers in the case studies, but they did not play an oversized role in the transitions. The transitions mostly emerged from a confluence of root and context drivers. The extreme event could act as a spark but only when the conditions are right. In the end, policymakers should not wait for a disaster event to provide a catalyst for the transition.

At the same time, the case studies also provide evidence that the most effective environmental policy transition proposals should be connected to the deeper societal conditions driving the crisis (e.g., unequal access to resources and exposure to pollutants and unsustainable patterns of growth) and not just address the simple surficial issues of the crisis (e.g., not enough water, polluted air, limited mobility). The policy proposals that embrace both of these aspects (the deeper and surficial issues) will be more attentive to the issues that are important for people's daily lives. These initiatives in turn often get more traction as a viable future policy option and seem to be those that most likely lead to unmistakable transitions, and possibly profound and meaningful subsequent transformations.

Several other consequential considerations for urban policy transitions coming from the case studies relate to conditions of governance. The case studies illustrate how urban environmental crises and policy transitions are driven by actors and institutions that collectively operate at all scales (local, regional, and national) and a diversity of interests, agendas, mandates, and capacity. These actors and institutions include residents, civil society, local and state/provincial, and national government. In many of the cases, the role of interests and political entities (including central governments) outside the city where the crisis was present grew over time and became highly significant in the definition of the transition and resulting transformation. It is clear from this analysis that urban climate change action and policy transitions will require a highly integrated governance response and collaboration. Interagency and intergovernmental action *and* collaboration, along with engagement of civil society, will be key to meaningful advance.

12.3 Adjustments to Current Urban Environmental Practice

Urban environmental crises are part of the experience of cities. As illustrated in the previous chapter (Chapter 11), a range of different practices in cities have emerged to respond to these conditions and circumstances. The case studies narratives reveal a range of activities that, when employed advance the opportunities to promote accelerated response to crises and eventual policy transitions. These observations are translated here to define a set of recommendations that city decision-makers and stakeholders should consider to create and boost prospects for climate policy transitions and transformations.

12.3.1 Approach to Research and Knowledge

To understand urban environmental crises and transitions, the focus should be directed toward understanding the role and significance of the underlying systematic issues. Attention is often directed at superficial aspects of the crises; however, it is when deeper societal drivers and their implications also are incorporated into the crisis narrative that broader understanding, comprehension, and potential support for responding to the crisis can more quickly be defined. Given that, as the crisis emerges, research and new knowledge generation should include notice of what the crisis is revealing about structural inequities and injustices, long-standing schisms and tensions, and similar issues. Crises take on multiple dimensions, and crises as lived experiences are especially important. Therefore, how the climate crisis is being experienced on the ground in cities is one type of research and new knowledge that should be developed and made available. This activity will help promote understanding about how people, households, neighborhoods, and institutions are experiencing the climate crisis. As noted in the case studies, how the crisis is experienced and the extent to which that knowledge is widely disseminated and acknowledged are key to driving the process of policy transition forward because of the increased general public and elite class support for such action.

Many other aspects of environmental crises also have significance with regards to how crises translated into transitions. For instance, the legacy of past decisions can become more important with time because they often can make actors more or less able to respond to a present crisis. In the case studies, it was shown that early, pre-crisis, resource allocation or infrastructure decisions tend to create conditions of lock-in. In Taiwan, for instance, a decision to build incinerators as an initial response to the waste crisis locked a specific managemental and policy approach that required significant effort, expenditure, and political will to overcome. Conversely, a legacy of change and action in other contexts was a powerful vehicle to accelerate present action. This is well illustrated by instances where cities had relevant previous experience with acute disease outbreaks (e.g., Seoul, South Korea; Marseille, France), which fostered a significantly better response when a disease outbreak struck again. Overall, it is valuable to understand the legacy of past decisions in the current context as much as possible, and to take advantage of this influence where relevant.

It is also critical to learn from successes and, especially, mistakes that occur during the build-up of each crisis. Stories of crisis and transition are full of incomplete solutions and failed ideas. These provide the narrative of the meandering and wrenching, often decadal, struggles that occur before an eventual policy transition takes place. It is important to promote better and more meaningful learning from these mistakes to provide advanced data and information on issues, pathways, or approaches to avoid mistakes and better promote the potential for new and effective strategies. In this way, connecting the climate crisis to the local context and legacies of past decisions embedded within it is essential to fully understand the crisis and its implications, and how a policy transition might occur. As an example, one can take from the case study narratives that it will be valuable to link the debate over climate action within a city directly to the pattern and pace of urbanization, the residents' well-being, and the impact on everyday life. When one can relate climate change material impacts (e.g., the level of damage and disruption and its costs) with how they are understood and perceived through the everyday experience of residents, meaningful climate action will be more likely to happen.

12.3.2 Approach to the Policy Transition Process

Several insights emerge from the case studies that could be used for city practitioners and stakeholders as they enter into a climate policy transition process. The case studies provide evidence of consistent themes, questions, and needs present during the transition process. For instance, it is important to be cognizant of the influence of social context (e.g., rapid economic growth, recession) and related drivers (e.g., entrenched inequities) in the decision-making and policymaking process. The different crisis narratives illustrate how one needs to not only understand these types of factors but also recognize that these social contexts and drivers are complex and sometimes relatively static while others might be highly dynamic. This complexity can be quite particular to different cities and crises. These local conditions need to be understood and incorporated into any climate policy transition debate and avoid any one-size-fits-all approach to problem solving, that is, what worked in one city might not work in another city.

The case studies amplify several basic elements of how policy issues are (re)solved in cities and how they will emerge when addressing urban climate crises. For example, power relations between competing interests are highly significant and structure much of how the conflict surrounding potential resolutions is debated and which various options are put forward for review and potential action. In many of the cases, the interests of nonlocal actors including regional and national issues were often brought into the discussion and played an oversized role in the process of crisis resolution and transition. These conditions, most typically focused on security issues (i.e., access to water) or identity issues (i.e., achieving sustainability), were evident throughout all the different crisis contexts. These interests when downscaled to the local level also greatly amplified the key enabling conditions (governance capacity, financing, and knowledge base) to promote an environmental policy transition. The same will likely be the case for urban climate crises as they emerge. While attempting to address issues locally, it will be often seen as preferable to bring in or drop down regional and national issues and/or partners to accelerate the movement toward significant environmental policy transitions.

Another key conclusion from the case studies is that in order to foster an environmental policy transition, one should focus on the resistance to that change and the resilience of oppositional interests and systems. Work could be done to proactively address and assuage these interests and concerns (often those of the elite) resistant to change while potentially forestalling further instability including civil protest, associated with urban crises. Policy changes inevitably involve the potential for winners and losers, and those losing can be quite resistant to the proposed change. If done in a manner to proactively incorporate and be responsive to the needs and concerns of these parties, the transition might occur sooner, more completely, and more successfully than otherwise. Most fundamentally, thinking strategically about limiting the resilience of the existing management system and policy regime has the potential to accelerate change.

The analysis also lays out how the character and pace of the policy change are important to the urban environmental policy transition process. It is clear that the time in number of years from when the full crisis emerges to when a significant policy transition takes place seems to have become smaller as noted in the analysis in Chapter 11. This description however masks a second issue. The case studies also reveal a much more complex history of transition than one being based on a single pivotal policy change. The histories present a series of proceeding conditions involving drivers, enabling conditions, minor transition or precursor events, and failed attempts or false starts at a major transition. From this perspective, major transitions almost can be imagined as a combination lock that only opens after all the tumblers in the lock are lined up and in sync.

This perspective forces another significant issue to arise – how to define and promote the process of climate action transition in a city. Within the discourse of climate transitions, this process is most often presented via the concept of pathways. Climate transition pathways are used to describe an evolutionary and flexible process of climate action that leads to transformation. Most often pathways are described in terms of gradual and incremental shifts that can also experience more abrupt, even large-scale disruptions possibly resulting from shocks. The case studies however illuminate a more nuanced sequence of change – one that is often punctuated by small shifts that individually are abrupt and significant in their own right, as well as massive shifts that result in wider impacts and are more likely to lead to transformation. So similar to when a smooth line becomes a jagged line when zooming down into a computer map to see greater detail, the process of transition is never really smooth but always is with a serrated edge.

The implications of this for urban climate policy action could be profound. Simply put, we need to alter our understanding of policy change. Instead of presenting it as smooth pathways with occasional shocks that result in dramatic change, policy change can be conceived as a continuous disruption. Such was the situation for many cases where small, limited shifts preceded the larger-scale transition that brought significant diminution to the crisis. For cities approaching the climate crisis, it will be important to articulate and make known the pattern and conditions of these numerous adjustments, each distinct yet linked. This acknowledgement will help facilitate debate and conversation about the process of change and enhance the capacity to foster a more effective and equitable response to larger-scale transitions when they occur and enhance the prospects for more successful and meaningful transformations. In the end, the connection of the policy transition to the resulting transformation will be key to understanding how to push and carry forward the broad new policy agenda and how to "win" the transformation.

12.4 Coda

The findings from the work provide a series of insights regarding how to better appreciate and push forward urban climate transitions. Perhaps most profoundly and simply, it argues that we should do all we can to learn from past decisions and actions to take stock of previous urban environmental crises and how they continue to inform us moving into the future. The analysis also simultaneously promotes a set of specific recommendations for policymakers and practitioners considering how to promote an aggressive and effective climate change agenda in their city. These recommendations are designed to build upon existing considerations that they might have on how to get things done in their town. The list of simple recommendations includes the following: (1) Address root drivers; (2) emphasize equity; (3) address the resilience of the existing management and policy regime and develop strategies to respond to it; (4) consider and focus on what government institutions should be changed and what new knowledge is needed; (5) define clear policy advances/breaks, minimize partial policy shifts, and side experiments, yet learn from them when they do occur; (6) enabling conditions matter but are not always sufficient to initiate change on their own; and (7) track the impact of the transformations and connections between transitions and transformations, even though these connections are fraught. And finally, we must recognize that and transformations might not result in the desired change and transformations might be incomplete, and that the accelerated demands of climate change and other acute demands (i.e., economic collapse, social disruption) might not allow for the results of the transition and transformation to fully play out before there is a need to change again.

References

Abu Dhabi Media Office. 2020. (DMT) announces 10 global winners of 'Cool Abu Dhabi Challenge.' October 6. www.mediaoffice.abudhabi/en/environment/dmt-announces-10-global-winners-of-cool-abu/

Abu Dhabi, Department of Municipalities and Transport. 2020. Cool Abu Dhabi Challenge. Coolabudhabi.com.

Adeleke, Oluwatobi, Stephen Akinlabi, Tien-Chien Jen, and Israel Dunmade. 2021. "Towards Sustainability in Municipal Solid Waste Management in South Africa: A Survey of Challenges and Prospects." *Transactions of the Royal Society of South Africa* 76 (1): 53–66. https://doi.org/10.1080/0035919X.2020.1858366.

ADGM (Abu Dhabi Global Market). 2020. Launch of the Abu Dhabi Climate Initiative. January 15. www.adgm.com/media/announcements/launch-of-the-abu-dhabi-climate-initiative.

Agyeman, Julian, Robert Doyle Bullard, and Bob Evans, eds. 2003. *Just Sustainabilities: Development in an Unequal World.* Cambridge, MA: MIT Press.

Alatout, S. 2008. "'States' of Scarcity: Water, Space, and Identity Politics in Israel, 1948–59." *Environment and Planning D: Society and Space 26* (6): 959–82. https://doi.org/10.1068/d1106.

Alcott, Blake. 2010. "Impact Caps: Why Population, Affluence and Technology Strategies Should Be Abandoned." *Journal of Cleaner Production* 18 (6): 552–60. https://doi.org/10.1016/j.jclepro.2009.08.001.

Allen, Adriana, Julio D. Dávila, and Pascale Hofmann. 2006. "The Peri-Urban Water Poor: Citizens or Consumers?" *Environment and Urbanization* 18 (2): 333–51.

Altimir, Oscar, Luis Alberto Beccaría, and Martín González-Rozada. 2002. "Income Distribution in Argentina, 1974–2000." *CEPAL Review* 78 (December): 53–82.

Anonymous. 2008. The Cairo Water Supply Source. *The British Medical Journal*, 1 (2456): 225.

Anonymous. 2013. US Lakes, Lake Sidney Lanier Water Levels. US Lakes Information. http://.uslakes.info/Level.asp.

Anonymous. 2016. "Moving towards Environmental Sustainability in Johannesburg for Future Generations," July 29, 2016, sec. *The Mail & Guardian*. Article. https://mg.co.za/article/2016-07-29-00-moving-towards-environmental-sustainability-in-johannesburg-for-future-generations/.

Anttiroiko, Ari-Veikko. 2021. "Successful Government Responses to the Pandemic: Contextualizing National and Urban Responses to the COVID-19 Outbreak in East and West." *International Journal of E-Planning Research (IJEPR)* 10 (2): 1–17. https://doi.org/10.4018/IJEPR.20210401.oa1.

ARC, Atlanta Regional Council. 2023. "Tri-State Water Wars – Background and History." Nonprofit. Atlantaregional.org. 011 2022. https://atlantaregional.org/natural-resources/water-wars/tri-state-water-wars-background-and-history/.

Arlosoroff, Saul. 2003. "Israel: A Case Study of Water-Demand Management." *Waterlines* 22 (2): 4–7.

Arsenault, Raymond. 1984. "The End of the Long Hot Summer: The Air Conditioner and Southern Culture." *The Journal of Southern History* 50 (4): 597–628. https://doi.org/10.2307/2208474.

Asonuma, Tamon, Mike Xin Li, Michael G. Papaioannou, Saji Thomas, and Eriko Togo. 2018. "Sovereign Debt Restructurings in Grenada: Causes, Processes, Outcomes, and Lessons Learned." *Journal of Banking and Financial Economics* 2 (10): 67–105. https://doi.org/10.7172/2353-6845.jbfe.2018.2.4.

Ashour, M. A., S. T. El Attar, Y. M. Rafaat and M. N. Mohamed. 2009. "Water resources management in Egypt." *Journal of Engineering Sciences* 37 (2), 269–79.

Atlanta Regional Commission. 2023. Tri-State Water Wars Overview. https://atlantaregional.org/what-we-do/natural-resources/tri-state-water-wars-overview/

Attia, Fatma Abdel Rahman. 1999. "Water and Development in Greater Cairo (Egypt)." *Revista CIDOB d'Afers Internacionals* 45/46 (April): 81–102.

Atwood, Sam. 1997. *Fifty Years of Progress toward Clean Air: Southland's War on Smog*. Diamond Bar, CA: South Coast Air Quality Management District.

Aozora Foundation. 2007. *The History of Japanese Air Pollution*. https://aozora.or.jp/lang/english/the-history-of-japans-air-pollution.

Bai, Xuemei, Richard J. Dawson, Diana Ürge-Vorsatz, et al. 2018. "Six Research Priorities for Cities and Climate Change." *Nature* 555 (7694): 23–25. https://doi.org/10.1038/d41586-018-02409-z.

Bai, Xuemei, and Hidefumi Imura. 2000. "A Comparative Study of Urban Environment in East Asia: Stage Model of Urban Environmental Evolution." *International Review for Environmental Strategies* 1 (1): 135–58.

Baker, M., and N. Letsoela. 2016. "Implementation of the Landfill Methane Gas to Electricity Project in the City of Johannesburg." In *23rd WasteCon Conference*. Emperors, Johannesburg.

Balch, Oliver. 2016. "The New Generation of Buenos Aires Trash Pickers Reenergizing Recycling in the Capital." *The Guardian*, January 20, 2016, sec. Environment. www.theguardian.com/environment/2016/jan/20/buenos-aires-litter-pickers-cartoneros-recycling-argentina-environment.

Ballard, Richard, and Christian Hamann. 2021. "Income Inequality and Socio-Economic Segregation in the City of Johannesburg." In *Urban Socio-Economic Segregation and Income Inequality: A Global Perspective*, edited by Maarten van Ham, Tiit Tammaru, Rūta Ubarevičienė, and Heleen Janssen, 91–109. The Urban Book Series. New York: Springer. https://doi.org/10.1007/978-3-030-64569-4.

Banerjee, Soumita. 2018. "An Analysis of Urban Flooding Scenario in the City of Kolkata West Bengal." *International Journal of Innovative Knowledge Concepts* 6 (5): 2454–515. https://doi.org/11.25835/IJIK-24.

Bao, Zhikang, Weisheng Lu, Ziyu Peng, and S. Thomas Ng. 2023. "Balancing Economic Development and Construction Waste Management in Emerging Economies: A Longitudinal Case Study of Shenzhen, China Guided by the Environmental Kuznets Curve." *Journal of Cleaner Production* 396: 136547. https://doi.org/10.1016/j.jclepro.2023.136547.

Barbieri, Rémi, and Michel Drancourt. 2018. "Two Thousand Years of Epidemics in Marseille and the Mediterranean Basin." *New Microbes and New Infections* 26 (August): S4–9. https://doi.org/10.1016/j.nmni.2018.08.009.

Barrientos, Armando. 2010. "Vulnerability and Social Protection in Small Island States: The Case of Grenada." *Social and Economic Studies* 59 (1/2, Social Protection in the Caribbean): 3–30.

Barry, John M. 1997. *Rising Tide: The Great Mississippi Flood of 1927 and How It Changed*. New York: Simon & Schuster.

Baysal, Emma, Adnan Baysal, Ali Umut Türkcan and Adam Nazaroff. 2015. "Early Specialized Production? A Chalcolithic Stone Bracelet Workshop at Kanlitaş, Turkey." *Oxford Journal of Archaeology* 34 (3): 235–57.

Beilin, Ruth, Nicole Tania Reichelt, Barbara Joyce King, Allison Long, and Stephanie Cam. 2013. "Transition Landscapes and Social Networks: Examining On-gound Community Resilience and Its Implications for Policy Settings in Multiscalar Systems." *Ecology and Society* 18 (2): 30. http://dx.doi.org/10.5751/es-05360-180230.

Bell, Michelle L., and Devra Lee Davis. 2001. "Reassessment of the Lethal London Fog of 1952: Novel Indicators of Acute and Chronic Consequences of Acute Exposure to Air Pollution." *Environmental Health Perspectives* 109 (suppl 3): 389–94. https://doi.org/10.1289/ehp.01109s3389.

Belshe, Robert B. 2012. "A Century of Influenza Prevention in St. Louis." *Missouri Medicine* 109 (2): 119–23.

Benati, Giacomo and Carmine Guerriero. 2021. "Climate Change and State Evolution." *Proceedings of the National Academy of Sciences* 118 (14): e2020893118.

Bender, Thomas. 2002. *The Unfinished City: New York and the Metropolitan Idea*. New York: The New Press.

Bennett, Nathan J., Jessica Blythe, Andrés M. Cisneros-Montemayor, Gerald G. Singh, and U. Rashid Sumaila. 2019. "Just Transformations to Sustainability." *Sustainability* 11 (14): 3881. https://doi.org/10.3390/su11143881.

Bentley, R. Alexander, Eleanor J. Maddison, P. Helen Ranner, John Bissell, Camila C. S. Caiado, Pojanath Bhatanacharoen, Timothy Clark, Marc Botha, Folarin Akinbami, and Matthew Hollow. 2014. "Social Tipping Points and Earth Systems Dynamics." *Frontiers in Environmental Science* 2: 35. http://dx.doi.org/10.3389/fenvs.2014.00035.

Berkes, Fikret, Johan Colding, and Carl Folke, eds. 2009. *Navigating Social-Ecological Systems: Building Resilience for Complexity and Change*. Cambridge, MA: Cambridge University Press. doi:10.1017/CBO9780511541957.

Berry, Brian J. L. 1990. "Urbanization." In *The Earth as Transformed by Human Action: Global Change and Regional Changes in the Biosphere over the Past 300 Years*, edited by Billie Lee Turner II, William C. Clark, Robert W. Kates, John F. Richards, Jessica T. Mathews, and William B. Meyer, 1st ed., 103–19. Cambridge, MA: Cambridge University Press.

Bhola-Paul, Helen M. 2015. "Tourism Challenges and the Opportunities for Sustainability: A Case Study of Grenada, Barbados, and Tobago." *Journal of Tourism and Hospitality Management* 3 (9–10): 204–13. https://doi.org/10.17265/2328-2169/2015.10.004.

Bianchi, Adriana, Wilfrido Cruz, and Masahisa Nakamura, eds. 2005. *Local Approaches to Environmental Compliance: Japanese Case Studies and Lessons for Developing Countries*. WBI Learning Resources Series. Washington, DC: The World Bank.

Birkmann, Joern, Torsten Welle, William Solecki, Shuaib Lwasa, and Matthias Garschagen. 2016. "Boost Resilience of Small and Mid-Sized Cities." *Nature* 537 (7622): 605–8.

Blake, Nelson M. 1980. *Land into Water - Water into Land: A History of Water Management in Florida*. Tallahassee, FL: University Press of Florida. 344.

Blaikie, Piers, Terry Cannon, Ian Davis and Ben Wisner. 2014. *At Risk: Natural Hazards, People's Vulnerability and Disasters*. London: Routledge.

Bojer, Hilde. 2011. "Prinsipielt Om Boligpolitikk: Bolig, Velferdsstat Og Rettferdig Fordeling (Principles of Housing Policy: Housing, Welfare State and Fair Distribution) Study for Housing Committee." *Hentet fra*, www.regjeringen.no/globalassets/upload/krd/vedlegg/boby.

Bonelli, Johanna Maldovan. 2018. "Environmental Protection, Work, and Social Inclusion: Formalizing the Recycling of Urban Solid Waste in Buenos Aires." *Latin American Perspectives* 45 (1): 91–107. https://doi.org/10.1177/0094582X17730372.

Borden, Skye. 2014. *Thirsty City: Politics, Greed, and the Making of Atlanta's Water Crisis*. New York: State University of New York Press.

Brandt, Willy. 1961. Speech to the Social Democratic Party of Germany Special Congress on April 28th. Quoted in Germany Federal Environmental Agency Press Release, No. 25/2011.

Bridgewater, Anthony V. 1986. "Refuse Composition Projections and Recycling Technology." *Resources and Conservation* 12 (3–4): 159–74. https://doi.org/10.1016/0166-3097(86)90008-8.

Brimblecombe, Peter. 2012. *The Big Smoke: A History of Air Pollution in London since Medieval Times*. New York: Methuen.

Brinkley, Catherine, and Domenic Vitiello. 2014. "From Farm to Nuisance: Animal Agriculture and the Rise of Planning Regulation." *Journal of Planning History* 13 (2): 113–35. https://doi.org/10.1177/1538513213507542.

Bruckmann, Peter, Ulrich Pfeffer, and V. Hoffmann. 2014. "50 Years of Air Quality Control in Northwestern Germany–How the Blue Skies over the Ruhr District Were Achieved." *Gefahrstoffe-Reinhaltung Der Luft* 74 (7–8): 291–98.

Brunkard, Joan, Gonza Namulanda, and Raoult Ratard. 2008. "Hurricane Katrina Deaths, Louisiana, 2005." *Disaster Medicine and Public Health Preparedness* 2 (4): 215–23. https://doi.org/10.1097/DMP.0b013e31818aaf55.

Burrows, Edwin G., and Mike Wallace. 1998. *Gotham: A History of New York City to 1898*. 1st ed. New York: Oxford University Press

Butzer, Karl W. and Georgina H. Enfield. 2012. "Critical Perspectives on Historical Collapse." *Proceedings of the National Academy of Sciences* 109 (10): 3628–31.

Carenzo, Sebastian, Paula Juarez, and Lucas Becerra. 2022. "Is There Room for a Circular Economy 'from below'? Reflections on Privatisation and Commoning of Circular Waste Loops in Argentina." *Local Environment* 27 (10–11): 1338–54. https://doi.org/10.1080/13549839.2022.2048258.

Castilla-Rho, Juan Carlos, Rodrigo Rojas, Martin S. Andersen, Cameron Holley, and Gregoire Mariethoz. 2017. "Social Tipping Points in Global Groundwater Management." *Nature Human Behaviour* 1 (9): 640–49.

Cha, Sangmi. 2022. "How One Country Is Beating COVID Despite 600,000 New Cases a Day." *Bloomberg US Edition*, March 17, 2022. www.bloomberg.com/news/articles/2022-03-17/how-south-korea-is-beating-covid-despite-600-000-new-cases-a-day?sref=z4R5TGTG.

Cha, Victor and Dana Kim. 2020. *A Timeline of South Korea's Response to COVID-19. Center for Strategic and International Studies*. www.csis.org/analysis/timeline-south-koreas-response-covid-19.

Chertow, Marian R. 2000. "The IPAT Equation and Its Variants." *Journal of Industrial Ecology* 4 (4): 13–29.

Chu, Eric and Kavya Michael. 2019. "Recognition in Urban Climate Justice: Marginality and Exclusion of Migrants in Indian Cities." *Environment and Urbanization* 31 (1), 139–56.

City of Johannesburg. 2011. "Jozi at Work." Government. Joburg. 2011. www.joburg.org.za/media_/Newsroom/Pages/2016%20&%202015%20Articles/Jozi-at-work.aspx.

Cohen, Aaron J., H. Ross Anderson, Bart Ostro, Kiran Dev Pandy, Michal Krzyzanowski, Nino Künzli, Kersten Gutschmidt, et al. 2004. "Urban Air Pollution." In *Comparative Quantification of Health Risks: Global and Regional Burden of Disease Attributable to Selected Major Risk Factors*, edited by Majid Ezzati, Alan D. Lopez, Anthony Rodgers, and Christopher J. L. Murray, 2, 1353–434. Geneva, Switzerland: World Health Organization. www.jstor.org/stable/resrep27829.22.

Colten, Craig E. 2005. *An Unnatural Metropolis: Wresting New Orleans from Nature*. Baton Rouge, LA: Louisiana State University Press.

Conlin, Richard. 2010. Waste Not: Seattle's Road to Zero Trash. Yes! Magazine. 54. Summer.

Corn, M. Lynne, Amy Abel, Stan Mark Kaplan, Eugene H. Buck, Cynthia Brougher and Kristina Alexander. 2008. "Apalachicola-Chattahoochee-Flint (ACF) Drought: Federal Water Management Issues." *Policy* 7: 9529.

Conyers, Zella Ann, Richard Grant, and Shouraseni Sen Roy. 2019. "Sea Level Rise in Miami Beach: Vulnerability and Real Estate Exposure." *The Professional Geographer* 71 (2): 278–91. https://doi.org/10.1080/00330124.2018.1531037.

Corporaal, Marguérite, and Lotte Jensen. 2022. "'But Most Brothers When in Misfortune': A Transnational Approach to Natural Disasters." *Nineteenth-Century Contexts* 44 (3): 265–83. https://doi.org/10.1080/08905495.2022.2084959.

Costanza, Robert, Lisa Graumlich, Will Steffen, Carole Crumley, John Dearing, Kathy Hibbard, Rik Leemans, Charles Redman, and David Schimel. 2007. "Sustainability or Collapse: What Can We Learn from Integrating the History of Humans and the Rest of Nature?" *AMBIO: A Journal of the Human Environment* 36 (7): 522–27.

Cronon, William. 1991. *Nature's Metropolis: Chicago and the Great West*, 1st ed. New York: W.W. Norton & Company.

Cutter, Susan L., Kevin D. Ash, and Christopher T. Emrich. 2014. "The Geographies of Community Disaster Resilience." *Global Environmental Change* 29: 65–77. https://doi.org/10.1016/j.gloenvcha.2014.08.005.

Czajkowski, Jeffrey, Vic Engel, Chris Martinez, Ali Mirchi, David Watkins, Michael C. Sukop, and Joseph D. Hughes. 2018. "Economic Impacts of Urban Flooding in South Florida: Potential Consequences of Managing Groundwater to Prevent Salt Water Intrusion." *Science of the Total Environment* 621: 465–78. https://doi.org/10.1016/j.scitotenv.2017.10.251.

Dakos, Vasilis, Egbert H. van Nes, Paolo D'Odorico and Marten Scheffer. 2012. "Robustness of Variance and Autocorrelation as Indicators of Critical Slowing Down." *Ecology* 93 (2): 264–71.

Darmanto, Nisrina Setyo, Alvin Christopher Galang Varquez, Natsumi Kawano, and Manabu Kanda. 2019. "Future Urban Climate Projection in a Tropical Megacity Based on Global Climate Change and Local Urbanization Scenarios." *Urban Climate* 29: 100482. https://doi.org/10.1016/j.uclim.2019.100482.

Davidson, Cliff I. 1979. "Air Pollution in Pittsburgh: A Historical Perspective." *Journal of the Air Pollution Control Association* 29 (10): 1035–41.

Davies, Stephen. 2015. "Terminal Dilemma: Hong Kong's Waterfront, 1841–1891." *Australasian Journal of Victorian Studies* 20 Special Issue: The Victorians and China (1): 5–23.

Daxbeck, Hans, Christoph Lampert, Leo Morf, Richard Obernosterer, Helmut Rechberger, Iris S. Reiner and Paul H. Brunner. 1997. "The Anthropogenic Metabolism of the City of Vienna." *From Paradigm to Practice of Sustainability*, 21: 250.

De Feo, Giovanni, George Antoniou, Hilal Franz Fardin, Fatma El-Gohary, Xiao Yun Zheng, Ieva Reklaityte, David Butler, Stavros Yannopoulos, and Andreas N. Angelakis. 2014. "The Historical Development of Sewers Worldwide." *Sustainability* 6 (6): 3936–74.

Demeritt, David. 2002. "What Is the 'Social Construction of Nature'? A Typology and Sympathetic Critique." *Progress in Human Geography* 26 (6): 767–90. https://doi.org/10.1191/0309132502ph402oa.

Dewulf, Art, Timos Karpouzoglou, Jeroen Warner, Anna Wesselink, Feng Mao, Jeroen Vos, Peter Tamas, Annemarie E. Groot, Annelies Heijmans, and Farhana Ahmed. 2019. "The Power to Define Resilience in Social–Hydrological Systems: Toward a Power-Sensitive Resilience Framework." *Wiley Interdisciplinary Reviews: Water* 6 (6): e1377. https://doi.org/10.1002/wat2.1377.

Dhiman, Ravinder, Renjith VishnuRadhan, T. I. Eldho, and Arun Inamdar. 2019. "Flood Risk and Adaptation in Indian Coastal Cities: Recent Scenarios." *Applied Water Science* 9 (1): 1–16. https://doi.org/10.1007/s13201-018-0881-9.

Diamond, Jared. 2011. *Collapse: How Societies Choose to Fail or Succeed.* Civilizations Rise and Fall Series. New York: Viking, The Penguin Group.

Dickens, Charles. 1913. *American Notes for General Circulation and Pictures from Italy – 1913.* London, England: Chapman & Hall, Ltd.

Dlamini, Smangele, Mulala Danny Simatele, and Nzalalemba Serge Kubanza. 2019. "Municipal Solid Waste Management in South Africa: From Waste to Energy Recovery through Waste-to-Energy Technologies in Johannesburg." *Local Environment* 24 (3): 249–57. https://doi.org/10.1080/13549839.2018.1561656.

Dodman, David, Bronwyn Hayward, Mark Pelling, Winston Chow, Eric Chu, Richard Dawson, Luna Khirfan, et al. 2022. "Cities, Settlements and Key Infrastructure." In *Climate Change 2022: Impacts, Adaptation, and Vulnerability. Contribution of Working Group II to the Sixth Assessment Report of the Intergovernmental Panel on*

Climate Change, edited by Hans-Otto Pörtner, Debra C. Roberts, Melinda Tignor, et al., 907–1040. Cambridge, UK, and New York: Cambridge University Press.

Du, Juan. 2020. *The Shenzhen Experiment: The Story of China's Instant City*. Cambridge, MA: Harvard University Press.

Echenberg, Myron. 2002. "Pestis Redux: The Initial Years of the Third Bubonic Plague Pandemic, 1894–1901." *Journal of World History* 13 (2): 429–49. https://doi.org/10.1353/jwh.2002.0033.

El Araby, Mohammed. 2002. "Urban Growth and Environmental Degradation: The Case of Cairo, Egypt." *Cities* 19 (6): 389–400.

Elkind, Sarah S. 2011. *How Local Politics Shape Federal Policy: Business, Power, and the Environment in Twentieth-Century Los Angeles*. Chapel Hill: University of North Carolina Press.

Emanuel, Elizabeth, and Charmaine Gomes. 2014. "An Assessment of Mechanisms to Improve Energy Efficiency in the Transport Sector in Grenada, Saint Lucia and Saint Vincent and the Grenadines." *ECLAC Subregional Headquarters for the Caribbean*, Studies and Perspectives Series – The Caribbean No. 38, 38 (October): 45.

Engineering Consulting Group ECG. n.d. "Greater Cairo Waterworks Master Plan." ECG Website. Accessed August 10, 2023. www.ecgsa.com/project/greater-cairo-waterworks-master-plan/.

Ensia, Marcello Rossi. 2019. "How Taiwan Has Achieved One of the Highest Recycling Rates in the World." *Smithsonian Magazine*, January 3, 2019. www.smithsonianmag.com/innovation/how-taiwan-has-achieved-one-highest-recycling-rates-world-180971150/.

Ermus, Cindy. 2015. "The Plague of Provence: Early Advances in the Centralization of Crisis Management." *Arcadia* 9 (Rachel Carson Center for Environment and Society). https://doi.org/10.5282/rcc/7029.

Ermus, Cindy. 2021. "Memory and the Representation of Public Health Crises: Remembering the Plague of Provence in the Tricentennial." *Environmental History* 26 (4): 776–88. https://doi.org/10.1093/envhis/emab046.

Ernstson, Henrik, Sander E. Van Der Leeuw, Charles L. Redman, Douglas J. Meffert, George Davis, Christine Alfsen, and Thomas Elmqvist. 2010. "Urban Transitions: On Urban Resilience and Human-Dominated Ecosystems." *Ambio* 39 (8): 531–45. http://dx.doi.org/10.1007/s13280-010-0081-9.

Fang, Wei-Ta, Mei-Hsuan Huang, Bai-You Cheng, Rong-Jeo Chiu, Yi-Te Chiang, Chun-Wei Hsu, and Eric Ng. 2021. "Applying a Comprehensive Action Determination Model to Examine the Recycling Behavior of Taipei City Residents." *Sustainability* 13 (2): 490.

Feitelson, Eran. 2013. "The Four Eras of Israeli Water Policies." In *Water Policy in Israel: Context, Issues and Options*, edited by Nir Becker, 15–32. Germany: Springer Netherlands.

Feldman, David L. 2009. "Preventing the Repetition: Or, what Los Angeles' Experience in Water Management Can Teach Atlanta about Urban Water Disputes." *Water Resources Research* 45 (4): 10.1029/2008WR007605.

Fiehn, H., and Jarod Ball. 2005. "Integrated Waste Management: Background Research Paper Produced for the South Africa Environment Outlook Report on Behalf of the Department of Environmental Affairs and Tourism." Pretoria, South Africa: Jarrod Ball and Associates.

Forsberg, Andrea. 2016. *The Impact of Growth on Urban Form in the Oslo Region* (Doctoral dissertation, Columbia University).

Fouquet, Roger. 2011. "Divergences in Long-Run Trends in the Prices of Energy and Energy Services." *Review of Environmental Economics and Policy* 5 (2): 196–218.

Frey, William H. 1979. "Central City White Flight: Racial and Nonracial Causes." *American Sociological Review* 44 (3): 425–48. https://doi.org/10.2307/2094885.

Fujikura, R., A. Bianchi, W. Cruz and M. Nakamura. 2005. Successful Air Pollution Control in Japan: History and Implications. *Local Approaches to Environmental Compliance: Japanese Case Studies and Lessons for Developing Countries*, 19–52.

Gadot, Yuval. 2022. *The Landfill of Early Roman Jerusalem: The 2013–2014 Excavations in Area D3*. University Park, USA: Penn State University Press. https://doi.org/10.1515/9781646022335

Galka, Max. 2016. "What Does New York Do with All Its Trash? One City's Waste – in Numbers." *The Guardian*, October 27, 2016, sec. Cities. www.theguardian.com/cities/2016/oct/27/new-york-rubbish-all-that-trash-city-waste-in-numbers.

Galusha, Diane. 1999. *Liquid Assets: A History of New York City's Water System*. New York: Fleischmann.

Gandy, Matthew. 2003. *Concrete and Clay: Reworking Nature in New York City. Urban and Industrial Environments*. Cambridge, MA: MIT Press.

Gao, Jing and Brian C. O'Neill. 2020. "Mapping Global Urban Land for the 21st Century with Data-Driven Simulations and Shared Socioeconomic Pathways." *Nature Communications* 11 (1): 2302.

Garschagen, Matthias, and Patricia Romero-Lankao. 2015. "Exploring the Relationships between Urbanization Trends and Climate Change Vulnerability." *Climatic Change* 133: 37–52. http://dx.doi.org/10.1007/s10584-013-0812-6.

Geels, Frank W. 2019. "Socio-technical Transitions to Sustainability: A Review of Criticisms and Elaborations of the Multi-level Perspective." *Current Opinion in Environmental Sustainability*, Open Issue 2019, 39 (August): 187–201. https://doi.org/10.1016/j.cosust.2019.06.009.

Gerritsen, Herman. 2005. "What Happened in 1953? The Big Flood in the Netherlands in Retrospect." *Philosophical Transactions of the Royal Society A: Mathematical, Physical and Engineering Sciences* 363 (1831): 1271–91. https://doi.org/10.1098/rsta.2005.1568.

Gilgen, Anina, Stiig Wilkenskjeld, Jed O. Kaplan, Thomas Kühn, and Ulrike Lohmann. 2019. "Effects of Land Use and Anthropogenic Aerosol Emissions in the Roman Empire." *Climate of the Past* 15 (5): 1885–911.

Gladtke, Dieter. 1998. "Air Pollution in the Rhine–Ruhr-Area." *Toxicology Letters* 96: 277–83. https://doi.org/10.1016/S0378-4274(98)00083-6.

Glavovic, Bruce, Richard Dawson, Winston T. L. Chow, Matthias Garschagen, Chandni Singh, and Adelle Thomas. 2022. "Cities and Settlements by the Sea." In *Climate Change 2022: Impacts, Adaptation, and Vulnerability. Contribution of Working Group II to the Sixth Assessment Report of the Intergovernmental Panel on Climate Change*, edited by Hans-Otto Pörtner, Debra C. Roberts, Melinda Tignor, et al., 2163–94. Cambridge, UK and New York: Cambridge University Press.

Glennon, Robert J. 2010. *Unquenchable: America's Water Crisis and What To Do About It*. Washington, DC: Island Press.

Godfrey, Linda, and Suzan Oelofse. 2017. "Historical Review of Waste Management and Recycling in South Africa." *Resources* 6 (4): 57. https://doi.org/10.3390/resources6040057.

Gonzalez-Quintero, Cristina, and V. Sophie Avila-Foucat. 2019. "Operationalization and Measurement of Social-Ecological Resilience: A Systematic Review." *Sustainability* 11 (21): 6073. https://doi.org/10.3390/su11216073.

González-Torres, María, Luis Pérez-Lombard, Juan F. Coronel, Ismael Rodríguez Maestre, & Bertoldi Paolo 2022. Activity and efficiency trends for the residential sector across countries. *Energy and Buildings 273*: 112428.

Gottdiener, Mark. 1985. *The Social Production of Urban Space*, 2nd ed. Austin, TX: University of Texas Press.

Greben, Harma A., and Suzan H. H. Oelofse. 2009. "Unlocking the Resource Potential of Organic Waste: A South African Perspective." *Waste Management and Research* 27 (7): 676–84. https://doi.org/10.1177/0734242X09103817.

Gregor, Alison. 2022. "House Hunting in Grenada: A Better 'Beach Shack' on the Caribbean Coast." *The New York Times*, April 13, 2022, sec. Real Estate. www.nytimes.com/2022/04/13/realestate/grenada-caribbean-house-hunting.html.

Grove, Kevin, Allain Barnett, and Savannah Cox. 2020. "Designing Justice? Race and the Limits of Recognition in Greater Miami Resilience Planning." *Geoforum* 117: 134–43. https://doi.org/10.1016/j.geoforum.2020.09.014.

Gunderson, Lance H., Crawford S. Holling, and Stephen S. Light, eds. 1995. *Barriers and Bridges to the Renewal of Regional Ecosystems*. New York: Columbia University Press.

Güneralp, Burak, Meredith Reba, Billy U. Hales, Elizabeth A. Wentz, and Karen C. Seto. 2020. "Trends in Urban Land Expansion, Density, and Land Transitions from 1970 to 2010: A Global Synthesis." *Environmental Research Letters* 15 (4): 044015.

Güneralp, Burak, and Karen C. Seto. 2008. "Environmental Impacts of Urban Growth from an Integrated Dynamic Perspective: A Case Study of Shenzhen, South China." *Global Environmental Change* 18 (4): 720–35. https://doi.org/10.1016/j.gloenvcha.2008.07.004.

Gustafson, Abel, Jennifer R. Marlon, Matthew H. Goldberg, Xinran Wang, Matthew T. Ballew, Seth A. Rosenthal, and Anthony Leiserowitz. 2020. "Blame Where Blame Is Due: Many Americans Support Suing Fossil Fuel Companies for Global Warming Damages." *Environment: Science and Policy for Sustainable Development* 62 (2): 30–35. https://doi.org/10.1080/00139157.2020.1708649.

Hallegatte, Stephane, Colin Green, Robert J. Nicholls, and Jan Corfee-Morlot. 2013. "Future Flood Losses in Major Coastal Cities." *Nature Climate Change* 3 (9): 802–6. https://doi.org/10.1038/NCLIMATE1979.

Han, Jiatong, Jie Yin, Xiaoxu Wu, Danyang Wang and Chenlu Li. 2023. "Environment and COVID-19 Incidence: A Critical Review." *Journal of Environmental Sciences* 124, 933–51.

Hansen, Teis, and Lars Coenen. 2015. "The Geography of Sustainability Transitions: Review, Synthesis and Reflections on an Emergent Research Field." *Environmental Innovation and Societal Transitions* 17: 92–109. https://doi.org/10.1016/j.eist.2014.11.001.

Hardy, Anne. 2020. "Death and the Environment in London: 1800-2000." In *A Mighty Capital under Threat: The Environmental History of London, 1800-2000*, edited by Bill Luckin and Peter Thorsheim. Pittsburgh: University of Pittsburgh Press.

Harvey, David. 1985. *The Urbanization of Capital: Studies in the History and Theory of Capitalist Urbanization*. Oxford, England: Basil Blackwell.

Harvey, David. 1990. *The Condition of Postmodernity: An Enquiry into the Origins of Cultural Change*. Cambridge, MA: Blackwell Publishing.

Harvey, David. 2005. *Paris, Capital of Modernity*, 1st ed. New York: Routledge.

Harvey, L. Danny, Katarina Korytarova, Oswaldo Lucon, & Volha Roshchanka 2014. Construction of a Global Disaggregated Dataset of Building Energy Use and Floor Area in 2010. *Energy and Buildings 76*, 488–96.

Harwell, Mark A., John F. Long, Ann M. Bartuska, John H. Gentile, Christine C. Harwell, Victoria Myers, and John C. Ogden. 1996. "Ecosystem Management to Achieve Ecological Sustainability: The Case of South Florida." *Environmental Management* 20 (4): 497–521. https://doi.org/10.1007/BF01474652.

Hashimoto, Michio. 1989. "History of Air Pollution Control in Japan." *Studies in Environmental Science* 38: 1–93.

Hatchett, Richard J., Carter E. Mecher, and Marc Lipsitch. 2007. "Public Health Interventions and Epidemic Intensity during the 1918 Influenza Pandemic." *Proceedings of the National Academy of Sciences* 104 (18): 7582–87. https://doi.org/10.1073/pnas.0610941104.

Heffron, Raphael J. 2021. *Achieving a Just Transition to a Low-Carbon Economy*. New York: Palgrave Macmillan. www.worldcat.org/title/1272869034.

Heidorn, Keith C. 1978. "A Chronology of Important Events in the History of Air Pollution Meteorology to 1970." *Bulletin of the American Meteorological Society* 59 (12): 1589–97.

Heynen, Nik. 2014. "Urban Political Ecology I: The Urban Century." *Progress in Human Geography* 38 (4): 598–604. https://doi.org/10.1177/0309132513500443

Hishida, Kohichi. 1974. "Tokyo To Ni Okeru Toshi Kogai No Rekishi (Urban Pollution in Tokyo Metropolitan Area)." *Kigyo Kankyo (Industrial Environment)* 4 (3): 25–67.

Hoehn, John P., and Douglas J. Krieger. 2000. "Economic Analysis of Water Service Investments and Tariffs in Cairo, Egypt." *Journal of Water Resources Planning and Management* 126 (6): 345–50.

Hofstad, Hege, and Jacob Torfing. 2017. "Towards a Climate-Resilient City: Collaborative Innovation for a 'Green Shift' in Oslo." In *Carbon Footprint and the Industrial Life Cycle: From Urban Planning to Recycling*, edited by Roberto Álvarez Fernández, Sergio Zubelzu, and Rodrigo Martínez, 221–42. Green Energy and Technology. New York: Springer. https://link-springer-com.ezproxy.gc.cuny.edu/book/10.1007/978-3-319-54984-2.

Homer-Dixon, Thomas, Brian Walker, Reinette Biggs, Anne-Sophie Crépin, Carl Folke, Eric F. Lambin, Garry D. Peterson, Johan Rockström, Marten Scheffer, and Will Steffen. 2015. "Synchronous Failure: The Emerging Causal Architecture of Global Crisis." *Ecology and Society* 20 (3). http://dx.doi.org/10.5751/ES-07681-200306.

Hone, Philip. 1889. *The Diary of Philip Hone, 1828–1851*, edited by Bayard Tuckerman. 2 vols. New York: Dodd, Mead and Company. (Often republished, most recently in 2023).

Horowitz, Andy. 2020. *Katrina: A History, 1915–2015*. Harvard University Press.

Hosseini, Seyedmohsen, Kash Barker, and Jose E. Ramirez-Marquez. 2016. "A Review of Definitions and Measures of System Resilience." *Reliability Engineering and System Safety* 145: 47–61. https://doi.org/10.1016/j.ress.2015.08.006.

Hsu, Shu-Hsiang. 2006. "NIMBY Opposition and Solid Waste Incinerator Siting in Democratizing Taiwan." *The Social Science Journal* 43 (3): 453–59. https://doi.org/10.1016/j.soscij.2006.04.018.

Inostroza, Luis. 2017. "Informal Urban Development in Latin American Urban Peripheries. Spatial Assessment in Bogotá, Lima and Santiago de Chile." *Landscape and Urban Planning* 165: 267–79.

IPCC. 2018. "Annex I: Glossary [Matthews, J.B.R. (Ed.)]." In *Global Warming of 1.5°C. An IPCC Special Report on the Impacts of Global Warming of 1.5°C above Pre-Industrial Levels and Related Global Greenhouse Gas Emission Pathways, in the Context of Strengthening the Global Response to the Threat of Climate Change, Sustainable Development, and Efforts to Eradicate Poverty*, edited by Valerie Masson-Delmotte, Panmao Zhai, Hans-Otto Pörtner, et al., 541–62. Cambridge, UK and New York: Cambridge University Press. www.ipcc.ch/sr15/chapter/glossary/.

IPCC. 2022. "Summary for Policymakers." [H.-O. Pörtner, D.C. Roberts, E.S. Poloczanska, K. Mintenbeck, M. Tignor, A. Alegría, M. Craig, S. Langsdorf, S. Löschke, V. Möller, A. Okem (eds.)]. In: *Climate Change 2022: Impacts, Adaptation and Vulnerability. Contribution of Working Group II to the Sixth Assessment Report of the Intergovernmental Panel on Climate Change*, edited by Hans-Otto Pörtner, Debra C. Roberts, Melinda M. B. Tignor, et al., 3–33, Cambridge, UK and New York: Cambridge University Press. doi:10.1017/9781009325844.001.

IPCC. 2023. "Summary for Policymakers." In: *Climate Change 2023: Synthesis Report. Contribution of Working Groups I, II and III to the Sixth Assessment Report of the Intergovernmental Panel on Climate Change*, edited by Core Writing Team, H. Lee and J. Romero, 1–34. Geneva, Switzerland: IPCC. doi: 10.59327/IPCC/AR6-9789291691647.001.

Jacobs, Jeffrey W. 2018. "Cedar Rapids Flood Risk Management: A Case Study in Disaster Recovery." 2018-R-02. USACE Institute for Water Resources. https://usace.contentdm.oclc.org/digital/api/collection/p16021coll2/id/2961/download.

Jiang, Jingjing, Ye Bin, Zeng Zhenzhong, Junguo Liu, and Xin Yang. 2022. "Potential and Roadmap of CO2 Emission Reduction in Urban Buildings: Case Study of Shenzhen." *Advances in Climate Change Research* 13 (4): 587–99.

Johnson, Cathryn, and Ananda Weliwita, eds. 2019. *The Story of Shenzhen: Its Economic, Social and Environmental Transformation*, 2nd ed. Nairobi: UN-Habitat. https://unhabitat.org/the-story-of-shenzhen-its-economic-social-and-environmental-transformation.

Jones, Lewis, John Fortuna, and Karen Johnston. 2013. "Updating Twentieth Century Water Projects to Meet Twenty-First Century Needs: Lessons from the Tri-State Water Wars." *Georgia State University Law Review* 29 (4): 959–86. https://readingroom.law.gsu.edu/gsulr/vol29/iss4/3.

Kaika, Maria, Roger Keil, Tait Mandler, and Yannis Tzaninis, eds. 2023. *Turning up the Heat: Urban Political Ecology for a Climate Emergency*. Manchester, England: Manchester University Press.

Kalnins, Irene. 2006. "The Spanish Influenza of 1918 in St. Louis, Missouri." *Public Health Nursing* 23 (5): 479–83. https://doi.org/10.1111/j.1525-1446.2006.00586.x.

Kates, Robert W., Craig E. Colten, Shirley Laska, and Stephen P. Leatherman. 2006. "Reconstruction of New Orleans after Hurricane Katrina: A Research Perspective." *Proceedings of the National Academy of Sciences* 103 (40): 14653–60. https://doi.org/10.1073/pnas.0605726103.

Kaza, Silpa, Lisa Yao, Perinaz Bhada-Tata, Frank Van Woerden, and Kremena Ionkova. 2018. *What a Waste 2.0: A Global Snapshot of Solid Waste Management to 2050*. Urban Development. Wahington, DC: World Bank. http://hdl.handle.net/10986/30317.

Keenan, Jesse M., Thomas Hill, and Anurag Gumber. 2018. "Climate Gentrification: From Theory to Empiricism in Miami-Dade County, Florida." *Environmental Research Letters* 13 (5): 054001. https://doi.org/10.1088/1748-9326/aabb32.

Kelman, Ari. 2006. *A River and Its City: The Nature of Landscape in New Orleans: With a New Preface*. Berkeley: University of California Press.

Kendall, Alissa, and Edward S. Spang. 2020. "The Role of Industrial Ecology in Food and Agriculture's Adaptation to Climate Change." *Journal of Industrial Ecology* 24 (2): 313–17. https://doi.org/10.1111/jiec.12851.

Khan, Mohd Afzal, Priyanka Pahuja, and Mohammad Arif Kamal. 2022. Appraisal of Aqueduct as an Ancient Water Supply Control System. *Journal of Advanced Research in Construction and Urban Architecture* 7 (3&4): 1–8.

Kim, Pan Suk. 2020. "South Korea's Fast Response to Coronavirus Disease: Implications on Public Policy and Public Management Theory." *Public Management Review*, 1–12. Advance online publication. 10.1080/14719037.2020.1766266

Kim, June-Ho, Julia Ah-Reum An, SeungJu Jackie Oh, Juhwan Oh, and Jong-Koo Lee. 2021. "Emerging COVID-19 Success Story: South Korea Learned the Lessons of MERS." *Our World in Data*, March 5, 2021. https://ourworldindata.org/covid-exemplar-south-korea.

Klingle, Matthew. 2008. *Emerald City: An Environmental History of Seattle*. Seattle: Yale University Press.

Koeppel, Gerard T. 2001. *Water for Gotham: A History*. Princeton, NJ: Princeton University Press.

Kondapalli, Srinivas, and Geetha Sakamuri. 2018. "The Great Flood of 1993: Can Catastrophic Flood Risk Be Better Managed?" *AIR Currents*, August 27, 2018. www.air-worldwide.com/publications/air-currents/2018/The-Great-Flood-of-1993--Can-Catastrophic-Flood-Risk-Be-Better-Managed-/.

Koren, David, Vojko Kilar, and Katarina Rus. 2017. "Proposal for Holistic Assessment of Urban System Resilience to Natural Disasters." In *IOP Conference Series: Materials Science and Engineering*, 245: 062011. IOP Publishing. https://doi.org/10.1088/1757-899x/245/6/062011.

Kuddus, Md Abdul, Elizabeth Tynan, and Emma McBryde. 2020. "Urbanization: A Problem for the Rich and the Poor?" *Public Health Reviews* 41: 1–4.

Lai, Ying-Ying. 2019. Head of the Taiwan Environmental Protection Administration's (EPA's) Department of Waste Management. Quoted in E. Marcello Rossi, 2019. "How Taiwan Has Achieved One of the Highest Recycling Rates in the World." *Smithsonian*, January.

Lakatos, Elena Simina, Geng Yong, Andrea Szilagyi, Dan Sorin Clinci, Lucian Georgescu, Catalina Iticescu, and Lucian-Ionel Cioca. 2021. "Conceptualizing Core Aspects on Circular Economy in Cities." *Sustainability* 13 (14): 7549. https://doi.org/10.3390/su13147549.

Langton, Ryan P. 2022. "Philadelphia under Siege: The Yellow Fever of 1793." *Pennsylvania Center for the Book*, Spring 2022. https://pabook.libraries.psu.edu/literary-cultural-heritage-map-pa/feature-articles/philadelphia-under-siege-yellow-fever-1793.

Larson, Larry A. 2019. "Assessing the National Policy Response to the 1993 Mississippi River Flooding." *Environment: Science and Policy for Sustainable Development* 61 (5): 44–49. https://doi.org/10.1080/00139157.2019.1637685.

Lee, Pui-Tak. 2013. "Colonialism versus Nationalism: The Plague of Hong Kong in 1894." *The Journal of Northeast Asian History* 10 (1): 97–123.

Lefebvre, Henri. 1991. *The Production of Space*. Oxford, England: Basil Blackwell.

Leichenko, Robin. 2011. "Climate Change and Urban Resilience." *Current Opinion in Environmental Sustainability* 3 (3): 164–68. https://doi.org/10.1016/j.cosust.2010.12.014.

Leichenko, Robin, and William D. Solecki. 2005. "Exporting the American Dream: The Globalization of Suburban Consumption Landscapes." *Regional Studies* 39 (2): 241–53. https://doi.org/10.1080/003434005200060080.

Li, Ting, Yuxiang Dong, and Zhenhuan Liu. 2020. "A Review of Social-Ecological System Resilience: Mechanism, Assessment and Management." *Science of The Total Environment* 723 (June): 138113. https://doi.org/10.1016/j.scitotenv.2020.138113.

Liao, Shu-chuan. 2003. "Taiwanese Women's Participation in Social Movements: A Case Study of the Homemakers' Union and Foundation (HUF) in Taiwan." *Convergence* 36 (2): 29–49.

Lin, Brenda B., and Brian Petersen. 2013. "Resilience, Regime Shifts, and Guided Transition under Climate Change: Examining the Practical Difficulties of Managing Continually Changing Systems." *Ecology and Society* 18 (1): 28. http://dx.doi.org/10.5751/es-05128-180128.

Lin, Dan, and Aidan H. While. 2022. "Environmentalism and Chinese Urban Order: The Ecological Control Line Policy in Shenzhen, China." *Political Geography* 97: 102685. https://doi.org/10.1016/j.polgeo.2022.102685.

Liu, Xiaozi, Gerhard K. Heilig, Junmiao Chen, and Mikko Heino. 2007. "Interactions between Economic Growth and Environmental Quality in Shenzhen, China's First Special Economic Zone." *Ecological Economics* 62 (3–4): 559–70. https://doi.org/10.1016/j.ecolecon.2006.07.020.

Lu, Li-Teh, Teng-Yuan Hsiao, Neng-Chou Shang, Yue-Hwa Yu and Hwong-Wen Ma. 2006. "MSW Management for Waste Minimization in Taiwan: The Last Two Decades." *Waste Management* 26 (6): 661–67.

Lu, Weisheng, Chris Webster, Yi Peng, Xi Chen, and Xiaoling Zhang. 2017. "Estimating and Calibrating the Amount of Building-Related Construction and Demolition Waste in Urban China." *International Journal of Construction Management* 17 (1): 13–24. https://doi.org/10.1080/15623599.2016.1166548.

Luomi, Mari. 2009. "Abu Dhabi's Alternative-Energy Initiatives: Seizing Climate-Change Opportunities." *Middle East Policy* 16 (4): 102–17. https://doi.org/10.1111/j.1475-4967.2009.00418.x.

Marcotullio, Peter J. 2002. "Why Are Urban Environmental Problems Different in Third World Cities? A Comparison of Western and Asia Pacific Experiences." *Comprehensive Urban Studies* 77 (3): 55–97.

Marcotullio, Peter J. 2003. "Globalisation, Urban Form and Environmental Conditions in Asia-Pacific Cities." *Urban Studies* 40 (2): 219–47.

Marcotullio, Peter J., and Yok-Shiu F. Lee. 2003. "Urban Environmental Transitions and Urban Transportation Systems: A Comparison of the North American and Asian Experiences." *International Development Planning Review* 25 (4): 325–54.

Marcotullio, Peter J., Sarah Rothenberg, and Miri Nakahara. 2003. "Globalization and Urban Environmental Transitions: Comparison of New York's and Tokyo's Experiences." *The Annals of Regional Science* 37 (3): 369–90.

Marín, Andrés, Stefan Gelcich, and Juan Carlos Castilla. 2014. "Ecosystem Services and Abrupt Transformations in a Coastal Wetland Social-Ecological System: Tubul-Raqui after the 2010 Earthquake in Chile." *Ecology and Society* 19 (1): 22. http://dx.doi.org/10.5751/ES-05633-190122.

Marin, Philippe, Shimon Tal, Joshua Yeres, and Klas B. Ringskog. 2017. "Water Management in Israel: Key Innovations and Lessons Learned for Water Scarce Countries." Technical. Washington, DC: World Bank. https://documents1.worldbank.org/curated/en/657531504204943236/pdf/Water-management-in-Israel-key-innovations-and-lessons-learned-for-water-scarce-countries.pdf.

Markard, Jochen, Rob Raven, and Bernhard Truffer. 2012. "Sustainability Transitions: An Emerging Field of Research and Its Prospects." *Research Policy* 41 (6): 955–67. http://dx.doi.org/10.1016/j.respol.2012.02.013.

Marshall, Rachael E., and Khosrow Farahbakhsh. 2013. "Systems Approaches to Integrated Solid Waste Management in Developing Countries." *Waste Management* 33 (4): 988–1003. http://dx.doi.org/10.1016/j.wasman.2012.12.023.

McGranahan, Gordon, and Jacob Songsore. 1994. "Wealth, Health, and the Urban Household: Weighing Environmental Burdens In…." *Environment: Science and Policy for Sustainable Development* 36 (6): 4–45.

McGranahan, Gordon, Jacob Songsore, Charles Surjadi, Marianne Kjellen, and Pedro Jacobi. 2001. *The Citizens at Risk: From Urban Sanitation to Sustainable Cities*. First. Earthscan Risk in Society. London, England: Earthscan. www.routledge.com/The-Citizens-at-Risk-From-Urban-Sanitation-to-Sustainable-Cities/McGranahan-Songsor-Surjadi-Kjellen-Jacobi/p/book/9781853835612.

McNeur, Catherine. 2014. *Taming Manhattan: Environmental Battles in the Antebellum City*. First. Cambridge, MA: Harvard University Press. https://doi.org/10.4159/harvard.9780674735989.

McShane, Clay, and Joel A. Tarr. 2011. *The Horse in the City: Living Machines in the Nineteenth Century*. Illustrated edition. Baltimore: Johns Hopkins University Press.

Meerow, Sara, and Joshua P. Newell. 2019. "Urban Resilience for Whom, What, When, Where, and Why?" *Urban Geography* 40 (3): 309–29. https://doi.org/10.1080/02723638.2016.1206395.

Meerow, Sara, Joshua P. Newell, and Melissa Stults. 2016. "Defining Urban Resilience: A Review." *Landscape and Urban Planning* 147: 38–49. https://doi.org/10.1016/j.landurbplan.2015.11.011.

Melosi, Martin V. 1999. *The Sanitary City: Urban Infrastructure in America from Colonial Times to the Present*. Baltimore: The Johns Hopkins University Press. www.worldcat.org/title/460694068.

Melosi, Martin V. 2005. *Garbage in the Cities*. History of the Urban Environment. Pittsburgh, PA: University of Pittsburgh Press. https://upittpress.org/books/9780822958574/.

Meng, Liting, Yan Sun, and Shuqing Zhao. 2020. "Comparing the Spatial and Temporal Dynamics of Urban Expansion in Guangzhou and Shenzhen from 1975 to 2015: A Case Study of Pioneer Cities in China's Rapid Urbanization." *Land Use Policy* 97: 104753. https://doi.org/10.1016/j.landusepol.2020.104753.

Merrifield, Andy. 2011. "The Right to the City and Beyond." *City* 15 (3–4): 473–81. https://doi.org/10.1080/13604813.2011.595116.

Meyer, Han, Anne Loes Nillesen, and Wil Zonneveld. 2012. "Rotterdam: A City and a Mainport on the Edge of a Delta." *European Planning Studies* 20 (1): 71–94. https://doi.org/10.1080/09654313.2011.638498.

Miami-Dade County, Department of Regulatory and Economic Resources, Office of Resilience. 2022. Extreme Heat Action Plan. December. www.miamidade.gov/environment/library/2022-heat-action-plan.pdf.

Middleton, Guy D. 2012. "Nothing Lasts Forever: Environmental Discourses on the Collapse of Past Societies." *Journal of Archaeological Research* 20 (3): 257–307.

Milkoreit, Manjana, Jennifer Hodbod, Jacopo Baggio, Karina Benessaiah, Rafael Calderón-Contreras, Jonathan F. Donges, Jean-Denis Mathias, Juan Carlos Rocha, Michael Schoon, and Saskia E. Werners. 2018. "Defining Tipping Points for Social-Ecological Systems Scholarship – an Interdisciplinary Literature Review." *Environmental Research Letters* 13 (3): 033005.

Miller, Donald L. 1997. *City of the Century: The Epic of Chicago and the Making of America*. Reprint edition. 1 vols. New York: Simon & Schuster.

Missimer, Thomas M., Philip A. Danser, Gary Amy, and Thomas Pankratz. 2014. "Water Crisis: The Metropolitan Atlanta, Georgia, Regional Water Supply Conflict." *Water Policy* 16 (4): 669–89. https://doi.org/10.2166/wp.2014.131.

Mithen, Steven. 2006. *After the Ice: A Global Human History, 20,000–5000 BC*. Annotated Edition. Cambridge, MA: Harvard University Press. https://onlinelibrary-wiley-com.ezproxy.gc.cuny.edu/doi/abs/10.1002/ajpa.20304.

Mohamed, Ahmed Shawky, and N. Vijay Jagannathan. 2009. "Egypt: Water Sector Public Expenditure Review." In *Water in the Arab World: Management Perspectives and Innovations*, edited by N. Vijay Jagannathan, Ahmed Shawky Mohamed, and Alexander Kremer, 554. Washington, DC: Middle East and North African Region, The World Bank.

Molinaroli, Emanuela, Stefano Guerzoni, and Daniel Suman. 2019. "Do the Adaptations of Venice and Miami to Sea Level Rise Offer Lessons for Other Vulnerable Coastal Cities?" *Environmental Management* 64 (4): 391–415. https://doi.org/10.1007/s00267-019-01198-z.

Mollenkopf, John Hull. 1983. *The Contested City*. Princeton, NJ: Princeton University Press.

Morse, Reilly. 2008. "Environmental Justice through the Eye of Hurricane Katrina." Washington, DC: Joint Center for Political and Economic Studies, Health Policy Institute. https://inequality.stanford.edu/sites/default/files/media/_media/pdf/key_issues/Environment_policy.pdf.

Mossberger, Karen, and Gerry Stoker. 2001. "The Evolution of Urban Regime Theory: The Challenge of Conceptualization." *Urban Affairs Review* 36 (6): 810–35.

Mukherjee, Alokananda Banerjee, and Suchandra Bardhan. 2021. "Flood Vulnerability and Slum Concentration Mapping in the Indian City of Kolkata: A Post-Amphan Analysis." *Water Science* 35 (1): 109–26. https://doi.org/10.1080/23570008.2021.1957641.

Mukherjee, Jenia, Raphaël Morera, Joana Guerrin, and René Véron. 2021. "Histories of Urban Deltascapes: A Comparison of Arles and Kolkata." *Global Environment* 14 (3): 505–34. https://doi.org/10.3197/ge.2021.140304.

Mumford, Lewis. 1961. *The City in History: Its Origins, Its Transformations, and Its Prospects*. First. New York: Harcourt, Brace & World.

Murdoch, Maggie. 2010. "Environmental Reviews and Case Studies: The Road to Zero Waste: A Study of the Seattle Green Fee on Disposable Bags." *Environmental Practice* 12 (1): 66–75. https://doi.org/10.10170S1466046609990470.

Muzenda, Edison, Freeman Ntuli, and Tsietsi Jefrey Pilusa. 2012. "Waste Management, Strategies and Situation in South Africa: An Overview." *International Journal of Environmental and Ecological Engineering* 6 (8): 552–55.

Muzzio, Douglas. 2018. "When Boz Came to Town, Remembering Charles Dickens's First Visit to New York." *City Journal*, 2018. www.city-journal.org/article/when-boz-came-to-town/.

Næss, Petter, Inger-Lise Saglie, and Tim Richardson. 2020. "Urban Sustainability: Is Densification Sufficient?" *European Planning Studies* 28 (1): 146–65. https://doi.org/10.1080/09654313.2019.1604633.

Næss, Petter, Arvid Strand, Teresa Næss, and Morten Nicolaisen. 2011. "On Their Road to Sustainability? The Challenge of Sustainable Mobility in Urban Planning and Development in Two Scandinavian Capital Regions." *The Town Planning Review* 82 (3): 285–315. https://doi.org/10.3828/tpr.2011.18.

Næss, Petter, Teresa Næss, Morten Skou Nicolaisen, and Esben Clemens. 2009. The Challenge of Sustainable Mobility in Urban Planning and Development in Copenhagen Metropolitan Area. Developed for the Institute of Transport Economic, Norwegian Transport Research Center. www.toi.no/getfile.php/1312261-1250076499/Publikasjoner/T%C3%98I%20rapporter/2009/1024-2009/1024-2009-nett.pdf.

Nahman, A., and L. Godfrey. 2010. "Economic Instruments for Solid Waste Management in South Africa: Opportunities and Constraints." *Resources, Conservation and Recycling* 54 (8): 521–31. https://doi.org/10.1016/j.resconrec.2009.10.009.

National Overview: Facts and Figures on Materials, Wastes and Recycling. 2017. Overviews and Factsheets. United States Environmental Protection Agency. October 2, 2017. www.epa.gov/facts-and-figures-about-materials-waste-and-recycling/national-overview-facts-and-figures-materials.

National Strategic Development Plan, Grenada. 2007. Grenada, Ministry of Economic Development and Planning. Grantham Research Institute. https://climate-laws.org/document/national-development-strategy-for-grenada_a2cb.

Navarro, J. Alex. Editor in Chief. 2019. The American Influenza Epidemic of 1918–1919: A Digital Encyclopedia. St. Louis, Missouri. *International Journal of Infectious Diseases*, *79*, p. 98. University of Michigan Center for the History of Medicine and Michigan Publishing. Accessed August 11, 2023. https://quod.lib.umich.edu/f/flu/browse/titles/i.html.

Neogi, Tathagata. 2018. "A Drowning City: Drainage and Waterlogging in Colonial Calcutta." Medium. *Immersive Trails Blog* (blog). July 13, 2018. https://medium.com/the-calcutta-blog/fighting-the-monsoon-drainage-and-waterlogging-in-colonial-calcutta-7fb0f5eb637c.

New, Mark, Diana Reckien, David Viner, Carolina Adler, So-Min Cheong, Cecilia Conde, Andrew Constable, et al. 2022. "Decision-Making Options for Managing Risk." In *Climate Change 2022: Impacts, Adaptation, and Vulnerability. Contribution of Working Group II to the Sixth Assessment Report of the Intergovernmental Panel on Climate Change*, edited by Hans-Otto Pörtner, Debra C. Roberts, Melinda Tignor, et al., 2539–654. Cambridge, UK and New York: Cambridge University Press. www.ipcc.ch/report/ar6/wg2/.

Nilsson, Anna. 2016. Challenges in Solid Waste Management in Buenos Aires: from a Sustainable Development Perspective. KTH, School of Architecture and the Built Environment. www.diva-portal.org/smash/get/diva2:970799/FULLTEXT01.pdf.

North Georgia Water. 2021. "Water Withdrawals per Capita Remain Steady." Nonprofit. Metropolitan North Georgia Water Planning District. 2021. https://northgeorgiawater.org/current-water-stats/water-withdrawals-per-capita-remain-steady/.

Nystad, Jens Fredrik, ed. 2004. *Building and Urban Development in Norway: A Selection of Current Issues*. Translated by Carol B. Eckmann and Walter Gibbs. Norway: Husbanken. https://static1.squarespace.com/static/5880e29ebe65940ff2702842/t/5899fd1120099e826d331b30/1486486818652/Norway+-+Building+and+Urban+Development.pdf.

O'Brien, Karen. 2012. "Global Environmental Change II: From Adaptation to Deliberate Transformation." *Progress in Human Geography* 36 (5): 667–76. http://dx.doi.org/10.1177/0309132511425767.

Obernosterer, R. and Paul H. Brunner. 2001. "Urban Metal Management the Example of Lead." *Water, Air and Soil Pollution: Focus* 1, 241–53.

(OCHA), UN Office for the Coordination of Humanitarian Affairs. 2020. "Grenada: Country Profile (as of July 2020)." Reliefweb. July 31, 2020. https://reliefweb.int/report/grenada/grenada-country-profile-july-2020.

Oh, Myoung-Don, Wan Beom Park, Sang-Won Park, Pyoeng Gyun Choe, Ji Hwan Bang, Kyoung-Ho Song, Eu Suk Kim, Hong Bin Kim, and Nam Joong Kim. 2018. "Middle East Respiratory Syndrome: What We Learned from the 2015 Outbreak in the Republic of Korea." *The Korean Journal of Internal Medicine* 33 (2): 233–46. https://doi.org/doi:10.3904/kjim.2018.031.

Olsson, Per, Victor Galaz, and Wiebren J. Boonstra. 2014. "Sustainability Transformations: A Resilience Perspective." *Ecology and Society* 19 (4): 1. http://dx.doi.org/10.1177/0309132511425767.

Pal, Jeremy S. and Elfatih A. B. Eltahir. 2016. "Future Temperature in Southwest Asia Projected to Exceed a Threshold for Human Adaptability." *Nature Climate Change* 6 (2), 197–200.

Pamuk, Humeyra. 2011. "UAE's Mission Impossible: Cooling the Desert." *Reuters*, July 13, 2011, sec. Environment. www.reuters.com/article/us-power-emirates-idUKTRE76C1OI20110713.

Pandey, Anamika, Michael Brauer, Maureen L. Cropper, Kalpana Balakrishnan, Prashant Mathur, Sagnik Dey, Burak Turkgulu, G. Anil Kumar, Mukesh Khare, and Gufran Beig. 2021. "Health and Economic Impact of Air Pollution in the States of India: The Global Burden of Disease Study 2019." *The Lancet Planetary Health* 5 (1): e25–38. https://doi.org/10.1016/S2542-5196(20)30298-9.

Park, Chulwoo. 2019. "MERS-CoV Infection in South Korea and Strategies for Possible Future Outbreak: Narrative Review." *Journal of Global Health Reports* 3: e2019088. https://doi.org/10.29392/joghr.3.e2019088.

Park, YYoojin, In Sil Huh, Jaekyung Lee, Cho Ryok Kang, Sung-Il Cho, Hyon Jeen Ham, hea Sook Kim, et al. 2020. "Seoul Metropolitan Government COVID-19 Rapid Response (SCoRR) Team. Application of Testing-Tracing-Treatment Strategy in Response to the COVID-19 Outbreak in Seoul." *Journal of Korean Medical Science* 35 (45): e396. https://doi.org/10.3346/jkms.2020.35.e396.

Pearcy, Matthew T. 2002. "After the Flood: A History of the 1928 Flood Control Act." *Journal of the Illinois State Historical Society (1998–)* 95 (2): 172–201.

Peckham, Robert. 2013. "Infective Economies: Empire, Panic and the Business of Disease." *The Journal of Imperial and Commonwealth History* 41 (2): 211–37. http://dx.doi.org/10.1080/03086534.2013.789272.

Pelling, Mark. 2010. *Adaptation to Climate Change: From Resilience to Transformation*. London; New York: Routledge.

Pelling, Mark, and Sophie Blackburn, eds. 2013. *Megacities and the Coast: Risk, Resilience and Transformation*. USA and Canada: Routledge.

Pelling, Mark, David Manuel-Navarrete, and Michael Redclift, eds. 2012. *Climate Change and the Crisis of Capitalism: A Chance to Reclaim, Self, Society and Nature*. New York: Routledge.

Pelling, Mark, Karen O'Brien, and David Matyas. 2014. "Adaptation and Transformation." *Climatic Change* 33 (Special issue on advancing climate change adaptation and risk management.): 113–27. https://doi.org/10.1007/s10584-014-1303-0.

Peters, Adele. 2021. "What U.S. Cities Can Learn from Abu Dhabi about Surviving Record Heat." *Fast Company*, July 13, 2021. www.fastcompany.com/90654190/what-u-s-cities-can-learn-from-abu-dhabi-about-surviving-record-heat.

Pierre, Jon. 2014. "Can Urban Regimes Travel in Time and Space? Urban Regime Theory, Urban Governance Theory, and Comparative Urban Politics." *Urban Affairs Review* 50 (6): 864–89. https://doi.org/10.1177/1078087413518175.

Platt, Brenda, Naomi Friedman, Carolyn Grodinsky, Pia MacDonald, and Margaret Suozzo. 1994. "Waste Prevention, Recycling, and Composting Options: Lessons from 30 U.S. Communities, Prepared by the Institute for Local Self-Reliance." EPA-530-R-92-015. US Environmental Protection Agency. https://ilsr.org/waste-prevention-recycling-and-composting-options-lessons-from-30-u-s-communities/.

Portes, Alejandro, and Alex Stepick. 1993. *City on the Edge: The Transformation of Miami*. First. Berkeley: University of California Press.

Preunkert, Susanne, Joseph R. McConnell, Helene Hoffmann, Michel Legrand, Andrew I. Wilson, Sabine Eckhardt, Andreas Stohl, Nathan J. Chellman, Monica M. Arienzo, and Ronny Friedrich. 2019. "Lead and Antimony in Basal Ice from Col Du Dome (French Alps) Dated with Radiocarbon: A Record of Pollution during Antiquity." *Geophysical Research Letters* 46 (9): 4953–61.

Pryor, Edward G. 1975. "The Great Plague of Hong Kong." *Journal of the Hong Kong Branch of the Royal Asiatic Society* 15: 61–70.

Qi, Yunfei, Faith Chan, Shun Chan, Colin R. Thorne, Emily C. O'Donnell, Carlotta Quagliolo, Elena Comino, Alessandro Pezzoli, Lei Li, Jim Griffiths, Yanfang Sang, and Meili Feng. 2020. "Addressing Challenges of Urban Water Management in Chinese Sponge Cities via Nature-Based Solutions." *Water* 12 (10), 2788.

Rankin, Caitlin G., Casey R. Barrier, and Timothy J. Horsley. 2021. "Evaluating Narratives of Ecocide with the Stratigraphic Record at Cahokia Mounds State Historic Site, Illinois, USA." *Geoarchaeology* 36 (3): 369–87. https://doi.org/10.1002/gea.21848.

Rapport, David J., Robert Costanza, and Anthony J. McMichael. 1998. "Assessing Ecosystem Health." *Trends in Ecology & Evolution* 13 (10): 397–402.

Raven, Rob, Johan Schot, and Frans Berkhout. 2012. "Space and Scale in Socio-Technical Transitions." *Environmental Innovation and Societal Transitions* 4: 63–78.

Raymond, André. 2000. *Cairo*. Translated by Willard Wood. Boston: Harvard University Press.

Ribeiro, Karina Braga, Ana Freitas Ribeiro, Maria Amélia de Sousa Mascena Veras, and Marcia Caldas de Castro. 2021. "Social Inequalities and COVID-19 Mortality in the City of São Paulo, Brazil." *International Journal of Epidemiology* 50 (3): 732–42. https://doi.org/doi:10.1093/ije/dyab022.

Ribeiro, Paulo Jorge Gomes, and Luís António Pena Jardim Gonçalves. 2019. "Urban Resilience: A Conceptual Framework." *Sustainable Cities and Society* 50: 101625. https://doi.org/10.1016/j.scs.2019.101625.

Roberts, Denise J. 2017. "Achieving Sustainability in Hazard-Prone Territories: A Case Study." Dissertation, Walden University.

Robinson, William. 1894. Speech from British Governor of Hong Kong regarding the outbreak of plague. Quoted in M. Echenberg, 2007, "An Unexampled Calamity: Hong Kong, 1894." *Plague Ports: The Global Urban Impact of Bubonic Plague, 1894–1901*, New York: New York University Press, pp. 16–46.

Rocha, Juan Carlos, Garry D. Peterson, and Reinette Biggs. 2015. "Regime Shifts in the Anthropocene: Drivers, Risks, and Resilience." *PloS One* 10 (8): e0134639. http://dx.doi.org/10.1371/journal.pone.0134639.

Rogers, Everett M. and D. Williams. 1983. *Diffusion of Innovations*. Glencoe, IL: The Free Press.

Rogers, J. David, and Independent Levee Investigation Team. 2006. "History of the New Orleans Flood Protection System." In *Investigation of the Performance of the New Orleans Flood Protection Systems in Hurricane Katrina on August 29, 2005*, Volume I: Main Text and Executive Summary: 4–1 to 4–55. National Science Foundation under Grants No. CMS-0413327 and CMS-0611632. New Orleans Levee System. https://biotech.law.lsu.edu/katrina/ILIT/report/CH_4.pdf.

Romagossa, Nicole. 2010. "Albert Baldwin Wood, the Screw Pump, and the Modernization of New Orleans." Thesis, M.A., New Orleans, LA: University of New Orleans Theses and Dissertations. https://scholarworks.uno.edu/td/1245.

Rose, J. Holland. 2014. *The Mediterranean in the Ancient World*. New York: Cambridge University Press. www.cambridge.org/us/academic/subjects/classical-studies/ancient-history/mediterranean-ancient-world,%20www-cambridge-org.ezproxy.gc.cuny.edu/us/academic/subjects/classical-studies/ancient-history.

Rosenberg, Jonathan. 2010. "Natural Disasters, Climate Change, and Recovery: The Sustainability Question in Post-Ivan Grenada." In *Community Disaster Recovery and Resiliency: Exploring Global Opportunities and Challenges*, edited by Desmond S. Miller and Jason David Rivera, 173–204. Boca Raton, FL: CRC Press.

Rosenzweig, Cynthia, William D. Solecki, Patricia Romero-Lankao, Shagun Mehrotra, Shobhakar Dhakal, and Somayya Ali Ibrahim, eds. 2018. *Climate Change and Cities: Second Assessment Report of the Urban Climate Change Research Network*. Cambridge, MA and New York: Cambridge University Press.

Rosol, Marit, Vincent Béal, and Samuel Mössner. 2017. "Greenest Cities? The (Post-) Politics of New Urban Environmental Regimes." *Environment and Planning A: Economy and Space* 49 (8): 1710–18.

Ruhl, J. B. 2005. "Water Wars, Eastern Style: Divvying up the Apalachicola-Chattahoochee-Flint River Basin." *Journal of Contemporary Water Research & Education* 131: 47–54.

Rumbach, Andrew. 2017. "At the Roots of Urban Disasters: Planning and Uneven Geographies of Risk in Kolkata, India." *Journal of Urban Affairs* 39 (6): 783–99. https://doi.org/10.1080/07352166.2017.1282771.

Sallares, Robert. 2002. *Malaria and Rome: A History of Malaria in Ancient Italy*, 1st ed. New York: Oxford University Press.

Sames, William J., Heung-Chul Kim, and T. A. Klein. 2008. "Evolution of Military Medical Entomology: Entomological Issues during the Korean War, 1950–1953." In *Proceedings of the DoD Symposium*, 29–44. Reno, NV: Armed Forces Pest Management Board (AFPMB).

Sanders, Jeffrey Craig. 2011. *Seattle and the Roots of Urban Sustainability: Inventing Ecotopia*. Pittsburgh, PA: University of Pittsburgh Press.

Sanderson, Eric W. 2009. *Mannahatta: A Natural History of New York City*. New York: Abrams. www.amazon.com/Mannahatta-Natural-History-York-City/dp/B0058M657W/ref=monarch_sidesheet.

Sanderson, Eric W., William D. Solecki, John R. Waldman, and Adam S. Parris. 2016. *Prospects for Resilience: Insights from New York City's Jamaica Bay*, 1st ed. Washington, DC: Island Press.

Schamber, Pablo J. 2010. "A Historical and Structural Approach to the Cartonero Phenomenon in Buenos Aires: Continuity and New Opportunities in Waste Management and the Recycling Industry." *International Journal of Urban Sustainable Development* 2 (1–2): 6–23. https://doi.org/10.1080/19463138.2010.507962.

Schär, Christoph. 2016. "The Worst Heat Waves to Come." *Nature Climate Change* 6 (2): 128–29. https://doi.org/10.1038/nclimate2864.

Scheffer, Marten. 2009. *Critical Transitions in Nature and Society* (Vol. 16). Princeton: Princeton University Press.

Scheffer, Marten, Stephen R. Carpenter, Timothy M. Lenton, Jordi Bascompte, William Brock, Vasilis Dakos, Johan Van de Koppel, Ingrid A. Van de Leemput, Simon A. Levin, and Egbert H. Van Nes. 2012. "Anticipating Critical Transitions." *Science* 338 (6105): 344–48. https://doi.org/10.1126/science.1225244.

Scheffer, Marten, Egbert H. van Nes, Darcy Bird, R. Kyle Bocinsky, and Timothy A. Kohler. 2021. "Loss of Resilience Preceded Transformations of Pre-Hispanic Pueblo Societies." *Proceedings of the National Academy of Sciences* 118 (18): e2024397118. https://doi.org/10.1073/pnas.2024397118.

Seattle City Council and Seattle Public Utilities. 2007. Seattle Solid Waste Recycling, Waste Reduction, and Facilities Opportunities. Prepared by URS Corporation, Herrera Environmental Consultants, Inc., and Norton-Arnold Company. Seattle, WA: Seattle City Council and Seattle Public Utilities. www.seattle.gov/utilities/about/plans/solid-waste/zero-waste.

Sequeira, Jessica. 2015. "Buenos Aires, Wasteland." *ReVista, Harvard Review of Latin America*, Winter 2015. https://revista.drclas.harvard.edu/buenos-aires-wasteland/.

Serge Kubanza, Nzalalemba, and Mulala Danny Simatele. 2020. "Sustainable Solid Waste Management in Developing Countries: A Study of Institutional Strengthening for Solid Waste Management in Johannesburg, South Africa." *Journal of Environmental Planning and Management* 63 (2): 175–88. https://doi.org/10.1080/09640568.2019.1576510.

SFWMD, South Florida Water Management District. 2021. "Quick Facts and Figures." 2021. www.sfwmd.gov/who-we-are/facts-and-figures.

Shen, Hung-Wen and Yue-Hwa Yu. 1997. "Social and Economic Factors in the Spread of the NIMBY Syndrome Against Waste Disposal Sites in Taiwan." *Journal of Environmental Planning and Management* 40 (2): 273–82.

Shen, Jianfa. 2008. "Urban Growth and Sustainable Development in Shenzhen City 1980–2006." *Open Environmental Sciences Journal* 2 (1): 71–79. https://doi.org/10.2174/1876325100802010071.

Shi, Linda. 2021. "From Progressive Cities to Resilient Cities: Lessons from History for New Debates in Equitable Adaptation to Climate Change." *Urban Affairs Review* 57 (5): 1442–79. https://doi.org/10.1177/1078087419910827. STOPPED

Shidong, Zhao, Bai Wanqi, Lu Jiehua, Qi Wenhu, Liu Guiping, Zhang Taolin, Qin Mingzhou, and Jiang Leiwen. 2001. "Population, Consumption, and Land Use in the Pearl River Delta, Guangdong Province." In *Growing Populations, Changing Landscapes: Studies from India, China, and the United States*, edited by Chinese Academy of Sciences and Indian National Science Academy, 207–30. Washington, DC: National Academies Press. https://doi.org/10.17226/10144.

Siegrist, Michael, and Joseph Árvai. 2020. "Risk Perception: Reflections on 40 Years of Research." *Risk Analysis* 40 (S1): 2191–206. https://doi.org/10.1111/risa.13599.

Simatele, Danny Mulala, Smangele Dlamini, and Nzalalemba Serge Kubanza. 2017. "From Informality to Formality: Perspectives on the Challenges of Integrating Solid Waste Management into the Urban Development and Planning Policy in Johannesburg, South Africa." *Habitat International* 63: 122–30. https://doi.org/10.1016/j.habitatint.2017.03.018.

Sims, David. 2003. "Urban Slums Reports: The Case of Cairo, Egypt." Understanding Slums: Case Studies for the Global Report on Human Settlements. University College London Reports. www.ucl.ac.uk/dpu-projects/Global_Report/pdfs/Cairo.pdf.

Slovic, Anne Dorothée, and Helena Ribeiro. 2018. "Policy Instruments Surrounding Urban Air Quality: The Cases of São Paulo, New York City and Paris." *Environmental Science and Policy* 81: 1–9.

Smith, Adrian, and Andy Stirling. 2010. "The Politics of Social-Ecological Resilience and Sustainable Socio-Technical Transitions." *Ecology and Society* 15 (1): 11. http://dx.doi.org/10.5751/es-03218-150111.

Smith, Kirk R., and Majid Ezzati. 2005. "How Environmental Health Risks Change with Development: The Epidemiologic and Environmental Risk Transitions Revisited." *Annual Review of Environment and Resources* 30: 291–333.

Smith, Rick. 2014. "Cedar Rapids Flood Buyout Is History." *The Cedar Rapids Gazette*, September 14, 2014. www.thegazette.com/news/cedar-rapids-flood-buyout-is-history/.

Soja, Edward W. 1989. *Postmodern Geographies: The Reassertion of Space in Critical Social Theory*. London, England: Verso.

Solecki, William. 2010. Abstract: Crisis, Transition, and Urban Environmental Change. UGEC Conference, Tempe, AZ.

Solecki, William. 2012. "Moving toward Urban Sustainability: Using Lessons and Legacies of the Past." In *Metropolitan Sustainability: Understanding and Improving the Urban Environment*, edited by Frank Zeman, 680–96. Cambridge, UK: Woodhead Publishing.

Solecki, William, Connor Murphy, and Allen Frei. 2025. "Critical Transitions in New York City's Drinking Water Supply Systems." *Anthropocene*, no. submitted to.

Solecki, William, Mark Pelling, and Matthias Garschagen. 2017. "Transitions between Risk Management Regimes in Cities." *Ecology and Society* 22 (2): 1–14.

Solecki, William, Lesley Patrick and Zoe Sprigings. 2019. "Urban Climate Change Policy Transitions Views from New York City and London." *The Adaptive Challenge of Climate Change* 41–62.

South Coast Air Quality Management District. 1997. The Southland's War on Smog: Fifty Years of Progress toward Clean Air (through May 1997).

St Clair, Peter. 2009. "Low-Energy Design in the United Arab Emirates–Building Design Principles." *Environment Design Guide*, February, 1–10. https://doi.org/10.2307/26151849.

Steinberg, Ted. 2000. *Acts of God: The Unnatural History of Natural Disaster in America*, 1st ed. New York: Oxford University Press. www.abebooks.com/9780195142631/Acts-God-Unnatural-History-Natural-0195142632/plp.

Stone, Rob. 2017. "Structuration Theory." In *The Wiley Blackwell Encyclopedia of Social Theory*, edited by Bryan S. Turner, Chang Kyung-Sup, Cynthia F. Epstein, Peter Kivisto, J. Michael Ryan, and William Outwaithe, 1st ed., 1–8. New York, Wiley-Blackwell. https://doi.org/10.1002/9781118430873.est0377.

Sullivan, Robert. 2005. *Rats: Observations on the History and Habitat of the City's Most Unwanted Inhabitants*. Paperback. New York: Bloomsbury Publishing.

Sun, Siao. 2019. "Water Footprints in Beijing, Tianjin and Hebei: A Perspective from Comparisons between Urban and Rural Consumptions in Different Regions." *Science of the Total Environment* 647: 507–15. https://doi.org/10.1016/j.scitotenv.2018.07.343.

Sutton, Keith, and Wael Fahmi. 2001. "Cairo's Urban Growth and Strategic Master Plans in the Light of Egypt's 1996 Population Census Results." *Cities* 18 (3): 135–49.

Swaney, Dennis P., Renee L. Santoro, Robert W. Howarth, Bongghi Hong, and Kieran P. Donaghy. 2012. "Historical Changes in the Food and Water Supply Systems of the New York City Metropolitan Area." *Regional Environmental Change* 12: 363–80. https://doi.org/10.1007/s10113-011-0266-1.

Swihart, Thomas L. 2011. *Florida's Water: A Fragile Resource in a Vulnerable State*, 1st ed. USA and Canada: RFF Press.

Swyngedouw, Eric. 2004. *Social Power and the Urbanization of Water: Flows of Power*. Oxford Geographical and Environmental Studies. Oxford, England: Oxford University Press. www.dawsonera.com/depp/reader/protected/external/AbstractView/S9780191543791.

Tàbara, J. David, Niki Frantzeskaki, Katharina Hölscher, Simona Pedde, Kasper Kok, Francesco Lamperti, Jens H. Christensen, Jill Jäger, and Pam Berry. 2018. "Positive Tipping Points in a Rapidly Warming World." *Current Opinion in Environmental Sustainability* 31: 120–29. https://doi.org/10.1016/j.cosust.2018.01.012.

Taing, Lina, C. C. Chang, Sophia Pan and Neil Armitage. 2019. "Towards a Water Secure Future: Reflections on Cape Town's Day Zero Crisis." *Urban Water Journal* 16 (7): 530–36.

Tal, Alon. 2006. "Seeking Sustainability: Israel's Evolving Water Management Strategy." *Science* 313 (5790): 1081–84.

Tal, Alon. 2017. "The Evolution of Israeli Water Management: The Elusive Search for Environmental Security." In *Water Security in the Middle East: Essays in Scientific and Social Cooperation*, edited by Jean Axerad Cahan, 1: 214. London, England: Anthem Press.

Tang, Shui-Yan and Ching-Ping Tang. 1997. "Democratization and Environmental Politics in Taiwan." *Asian Survey* 37 (3): 281–94.

Tariq, Hisham, Chaminda Pathirage, and Terrence Fernando. 2021. "Measuring Community Disaster Resilience at Local Levels: An Adaptable Resilience Framework." *International Journal of Disaster Risk Reduction* 62 (August): 102358. https://doi.org/10.1016/j.ijdrr.2021.102358.

Tarr, Joel A. 1996. *The Search for the Ultimate Sink: Urban Pollution in Historical Perspective*, 1st ed. Akron, OH: The University of Akron Press.

Tate, Eric, Aaron Strong, Travis Kraus, and Haoyi Xiong. 2016. "Flood Recovery and Property Acquisition in Cedar Rapids, Iowa." *Natural Hazards* 80 (3): 2055–79.

Tellman, Beth, Hallie Eakin, and Billie Lee Turner. 2022. "Identifying, Projecting, and Evaluating Informal Urban Expansion Spatial Patterns." *Journal of Land Use Science* 17 (1): 100–12.

The 6th National Climate Risk Assessment: Hazardous Heat. 2022. First Street Foundation. https://report.firststreet.org/heat.

The History of Japan's Air Pollution. 2011. Aozora Foundation. http://aozora.or.jp/lang/english/the-history-of-japans-air-pollution.

Thi Hoang Duong, Tong, Avner Adin, David Jackman, Peter van der Steen, and Kala Vairavamoorthy. 2011. "Urban Water Management Strategies Based on a Total Urban Water Cycle Model and Energy Aspects–Case Study for Tel Aviv." *Urban Water Journal* 8 (2): 103–18.

Thomas, Alexander R. 2005. *Gilboa: New York's Quest for Water and the Destruction of a Small Town*. Lanham, MD: University Press of America.

Thomas-Hope, Elizabeth M., ed. 1998. *Solid Waste Management: Critical Issues for Developing Countries*. Kingston, Jamaica: Canoe Press, University of the West Indies. https://libraries.sta.uwi.edu/uwipress/index.php/main/catalogueDetails/520.

Tonsmeire, Drew. 2012. "Georgia Wins, Where's the Equity?" *Atlanta Forward*, July 6, 2012.

Tri-State Water Commission. n.d. Map of ACF Basin and Adjacent Alabama-CoosaTullapoosa (ACT) Basin Showing Major Urban Areas and Reservoirs. https://water.sam.usace.army.mil/wm/

Trounstine, Jessica. 2018. *Segregation by Design: Local Politics and Inequality in American Cities*. Cambridge, England: Cambridge University Press.

Tsuda, Toshihide, Takashi Yorifuji, Soshi Takao, Masaya Miyai, and Akira Babazono. 2009. "Minamata Disease: Catastrophic Poisoning Due to a Failed Public Health Response." *Journal of Public Health Policy* 30: 54–67.

Uekoetter, Frank. 2009. *The Age of Smoke: Environmental Policy in Germany and the United States, 1880–1970*. Translated by Thomas Dunlap. First. Pittsburgh History Urban Environment. Pittsburgh, PA: University of Pittsburgh Press.

UN Habitat. 2019. The Story of Shenzhen, Its Economic, Social, and Environmental Transformation. Nairobi, Kenya, ISBN 978-92-1-132840-0

UNGA, UN Secretary-General. Open-ended Intergovernmental Expert Working Group on Indicators and Terminology relating to Disaster Risk Reduction. 2016. "Report of the Open-Ended Intergovernmental Expert Working Group on Indicators and Terminology Relating to Disaster Risk Reduction : Note /: By the Secretary-General." Transmits report of the Working Group. A/71/644. United Nations. https://digitallibrary.un.org/record/852089.

UN Human Settlements Programme via UN SDG Indicators Database. 2024. (https://unstats.un.org/sdgs/dataportal), UN Department of Economic and Social Affairs (accessed 2024). More information available at: https://unstats.un.org/sdgs/metadata/files/Metadata-11-01-01.pdf.

United National Environmental Programme. 2002. The Global 500: Roll of Honour for environmental achievement. UNEP(02)/G5/2002. Nairobi, Kenya. 21p.

Unwin, Tim. 2000. "A Waste of Space? Towards a Critique of the Social Production of Space…." *Transactions of the Institute of British Geographers* 25 (1): 11–29. https://doi.org/10.1111/j.0020-2754.2000.00011.x.

Urban Land Institute. 2009. "Cedar Rapids Iowa Strategies for the Downtown." An Advisory Services Panel Report, Report Summary: 09-255002_Cedar Rapids.

US Department of Housing and Urban Development, HUD, and ESA US Department of Commerce Economics and Statistics Administration. 2014. "Characteristics of New Housing." US Census Bureau. www.census.gov/construction/chars/pdf/c25ann2014.pdf.

US Environmental Protection Agency. 2025. National Overview: Facts and Figures on Materials, Wastes and Recycling. www.epa.gov/facts-and-figures-about-materials-waste-and-recycling/national-overview-facts-and-figures-materials#Trends1960-Today

US Lakes, Lake Sidney Lanier Water Levels. 2013. US Lakes Information. April 10, 2013. www.uslakes.info/Level.asp.

Velis, Costas A., David C. Wilson, Ondina Rocca, Stephen R. Smith, Antonis Mavropoulos, and Chris R. Cheeseman. 2012. "An Analytical Framework and Tool ('InteRa') for Integrating the Informal Recycling Sector in Waste and Resource Management Systems in Developing Countries." *Waste Management & Research* 30 (9 Supplement): 43–66. https://doi.org/10.1177/0734242X12454934.

Wallace, Deborah, and Rodrick Wallace. 2008. "Urban Systems during Disasters: Factors for Resilience." *Ecology and Society* 13 (1): 18. http://dx.doi.org/10.5751/es-02386-130118.

Wang, Xinxin, and Kevin Lo. 2021. "Just Transition: A Conceptual Review." *Energy Research & Social Science* 82: 102291. https://doi.org/10.1016/j.erss.2021.102291.

Wang, Ye, Zhe Jiang, and Lin Zhang. 2022. "Sponge City Policy and Sustainable City Development: The Case of Shenzhen." *Frontiers in Environmental Science* 9 (772490): 1–5.

Ward, David, and Oliver Zunz, eds. 1992. *Landscape of Modernity: Essays on New York City, 1900–1940*. Baltimore: John Hopkins University Press.

Weaver, Timothy. 2017. "Urban Crisis: The Genealogy of a Concept." *Urban Studies* 54 (9): 2039–55. https://doi.org/10.1177/0042098016640487.

Weesjes, Elke. 2015. "The 1953 North Sea Flood in the Netherlands: Impact and Aftermath." *Natural Hazards Observer* 15 (1). https://hazards.colorado.edu/article/the-1953-north-sea-flood-in-the-netherlands-impact-and-aftermath.

Wellesley, R. C. Lord. 1803. Governor General of British India, detailed minutes condemning the sad state of municipal affairs and flood management in Kolkata, India. Quoted in S. W. *Goode, 1916. Municipal Calcutta: Its Institutions in Their Growth and Origin;* Kolkata: Corporation of Calcutta.

Weng, Qihao. 2007. "A Historical Perspective of River Basin Management in the Pearl River Delta of China." *Journal of Environmental Management* 85 (4): 1048–62.

Westley, Frances, Per Olsson, Carl Folke, Thomas Homer-Dixon, Harrie Vredenburg, Derk Loorbach, John Thompson, Måns Nilsson, Eric Lambin, and Jan Sendzimir. 2011. "Tipping toward Sustainability: Emerging Pathways of Transformation." *Ambio* 40: 762–80.

White, Rachel H., Sam Anderson, James F. Booth, Ginni Braich, Christina Draeger, Cuiyi Fei, Christopher D. G. Harley, Sarah B. Henderson, Matthias Jakob, and Carie-Ann Lau. 2023. "The Unprecedented Pacific Northwest Heatwave of June 2021." *Nature Communications* 14 (1): 727. https://doi.org/10.1038/s41467-023-36289-3.

Wildman, Wesley J., Joseph Bulbulia, Richard Sosis, and Uffe Schjoedt. 2020. "Religion and the COVID-19 Pandemic." *Religion, Brain and Behavior* 10 (2): 115–17. https://doi.org/10.1080/2153599X.2020.1749339.

Wilson, Geoff A. 2013. "Community Resilience, Policy Corridors and the Policy Challenge." *Land Use Policy* 31: 298–310. http://dx.doi.org/10.1016/j.landusepol.2012.07.011.

Wise, Russell M., Ioan Fazey, M. Stafford Smith, Sarah E. Park, Hallie C. Eakin, ERM Archer Van Garderen, and Bruce Campbell. 2014. "Reconceptualising Adaptation to Climate Change as Part of Pathways of Change and Response." *Global Environmental Change* 28: 325–36. http://dx.doi.org/10.1016/j.gloenvcha.2013.12.002.

Wolfram, Marc, Sara Borgström, and Megan Farrelly. 2019. "Urban Transformative Capacity: From Concept to Practice." *Ambio* 48: 437–48. https://doi.org/10.1007/s13280-019-01169-y.

Woolf, Greg. 2020. *The Life and Death of Ancient Cities: A Natural History*. Illustrated. New York: Oxford University Press.

World Health Organization. 2016. "Ambient Air Pollution: A Global Assessment of Exposure and Burden of Disease." Geneva, Switzerland: World Health Organization. https://apps.who.int/iris/bitstream/handle/10665/250141/?sequence=1.

World Health Organization. 2022. "Drinking-Water." Fact Sheet. www.who.int/News-Room/Fact-Sheets/Detail. March 21, 2022. www.who.int/news-room/fact-sheets/detail/drinking-water.

Wu, Yangyi, Yehua Dennis Wei, and Meitong Liu. 2023. "Urban Form and Spatiotemporal Vulnerability of Local Communities to COVID-19." *Geographical Review* 113 (4), 482–501.

WWAP, UNESCO World Water Assessment Programme. 2019. "UN World Water Development Report 2019- Leaving No One Behind." Paris, France: UNESCO. www.unesco.org/en/wwap/wwdr/2019.

Yoshida, Aya. 2022. “China’s Ban of Imported Recyclable Waste and Its Impact on the Waste Plastic Recycling Industry in China and Taiwan.” *Journal of Material Cycles and Waste Management* 24 (1): 73–82. https://doi.org/10.1007/s10163-021-01297-2.

Yuan, Yiming, Hongyi Guo, Hongfei Xu, Weiqi Li, Shanshan Luo, Haiqing Lin, and Yuan Yuan. 2010. “China’s First Special Economic Zone: The Case of Shenzhen.” In *Building Engines for Growth and Competitiveness in China*, edited by Douglas Zhihua Zeng, 55. Washington, DC: World Bank Publications.

Zeller, Vanessa, Edgar Towa, Marc Degrez, and Wouter M. J. Achten. 2019. “Urban Waste Flows and Their Potential for a Circular Economy Model at City-Region Level.” *Waste Management* 83: 83–94. https://doi.org/10.1016/j.wasman.2018.10.034.

Zhang, Sheng, Meng Xu, Yifu Yang, and Zeyu Song. 2021. “Technological Innovation, Production Efficiency, and Sustainable Development: A Case Study from Shenzhen in China.” *Sustainability* 13 (19): 10827. https://doi.org/10.3390/su131910827.

Index

For EU product safety concerns, contact us at Calle de José Abascal, 56–1°, 28003 Madrid, Spain or eugpsr@cambridge.org.

www.ingramcontent.com/pod-product-compliance
Lightning Source LLC
LaVergne TN
LVHW052250200926
848481LV00002B/329